CYCLING BACK TO HAPPINESS

Adventure on the
North Sea Cycle Route

Bernie Friend

Pen Press Publishers Ltd

First published in Great Britain by
Pen Press Publishers Ltd
25 Eastern Place
Brighton
BN2 1GJ

ISBN 13: 978-1-9062-0671-0

Printed and bound in Great Britain by
Cpod, Trowbridge, Wiltshire

A catalogue record of this book is available from
the British Library

Cover design by Jacqueline Abromeit
All photographs taken by Bernie Friend and Rhys Chisam

Map Design: Simon Bishop

For Marylyn Friend,
Simply the best.

Acknowledgments

Thanks for equipment go to nice people from Leigh-on-Sea. Erik at Richardsons Cycles for wheels, spares and comfy padded pants. Daniel Hull at TopGear for a dry tent, warm sleeping bag and a good jacket for fighting the wind and rain.

Cheers for help with the book go to Eli Viten at Rogaland Council, Norway, for helping piece together the many parts of my trip. Rhys Chisam for arriving in the nick of time and Neil Holland for finally paying back his debts via computer donation, IT backup and constant ciggie rolling.

For food and shelter, praise be to Monique Kool, the ten Harkels, Radmers, North Sea Wife, Ganters, Gudrun Rishede, Maria Hürlimann, Jenny Engström, Zelda and anybody else who took pity and showed kindness.

Writing inspiration thanks go to Tom Baker for making me pick up a primary school pen, Mark Vinal for encouraging me to make a living using one and Emma Stonex for a nice letter which got me on my bike to chase the ultimate dream.

Massive respect to my publisher Lynn Ashman, e-mail's answer to Dear Deidre, everyone who helped me raise £3,640.51 for Cancer Research UK, especially Chas at the Pink Toothbrush, plus all my friends and family, especially you Karl.

Saving the best until last, thanks to the love of my life, Katie, who let me go and do this stupid thing and remained patient (through some dark times) while I tapped it into a screen with all the dexterity of a sloth. Love you babes x x x

About The Author

Bernie Friend was born in 1971 and lives in Leigh-on-Sea, Essex. He has an unhealthy Doctor Who obsession, supports Southend United and enjoys pulling funny faces at himself in the bathroom mirror. He has followed a career path of digging holes, pulling pints, spinning records, delivering letters, selling market stall hats, number crunching and getting sacked for illegally swearing and smoking at his desk, all in the same breath, before becoming a journalist and writing his first book 15 years later. His only remaining ambitions in life are to sit on Richard and Judy's couch and spend an evening playing drunken Trivial Pursuit with Tom Baker.

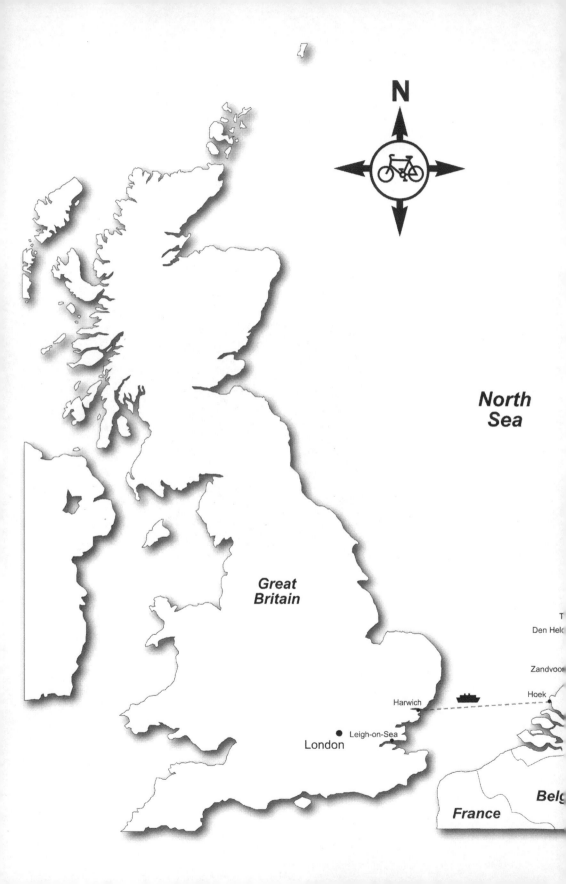

Prologue

Look at the silly humans, aren't they funny. Reading the sunlit expressions of the smiling seals as they bobbed around lapping up the free morning entertainment wasn't difficult. The grey and black spotted faces could hardly contain their amusement as they observed the land dwellers scurrying across the beach from the comfort of their floating auditorium. Shoes and socks had been abandoned and soggy trouser legs rolled up right to the knees as the Grenen pilgrims readied themselves for the show's big climax.

The two-legged ones had climbed to Denmark's most northern point to do more than just dip their toes in the water. This was the meeting place of the Skagerrak and Kattegat seas – a relentless head-on collision of crashing waves and high flying spray. And the foolish humans were convinced they held some mastery over these turbulent powers of mother nature. By scuttling across a small fin of white sand it was possible to safely plonk a leg in each separate channel at the same time, before claiming a hollow victory with an excited scream and a frantic wave which was captured on camera for evidence.

With my left hand clamped to my eyebrows as a sun visor, I watched the illuminated conveyor belt of people going through the same ritual of jettisoning their footwear ahead of bravely jumping up and down in only a few inches of water. The tables had not just been turned, but sent tumbling across the drink towards Sweden, as the fascinated seals were held trance-like by the planet's so-called superior race reduced to no more than circus clowns in their black marble eyes. It wouldn't have been a surprise to hear a rousing, but wet round of applause from the flippers of an appreciative audience.

Sticking out like a sore thumb, after resisting the temptation to get in with the in-crowd by losing my cycling boots, the irony of the situation wasn't lost on me. I even had a little giggle to myself. Hardly anyone else gave the seals a second glance after firing off a quick, 'ah… look at their little faces… aren't they just so cute.' This was followed by a frenzied shower of shoes, trainers and flip-flops in a mad dash to book a spot on northern Europe's most exclusive, congested and minuscule beach. Better pump up those orange balls and practise balancing them on your little moist noses again, chaps, if you have genuine aspirations of being more than a quickly forgotten warm-up act for a feverish splash into the shallows of the converging seas.

A month ago I would have been at the head of the queue, thrusting out legs and elbows in a determined attempt to get over the finishing line first. That's if I had even managed to get this far at all. The last few weeks had been a life-changing experience for this quiet backseat spectator. I had started to look at the outside world much differently. Step back, stop rushing, take in all the wonderful things around you. But, most importantly, this transformation had blossomed from new-found buds of optimism, which were flowering confidently and forcing my fears to shrivel in the dirt below.

Four weeks of hard graft, propelled by nothing more than a sweat welded fusion of scratched aluminium, aching lower leg muscles and rust dotted chains and cables had driven me on to Grenen. Just being here was such a huge achievement. I had rarely lowered my backside on to a saddle since abandoning the stabilisers as a wobbling whipper-snapper. But keeping the pedals turning on a big boy's bike for hundreds of miles was proving to be a real tonic.

For longer than I care to remember this born-again rider had found it impossible to leave the security of his English castle. Previous plans to seek out adventure had been paralysed by a terminal travel phobia, fuelled by a long list of other mind-bending anxieties. But here I was, being winked at by a proudly burning sun, without a care in the world. There was no desperate gasp for breath and my heart hadn't rocketed into a rapid pulse countdown in readiness for a chest launch into the sedate sky above. Even the terrifying urge to crank into reverse and panic pedal back to the safety of home as fast as possible had kept its distance. Completely relaxed and soaking up the natural beauty around me like a sponge, I was actually taking uninterrupted pleasure from this moment.

I knew I could do it. I could be normal. I'd made so much positive progress over the past few weeks and was rightly pleased with myself. But this wasn't mission accomplished. Trudging back across the bone-dry sand I was well aware that rooted right down deep in the darkest recesses of my overworked brain, fear was working overtime. My resourceful arch nemesis was back at the drawing board preparing a future assault on my sanity. As he planned and plotted brand new horrors and nightmare scenarios individually designed to test my mental breaking point, a faint, blood-curdling inner cackle attempted to splinter my tranquillity

But it wouldn't be so easy from now on. Left battered and bruised on the ropes for far too long, this walkover had finally lifted himself away from the canvas and started to fight back. I was growing stronger every day and the weeks, months and years of taking an easy fall were over. There was still a long, long way to go yet. And the odds were stacked against me winning every round of this non-stop bout against a dark destroyer hell bent on knocking me down at every opportunity. But I was prepared to go the distance or go mad trying.

1   Mad World

The way Katie looked at me across the dinner table just about summed everything up. Announcing my grand plan to cycle across northern Europe in a last ditch bid for therapy was never going to be an easy subject to approach. The fall-out from this unexpected bombshell exploded into a shell-shocked stare from my fiancée, betraying her inner desire to carry out one final act of undying love by signing the consent forms for the nuthouse right there and then. To be honest the girl might have been doing me a favour.

Long doses of daydreaming encouraged me to seek out far off places, dip an inquisitive toe into different cultures and wrench open my slammed shut eyes to the many wonders of the big wide world. The only thing that put the block on doing it for real was being scared stiff. Sorry, let me rephrase that, I was petrified of suffering a horrible, ugly death in a foreign country surrounded by complete strangers who didn't know and didn't care about me. Does that sound just a little bit over the top? Well, welcome to the twisted reality of my mixed-up existence.

My track record of emulating millions of normal people who jump on a plane or boat in search of new thrills and spills without batting an eyelid reads MISERABLE FAILURE. But we had nothing in common. I was waging a one-man war against a mucked-up mind which projected a stubborn red stop sign if anything threatened to scale the safety perimeters of my everyday routine; go to work, come home, have dinner, slop out in front of the TV, read a few chapters and go to bed. A serial offender inside a mental prison, long sentences had been served for anxiety, panic attacks, depression, obsessive compulsive disorders and a cheery fixation with my own mortality. These powerful phobias paralysed any travelling aspirations, fuelling the pessimistic belief that attempting anything too adventurous would topple a set of delicately balanced bails and prematurely end this earthly innings. My one big wish was to have enough puff left in my decrepit lungs to blow out 122 candles on the mother of all birthday cakes. Becoming so old and weak that I was bed ridden and needed my bum wiped every day didn't matter – I just wanted to live forever.

Being a professional hypochondriac is a multi-skilled job. You need a huge imagination, high energy levels and more dedication than Roy Castle's trumpet to make the grade. If these special talents could be channelled into the employment sector then a big queue of expensive suits would be tripping over themselves to offer me a fat £100,000 a year salary, plus gleaming company Audi to match. I wouldn't even have to pay for the petrol. Unfortunately, my CV had another entry right at the top – the ability to crumble and crack under the routine pressures of day-to-day life, which is why I'll never sing sweetly from the cloud piercing perch of a giant gleaming skyscraper owned by Goliath Enterprises.

A slight twinge across the forehead – not even a proper headache – or a runny nose, was enough to convince me my time was nearly up. I've had to fight so many deadly brain tumours and killer strains of meningitis I've lost count. Yes, I know it sounds terrible and of course I was brave, but spare a thought for somebody else before wringing out your hankies – my dear mother. The old bird could have taught Job a thing or two about patience and should qualify for a sainthood, having endured my back catalogue of phantom menaces on a daily basis in the desperate search for reassurance.

Even when the sobbing son was peeled off the sticky kitchen lino, after releasing his best wrestling grip from the lower part of a submitting mother's leg, he would still need to tick off the terminal illness checklist. A bull-like stampede upstairs to the bathroom was followed by a sweaty palm slap on the forehead for a quick temperature check. Stage two consisted of a long, hard stare at the eyes in the toothpaste splattered bathroom mirror to make sure the pupils were the same size. Any difference in shape was a definite sign of oncoming brain haemorrhage I'd once heard. A stopwatch was needed for stage three to count out 60 seconds and perform a one-fingered pulse check on my wrist. Anywhere between 60 and 80 beats per minute ruled out heart failure, somewhere in the 50s was a sure sign of athletic health, but 81 plus and I was shitting myself again. The grand finale required another piece of delicate apparatus, a pint glass, which was hysterically rolled backwards and forwards across the arm to see if any blotchy red skin (usually a colony of zits building up to a juicy pus squeezing fest) turned white, giving meningitis the all clear too. And guess what? I survived every time. But not because I'm a miracle of medical science, just a neurotic slave who blows the tiniest sniffle into a BAFTA winning bodily drama.

Sometimes I feel ready to collapse just walking to the shops for a pint of milk. It's like being pissed, but without the alcohol or expense, a giddy sensation most normal people would be happy to experience when they are short of a few quid at the weekend. But not me. My broken down brain suddenly thrusts into psychotic overdrive and the miniature cinema inside my cranial auditorium projects vivid pictures of my legs and arms writhing around in a frenzy on the cold High Street concrete with foam bubbling out of my mouth.

Pull yourself together, you must be thinking. That golden nugget of advice has been prescribed once or twice. But unless you share my experience of unwilling propulsion into a similar nightmare scenario you can't possibly understand how terrifying fear can be when it seizes control of the body without warning.

Imagine leaping out of bed in the dead of night, with the gold medal winning agility of an Olympic high jumper, as your sleep is invaded without invitation. At the same time a hot feverish sweat washes across the body and you are gripped by a state of confused disorientation, not knowing quite where you are or what is happening. This is a panic attack and when it hits you receive a massive injection of adrenalin free of charge, whether you like it or not. Taking complete control, this rush of energy is part of the body's natural defence system, designed to get you out of the starting blocks in a flash. Usually reserved for escaping a deep pan frying in a burning house or throwing yourself clear of a car with your name written on its bumper, anxiety can also trigger the process unexpectedly. In both instances the mechanics work just the same, but in my case this powerful inner force breaks the emergency glass around my fragile mind and sounds the run for your life alarm when I'm trying to recharge the batteries.

I can be dribbling contentedly on my pillow, dreaming about a shady polar bear salesman – complete with ice cool sunglasses and property portfolio – trying to flog me one of the last remaining igloo timeshares at a globally thawing out Arctic resort, when a huge snowball hurtles out of nowhere and rudely crashes with a large splash, bang in the centre of my salivation pool of relaxation. Bolting upright and ripping back the duvet, I grab my throat and gasp for air, with my heart thumping inside my chest like the bass speakers of an Essex boy racer's Fiesta. In that split second, when the tranquillity of your peaceful slumber is savagely interrupted, you expect your ticker to explode like a French banger, if you don't choke to death first. But you never get the chance to pump 999 into the mobile on your bedside table for paramedic back-up, as the whole frightening episode finishes as quickly as it started. Shaken-up and definitely stirred, but back on planet bedroom, I usually find myself trembling naked in the wardrobe mirror (nothing to do with admiring my well-toned build I might add), while Katie snores away like a deep-sleeping hippo with serious sinus problems, completely oblivious to the terror her nearest and dearest has endured.

These silent assaults are not confined to the behind closed doors privacy of the sleeping quarters either. They can strike anytime, anyplace, anywhere, and it's definitely not a feeling you would want to share. It can happen on a packed train as you reluctantly sniff another sardine's briny armpit, during a round of wage increase discussions with the boss or just down the pub in front of your mates, who aren't privy to what you have hidden away as an embarrassing secret. Panic has no respect for its victims and will come out to play when it is in the mood to fuck you right up.

Brainwashed by a Catholic upbringing (the word guilt is branded in huge red steaming capitals on my soul), church kneeling was a regular occurrence during the formative years and I even did a turn smoking out the congregation with a wild choking swing of the incense burner as an altar boy. I've always acknowledged a God and we've had some good chats, especially when I'm in a flap and need a quick fix of salvation. But the true sum of my faith is a desperate hope that something else really exists on the other side. Those of us who make a decent job of it down here will get gold stars slapped on our coffins by the man upstairs and promotion to the Premier League of paradise. If my prayers are answered then special treatment will be reserved for this warped piece of God's Game of Life, Planet Earth AD (21st-century edition).

What really keeps the neurotic fires glowing brightly is the uncertainty about what happens next. The possibility that death boils down to a quick stint in the undertaker's freezer straight after the final credits have rolled, before being burned or buried without any sign of a sequel, is not acceptable to me. Just ceasing to exist seems such a waste.

My perfect paradise would be a huge piss-up where you could party away with all your deceased family and friends again. There would be no licensing laws and the drink would flow for eternity. It wouldn't be another world or some spiritual dimension, more like a toga party for the resurrected in a massive pure white marquee stretched across an endless cluster of fluffy cotton wool clouds. Imagine the alcohol bill for that rave-up! Being God's gig, he would have to stick an enormous wad of notes behind the bar to cover it. But I'm sure he'll have a red-hot contact down below who can get a pair of claws on some cheap hooch which had tumbled off the back of a fallen angel. After sorting out the booze, the number one Lord of the Dance would get behind a turntable and spin the decks, whipping the born-again revellers up into a right old frenzy. And I'm certain the creator of all things will be big enough to admit his mistakes, trashing Black Lace, Jive Bunny mega-mixes and the Birdie Song from his play-list.

And what about God's other once breathing works of art, the pet rabbits, goldfish, cats and dogs we all adored? Are they invited to the reunion or exiled to a separate doggy heaven? Will there be flies to sniff around their cleansed shit (which obviously won't stink now)? And what happens to some of the great architect's other magnificent designs for life – giraffes, dinosaurs and woolly mammoths? I'm certain God is a fair bloke and all invites will get careful consideration, but he did create the human race in his own image and maybe St Peter and his burly bouncers will have a strict no tusks, tails or whiskers door policy at the Pearly Party Gates.

Uninterrupted sleep is the main topic which tortures my overworked grey cells. Becoming an underground restaurant for slow chewing earthworms or resembling a Silk Cut ash convention in an old rusty pot – unable to rewind back to my first kiss, my children being born and a lifetime of loving the one girl who truly captured my heart – what's the point in that? Arise Sir Morbid, you may think. What makes me so special that I should have all the pieces of the universe's greatest jigsaw puzzle slotted neatly into place? But I can't help it! And it's this relentless battle against the pitch black abyss of the unknown which inflates my fears and consistently leaves me sitting broken in the losing corner.

This couldn't carry on. Just for once I had to take the shit or bust approach and stop worrying about things which were out of my control. Past opportunities had slipped through my grasp because I was afraid of pushing myself to the limit, allowing this stranglehold to take an even firmer hold on my negativity. Memo to brain: 'I have been invited on a weekend drinking retreat to Nottingham with the lads.' Brain's reply: 'Following a long deliberation with the council of fears department, deep in the darkest chambers of your squishy mass, it has been unanimously decreed to turn down your request. It sounds far too perilous for a fragile little thing like you. Stay at home where you will be out of harm's way as all sorts of dangerous things could happen up there (like turning into a Nottingham Forest fan). What would happen if you started feeling ill? (Or maybe Notts County.) Better to be safe than sorry.'

I was in my prime, but living in a time-warp. I had transformed into one of those medieval textbook settlers from a stuffy school classroom history lesson, who never ventured further than a five mile radius from their farm right until the day they kicked their last bucket of potatoes. Sick and tired of being a town-bound hermit, I was determined to have one final crack at breaking my mental bonds. This was the last chance saloon and it would take a quick draw of my positive pistol to get in an accurate shot at silencing the intimidating snarl of the vicious circle which had me surrounded. Something as precious as life couldn't continue to pass me by. I had to stop stressing about the one thing nature had made inevitable because of some greedy geezer and his selfish bimbo scrumping apples in the orchard of Eden thousands of years ago. This bloated mental parasite had gorged itself on more than a decade of my sweet tasting anxieties and now was the time to drag it kicking and screaming to fat camp.

Most normal things were ticking along quite nicely on arrival at the crossroads of life. I had a decent job, a cosy flat and a far too attractive girlfriend who knew all about my inner conflicts, but still wanted to shack up with me for the rest of her life. What a trooper! I even had a bloody dog. The only thing missing was the 2.4 children and they wouldn't be far away.

But there was no planned fitting for a smoking jacket, pipe and slippers, before giving myself a congratulatory pat on the back, basking in the comforting glow of intimate fulfilment which some people never find in a lifetime of trying. Deep down inside there was this whopping great Grand Canyon sized hole – not a good sign six months short of making the biggest commitment of my frustrating existence.

The past 15 years had been an undisturbed plod of self-indulgence. Work to earn money, spend it on football, bars, beer, nightclubs, more beer, a few shots and the occasional bed and breakfast jackpot. Then right out of nowhere you meet the female of the species known as 'The One' and a long haul of self-gratification has been replaced by the ringing of wedding bells, swirling confetti storms and a cake constructed from the same blueprints as North Sea oil rigs. I wasn't ready for this.

Don't get me wrong, there were no doubts about Katie. She was the one thing I was concrete about. This remarkable woman had the power to raise the force-shields, conjuring a magical feeling of calm which lifted away the doom and gloom of my self-destructive pity and took me to a temporary plain of optimistic invincibility. Selfishly, though, it wasn't enough. There were still loose ends to lash tight ahead of walking down the aisle and handing myself over to her completely, malfunctioning mind, body and soul. I wanted our unison to be whole more than anything, but until I soared over one last hurdle, without scraping more skin off my battle scarred knees, our big day could never be perfect.

A powerful yearning for adventure and believing the freedom it brings might deliver some respite from my personal torment would not leave me alone. It didn't matter where I was, sitting on the toilet balancing the bog roll in my hand, watching a film or supping a pint, it kept eating away at me. Repeatedly goaded by my spiteful subconscious (which was wetting itself with laughter at this stage) about unfinished business away from the safety zone of the British Isles, the only way I could make the teasing stop was by getting out of the country. No real man spent his life at home cowering behind a woman. Sympathising with the Tin Man from the *Wizard of Oz* was easy in my situation. In fact, I shared an immense empathy with most of the film's main characters. I could certainly do with a dose of courage like the Lion and I looked like a Scarecrow, so would that make Katie my Dorothy?

Wasting time, playing on the internet at work, my Googled eyes stumbled across the ultimate quest, my Holy Grail, the North Sea Cycle Route. Having read heaps of travel novels, to compensate for an inability to walk out of my own front door, I was quite clued up on European destinations. But this two-wheeled masochist's dream – proudly boasting to be the world's longest signposted coastal track – was news to me and maybe, just maybe, achievable. The route circled around 6,000 killer kilometres of the Netherlands, Germany, Denmark, Sweden, Norway, Scotland and England. Could undertaking this hard slog be the key to curing my continental agoraphobia?

It seemed an ideal mission. Close to home, I would have peace of mind, but my crumbling resolve would still be tested to the limit. If everything did go pear-shaped and I needed to bail out quickly there was the added security of making a quick escape on numerous ferries as all the foreign coasts on the tour faced the UK. It would be like playing the Northern European edition of Monopoly with a 'Get out of jail free Card' tucked under the saddle. I just wanted to pass 'Go'. It would be difficult severing all ties with the visual and written aid of my permanent travelling companions, Michael Palin and Bill Bryson. The three of us had grown intimately close during our numerous living room expeditions. But I'm sure they wouldn't begrudge a fellow adventure seeker his own taste of the action completely unaided by DVDs and books.

Initially this bolt from the blue didn't sit well with Katie, who at this point may have regretted the generous offer of wet nursing my insecurities for the rest of her life. I tried to make her understand that circumnavigating hundreds of kilometres of North Sea shoreline on a push-bike just months before the biggest day of both our lives was pretty much normal behaviour for a confused thirty something preparing to hang up his boots and settle down. Katie finally surrendered after high level talks across the kitchen war zone negotiated a ceasefire of crockery mortars exploding above my head (hurrah for the wedding present list and all those Debenhams vouchers).

If deserting her for a couple of months to get on with the final wedding arrangements was really going to make me less of a paranoid pain in the arse then I just about had a full blessing. Although I really didn't understand Katie's problem. Like most blokes, my side of the 'Big Day' bargain had been completed, perfecting the delivery of those two sacred words, 'I will'. But I had to promise to phone every day, not talk to any Scandinavian girls (who I tried, unsuccessfully, to pretend weren't very attractive with all their lovely blonde bunches and... stop it) and make sure my triumphant return wasn't in the church car park on the day of our wedding. Then, with a quick shake of the head, Katie pulled out the dust pan and brush and started to remove the new blue and white crushed floor mosaic of broken cups, plates and bowls.

I knew Katie's game. She had given me the green light in the firm belief I would return home swiftly with my tail firmly tucked beneath my backside, instantly ending any future plans of going it alone. I would probably get the whole 'adventure thing' out of my system after spending the opening night camping in a passport photo booth at Harwich ferry port, wrapping myself in the itchy orange dividing curtain to hide from the dangers outside. Oh she of little faith.

We'd been an item for three years and during that time Katie had grown to realise her perfect partner wasn't just a tad eccentric with a knack of making people laugh in the pub, but definitely had a crazy streak. Wild allegations that I am totally bonkers are cruel and untrue. Only once or twice (maybe three times) had I genuinely visualised clasping my hands around Katie's soft throat and throttling her to death as she slept. But aren't all serious relationships like that?

There were no guarantees of surviving total meltdown by standing tall on my own two pedals in a last ditch attempt to shake off these unhealthy obsessions. Convinced now that a spell of cycling solitude was a vital ingredient in solving a large chunk of my problems, I hadn't set my sights too high and knew I could get through this trip.

Full of bravado behind the pad, pencil and paper tray fortifications of my office computer, I was a rookie explorer, complete with padded khaki cycling shorts, on the verge of achieving greatness. Laughing in the face of adversity, my handlebars would steer past any hazards that tough, unforgiving countries like the Netherlands, Sweden and Norway could throw in my path. Although nothing more taxing than the sobering super-inflated alcohol tariffs of Scandinavia sprung to mind. This intrepid hero would return home triumphantly, spreading tales of newly discovered people talking in strange gibberish and their even weirder food and customs. There would be rough days ahead on the open cycle paths, but I would relish the punishing challenge of breathing new life into punctured tyres and getting my hands dirty tangling with awkward, greasy bike chains. These hardships would be character building and miraculously transform the anxiety ridden weakling into the complete 'man' husband Katie deserved to spend the rest of her days with.

My snug spell in the comfort zone was cruelly shattered by a scrunched up piece of A4 hitting me on the cheek, accompanied by a sighing 'wake up Bernie' from the thrower. Wiping daydream dribble from my chin, I began to realise the fantasy could so easily become the reality. That was it, make your mind up time. I was going to play this gig. It was time to finally get my shit together and return home a level headed, sane cycling Adonis with a very sore rear bumper.

2 All the fun of the Fear

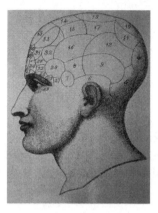

Anxiety and me first got hitched on a teenage trip to Amsterdam. It was fear at first sight. If there was ever a living advert for never legalising cannabis then my deranged features would be plastered across advertising boards on the side of laundrettes up and down the country. Eighteen and naïve, I went searching for liberation underneath the only Red Lights which never order anybody to stop indulging in the many pleasures the famously tolerant Dutch capital had to offer. But my only new discoveries were uncontrollable panic and the persistent paranoia which still haunts me 17 years down the line.

I'd never been into drugs, despite being surrounded by close friends who will smoke, swallow and sniff anything they can get their hands on as often as possible. They love to see it snowing all year round and if they can't pilot their blistered nostrils along a runway of cocaine they will turn to acid, ecstasy, speed – any chemical cocktail for that extra buzz. Maybe I never got enrolled in the small town narcotics society because I've got such a large nose (my bulbous bugle would probably make King Dong blush) that nobody wanted to share with me, which was a blessing in disguise. The thought of having an illegal substance, which I don't have control of, taking over my body would finish me off once and for all. I can't even drop an aspirin or Lemsip capsule without worrying myself sick about it, so anything riskier would definitely rubber-stamp my one-way ticket to the funny farm.

Like most fresh-faced youngsters on their Amsterdam debut, two pals and I were well up for a dabble with the hospitality of the city's legendary café culture. What a mistake! We'd gone to watch pensionable indie punk rockers *Carter the Unstoppable Sex Machine* play the Paradiso, a venue which had become a well known worship place for music lovers needing a live sermon as it used to be a church. I helped Carter run their fan club and had cashed in a promise of a plus one or two freebie at any of their European gigs, following weeks of mastering cramp, sitting cross-legged on the floor of an untidy Brixton living room stuffing pre-paid envelopes for the band's mailshot.

A strange edginess took over when we entered the thick fog of an Amsterdam smoking emporium for the first time. The green neon light of a big fat spliff hanging on the side of the building had beckoned us inside after being spat out of a grubby narrow snake-like alley. But on approaching the crowded bar of the back-street puffing paradise with a fistful of jangling guilders the atmosphere was far from welcoming. Someone turned off the chatter switch and raised the hard stares lever. It didn't take a posse of stoned rain-macked Columbos to have a hunch we were from out of town – the baseball caps, back-packs and waterproofs sort of gave it away. For the not so super sleuths, the other clue was in the painfully slow English my mate punctuated patronisingly with hand signals as he tried to translate his intention to score from the barman. It was just like the Slaughtered Lamb pub scene at the start of *An American Werewolf in London*, but minus the eerie wall pentagram and unfriendly superstitious bitter-drinking old boys in their flat caps, sporting giant lamb-chop sideburns which were crying out for a dab of mint sauce.

The whole scenario made me nervous, which probably wasn't the right frame of mind to be in as I saddled up for a first, and last, trip along the super-skunk highway. On the rare occasions I had sucked on a joint back home it had been much weaker solids, soap bar, and as the green smoke of one reefer after another curled towards the ceiling from my mouth I had no idea how potent it was.

Everything started off fine. Comfortably numbed by our experimental inhalations, the negative vibe had passed, leaving us slumped giggling in our battered brown leather chairs. But it was the calm before the storm and 15 minutes later Hurricane Panic ravaged my body. Feeling more chilled out than Bejams (it was the early 90s, Iceland hadn't won the frozen store war yet), I was sipping one of those silly coffees from a thimble-sized cup, when right out of nowhere my heart felt like it had caught an express elevator to my throat. I sprung up from the café armchair and spilled on to the street, tripping out of my head and convinced that something terrible was going to happen. Breathing was a major struggle as the first panic attack of my life let rip and it suddenly dawned on me that home was far away. OK, it was only the Netherlands, but at the time I felt so helpless and alone I could have been a wandering yak farmer stranded in the Outer Mongolian plains without a Ger to his name.

My worried comrades soon caught up and found their travelling companion pacing up and down the street like a madman, mumbling a desperate plea to God and begging for help. 'Please make it all right, make it go away and I'll never do anything like this again, promise.' They grabbed hold of my jacket and attempted to calm me down, but it took more shakes than a Tic-Tac packet to help me get to grips with this alien sensation. Eventually catching my breath, the tightness across the chest began to release. But I felt like my head had been sandpapered, turning my legs into a couple of custard stilts, which were tricky to balance on as we headed for the haven of the Paradiso. Seeing I was in a right mess, the club's understanding owner granted us early admission and I somehow shut out the raging electric guitars, pounding drum machine and screaming vocals of Carter's sound-check, stretching out on an old wooden pew and sleeping off the mind-altering effects of the skunk. Life would never be the same again.

My only memory of the gig itself was a one-armed stage diver with a death wish throwing himself into the crowd all night long, much to the amusement of the band's smiling guitarist Fruitbat. I was fortunate enough to make the sweat soaked Utrecht madman's acquaintance in the toilet after the show. He in turn felt honoured to receive an Englishman's praise for his sterling efforts and excitedly offered his only hand in friendship and promptly pissed down the front of his jeans.

Amsterdam was just the tip of an enormous iceberg and my problems mushroomed back in Blighty. Mum had binned my dad and moved in a brick shithouse, Freddy Mercury look-alike. He certainly sent me Radio Ga Ga. Under strict order of violence, Major Mercury would conscript my younger brother Karl to join me in carrying out a military style clean-up operation in our shared bedroom each week, before holding a meticulous inspection of the sleeping quarters.

This bloke was very scary, he was a loose cannon happy to fire, and things were worse when mum wasn't around. My head had already made a close acquaintance with a bowl full of washing-up, miraculously failing to get really intimate with a number of upward facing forks and knives. Another time, I was a terrified spectator as Karl was forced to run up and down the living room stairs 100 times. The twisted bastard rewarded my worn-out sibling with a glass of Coke, which he rapidly necked to quench his thirst, but it turned out to be vinegar and made him spew everywhere. This sort of behaviour couldn't go unpunished. How dare he throw his guts up, my tortured brother should have drained his cup of cruelty and kept it down. Out came the flesh stripping bamboo garden canes.

My frightened focus on finishing the bedroom drill soon sprouted another branch of the madness tree – obsessive compulsive disorders. Any pieces of fluff on the floor would have to be picked up quickly and stuffed in my pockets. Shoes and books had to be left in exactly the right position and lights needed to be clicked on and off in a certain sequence before going to bed or a new day would never come. These rituals soon manifested themselves in more bizarre ways. I started having urges to twist my arms and legs into painful knots, press myself up against the wall at the same time and recite multiples of the number eight in my head, believing this oddest of behaviour would save me from harm.

But I wasn't cut out for this new career as a mathematical contortionist. Carrying out these energy draining procedures was equalling the efforts of a runner in training for the London Marathon and it couldn't carry on. I was heading for burnout at the end of my teens. Home help came from a stocky Care in the Community nurse with a ginger beard (yes, it was a man, worst luck) who prescribed a diet of antidepressants for the next six months. After forcing down the pills with gallons of water, the side-effects of the drugs filtering into my blood stream put the frighteners on again at first. This was strong gear and I found it difficult to get up from a sitting down position. The first 48 hours turned into a giddy rollercoaster ride, before the calming effects of the medication kicked in for real and slowed everything down, giving me the self-assurance to relax and attempt a more normal life.

Another bonus was my mum's decision to ditch the resident headcase, who by a happy coincidence turned out to be a psychotic schizophrenic and was having regular therapy himself. I remember hearing him having a heated argument with my mother one morning when she was 15 miles away at work. Now that's what I call crazy. I can appreciate the funny side of it now, but at the time there wasn't much laughter around the house.

The medication was finally ditched after attending group therapy and relaxation sessions. It certainly is good to talk and listening to and learning from other anxiety addicts made me realise three things – I was not alone, most of them were even more loopy than me and I was well on the road to recovery. All meetings ended in the same way, shutting off the outside world by lying down in a darkened room on karate style crash mats alongside the rest of the barmy army, listening to the calming calls of nautical mammals. Replacing the drugs with breathing exercises during these sessions, to control the feelings of panic naturally, was a huge help. But the biggest bonus was definitely picking up which high-pitched chat-up noises to make if I ever fancied getting it on with a dolphin or whale. We could be Mr and Mrs Flipper Friend.

During the cosy group chats, one veteran nutter would chirp on about her pigeon phobia. She was radio rental at a high frequency and would happily reminisce about running through Southend town centre screaming like a banshee if any of our winged friends decided to use her as a landing pad. I visualised how funny it would be to glue bits of bread bait to her coat and watch the sprint for cover as she was pecked by an attack squadron of airborne rodents.

Having already accepted complete normality was out of my reach, I started to adapt and survive. I certainly didn't need four pink pills and a couple of radioactive-looking yellow and black capsules to get through the day. It may sound cruel, but sniggering at the likes of the pigeon lady made me realise some rehabilitation was possible and this lunatic wasn't as badly off as some of his cell mates. Although, to this day, there are still the odd moments when I pull funny faces at myself in the bathroom mirror, make gurgling noises and flick my tongue in and out of my mouth as fast as I can.

My quality of life did improve and I started to wrestle back control, slowly growing stronger. Learning to keep a tighter leash on my anxieties helped me bounce back to achieve a lot on a personal level. But I'll never be 100 per cent cured as this is a life sentence. I don't have to put my boxer shorts away in my cupboard at right angles anymore, but I'm still a glutton for the odd spot of mental torture.

There's the claustrophobic feelings on coaches and tube trains. I've already persuaded myself before I climb on board that I'm going to cover anybody in a three seat radius in a projectile vomit launch. Just think how much a lap full of my recycled bacon, eggs and beans would improve the miserable existences of those glum underground sentinels who tunnel through London's rabbit warren every day.

And flying is a complete no-go. There's more chance of Mr T and Dennis Bergkamp parking their arses on a plane seat next to each other before me. If man was meant to fly free through the air evolution would have given him a pair of wings, but there are no feathers sprouting out of anything of mine. No, my feet stay firmly on the floor, which is a barrel of laughs for the other half during the summer holidays. 'Guess what? Thanks for putting up with me again this year when you could have just chosen a normal boyfriend and had an easy life, as a reward I've booked up the caravan in Dawlish. It's buckets and spades, fish and chips, plus toffee nut brittle rings all the way for us this June.' Who needs a proper Costa bronzing anyway?

My one and only flight was a strictly one-way affair five years ago. The mission was to hook up with a Canadian girl I first met in a Bruges youth hostel on FA Cup final day, following a Trappist monk brew-inspired session at the aptly named De Pub. Let's just say that Arsenal's Ray Parlour wasn't the only person to score that day and if Little Miss Maple Leaf's name had been Chelsea then life would have been perfect.

14

Living in sin at the time, I could feel the unforgiving fires of hell burning ever warmer beneath my backside after remaining in contact with Miss Issauga via email (the greatest adultery tool ever invented on a par with text messaging by the way). A few weeks after returning home from the Belgian tryst, the Canadian cutie offered to demonstrate her extreme stamina by inviting me on a Spanish shagfest (not a traditional festival), before jetting back home after four long months back-packing around Europe. Determined to make the rendezvous of lust and lying through my back teeth, I quickly invented a story for the long suffering girlfriend about a free press trip to Alicante, awarded in recognition of all my hard work on the local rag. She bought every word, but this was the bloke who could sell a fortnight in Cleethorpes to Judith Chalmers, and I was soon making my maiden flight from Gatwick to the Spanish seaside resort with a *Southend Echo* colleague Steve, making my big fat fib even more convincing.

But I got my comeuppance and went through every pair of pants in my suitcase just getting there. The flight was only two-and-a-half-hours long, but it was the most topsy-turvy 150 minutes of my life. Our cabin crew were buckled in tight for the whole journey and my companion, Mr 'I've flown 17 times and it's a piece of Piss', was equally afraid of becoming a huge tangled mess of wreckage on the *Six O'Clock News*, which was a great comfort.

Just to make the journey even more snug, I was wedged in between Steve and a massive meathead in an Australian rugby shirt, who looked hard as nails, was oblivious to the turbulence and hadn't flinched once. In slight contrast, I ripped off my wooden cross and St Christopher necklaces, clutching them so tightly they left imprints in my greasy palms which threatened to become permanent holiday souvenirs.

The Catholic guilt factor soon kicked in. Death was my destiny in divine retribution from God for going away to do the dirty on my other half. My stomach lurched every time the fragile feeling craft bobbed to the side or suddenly dropped. Tidal waves of sweat washed across my forehead at every movement, no matter how big or small. And inside my head it was just like being back in Amsterdam, except this time I wasn't making a panic pact with the Lord Almighty because of a few spliffs, I was promising to keep my dick in my shorts and never be unfaithful again if we landed safely. But God's no mug and knew this fast tracked, newly born Christian, would break his pledge as soon as we were back on the tarmac. He opted instead to carry on using the plane as a holy yo-yo all the way to Spain, wasting away a couple of hours of what must sometimes be a monotonous immortality.

The skipper put the icing on the cake. 'Hello boys and girls this is captain Johnny speaking,' bleated the intercom in an insanely calm sounding voice. 'Sorry about the turbulence, I know it's a poor old show, but it's just like little ripples in the bath, nothing to worry about.' Yeah right, not only does the bloke holding my life in his altitude levers think he is Biggles (complete with smart tash, sticky out trousers, goggles and wire supported scarf), but he's trying to stop me going out of my mind by quoting lines from the 'We're going to nosedive to our doom, but let's calm down the passengers anyway Manual.' I think it was section 12, paragraph 6.

Of course, the big man upstairs spared my life, but things were just as rough back on solid ground. I was soon wobbling like a toddler's party jelly as stowaway anxiety sneaked out of my suitcase, bringing a premature end to a planned programme of sun, sea, sex, sangria and sanity. Miss Mounty (and no, she wasn't a moose) didn't seem too impressed with her English stallion's inability to make the final furlong. Missing out on a sun tan in the hotel room, I only kept the pace for three days before abandoning ship, but let's face it, we never had a long-term future. Having a big affinity with chickens now, my wings were firmly pinned and I would never have the bottle to take-off again, it was never going to last. I certainly didn't like her enough to pull on a black roll-neck jumper and spend 10 days getting smashed around by the freezing waves of the North Atlantic on a cargo ship, just to deliver a box of Milk Tray with the personal touch to Canada.

This left one route back – the train – and I was soon on my way to the ticket office, despite frenzied protestation from my holiday chum Steve. He was right to think I had lost the plot, but came anyway because his pulling technique stunk (standing in the same spot at the bar all night, undoing more shirt buttons as he got increasingly intoxicated and staring creepily with growing deviancy) and I was paying. It may have taken 25 hours longer than the flight, but was the best part of the trip, just chatting freely with strangers who tumbled into the same carriage grimacing under the weight of monstrously overloaded back-packs with tea-towels and spatulas dangling from the side. Most were American and Canadian travellers who were only too happy to share favourable tales of the mysterious new places they had discovered. There was even one German guy eager to steal the limelight by telling us he had visited England once. But it didn't count. Gunther had spent one day in Hull which, trying to impress us with his accurate grasp of the English language, he correctly described as an 'armpit'.

The point I'm trying to make is that a long rail journey back to London, blinking past Barcelona and Paris, sowed a seed which has never been allowed to germinate. I have been restless ever since and never stop craving for my own chance to get out there and throw myself headlong into the great unknown. But my constant unwanted companion, paranoia, has prevented me from fulfilling my one burning ambition.

All of my mates have been on their holidays of a lifetime, mostly beer, drug and prostitute-fuelled trips to Thailand, followed by endless lazy months in Australia. But I have to pull on my brown trousers as soon as I leave the safety of Essex.

Following Southend United's sinking fortunes for an evening newspaper caused me enough aggro, travelling a few hundred miles across the motherland to report on games at footballing hotbeds like Hartlepool and Scunthorpe. Although, I did make a lot of new friends, generously sharing my shaking half-time coffee and flaky meat and potato pie with the other gentlemen and ladies of the press, hemmed into a lower division theatre of rust like battery hens.

Other efforts to launch non-flying expeditions abroad have all ended in the same miserable failure. There was the time I caught the train to Malmo, another 24-hour slog, but no sooner had my trainers kissed the soil of Sweden's southern coast, it was time to turn around and flee back home because I felt insecure and couldn't handle being so far away. Another futile attempt to go private and unearth an expensive cure for my travel phobia was splashing out £6,000 on a camper van with the aim of driving around Europe for six months. The plan was to grip a stubborn bull by the horns and become the master of my own destiny, steering myself along the open road towards craggy peaks, wild untamed forests and golden sandy beaches. Sounds great, doesn't it. The harsh reality was a four day chug up and down the Netherlands' motorways in a right old flap before again waving my little white flag and scrambling back home a quivering wreck.

Pathetic I know, but when you start suffering stomach cramps, nausea and light-headedness, cranked up to the max by unshakeable thoughts of an untimely end away from the protection of your loved ones, the desire to be back in familiar surroundings is quite strong. But the determination to put this constant negativity behind me was still fervent. We all meet our maker one day, although I hadn't given up hope of becoming the first member of the human race to live forever, and I didn't want to take my place in heaven without having been anywhere on earth.

The North Sea Cycle Route had become an all consuming obsession which was eating away at my days and nights. Every spare moment was spent pouring over maps and internet pages, scanning the towns and cities I hoped to pedal through as part of the experience. It was impossible to leave it alone. Sleeping was becoming a difficult pastime as my brain refused to switch off in unison with the bedroom light, filling the restless little hours with travelling fantasises and visions of what may lay ahead.

Forgive me for stating the bloody obvious, but 6,000 kilometres was a long way to cycle. Undecided whether I was going to attempt the whole thing, I didn't even know if my body was up to the punishing demands of going all the way. That decision would take care of itself once I was out there and doing it for real. The fitness levels would need to be higher than struggling through 90 minutes on a muddy football pitch, blowing out of my backside on a hangover blighted Sunday morning. But there would be no rush, just pedalling at my own pace and taking in the scenery.

Cycling parallel to the sea every day and tapping into its ancient calming influence sounded like soothing therapy to me. After all, what was the worst thing that could happen? I could return home the conqueror of my troubles with calf muscles the size of tree trunks having won this mental tug-of-war. Alternatively, the marbles might fall out of the bag completely, forcing me to sprint stark bollock naked through an obscure fishing village, flapping my arms around frantically and squawking like an angry parrot. What else was there to worry about?

My mission, and I had accepted it, would begin at Harwich ferry port, with the first turns of the pedals on Dutch soil following the six-hour crossing to the Hoek van Holland. Then I really would be on my own. After leaving the flat cycling haven of the polders, which was the best place for a complete novice to start, the route crossed the top of Germany and climbed up, across and back down Denmark to Sweden, before reaching out towards the Norwegian port of Bergen. If breathing was still an option, another ferry could then whisk me across the North Sea stepping stones of the Shetland and Orkney Islands, before landing on mainland Scotland and freewheeling down the east coast of England back to my Harwich starting point, which should be a doddle as it was all downhill on the map.

To the normal man on the street, this may sound as far removed from a dream vacation as a stinking, rotten molar, but in my eyes the opportunities were endless. It was definitely on a par with losing my shirt in Las Vegas, picking up Yeti sized blisters trekking across the Himalayas or getting to grips with a pair of flippers and snorkel for a spot of scuba-drowning on the Great Barrier Reef. All I had to do was jump on the saddle, keep my travel-allergic mind together, and start pedalling my way back to mental health.

3   Christmas Cancelled

A grim December sent all the baubles crashing off my Christmas tree in one loud bang. As everybody else got into gear for the fun and frolics of the festive period, I was gifted the shattering news that my mother had a maximum of 18 months to live. She only lasted seven weeks.

It started with a simple slur in the speech, which all the arrogant health professionals fobbed off as previous painful dental treatment, before having another guess at a mini-stroke. If only their diagnosis had been right. It had taken three months and three ambulance trips to get my mother admitted to hospital as her condition grew worse. We all raise our eyebrows at horror stories in the newspapers about shoddy treatment on the wards, but it is forgotten as soon as the page is turned. Witnessing first hand how hard it was to get urgent help for a loved one from the great crumbling British institution of the NHS was a much more difficult pill to swallow.

The Nothing but Hassle Service gets a big no vote of confidence from this tax payer. Not one of the handful of doctors who examined mum were willing to stick their necks out and admit her as an inpatient, or give the green light for a scan to find out what was happening inside her head. 'We just haven't got the room,' one said. 'She's better off at home,' diagnosed another. But I'll save the best until last, 'All you can do is take her back to her house and keep your fingers crossed.' The whole nightmare experience was so energy draining as the patronising know-it-all guardians of our well-being kept in tune with the festive theme by doing a cracking rendition of the beleaguered inn keeper of Bethlehem. This could have been an undercover special on the *Cook Report*, with the portly champion of the underdog warning: 'Don't ever get ill folks, as those

National Insurance payments on your payslip may as well be printed on the same paper as Christmas cracker jokes.'

Weeks of virtually crawling on my hands and knees begging health workers for assistance, plus forcing my ailing mother to invent terrible headaches, eventually paid off. But my fingers weren't crossed tightly enough. The expected relief gained from watching her take the first steps on the road to recovery, aided by special drug concoctions and speech therapies, evaporated overnight. Results of the long campaigned for scan delivered the unexpected and crushing news that mum's brain was being ravaged by the most aggressive cancerous tumour on record anywhere – a grade four glioblastoma.

Sitting in a hospital room beside my mother, who was sobbing uncontrollably about her life being prematurely stolen away, shattered my world. This woman had not just been my rock, but a towering mountain, who was now destined to crumble away far too early in the cruellest of fashions, leaving behind an almighty void in her absence. Squeezing her hand tightly against a torrent of tears, the roles had been reversed and I was the one doing the reassuring now. I tried to make her believe everything would be OK, just as she had done for me thousands of times in the past. But this was terrible. I'd never seen my mother look so scared and washed-out before. The terrified childlike expression on her face soon turned to complete horror as she began having future visions of lying in a coffin at her own funeral. This screaming description was so harsh and instantly choking, the most difficult to ever pass through my ears, which will take some beating.

Here was my mum, a young 56 in the prime of her life and a keen swimmer in good physical condition, so why was this happening? This sort of thing only happened to other people, not me. Mum had never hurt anyone and worked her fingers to the bone. How could she be dealt this stinking hand when winding down and a relaxing retirement should have been on the cards?

My first feeling was of complete guilt. Here was the human being dearest to my heart coming under ferocious attack from something I had consistently hammered on about during my own unsubstantiated delusions. Recalling all the anxious sprints to the security of her apron strings bleating 'please mum, tell me I haven't got a brain tumour', because of a slight twinge in my temple filled me with shame. And here she was being destroyed by the real thing – how could I have been such an idiot? Wiping the tears from both of our eyes I apologised for being such a fool in the past. But now the initial shock had passed she found the courage to smile, telling me to dry my eyes and stop being so silly, as only a mother can.

Guilt soon gave way to anger. The tumour had grown two inches in diameter – the size of a satsuma – in just two months, time we had spent being pushed from pillar to post in the hope of securing a hospital admission. Could something positive have been done if the dithering doctors had taken action straight away? Private internet investigations soon uncovered the awful truth – there was no cure. All the money in the world couldn't buy you freedom as there was no recovery rate, not even one per cent. Forget all the breakthroughs of modern medicines and brand new wonders of the scientific universe, the harsh facts were that nobody who has this disease gets well. We were powerless and talking damage limitation at best.

I kept a nervous vigil, following the waiting-room clock hands as they slowly crept around a cracked face for seven hours, while mum fought a winning battle for survival in emergency surgery. No matter how skilful the surgeons were with the knife, it was almost impossible to dig out the whole tumour – which wraps itself around the brain like a tightly clinging poison ivy – for fear of causing irreversible damage to the other primary functions of the mind. Always a quick healer and a veteran of routine trips to the operating theatre, she made the expected almost super human recovery. Speech was much improved and she was soon chasing nurses up and down the corridor to give them a telling off about her lukewarm morning tea, but it was no more than a heartless illusion and brief return to near normality.

Two weeks after the operation we were back holding hands again when the consultant confirmed our worst fears, mum could finally be discharged, but the sands of her time were draining away fast. Remarkably, this terminal revelation was digested outwardly comfortably by the shaven headed, bruised and skull scarred figure gripping me. Mum thanked the doctor for his honesty, before opening up about a host of targets she was determined to struggle on and meet, spending special final moments with all her friends and family during the months ahead. This act of bravery left me completely gobsmacked, but 'what was the point in worrying about the inevitable, it wasn't going to magic up a cure', was her response.

We started hatching plans about Caribbean cruises and even more ambitious trips. A keen £20 a week gambler, it had always been a lifelong ambition of my mother to blow some real cash at Las Vegas' casino heaven. 'What have I got to lose,' she chuckled. 'I may as well go out on a high having a flutter on the roulette wheel. Collapsing and dying inside Caesar's Palace with a load of chips in my hand would be just as good as anywhere else. But I'd stock up on all those free sandwiches and drinks they give you before I went.' That was typical of my mother, here she was holding the Grim Reaper at arm's length, but was too busy contemplating an expensive freebie on the other side of world to worry about it.

This spiteful twist of fate didn't grant last wishes however and she was taken away swiftly one February morning, just weeks after the final diagnosis. Beginning a course of radiotherapy, in a last ditch attempt to fight back and give this nasty tumour a taste of its own medicine, she had been given a bed on the cancer ward for observation. They can't do enough for you once they know you're going to die, but the speed of her final exit was a shock to everyone – doctors, nurses and family. I was supposed to be picking her up on that final Friday and taking her home, but she had already slipped away on my arrival. There was no warning. Mum had been fine all morning, watching a film on a portable DVD player and larking about with the nurses, when suddenly there was a short, sharp struggle for breath and it was all over. Complications with a lung clot was the official cause of death – a pulmonary embolism apparently – and in all honesty I should be grateful for this one small mercy.

I would have done anything to keep her here. You could have chopped off my arms and legs if it had made any difference. But in the long run it was better this way, better than watching her continue to deteriorate in agony or become a vegetable who turned into a complete stranger and didn't even recognise me. That would have been a nightmare image I couldn't handle, haunting me every time I closed my eyes until my own dying day.

She couldn't grow old now and in an increasing number of night time prayers I pleaded with this heavily cherished, bold woman to zap me with a shot of her immeasurable strength from the other side. If she could be so tough in her darkest hours of despair, then I could shake off my own demons and make the most of the greatest gift any mother can give her child – life. This was a huge wake-up call and stuffed a plug in my own paralysing worries, which were still leaking out, but beginning to pale into insignificance.

If my mother was brave enough to stare death in the face each day with a smile on her face, then I could jump on a bike and cycle a few hundred miles safe in the knowledge I was both fit and healthy. She was on top of my unfulfilled travelling plans and always pointed out the funny side of my past failures, encouraging me never to give up and chuckling that I would leave England for more than a few days eventually.

Those last few weeks together were so precious and I will hold them tight forever. She had got worse. Her voice was fading badly and a violent facial tick made the garbled words come out like a scratched record. Mum did get upset, especially by the possibility of missing my wedding, which she would, and knowing the chance of cradling her future grandchildren had vanished. But she never threw in the towel and made me promise to be the same, seeing my plans through and giving the North Sea Cycle Route a go. I'm not trying to place her on an unassailable pedestal as some sort of martyr, because she certainly wasn't the first person to die this way or a perfect mother by any means, leaving my father and residing with a violent nutcase who mentally scarred her children for starters. But show me someone who is perfect. We all make mistakes and she was always there when it mattered most, wedging herself into the bathroom doorway to form a body barrier between me and Corporal Aggression during a *Dallas* length series of two hour stand-off specials which saved me from a bloody beating.

Even right at the end my mother was an influential force (at senior school she forced me to wear a black bomber jacket for so many terms that the birth of the Beastie Boys made this newly crowned Brooklynite the toast of the playground), giving me one last push to accomplish the goals she wouldn't be around to witness on this mortal plain. Renewed determination filled me to carry out my journey, which would now double up as a fitting tribute to this remarkable woman. Calling on her ability to face the greatest personal adversity headlong without a whimper for motivation would keep the pedals turning. Mum always made the most of life and her motto was: 'If you've got, it flaunt it.' Her favourite catchphrase was accompanied by a staged wobble of her two biggest assets and that's what I had to do (make the most of every second, not the boob shaking part).

The comfort gained from knowing a proud person like my mum had gone out with her dignity fully intact grew stronger as the weeks raced by. What still felt strange was that mum was actually gone forever, when only a few weeks before her passing she had been bursting at the seams with life. We had spent a precious week at a holiday camp with her two sisters and Katie. She had been stuffing cream cakes down her face, jigging with the girls to the sound of the 60s and filling her big rosy cheeks with laughter after being serenaded by an Elvis impersonator whose over the top quiff resembled a jet black broom head. And then she was gone, snuffed out like a candle flame in the swift click of a finger. I felt both robbed and cheated.

The good memories outweighed the dark ones, lifting my deflated spirits and damming the intermittent floods of tears which were still seeping through. It was time to stop moping around and start picking up the pieces of my own life. That was easier said than done of course, but no amount of rewinding past painful events in my head was going to bring her back from the grave and it was time for me to start living again.

A finger piloted test run around my European motoring atlas took in a long list of weird and wonderfully named destinations on the North Sea

Cycle Route. Monster, Tzummarum, Brunsbüttel, Pellworm, Ringkøbing, Klitmøller, Fiskebäckskil and Mosterhamn all stuck out at first glance. And let's not forget Hull and Hartlepool. What happened in these places and how were they christened in such strange ways?

Monster was one of the first places to trundle past after docking in the Netherlands. Would it be a case of pedalling frantically through the streets of this small coastal town to escape the hungry, slavering attentions of giant furry Edams with eight arms and sharp blood stained teeth, geared to swallowing both me and the bike in one sitting? (A bit like trying to get past a gang of inebriated ladies unscathed on any Saturday night in Hull city centre.)

Was Fiskebäckskil the top secret training camp for a special breed of super female Swedish gymnastic goddesses in tight yellow Lycra costumes, hell bent on striking gold at the next Olympics? Please, please, please let it be so. I wanted to do my bit to help them prepare for an assault on the awards podium by generously taking a break from my tight cycling schedule to get them working up a sweat with some thorough testing of their suppleness. Maybe they would keep me prisoner against my will and force me into coaching them for the next World Nude Twister Championships. It sounds like a hard job, but somebody had to do it, preferably with every single one of them.

And how about the pig farmers of Mosterhamn, did they breed giant porkers in an effort to fill all the ham sandwiches in Norway? It was a big place after all and with that much trotter flying about you would expect bacon sarnies to be the only cheap commodity in this expensively silly country. Let's just hope it wasn't the bordello capital for thrill seekers trying to get their grubby paws around a big sausage. It's not illegal to bonk animals in Norway, but the Danes are the true masters of the beast, actually running farm style brothels (maybe the madam is a buxom sheep known as Dolly Baa-ton). Hundreds of Norwegian sex tourists flock (sorry) to Denmark for their hard earned holidays, so they can forge a bond with that special lamb, cow or donkey every summer. What else was I going to find out by visiting these places? God only knows, but I definitely wouldn't be practising safe sex on Daisy with a dustbin bag. I'm all for being at one with nature, but I'll stick to puckering up to a pickled herring, hugging a tall tree and tickling a good looking elk under the chin if that's OK.

I would strive to discover the answers to all these questions and much more, but a mountain of groundwork had to be tunnelled through before I could unscrew the stabilisers and disappear into the sunset. The North Sea Cycle Route was the brainchild of a group of crack Norwegian fanatics, who must have lost their skis mid-air and landed on push-bikes. A European funded international partnership between all seven countries covered by the 6,000 kilometre course, the Norse County Council of Rogaland is credited with painstakingly fitting all the pieces of this complicated jigsaw across land and sea together, before announcing its birth to the world with a deafening silence of handlebar bells in 2001.

Sure, there is limited knowledge of the route in secret cycle circles and on a now much improved official website. But does your average man or woman in the pub know anything about it? Try dropping this one into the conversation next time you are engaged in idle banter with a stranger at the bar of the Dog and Duck. 'Did you know there is a cycle track which starts in Harwich and spans a huge 6,000 kilometre loop of Northern Europe before returning home again? All we need to do is drink up, jump on our bikes and be back here again before last orders in three months. Did I mention it had a Guinness World Record certificate? Another pint of the black stuff while you mull it over?'

Nobody in their right mind was going to escort you, completely battered or stone cold sober, so it was worth taking a pop shot at a random drinker. But don't be offended when your new ex-friend ploughs his drinking arm through a valley of beer mats (without spilling a drop) to sit alongside the token village idiot and enjoy a chat of superior intellectual substance. He may also take the safety precaution of slashing the tyres on your bike in the pub car park on the way home. But don't take it personally. You did make an impression as this was for your own long-term benefit as well as his.

The first thing I discovered was the continental translation for North Sea Cycle Route was 'come and find your way around our coastal maze if you can'. Any thoughts of cycling carefree around a nice little circle of neatly packaged countries with a soppy deranged look on my face were soon destroyed. A closer inspection unveiled a three month grind of psychological as well as physical tests which would have been right at home on the *Krypton Factor*. The route was nowhere near as clearly signposted as suggested on the official internet web of lies. There was also more than one way to traverse this imperfect circle and maps for the journey were like gold dust.

Now this was a big problem as I was no Peter Pathfinder. Weekends away camping with the cubs were frustrating enough (for everyone else) as yours truly was the only Dib-Dibber who had a problem reading a compass no matter how many times he recited 'Never Eat Shredded Wheat' to himself. Getting in a right old muddle, my pitiful attempts to arrange mental breakfast cereal substitutes for bearings in the correct north, east, shredded, west order, would end any chances of being back around the campfire in time for beef stew, mash, carrots and a quick Ging-Gang-Gooley.

It wasn't something I grew out of either as I'm still useless with directions. Getting lost in a toilet cubicle is a possibility when the door is shut. This can be embarrassing in pubs and clubs as most people don't want to watch you sitting on the can preparing to unload. It's just as bad standing up for a number one with the door ajar as you are dismissed as a snob who shuns the company of other men for a posh piss alone. Alternatively, you are the band leader of the small weener brigade, frowned upon by superior members of the Gents club who snigger at your expense as they unzip their trousers and rub shoulders (and who knows what else) alongside real men as you tackle your stage fright in solitary confinement.

But in times of crisis you can always rely on the services of an experienced professional and help was at hand. Not with the lavatory problem, that was personal, but with plotting a smooth course around the North Sea circle. Another quick browse across the information super cycleway helped me link-up with a real life legend in the saddle, North Shields' John Taylor, who claims to be the only cyclist still pedalling to have covered every inch of the route.

Maths teacher John traded in his geometry set and abacus beads to take up early retirement in his late fifties a few years ago. But wasting away the days with a green finger or two in the back garden cabbage patch and among the runner-beans, before a game of cribbage down the British Legion, were the last things on John's twilight itinerary. Instead he plonked his backside on a firm seat and set his sights on the greatest challenge of his life, conquering the North Sea Cycle Route and raising £20,000 for the MacMillan Nurses and NECCR Childrens Cancer Research charities.

Having made the mistake of leaving a phone number for stalking website freaks to feverishly take advantage of, no time was wasted in interrogating my new found mentor. 'It was something I will never forget and I'm so pleased I did it,' John fondly recalled. 'Of course I had the added incentive of doing the whole thing for charity. But the entire journey was full of wonderful sights and amazing experiences which will stay with me forever.'

My North Sea Cycle Route tour guide promised me a diversity of stunning scenery. Big cities and tiny villages, endless sand dune guarded golden beaches, grassy lowlands and uplands, as well as steep, rocky cliff pathways and deep icy fjords – the full Monty. But after settling into a snug daydream of lazy lost cycling days, John quickly brought me crashing back to reality with a sore thump by confirming my worst fears.

'The route maps are a nightmare to get hold of,' he added. 'There isn't just one simple guide for the whole thing. You have to buy numerous maps for every country and they are not all easy to find. The English and

Scottish parts are straightforward as they are part of the National Cycle Network and there are excellent books published for the stretches through the Netherlands and Germany. But it all gets complicated when you hit Scandinavia. There is no guide for one of Denmark's coasts and you need two booklets for the Norwegian leg, one of which I had to track down and buy while I was out there in Kristiansand. I had the same problems in Sweden. I paid for the map on my credit card and they sent me a tourist brochure. I couldn't get the maps anywhere and had to follow normal road atlases, which were in Swedish, but did have the cycle route marked all the way. It caused more than a few problems, but certainly added to the adventure of the trip.'

It was at this point that I should have slammed down the phone, accepted my limits as a human being and conceded defeat by booking week long reservations for Bucks Fizz's 'Flogging a Long Dead Horse' tour at Butlins in Bognor Regis. But after a long pause, wondering if I could stomach the Eurovision Vomit Test of Cheryl Baker having her skirt ripped off in the middle of 'Still Making your Mind Up after 20 odd years', a concerned voice on the other end of the receiver tried to offer soothing reassurance.

'There's no need to worry,' John cheerily explained. 'You will be part of a big cycling family when you are out on the road. Everybody looks out for each other. When I was having trouble on the Norwegian leg of the journey I met up with a German girl at a campsite and we helped each other out. She was cycling the opposite way to me and we solved our problems by swapping maps. All these little glitches have a way of sorting themselves out on the road.' Now I really felt all warm inside.

John affectionately recounted many happy tales of meeting new comrades on two wheels and forging evening friendships, which are still strong today thanks to email, next to the warmth of a campfire. Comforted by the knowledge that all troubles in the field could be resolved by sending up a Bat Signal for a cycling Helga, I asked my new buddy which was the best way around the course. I was planning to start at Harwich and head for the Netherlands, following the route anti-clockwise. John had decided to follow the hands in numerical order, setting off from his north-east home and progressing up to Scotland, before island hopping to Norway. Big mistake.

'I chose the tougher way for sure,' he said. 'The elements seem to be a lot worse on the clockwise route and the winds are terrible. I was up against these horrible gales and got buffeted about all over the place.'

John was soon fast-tracked on to my all time greatest heroes list. He was sandwiched between my role models of insanity, the fourth *Doctor Who* Tom Baker (that reminds me, I must pack some Jelly Babies) and 'Red Card' Roy McDonough, the former Southend United targetman and

Basil Fawlty look-alike (even the silly walk) with the worst disciplinary record in the history of English football. But John was soon pulling away from the flying elbows and dragging himself up the Time Lord's long scarf past a mass of teeth and curls to the number one spot. This pride of place was awarded after Mr Numbers revealed the level of perfection he reached on those three solitary months of endeavour.

'I had to make sure I covered every inch of the route to boost my charity fund,' he said. 'One of my sponsors had promised to give me £500 alone to do the whole thing. There are various interpretations of the route, which I clocked up as 6,076 kilometres in total, and some that are shorter. The biggest problem I had perfecting the course was arriving on Shetland. The ferry missed out half the official route by dropping me off on the middle of the island. So I backtracked and cycled down to the southern most tip before returning up to Lerwick to make it qualify. There are lots of little interruptions on the route. You have to catch about 14 ferries on the journey, mostly in Norway, to get across small estuaries and parts of the path which just break off into the sea. It would be geographically impossible to cycle along all the coasts in an unbroken circle.'

John went on to make a warning, with a capital W, about the Norwegian leg of the journey. It was the hardest as most of the track followed an upward gradient, with howling winds doing their best to blow you back down the hillside. But he wasn't prepared to agree with my theory that this was the mischievous work of Scandinavian mountain trolls with a serious case of bad breath. 'Norway was rough,' he added. 'The mountainous scenery is breathtaking, but it gets very steep up the hills and you can almost feel yourself slipping backwards. There was more than one time I was forced to dismount and just push my bike to the top.' Hmmm... Does that still count John?

But there was good news for non-athletic tightwads like me, with the mathematician calculating the trip as both cheap and not necessarily tailor-made for cycling fitness fanatics. 'The whole journey only cost about £500 and I came home with change in my pocket,' confirmed John (sounds like a typical Northerner to me). 'Most nights I used campsites, so I could have a refreshing shower after a long day's cycling. There were a few occasions when I pitched up tent in the wild, especially in Norway where everything is so expensive, but I didn't encounter any beasties. And you don't need to worry about fitness. I enjoy cycling, but I had never attempted anything on such a massive scale before. In the past, I've completed the odd local Coast to Coast ride, but it's not something I do religiously all the time. You can go at your own pace, beginning at about 50 kilometres a day, but as the weeks pass you will clock up much greater distances.'

Wow, £500, and loose change. Where else could you go on a package holiday for the best part of three months for such a pittance and get transport, full bed and board thrown in? But I wasn't so sure about showering, I was quite happy to smell like a real man after a hard day's toil.

And as for the camping out in the wild part, I might just take a rain check on that one too John, after discovering that Scandinavia has four hungry predators on the prowl; the bear, lynx, wolf and wolverine. (Mental note: Don't leave any smelly, bloodthirsty creature attracting, ham sandwiches at the bottom of sleeping bag.)

The fitness side of things was a relief. Ambitious, and unrealistic, plans of building up to this event with a strict cycling regime went straight out the window. I could now plot my whole training programme around cycling a few hundred metres to the shops, before testing out my heavy pannier carrying skills by balancing bags full of groceries on my wobbling handlebars all the way home. Sheer practice perfection.

4 Into the Void

The protective growl of a mother fox greeted me good morning from next door's overgrown jungle. Banging and crashing heavy cycling bags down the back garden stairs at 4am had unsettled the poor urban scavenger. That's what's known in the trade as pay back missus, for all those times your cubs' terrifying screams have kept me awake. Deal with it!

It was D-Day. In an hour's time I would be sitting on a train, heading for London and ultimately Harwich. You never think departure day is going to arrive. The big launch had always seemed months away, even a few hours before setting off it hadn't seemed real, like it was never actually going to happen. But this was it. Here I was dressed in cycling shorts, a bulky red hooded waterproof and attaching my two back wheel panniers, front box, tent and sleeping bag to the bike. I looked like a postman.

But I wasn't worried. The adrenalin pumping through my veins was positive for once. Making those first few turns of the pedals wasn't going to be as difficult as bidding an emotional farewell to a half asleep Katie, who had dragged her tired body out of bed to wave me off. She was putting a brave face on it, but this was the moment she had been dreading.

As my focus left her heavy eyes and switched to the grassy path stretching away through the darkness from our garage to the road outside it felt very strange. I wouldn't be standing in this spot again for weeks. I wasn't going to see her little face, hold her warm body close against mine or plant a smacker on those loving lips for what would seem like a lifetime. But we both knew it was something which had to be done.

The clock was ticking and I had to get my arse in gear and make the station in time for the early morning train. Switching on my front and back lights I dispatched the last and most difficult of 30 goodbye kisses and climbed on to the bike, pushing forwards and ignoring the temptation to look back one more time. I was really on my own now.

The roads were empty and cycling to the station under the reflection of the orange street lamps felt good. Despite lugging 56 litres of weight in the two bags, plus my mobile hotel room, everything felt effortless. Training for take-off had been minimal and I was getting carried away far too early. Talk about bursting into a sprint before you can even crawl along the floor.

Trying to pump my skinny frame towards the perception of physical well being's cut-off point had added up to cycling the 26 mile round trip between home in Leigh-on-Sea and work in Basildon for two weeks. Plodding along beside the busy A127 carriageway was a killer in more ways than one. Southend isn't a very cycle friendly town, it isn't even curious, and this route was about as good as it got. There was the added bonus of filling my lungs with foul car fumes on a daily basis, while steering through the obstacle course of rusting exhaust pipes, broken glass sprayed by every colour of the rainbow, old splintered pallets and the occasional blackened burnt out abandoned caravan.

After wrestling my back heavy transport on to the dosing train and plonking myself on a ripped seat, numbness took control. What the bloody hell was I doing? It was much easier to hermitize in my safe, cosy bubble at home. Was this adventure lark really a bit of me or had I bitten off more than I could swallow (nobody chews) this time? Escaping this carriage would only take a second. I could hide in my cocoon for two months, gag Katie from spilling the beans and return to the world with a convincing concoction of lies about my life changing trip. Shut up – you're going through with this! That was the end of it.

My old man had to take his share of the blame for this hair-brained sink or swim scheme. It was definitely in the genes. Bernard senior was an elite member of Baden Powell's crew – a King Scout – and spent the summer months of his youth hiking across Switzerland, kipping rough in Alpine hay barns and hand-milking grazing cows for his morning billycan brew.

This passion reached out farer and wider in adult life, with dad regularly disappearing with his other half on last minute cheapo Teletext flights. And wherever he went, the faithful hand-held camera would follow. Father had a holiday fixation with filming everything and anything. A drugged up tourist trap crocodile snoozing next to a Gambian swimming pool, the disturbed resting places of Egyptian pharaohs, plus the warped curvatures of Barcelona's Gaudi Park all featured on these masterpieces of cinematography. On returning home to Harlow, it was compulsory to sit through the premier of dad's latest Alan Whicker style documentary, complete with rambling commentary, followed by revisory discussion at the end of the screening just in case the audience had missed anything.

Bore off father, was always my first thought. But I would give anything to wince through one of those painful DIY answers to Wish You Were Here now. Dad had checked out before mum six years ago at 54, again no age at all. A quick dash to hospital for an appendix operation had gone to plan, but swelled into an enlarged heart and fatal attack just moments after coming round and cracking a joke with the nurses.

So I was doing this for him too. Emulating that same desire to head off into the void and see what sprang out. And keeping my fingers-crossed that this attempt to go it alone would unearth the same excitement which the old fella would embrace from a similar experience.

As the train slid off into the dusky gloom other odd thoughts filtered into my think tank. I began pondering the theory of some religious nutters who believe we are put on this Earth by God so he can test us out. A sort of Big Brother reality gameshow, but in this version the evictees actually pay the ultimate price – with their lives. The big guy had certainly tested me to the max after taking away my folks so early in life.

I was an orphan now, but the coin had finally dropped – well it was more like the entire contents of the Bank of England safe – that life should be cherished and making the most of it was the best policy as you never know what is around the corner. If God was testing me, then now was the time to flex my muscles in response and show him this player was equal to any Japanese gameshow goon when it came to undertaking the definitive cycle rally of endurance.

As for the not so olds, the adage 'the good die young' could have been penned just for them. I hoped mum and dad had patched things up on the other side, as nobody wants to be at loggerheads for eternity, and would join forces to act as my guardian angels on the road ahead. Maybe we'll be a family again one day, even if that means coming back as a lettuce lunching, reincarnated rabble of chilled out rabbits, wiling away lazy summer days humming 'Bright Eyes' in perfect unison. It would beat working, paying bills and eating chips on a daily basis anyway.

Changing at London Liverpool Street, my Stena Line Express ticket was supposed to ferry me straight to the north Essex port. But nothing's ever that simple on British public transport and finding the word Harwich sandwiched anywhere between the other numerous destinations was becoming a perplexing ordeal. With their usual eye for meticulous detail, the rail operators hadn't bothered to inform the crowd of bewildered travellers staring blearily up at the computerised departures board that the plan had been changed.

After collaring three clueless numbskull platform attendants without making any headway, I was finally pointed in the right direction by a bunch of foreigners. Plotting a successful course across alien soil suddenly seemed an increasingly daunting prospect after finding it so difficult to get past the most minor of hindrances in my own back yard.

The head of the Dutch group informed me I would have to catch the Norwich train to Manningtree and then struggle with my bike on to a local Harwich service. Paying no attention to the protestations from a platform numpty, I frantically pedalled down the side of the Norfolk bound train, took off all my packs and strapped the bike into the guard carriage with minutes to spare.

Mist curled around the fields and dawn light was breaking out everywhere as the train pounded north along the track. Irritation soon turned into smugness as miserable looking commuters jostled for space at Chelmsford and Colchester ready to fight anyone to the death in the race for a sacred seat on their daily grind to London. How great it was to be heading off on my journey in the opposite direction to all that self-orientated stress, overpowering deodorant and broadsheet newspaper origami, not conforming to the slave-like norm of the big city drones.

My train was dead and I informed the guard, who had doubled up as a ticket inspector, that the bike carriage would need to be opened at the next stop. Surprise, surprise, he was nowhere to be seen when I jumped out of the door. Pressing down the green button on the guard carriage was having no effect at all and memory man was still nowhere to be seen.

'Open the door,' came an aggressive shout from the front of the train. 'I can't open it,' I replied to Mr Angry train driver, who had squeezed the top half of his body through a small side window. 'Open the door,' the red faced arsehole screamed again.

'I can't, it is locked and the guard told me he was going to open it here for me so I can get my bike off.'

'Just open the fucking door will ya, there's people on the train and you're making it late.'

Charming, but of course it was my fault. How rude of me to expect a guard with the brain retention of a lobotomized tadpole to remember a conversation two minutes earlier on a ghost train. And stupid me for not passing my City and Guilds in safe cracking so I could prise open a locked secure door specifically designed to stop people stealing the items inside. On arriving at Harwich, I would quickly locate the nearest thorny stick and whip myself profusely as penance. Then, as if by magic, in a begrudging act of kindness, ranting and raving train twat actually did the unthinkable and climbed out of his cab to open the door for me. What a sweet guy.

The relief soon drained away when I realised that leaping away from the hot fat of the frying pan was threatening to singe my toes in the fire. After taking five minutes to clip and strap everything back on to the bike, I spotted an anxious looking station master on the other side of the double track holding a long white table tennis bat signalling type thingy.

'Don't tell me, that's the train to Harwich and you're waiting to wave it off,' I concluded after catching the impatient faces of the passengers on the other side of the grubby glass.

'Sure is,' he nodded, before adding in a much calmer manner than his Norwich bound compatriot, 'but don't worry, I'm holding it for you.'

Manningtree station was basic and right out in the sticks. I already knew the answer before calling: 'I take it there's no lift here for my bike, I've got to use the stairs I suppose?' Another slow downward movement of the head in reply confirmed the worst.

There was no time to de-bag again. Holding down the breaks tightly and using my meagre resources of strength to navigate the 40 steep concrete steps, the descent started slowly, but accelerated into a jerky jog to the flat floor below as the weight on the back nosedived forward. Mr Nice Station Man was waiting for me at the bottom of the upward stairwell and grabbed the front of the handlebars, while I nudged my shoulders into the saddle and lifted the backside. Helping me on to the carriage puffing and panting, he picked up his bat and served the train down court to Harwich.

The ferry terminal was blessed by a sunny spring morning which washed across the car park, cranes and cargo containers. This surely added up to a smooth crossing and equalled a settling of the nervous system. The head felt fine, a definite brief spell of mental stability, and even the screaming warnings from the seagulls to turn back right now couldn't put me off.

Then I saw the ferry. I've got about as much stomach for boats as I have for flying, but maybe that hasn't been mentioned. This reluctant sailor hadn't set foot on deck for years. The only reason he was willing to do so now was because there was a minimal chance of living to tell the story about a sinking ship. Planes just crash and it's all over in seconds. It doesn't matter how many pre-flight safety videos you watch, your chances of survival are equal to jumping off the top of the Empire State Building in your birthday suit, clutching a single feather in each hand and flapping about as fast as you can. Splat! At least I could prolong the agony by drowning or freezing to death in the North Sea if anything went wrong this way.

But the *Stena Britannica* was a real boat, a big bugger built like a floating block of flats. The one and only other time embarkation had been suffered from this shore was on an oblong red hulk attached to the ramp which wasn't sturdy enough for my liking. There were no big funnels and little rows of round portholes dotted around the decks, sitting above the curvy, weather stained body of the hull. The now defunct catamaran resembled the space shuttle used in *Star Trek* to land on planets the Enterprise was orbiting when Scotty was having trouble fixing the transporter.

My eyes flicked across the decks of this superior replacement for lifeboats, which were hanging off the side of the vessel on support chains in adequate enough numbers. There seemed to be enough back-up for 200 frenzied people scrambling for their lives. But I cursed under my breath for not squeezing a mouth inflated rubber dinghy into my panniers and slowly cycled behind the goods trucks into the open mouth of the ship, before parking up against *Britannica's* left gill.

It was six hours to the Netherlands on the opposite side of the North Sea and an undercurrent of palpitations were trying to pierce what had been a tense, but successful start to the day. My thoughts turned to mum for inspiration. She wouldn't be happy with me if I turned back now. It was time to grin and bear it just like she did. The sea was calm and the sky rolled out in front of me like a carpet of pure cloudless blue. Maybe mother had pulled a few strings up there to arrange this composed start to the campaign, and it would be rude not to take advantage.

Claiming a tactical seat a stride away from the toilet, just in case a spell of private panicking or vomiting was required, and being careful not to make direct eye contact with the water through the window, the hum of the engines powering up flowed through my shaking body. This was it, we were setting sail. There was no turning back.

But I didn't have to like it. To quote Han Solo in *Star Wars* as he flew towards the ominous shape of the Death Star in his ship the Millennium Falcon, 'I had a bad feeling about this.' I felt a great affinity with Harrison Ford right now. This reluctant Rebel could relate to his cheery forecast just by being on a boat. Except in my case it was of course worse and this pilot would be racing towards the entire might of the evil Empire armed with a weaponless intergalactic dustbin truck. As I pondered the possibility of trashing a fleet of Imperial tie-fighters by blasting them with space garbage and whether my real actions were equally futile, the ferry slowly jerked into life. Pulling away from the dock and the safety of dry land I closed my eyes and hoped for the best – it was just like using the Force.

5   Punk'd

The ear-splitting chinking of glasses and smashing of plates woke me up. Sprawled across one side of a table booth, with the clip-off front bike box containing my valuables held in a vice-like safety grip between my legs, I groggily wondered what all the racket was about.

With the entire boat to choose from the cleaning staff had decided to park the dirty cutlery trolley right next to my head. Totally oblivious to my hopes of spending the next six hours asleep, the blue waist-coated Apollo Creed twins, complete with tightly trimmed pencil tashes, continued to increase the decibels of their concert of noise.

I'd set up camp in the boat's disco bar, which provided entertainment for the passengers and truckers on the second scheduled crossing of the day, which was overnight and took nine hours to reach dry land. Looking around the half empty ship, I was in the company of teenage delinquents and middle-aged should-know-betters wearing their rugby club tracksuits, who had caught the Stoner Line en-route to 'The Dam' for a big smoke and the best of eastern European imports.

To my left was the glass walled smoking compartment, with a series of famous faces pixilated together from green dots adjourning the panels. David Bowie, Rod Stewart and Little Richard were all staring straight at me. But where was the Dutch influence? Surely there should have been room for Johan Cruyff perfecting his famous turn, Van Gough holding up his bloody ear or even 2 Unlimited.

In an age dominated by low-cost air travel I wondered just how much longer these ferry crossings could stave off extinction. *Britannica* was a big boat, but there was no more than 50 other passengers on board. Apart from weirdos like me, who wanted to sit on a ship for half-a-day when they could fly to their destination in under 60 minutes? The cancelled catamaran was a better option as it charged across to the Netherlands in just three hours, but raising fuel prices and falling passenger numbers had sounded her death knell. The ferry business couldn't compete with the customer friendly economics and speed of their sky-high competition. It wasn't a great distance to the other side, only 106 nautical miles, which made the sloth-like crossing seem a huge drain on time. Even the captain's best efforts to slow down the boat to try and rake in extra cash through the duty free tills on cheap ciggies, booze and perfume surely couldn't continue to keep these fast fading out of fashion services afloat.

It was hard to believe I was sitting on a boat. Braving a quick glance through the window there was hardly a ripple breaking the dark grey water outside. The sailing conditions were as smooth as a baby's bottom and it was hard to believe, but very reassuring, that we were moving at all.

Feeling more confident I asked the guy on the table next to me if I could have a peek at the football programme he had just finished reading. It was from a Championship match between the small town farmers of Colchester and fallen Premiership lords of the manor Leeds United, whose financially blighting slump had continued with an embarrassing defeat at ramshackle Layer Road on Easter Monday. The Yorkshire giants would make the unthinkable drop into English football's third tier at the end of the season, alongside Southend, for the first time in their history. Playing Real Madrid in the elite of European footballs' Champions League only six years ago would seem a million light years away for the distraught Elland Road faithful.

The white-haired Leeds fan joined me at my table and a long conversation about football tailored off into a self-imposed exile away from the UK. Stephen Cannell was in his late forties and had spent the last decade working abroad in Dubai and Thailand, where he was now an English lecturer at Kasetsart University in Bangkok. He'd flown back to regrettably watch his beloved Leeds and was on his way to visit a former employer from another stint working as a chef in The Hague. She was apparently the daughter of a Dutch gangster who liked his grub, so it seemed sensible to open a restaurant.

Before taking up country hopping as a profession, Stephen had been the bass player in one of the various incarnations of *Alternative TV*. The 70s punk band were the brainchild of Mark Perry, the editor of *Sniffin' Glue*, the most revered music fanzine for a generation of aggressive safety-pin obsessives, which gave away their first single 'Love Lies Limp', for free. By coincidence, he also toured America with Southend born Danielle Dax, who was the figurehead of avant-garde punk outfit the Lemon Kittens. She was once interviewed by a computer for Channel 4's *Star Test* show, which asked: 'If you met God, what would you ask her?'

Her poignant reply: 'Why are the nicer people not as successful as the shitty people?' Amen sister!

Alternative TV are still floating around in some shape or form today, but Stephen didn't miss the punk rock lifestyle, or the drug taking that went with it. Escaping the suffocation of being a narcotic powered musician had inspired him to seek out the world. Something I could relate too.

He had a thin Thai male companion who was busy wandering around the deck, taking photos and popping back every now and then to check in and mutter a few words in pigeon English. I already knew the answer to my next question before carefully delivering: 'Is that your son?'

'No, he's my boyfriend. I know what you're thinking. He looks very young.'

'He could easily pass for about 16 or 17, easily a teenager,' I quickly butted in.

'But he's not. We've been together for years and his 30th birthday is coming up very soon. The Thai people just have better skin than us and don't age as quickly.' Who was I to judge? Whatever floats your boat.

Stephen had been an ardent campaigner for homosexual equality in the 80s and had even spent a night in the cells for his strong beliefs. He was caught up in the Section 28 fiasco when the gay and bisexual community were frowned upon from up high in a prejudicial world running scared from the spread of the AIDS epidemic. Three quarters of HIV infected people were from this cross-section of society

Section 28 was an attempt to censor the gay community by making a controversial amendment to the *United Kingdom's Local Government Act 1986*. The amended statement ordered local authorities not to: 'intentionally promote homosexuality or publish material with the intention of promoting homosexuality', or 'promote the teaching in any maintained school of the acceptability of homosexuality as a pretended family relationship.' In other words, queers and fags were abnormal and we couldn't let this disgusting disease spread any further. School kids needed to be brainwashed at an early age and not allowed to make their own choices. Books, plays and leaflets mentioning the horrible 'gay' word should also be eradicated.

Section 28 became law on May 24, 1988. The night before a group of daredevil lesbians protested by abseiling into Parliament and more famously another woman invaded the BBC's *Six O'Clock News* studios and chained herself to a startled Sue Lawley's desk as she was running through the nation's headlines.

Stephen was in the thick of the action, breaking into the House of Commons with a couple of dykes, and was arrested and thrown in irons along with his two lady friends (they weren't into bondage). Section 28 wasn't repealed until November 18, 2003, with many prominent MPs, who had originally supported the bill, voicing regret over their actions.

The Hoek van Holland loomed bleakly on to the horizon as the port's sea bedded lighthouse guardians strained to pierce through the gloom. *Britannica* steered herself straight towards the throat of the Nieuwe Waterweg, the coastal inlet waterway which flowed 30 kilometres inland, giving the largest seaport on the globe, Rotterdam, direct access to the North Sea. The Hoek or 'Corner of Holland', as it is also known, sits directly on the mouth of the shipping highway and it was here that my own journey would get underway for real.

As I rubbed shoulders with truckers on my way downstairs to the bowels of the vessel a vibration in the pocket of my shorts alerted me to a text message. The electronic telegram on the mobile phone was from my good mate Neil. It read: 'Sorry I didn't get a chance to say a proper goodbye the other night, but I was hammered and fell asleep. Remember you are a special bloke doing a very special thing'. I was special alright!

6   Into the Dunes

Land ahoy! It was 4.15pm and the hard slog began right here. Double-checking everything was properly attached to the bike, I lowered myself on to the saddle and found my pedal biting point. The dreariness engulfing the ship as it docked had been no more than a brief illusion as the open doors in front of me sucked in the bright sunshine from outside.

Criss-crossing truck drivers as they climbed up into their cabs eager to hit the road with precious cargos, I raced the slow sluggish diesel puffing hulks out of the vehicle deck. One of the *Village People*, a dock worker with trademark Dutch orange boiler suit, directed me towards the terminal exit with a cheery wave and a smile half hidden by a bushy handlebar moustache. Given a guard of honour on my arrival by a procession of tall wind farms and cranes building Lego style stacks with red containers I couldn't wait to get started.

Something wasn't right here. I was supposed to be shitting a brick at this stage and skulking around in the ferry waiting room for a few hours before booking myself on the overnight crossing back to Harwich. But as the pungent whiff of brine flew up my nostrils the only sensation to take a grip on my body was excitement. Deep curiosity about what lay ahead took control and the thrill of propelling myself forwards energised by muscle alone. But I wasn't getting carried away as this trip was still at the melting pot stage. In the grand scheme of things, jelly amoebas hadn't evolved into land conquering fish yet, monkeys were still a long way off walking upright and Ken Barlow hadn't sunk his first pint in the Rovers. But even an eternal pessimist like me had to admit this was turning into a damn good start.

This was my first port of call on the way to becoming a fully paid-up member of the stereotyped tourist club. Just what would the next few days bring? After getting ahead with a few hundred kilometres on the clock, I could reward myself and park the bike up for a rest under the turning sails of a windmill. Slumped by a reedy river bank, armies of tulips would be saluting each other in a cool breeze while I greedily stuffed cheeses full of holes and crusty bread inside my mouth at the same time. Maybe I'd even spot that little white mouse, who is probably still sitting right there on the stair, forcing yet another generation of tortured Netherlanders into singing that annoying song. How I prayed that somebody had seen the sense to go clip-clippidy-clop on the rodent's head with a heavy wooden clog. Miracles do happen, especially in a country where one little boy's finger was enough to prevent the break up of the *Women's Liberation Movement*. Sorry, a bulging fat dike threatening to wet herself.

And there it was, my first major worry evaporating instantly in a white weather-stained sign with a green bike printed on it and the magic words 'North Sea Cycle Route' accompanied by a directing arrow. This was far too easy and I reminded myself to 'beware the sting in the tail', which would become a recurring theme. The first part of the trip would take me straight up the west coast of the Netherlands to the naval port of Den Helder which nestled crow's nest like on its summit. And to make things simple for a map-a-phobe like me the track followed a single cycle path – the LF1 Noordzee route. Starting in the province of Zuid Holland, the road ahead followed a fairly straight forward line, with the occasional twist and turn, across the county border into Noord Holland for 170 kilometres. The names of these two provinces (there are 12 in total) are the main source of Dutch peoples' irritation when outsiders refer to their country as Holland. It's a bit like downgrading the whole of England to Rutland. Quite fitting for a small island still clinging on to its empire building delusions of grandeur, which have long been replaced by the modern face sculptures of hoodie gangs, obesity, immigration problems and ASBOs.

Most of this first challenge would send me burrowing into the dunes, the Netherlands' natural defence against its mortal foe, the land eroding tendrils of the North Sea. Half of this low lying country was less than a metre above sea level and you could have forgiven me shoving a snorkel inside my gob as the current day west coast should be engulfed by the wet stuff. The Dutch asserted mastery over the sea long ago, draining away water by pump and building high banks called dikes to prevent the large chunks of land they had reclaimed for habitation and agriculture from being flooded. Thus the old saying: 'God created the world except for the Netherlands. The Dutch took it from the sea.'

Most of the way to Den Helder was below sea level and the towns and villages which dotted this coast were living testament to the ingenuity of those Dutch pioneers. But the Netherlanders can't afford to relax as their battle with the sea is far from finished. The domino effect of global warming and melting ice caps could have catastrophic future consequences as rising sea levels threaten to breach the dikes, dunes and dams which shield this nation. The last warning came back in 1953 when 1,835 people lost their lives after a combination of high spring tide and a severe windstorm caused the North Sea to flood across the country. Dutch brains need to think fast and come up with new ways of emulating their forefathers from hundreds of years ago in keeping their natural enemy at bay. The Netherlands has 16 million inhabitants and is one of the most densely populated countries in the world, with 484 people occupying every square kilometre of land, and the climbing seas threaten to spring an unthinkable devastation on future generations. It promises to be a long fight, which sadly may inevitably prove futile.

People use the other side of the road abroad. Everybody knows that, but being a complete buffoon I forgot and only just escaped unscathed to tell the story. Chatting merrily to a trio of Bristolians who had glided out of the ferry for a cycling holiday, I stuck to good old UK tradition and hugged the left hand of the cycle path. That was my first mistake. Vroom… vroom… vroom. My second navigation cock-up, as my rightful place was cemented through an evasive lean to the opposite part of the track, was that I hadn't seen the three teenage charged mopeds hurtling towards me. Some motorised bikes are also allowed to use these paths, they are not exclusive to pedal power. An important life saving lesson learnt.

Pushing through arteries of alleys, parallel to waterways and row upon row of giant greenhouses as large as houses, I reached the heart of 'Glass Town'. There were hundreds of the things, stretching out ahead of me as far as the eye could see. Variations of vegetables, fruit and flowers were topping up their tans, as well as a familiar looking green plant which I hoped was legal. It was like *Springwatch* everywhere. Bill Oddie would have been creaming his pants watching the lambs resting in the shade of the greenhouses under the watchful eye of their mother, herons stalking prey on stilted legs and getting a right ticking off from irate ducks trying to sneak a few winks on the brown water.

Percy Thrower's paradise spread its transparent canopy for 15 kilometres, past Monster (no carnivorous Edams thank God) and along the outskirts of The Hague, the seat of the Dutch Government and home of Queen Beatrix. Slender dunes began to break through the dominance of the panelled metropolis and the coastal wind brushed through my hair, although there was still no sign of the sea which was well hidden behind the yellow and green patched humps all around.

My first major town zoomed into view, Scheveningen, and it wasn't long before the sniff of the trail would evade me. The first taste of Dutch civilisation was a frustrating one. Joining the main road, I breezed past the tall red apartments, general stores and off licences into the centre of Scheveningen. People were walking their dogs, drinking cold beer outside bars and unlocking bikes at the supermarket to travel home with a basket full of groceries. Everyone seemed to be taking life at a slow pace, it was nothing like the hustle and bustle of home. But my full immersion into this laid-back existence was cruelly shattered by ugly lumps of broken concrete jutting about all over the place. Some bright spark had decided to mutilate the tram lines and half the road in front of me. The road works were impeding my progress and to make matters worse the guiding lights of the North Sea Cycle Route signs had stopped twinkling.

Whacking the bike into reverse and re-tracing my route into town, past the small harbour and scattered shops, I confirmed from previous directions that my route had been spot on. Back to the road works. No sign. Taking a gamble and leaving the mishmash of steel and stone behind me, I forged straight ahead, but after 10 minutes of getting nowhere returned to the stumbling blocks.

Great. I've only been here two hours and 20 kilometres and I'm lost already. What now? I might actually have to try and hold a conversation with someone. But they all speak good English here so it won't be a problem. And if in doubt, give the sea a shout. Pushing the bike down a pedestrianised shopping street a couple of hairy dudes chin-wagging outside a surf shop pointed me past the high clock tower and towards the seafront.

The promenade was busy with early evening strollers investigating the tacky souvenir shops, restaurants and beach bars. My particular favourite spot was the *Golfslag*. Obviously a popular drinking den for lusty women golfers who like balls and weren't too fussy about receiving a front or back nine at the end of the night. Passing the domed spectacle of the Kurhaus hotel, which was built in 1884 and once played home to a Rolling Stones concert, probably before the end of the same century, the odd shape of the pier lay ahead of me.

Coming from Southend I am a bit of a pier connoisseur. We have the longest one in the world you know, which is still standing proud despite being set on fire on numerous occasions and rammed by drunken sailors with a worse sense of direction than me. But it's still hanging on, an elegant wooden and iron cladded Victorian construction which stretches 1.33 miles out to sea in a straight line, still doing her jobs after all these years. This creation on the other hand was a monstrosity for a traditional pierilist like myself. Yeah, it did the basic going out to sea thing, but the architect must have taken one or two many tokes on the wacky-backy when he pencilled in the drunken steps and meringue-shaped centrepiece, with the cherry on top being a yellow bungee cage on a crane. All the tulips in Amsterdam couldn't get me on that thing.

Still no signs and the promenade ended in a double bank of steep steps which were the only way down. Smack! One of the pedals spun back and cracked me straight in the shin as man and bike bumped their way downwards in an awkward unity. Bastard steps. I was bleeding and had also managed to get a nice stinging scrape up the back of the same limb. If these fucking signs weren't here I was going to scream. But hey, anger's fine! At least I wasn't worrying about other stuff. Take a few deep breaths and think 'lush green grass' and it will all be OK!

There she blows. The North Sea Cycle Route picked up straight in front of me, but how it disappeared at the mysterious tram triangle and materialised here I'll never know. Bare-footed walkers patrolled the white pebble-less beach below the sea wall. It was hard to believe this same spot was packed with thousands of hecklers in 1654, cheering on the home team against England in a naval battle dubbed the Battle of Scheveningen. I couldn't tell you the outcome, they weren't selling commemorative shirts or mugs in any of the souvenir shops. But they say you're only as good as your last game and we gained revenge more than 300 years later in our last altercation, the 4-1 clogging of the Dutch at Wembley in Euro 96.

Back into the dunes and the raised mounds had grown into mini-mountains. They were much higher and wider now, dwarfing me completely as I continued along the remarkably level concrete paths which wind around the grassy hair on their toes. The whole area was a hive of activity with all different types of physical exertion taking place. But it made perfect sense, getting out in the clean open air here, which beat an old creaky church hall or sweaty gym back home.

There were *Footloose* style joggers tuned into personal stereo headphones on long tangled chords, the black leggings and shell suits of a curved arm stretching female fitness class and a father and son were flying a remote control aeroplane. All sorts of cyclists were using the paths, ranging from a hit squad of serious wheelers in skin-tight genital hugging Spandex, sunglasses and helmets (who delighted in lapping me and my packs more than once) to a couple of freewheeling lovers holding hands side-by-side and absorbing the beauty around them.

And then there was the other end of the work-out scale, the human snails. I don't understand the benefits of walking sports. How does it do anything for you? You may as well take a really brisk walk to the shops. Don't bother getting all track-suited up and wearing head bands. As if you actually sweat. Although, there is some justice out there as these pathetic sporting tortoises do a great impression of somebody who has shit themselves as they waddle through the motions.

And what about Nordic walkers? Granted, it would be hard work pulling yourself through the thick snow and ice of Norway. But does anybody seriously believe that half-heartedly dragging along a couple of ski poles on a firm piece of ground is making you fit and healthy? The answer of course is a resounding no. And don't say it's good for the arms, because so is wearing a watch on both wrists or taking up tiddlywinks in that case. Just get out there and get the blood pumping by breaking into a jog you lazy tossers. Yes, even a slow one!

Wetlands are dotted around the feet of the dunes, which are filtered into drinking water for The Hague and town of Leiden. This area was originally used for farming, but the financial turnover was poor forcing the owner to flog off his land for house plots and expensive villas in 1916. Concerned that building on such a major scale would lead to heavy water extraction, The Hague intervened and slapped a compulsory purchase on the site. Since then, the Dutch Water Company have become the dunes' green keepers, preserving the rugged charm of this coastal stretch, as well as planting various native shrubs and trees to boost the aesthetics. These strips of dune defence closest to the sea are also the most vulnerable, not just because of the relentless waves hitting the shores, but the fierce winds which can blow through these parts. Extra protection has been provided in the form of specially planted marram grass and black and coarse pine trees to beef up the fight against mother nature.

A lavish Indian-style construction of squared-off walls topped by a small circular hat poked its head out of the sand. Starting to feel peckish, I quite fancied a chicken biriani, but determination pushed me on to Katwijk and a first glimpse at the North Sea (Scheveningen didn't count – that was a detour). Like most of its neighbours along the coast, this village had inherited an adapt and survive policy, growing from a small fishing community into a seaside resort. But it seemed to be flourishing quite nicely as canoeists and surfers splashed about in the white foam with their oars and boards. Katwijk had a touch of quaintness about it, with its cosy orange glowing eateries and large square windowed apartments acting as a magnifying glass for its owners out to sea. It is also the mouth of the Old Rhine, which dissects the middle of Europe to Switzerland, and a memorial stone commemorating the connection of the great river with the North Sea in 1807 stands here. This little gem also boasts the second oldest lighthouse in the Netherlands, the *Vuurbaak*, which dates back to 1605.

Next door was nowhere near as cosy. Noordwijk describes itself as being an ultra-modern holiday retreat, but in all honesty it felt like a grimy council estate with a beach. The repulsive yellow and gold brick flats were a tired eyesore and even the lighthouse at the end of the boulevard was a token effort which could have been popped out of a basic cement mould.

As light began to fade I plunged back into the dunes eager to gobble up the last 20 kilometres to my target destination, Zandvoort. The body still felt good and it wouldn't have been a problem to continue through the night. But I had been on the go for five hours, which seemed a decent enough introduction to this cycling business for my liking. Already, nearly half way up the coast to Den Helder, it was time to set up camp.

These dunes were owned by the Amsterdam Water Company, who began extracting here in 1851 after a pollution of the existing water supply caused a cholera epidemic. They were a much bleaker place as the shadows of the setting sun started to take control and dropped a nasty nip into the air. The joggers, walkers (grrrrh) and two-wheeled romantics were long gone, meaning I had the gaff all to myself. Apart from the quiet lapping of waves against the hillock hidden beach to my left, there was no other noise to be heard. No car engines revving, grannies whingeing about the price of cucumbers or those tinny *EastEnders* theme tune drums blaring out a TV set through an open window. There was nothing else here, just great sloping hills of sleeping sand and the soothing, but slightly eerie sound of silence which wrapped itself around me.

But I wasn't completely alone after all. As I scooted along the sand-dusted trail other dune-trippers began to spring out of the darkness, drawn magnet-like to the tranquillity on offer. Tiny black dots fidgeting about in the distance soon morphed into the recognisable shape of rabbits who had come out to play in the cooler evening breeze. I had quite a bit in common with Flopsy and friends as we were both from out of town originally. Rabbits were imported to the dunes by the Spanish in the 13th century as a hunting quarry. The nobility owned the hunting rights to this area and leased them to professional hunters known as *Duinmeiers*, who stalked the rabbits for their fur. But they also acted as guardians for their prey, feeding them during the winter and seeing off natural enemies hoping to muscle in on the action. Poachers risked having their eyes gouged out, farmers were only allowed to put up fences and hedges to keep out the bunnies and it was even worse for their animals. Dogs would have a leg amputated to stop them chasing the guarded creatures and poor old cats had both their ears lobbed off to deter them climbing into burrows for fear of getting sand in the holes left behind on either side of their heads. Don't fuck about in Bunny World!

But I'm sure I'd seen something bigger stirring out there in the blackness. It was probably just my eyes playing tricks on me, but I put an extra bit of humph into the pedals to fend off a chance meeting with the Netherlands' answer to the Beast of Bodmin. Just short of leaving the cover of the dunes and ducking into the street lights of Zandvoort a hefty gnarled branch poked out into the path. Dropping anchor for a glance over my shoulder I was staring straight back into the face of a curious stag. It wasn't bothered about me at all and proudly stood its ground with a twist of boney antlers reaching far above his head. It really was a magical moment as it's not every day you virtually go nose to nose with such a regal being. What would Barbara Woodhouse have done in this situation? I wasn't going to try and blow up his nose and there were no sugar lump treats in my packs, so I tried to muster up some primitive form of deer speak. It was something like a strangled dog calling noise and I really couldn't tell you what I was hoping to achieve. It wasn't like he was going to trot back to my tent and volunteer services as a mobile washing horse. Growing concern about the twitching antlers which could puncture my behind forced me to ditch the *Doctor Snuggles* act and leave this lord of the dunes to it, giving one last K-9 call goodbye.

It was 10pm and darkness was in full swing when I arrived at the seafront facing Camping de Branding. It was a pretty basic site sitting in the bottom of a dune surrounded crater, but it was home for the night and more importantly it was free. Whoring my trip out to every campsite, hostel and hotel I could find on the internet, with a promise of free publicity (this is it by the way), some kind people offered to put me up. Other tight-fisted bastards didn't – you know who you are.

The owner of this patch of toilet blocked grass, Andre van Dijk, was one of those charitable souls who took pity on me after reading my circular about the journey, my mother and the added incentive of raising money for Cancer Research UK.

'Dear Bernie. I hope you don't mind me calling you by your first name, but if you do it is too late and I am sorry,' he replied. 'I of course would be more than happy to give you a place to put your tent. Even if I didn't believe your story I would still have given you somewhere to stay as you tried very hard.'

And here I was, my first night away from home on my own, and using my torch to scan two tent skins, a set of elasticated click-together poles and a bag of pegs which I didn't have a clue how to assemble in the correct order. Why didn't I bother putting this thing up in my back garden in the daylight before setting off? It would have made things a lot easier, but that's not my way. Well the good news was that it wasn't raining and my thoughts turned to unzipping the inside shell of the tent, clambering into it with my sleeping bag and using it as a big floppy duvet. I continued staring blankly at all the different pieces for 30 minutes, but nothing happened. It didn't move. There were no instructions and there didn't seem to be any help at hand as all the other canvas capsules, caravans and motor homes were deathly quiet. I was going to start crying any minute.

'He-he-he.' What was that? 'Oh, ha-ha-ha.' Somebody was laughing, or was that people. They were taking the piss out of me. Where were they? Show yourselves! Not that I knew how to abuse them in anything but English and I didn't feel entitled to as this was a mess of my own making.

'Er… hello there,' came a call from a skinny blond-haired lad crawling out of a gigantic tent opposite my shambles.

'Hello… do you speak English?' I begged desperately. 'I'm having trouble with my tent. I've been standing here for half-an-hour and I don't know what I'm doing. There's no instructions you see. I'm usually very good at this sort of thing. Honest.'

'Ja… okay… give me one minute please and I will get help for you in putting up ze tent.'

He disappeared back inside his well constructed marquee under the stars, called out some sort of rallying call in German and appeared with three other friends, all carrying torches and bottles of beer. Martin, Thomas, Alf and Carsten were all from Dortmund and spending a few days driving up the Dutch coast. Luckily for me they were also tent experts and got to work with the speed and skill of the mechanical mice from *Bagpuss*. It still took them 20 minutes to figure it out though, which made me feel better as I just stood and watched, trying to make up other excuses for my outdoor inadequacies.

Putting the bottle of Grolsch they had given me on the floor, I began transferring the gear off my bike into the tiny blue one-man tent which was specifically designed for mountaineering specialists, not housebound hermits. Happy with my efforts, which consisted of throwing everything either side of my sleeping bag and rolling my fleece into a pillow, I wandered back over to the guys to say thank you. But they had already gone to bed, the Germans had surrendered again.

All I'd eaten all day was a couple of acclimatizing cheese rolls and the rumbles in my stomach were pleading for sustenance. Shovelling coal into the furnace was a must to keep me going, but it was getting on for midnight and everything was closed down. Raiding the camp vending machine for a bottle of water and two gooey honey waffle wafers it was time to settle down for a quick feast and some pillow time. The ground under the tent was getting cold so I laid my thick waterproof jacket under the sleeping bag to keep out the chill, before zipping up and holding on tightly to Katie's vest.

We'd decided to soil our night tops for a whole week before I left so we could still get a good whiff of each other at bed time. I definitely got the better side of the bargain, taking a deep inhale of vest which reeked of perfume and fake tan. Much better than my offering of sweaty armpit juice and crusty bogies wiped down the front. It was so odd going to bed on my own without the missus, but my pining was quickly overwhelmed by a strong sense of pride. I'd clocked up 70 kilometres on my first day and more importantly I was still here. Bring on Den Held… zzz… zzz… zzz… the hay was well and truly hit like a hammer.

7   Give me Shelter

All the excited morning chatter in the campsite office was about Manchester United's 7-1 demolition job on Roma the previous night. Fergie's boys booked their place in the Champions League semi-final with an Old Trafford romp over the Italians and the Dutch had enjoyed every minute of it. Huge fans of the English Premiership, the campers felt justice had been done following the horrendous scenes in the Eternal City during the first leg, which had left United's travelling fans bloodied and beaten by over-zealous baton-wielding police.

Looking around the cluttered desk the only breakfast on offer was a basket of crusty rolls and little packets of jam and honey. Disappointment set in as I had my heart peeled on potatoes. Zandvoort is well known for its race circuit and casino, but nothing beats its reputation for growing a decent spud. The sandy soil of the dunes is a fertile ground for potatoes and the townsfolk turned to the bosom of their bumpy neighbours for food in the 19th century. Occupying French forces had banned fishing in the seas as they were kicking-off with England at the time. High unemployment followed, but the canny locals were saved by the starchy plant tuber. Zandvoort potato mania was bigger than the Beatles and became famous both home and abroad. The sturdy buggers were so tough in these parts that they still continued to grow when the Netherlands was plagued by a potato disease which wreaked havoc in other parts of the lowlands. But there wasn't a chip or jacket in sight here.

Moving on to the shower block a smiling man in his mid-thirties with hair flicked over to one side was holding a hot water token lottery with three German lads. One of the teenagers correctly answered that former Dutch football captain Frank de Boer wore the number four shirt and was rewarded with a free shower. I deduced the quiz master must have been camp owner Andre and introduced myself.

'Ah... so you made it then. I hope you slept well. I wondered if you would be coming. Pleased to have helped you,' he said, with a friendly grin.

The conversation rambled from United and Chelsea's progression to the Champions League semi-finals, where they would be up against AC Milan and Liverpool respectively, before turning to the weather.

'You will have very good weather today I think,' Andre added. 'It is going to get hotter and hotter this week. The weather is far too good for this time of year, but excellent for business.'

'That will be global warming,' I said. 'It was snowing in England a few weeks ago and now it is boiling. Weird.'

'Yes it is strange. We had frost in the Netherlands only a few weeks ago, but now it is so warm. It must be to do with climate change, but it is not the planet which will suffer, it is the people.'

Ever since receiving Andre's hospitality invite, I was curious about his email address which started with the distinctive numbers 007.

'I take it you are a big James Bond fan from your email address Andre?'

'Yes, I like James Bond, but don't tell anybody else that I am a top secret spy.'

'I think the address has blown your cover wide open if I guessed it straight away.'

'I see your point. But nobody knows what I do away from the campsite. It is all mysterious.'

'You weren't here last night when I arrived. Were you on some sort of secret mission then?'

'I may have been, but I cannot give too much away. You haven't seen the operations room under the toilet block or the hi-tech gadgets in my car,' laughed Andre pointing to an old Ford Fiesta in the car park. It was hardly the Aston Martin, but he definitely had a licence to camp.

Making my way down to the beach the daylight revealed a parade of cafes, complete with wooden decked porches, tables and umbrellas. My belly was still growling and it was time to refuel before getting back on the road.

Now, if you want a fry-up abroad you are struggling big time. Even a bowl of Coco-Pops is out of the question. Continental Europeans breakfast on what I would nibble on for lunch. Forget the croissants and jam, more popular in Belgium and France, it's bread, rolls, ham and cheese all the way here.

Tea is another sore point abroad. You can't get a decent cuppa away from home and coffee needs to be called off the substitutes' bench. If you're like me then nothing can take the place of a refreshing brew to get you going in the morning and I drink gallons of the stuff. Tea here can be summed up politely as a cup of hot water with a slight staining, or more to the point, a cup of cat's piss. Both are weak and completely inexcusable for an Englishman to consider drinking. I was tempted to pack a 250 bag blister pack of Typhoo, but it fell to the wayside of bike weight limitation.

Coffee can also be a perplexing pursuit. It's always strong, freshly filtered, not from a jar, and slips down a treat. But just ordering a coffee is a horrifying experience when the waitress returns with a mouthful of black liquid in a midget's cup. Therefore, you have to ask for a 'big coffee' which earns you a strange look as if you were some sort of hot drink swilling pig. The same stare is reserved for the added request of milk and sugar. Very uncivilised.

Cycling parallel to the train line to Haarlem a patch of mini dunes shrank into grassy lumps. A dotting of lanky pine tree foot soldiers began to break cover, before the bulkier marines launched a full scale invasion and became the dominant power with muscular roots forcing their way through the submitting sand below. Exiting the wooded area the path followed a quiet road past a sprinkling of pretty fairytale white houses with red shutters and led into the undergrowth of the Kennemer National Park.

The dunes had given up the ghost now and were replaced by a thick procession of sky-reaching pine and silver birches, with discarded cones and brown leaves carpeting the floor. White spring blossoms complimented the trees and my first lesson in cycling with my mouth shut soon arrived as I swallowed a swarm of black flies buzzing in from the opposite direction. Possible vitamin content?

Popping out of the park into rural land, sitting cows were on sentry duty outside the ruins of the red brick Brederode castle, while chickens and geese co-existed in perfect farming hutch harmony. The leafy suburb of Driehus with its stables and dusty horse training circles flashed past and it was like travelling back in time on arriving at Velserbeek Park. A popular summer haunt of the 17th-century Amsterdam aristocrats, the park was purposefully transformed into a mirror image of the fashionable English countryside. Small lakes, little islands and meandering paths and streams lay at the centre of this pleasant green open space. Visitors peered inquisitively into the aviaries and children approached a majestic light brown horse with a black and white striped Mohican with a handful of grass. Ducks and sheep shared the powerfully built animal's railed off quarters opposite the magnificent white wooden panelled townhouse, topped off by a golden crest of a lamb holding a flag up to its woolly brethren.

Zooming under a road tunnel brought me into poor old Velsen Zuid which had fallen victim to the land hungry Noordzeekanaal. The Dutch equivalent of the River Thames allows freighters and mammoth sized barges to pass through to the capital city Amsterdam from the North Sea and the shrinking village has paid the ultimate price for increased shipping commerce. During the course of the last century almost half of Velsen Zuid has been sacrificed to widen the busy waterway. The other side of the sandwich has swallowed up even more of the village with car congested provincial road networks to Amsterdam and Haarlem taking their slice of the pie. It wasn't until 1970 that a preservation order was slapped on its oldest buildings which are safe for now.

A queue of cyclists were waiting for the small passenger ferry which crossed the Noordzeekannal, so I made a pit-stop next door at Bastiaans Friture. The Dutch love their hot-dog style foods, called *broodjes,* which come in all different flavours, usually sinking in a pool of tomato sauce or splodge of mustard. Not sure what to order, I asked the bemused girl behind the counter to choose for me. What a stitch-up! After gulping down what had seemed quite palatable, I returned to the counter and enquired about the contents of the *broodje fricandel.*

'A little bit of chicken, a small piece of pork and some horse,' she smirked. Oh well, when in Rome. Sorry Shergar!

The small yellow ferry ran every 20 minutes and was free to cyclists who packed both sides. Chugging across to the opposite bank you could just make out an island which served as a fortified point of the German's Atlantic Wall during the Second World War. The Nazi barrier was an extensive system of bunkers, batteries and minefields, strategically built along the western coast of Europe - stretching from the French-Spanish border right up to Norway - to defend against an anticipated Allied invasion from Great Britain. I would see plenty more of the Atlantic Wall's disfigured crumbling concrete relics along the way. Docking at Velsen Noord a long line of cyclists split off in all directions. My route glided past the industrial plants, loading wharfs and fat snaking factory pipes which lived here by the water.

Taking forever for the lights to change at a chaotic main road, a couple of baseball capped homeboys hit me with eyeballs of attitude before disappearing in a cloud of window filtered skunk smoke towards Amsterdam. It was early afternoon and the weather switch had been turned up to sweltering. My thoughts turned to Texel, the Frisian Island north of Den Helder across the Wadden Sea. I'd been offered a free bed on the island and decided to try and take up the offer a day early by totting up another 70 kilometres.

Doubling my efforts and cutting through the market gardens of Beverwijk and Heemskerk the surrounding landscape transformed into a dazzling artist's palette of red, purple, white and yellow tulips and daffodils.

A famous region for strawberry growing, manure mounds and straw were littered around the fields along with rusting antiquated irrigation pipes and sprinklers lying idle. There were also a number of sturdy secure units with computerised locking systems, which would have put Fort Knox to shame. It's obviously a serious thing this flower growing business, especially if you are working tirelessly on a top secret brand of tulip which will be the envy of rival Dutch farmers everywhere. Not much chance of the precious formula falling into enemy hands here.

Back into the dunes and skirting round the back of another seaside resort, Egmond aan Zee. The cycle signs had changed now, downsizing into mushroom shaped stubs with numerous destinations marked on them to feed the addiction of this cycle crazy country. The choices were now top, middle or bottom. It was like being on *Play Your Cards Right*.

Continuing north I looped around a corner and came within a sharp horn of colliding with a group of Scottish Highland bulls who were grazing on the move at the side of the path. Taking evasive action and ducking into a side lane I waited for the shaggy beasts to plod past. Then my phone rang, it was Katie, and after pressing the cancel button quickly I closed my eyes awaiting a painful stampede. But it never came, the foursome, three brown and the black bull of the family, were too preoccupied with their lazy munching to offer me any unwanted attention.

Standing taut in motionless straddle mode the docile quartet continued chewing slowly and weren't budging anywhere fast. They were at the centre of a t-junction, but barring my path. Edging slowly towards them I was still wary and took great care not to startle them into action.

What a wally! Just around the corner a woman and her two children had abandoned their bikes on the floor and were actually trying to stroke the things. Taking that as my cue, I belted past, not giving a second thought to my own sudden movements ending in a bloody gorging of the stupidly brave family. I hadn't seen a thing if anybody asked.

We English pride ourselves on being a nation of animal lovers, but on the evidence of what I had witnessed the Dutch beat us hands down. There were four-legged friends on the ground and winged creatures in the air everywhere. Parks, dunes, woods and even towns had a goat pen plonked in the centre of the shopping streets, which beat a mini roundabout I suppose. In another field a group of parents and children had hurdled a fence to pick up, hug and kiss a posse of young goats. The adult animals were far too busy worshipping an important looking ram who was strutting his stuff on top of a mound of hay in front of his bowing subjects. But it warmed the heart and was lovely to see. No wonder a recent European survey revealed that Dutch children were the happiest on the continent. They were in touch with nature, all seemed fit and healthy and were doing much better things with their time than sitting at home playing computer games or loitering outside the High Street kebab shop at all hours smoking cigs and sinking Tenants Extra.

I hadn't seen one hoody or fat kid since I'd been here. Alright, it was only two days, but I'd covered a lot of ground. The biggest black mark on Dutch society so far was an anorak wearing Alan Partridge lookalike who was slumped peacefully in the middle of the dunes on a bench having a quiet beer. He was even putting his empties in a recycling bag!

All the youngsters are physically active, playing football, golf, water sports or, of course, immersing themselves in this cycling nirvana. But that's no surprise as so much thought has gone into the Netherlands' cycling network which is on a complete par with the road system. They have all these whopping great car-free areas of unpolluted dunes to cycle around in complete safety, filling up their young lungs with fresh air. It's a million miles away from the token cycle paths at home which are usually nothing more than a thin white stripe of paint between the road and kerb which cars are still magnetically drawn towards. Don't think I've got a big downer on England, I just think we could do the simpler things better sometimes and can learn a lot from the infrastructure of so-called 'smaller nations' like the Netherlands.

Thatched bobbed cottages and huge triangular roofed houses hugged both sides of the road, as well as abodes with a traditional iron curved Dutch topping. This was a brief respite as I made my way back into the never-ending shoulders of sand which would whisk me past Bergen ann Zee (not Norway's Bergen – I wasn't that quick) and on to Camperduin.

The entrance to the latest dune range was watched over by a grey statue of Dutch poet and Socialist Herman Gorter, who in 1909 helped form the Social Democratic Party, believed to be the world's first Communist political group long before Lenin offered the revolution hungry Russians 'Peace, Lane and Bread.' Old Herman had a touch of the Harold Lloyds about him as he stood there supported by his walking stick. Well he had a pair of glasses, but I couldn't quite make out a smile.

The dunes were like an oven now. It may have been disorientating sun stroke cooking my brain, but Erika and I seemed to be going nowhere fast. Erika? She was my cycling soulmate, the slender, stunningly curved and well toned bike who was sharing the whole experience with me. We had begun conversing regularly, but now it was mostly a grumble as foot to pedal, man and mistress bolted blindly around the thickly wooded sandbanks. But our relationship wasn't just born out of reduced contact with fellow humans. That would be far too shallow, I wasn't a user you know! We were just getting familiar with each other's little ways on the road and had already become intimately close. Erika had stopped taking offence and was now comfortable with my screams of 'fuck, shit and piss,' every time something went wrong. And showing she cared would send out a responsive screech of the brakes or rubbing sound of the tyres. It was turning into a beautiful relationship.

Erika was christened after my local bike dealer Erik, who had been kind enough to lend me a trusty steed for this crusade. Over the last few months Erik had taken me under his wing at the shop and handed out a crash course in roadside repairs in case the old girl got injured. Feeling awkward and having no sense of co-ordination at all when it came to carrying out menial tasks with my hands, this had been difficult. I had a strong dislike for getting grease on my palms, whereas Erik loved to smother himself in the stuff and always seemed to have a black smudge on his head like some sort of cycling commando camouflage. The fear of getting my hands dirty had nothing to do with a washing obsessive compulsive disorder. I still needed that one to complete the set.

My cycling mentor showed me how to dismantle break pads, quickly release wheels and inner tubes and fix broken chain links with complicated Swiss Army Knife style tools. I just nodded and did my best to convince the cycling master that this vital knowledge was sinking in. What was the point in worrying about breaking down in the middle of nowhere? There would be a cycling shop in the next town. I would just have to push for a few hours.

The best bit of advice Erik had given me was to smear a banana around the crack of my bum if I got too saddle sore. Apparently it was what all the professional cyclists do. I told Erik that the real pros would eat it afterwards!

The signs were starting to annoy me now. One would read seven kilometres to Bergen, the next five and then seven again. I was going round in circles and the heat wasn't helping to improve my mood. The pine sprinkled dunes were five kilometres wide in some places and 50 metres high. Dune lakes provided an inland haven for seagull colonies. And only 600 metres from the sea this was the nearest trees got to the coast in the face of strong opposition from the sea winds and salt air.

After two dragging hours of strength zapping trundling, Camperduin blinked onto the radar. A sand bowl outpost in the middle of nowhere it had nothing to offer and with the time getting on for 7.30pm I decided to put in a call to Monique Kool at the StayOkay hostel on Texel to reserve my blagged sleeping quarters.

The news wasn't good. 'Sure, you can stay here, but I don't know if you will make it,' she said. My face contorted into a miserable grimace.

'The last ferry to Texel from Den Helder is in two hours and you are still 30 kilometres away.'

'Not a problem. I can make that. Get the bed ready and I will see you in a couple of hours,' I attempted to convince Miss Kool.

'OK. But you must have a rocket pack on your bike to get here so quickly. We have very cold beer here and I will have one waiting for you if you make it. If you have any problems call me back.'

Beer! What was she trying to do, torture me? Talk about dangling a juicy carrot in front of a famished donkey. Hurdling back on to Erika I cracked the whip and pedalled away frantically down the dusty yellow path. Systems shutting down. A couple of kilometres down the road I was cream crackered. My legs felt like dead-weights. I was still a novice at this game and every turn of the pedal stabbed me painfully in the calf and thigh muscles.

But I could make it. The route ahead was smooth and flat as an airport runway. It was time for take-off. To my right the surrounding scenery was agricultural with a colourful splash of hyacinths and traditional Dutch windmills dwarfed by the slashing blades of modern day wind farms. On the other side loomed an immense green sea dike, *Hondsbosse Zeewering*, which made me feel completely insignificant. It was first built at the beginning of the 17th century after the village of Hondsbos was devoured by the sea. Three dikes were originally constructed, called the Guard, the Sleeper and the Dreamer. But if you snooze you lose and the latter two were removed when the Guard was considered strong enough to puff out his chest and hold the sea at arm's length alone.

Carrying on at snail's pace, the motor home encircled town of Callantsoog lumbered away behind me and it was now only 12 kilometres to Den Helder. Even at half pace this was a piece of piss. I still had an hour to board the last ferry to Texel and my hand was getting closer to gripping that dripping wet glass of beer which wouldn't leave my mind. I hadn't taken into account another stint in the dunes though.

Darkness was falling and the wind was kicking up, making my dead legs work three times as hard. And then it got hilly as the path ahead climbed up and down, zig-zagged round and inevitably shifted upwards again. Typical, nothing but even surfaces for 160 kilometres and just when I needed a bit of help the North Sea Cycle Route sprung the first of many irksome surprises.

The Wadden Sea should be straight ahead of me. I could even smell it, but it wasn't getting any closer as I plundered my way, lights on, through the dark. I did have another shining star. The beams of the *Lange Jaap* cut a hole in the dim horizon which faced me. The tallest iron clad lighthouse in Europe, at 63.45 metres, it stood right on the spot where I wanted to be, but refused to get closer despite taunting me with its highly visible presence.

But it couldn't escape me forever and after another 20 minutes of *Benny Hill* type antics, ducking up and down in the dunes, I was rewarded with my first glimpse of the sea since Zandvoort. The faint sparkle of

Texel's lights beckoned me over the Wadden Sea which stretched across the top of the Noord Holland peninsula. Pitch black darkness laid between my tyres and the largest of the Dutch Frisian Islands, barely illuminated by the timid glow of distant buoy markers. It was a cruel joke. I could see it, but with only 15 minutes until ferry o'clock my hopes of touching it tonight were evaporating fast along with that pint.

Racing past the sniggering lighthouse and offering a two-fingered salute in return I found one last burst of energy to nudge into Den Helder. I'd missed the boat by five minutes. Fuck it! Sluggishly moving into town it was nearly 10pm and my spirits dropped like a heavy anvil as I inspected the bleak outlook of tumbleweed central.

A deserted shopping parade and square were surrounded by bars and restaurants whose under the arm tea-towel balancing barmen were dragging in specials boards and shutting up shop. It was time to get on the blower to Monique, who promised to ring around and try to find me somewhere to put my head. The beer would also still be there tomorrow. Small pangs of panic began to bite at my body, but I suppressed them long enough to pick up the slightly shaking phone.

'The first place will not take you as you do not have a Dutch Friends of Cycling card, but I have another number and will get back to you.'

Preparing for a humid night on the bench my bike was propped against, the ring-tone blasted out again and Lady Kool was certainly living up to her name.

'I have found you somewhere with a family in Java Street. They will give you a room for the night. Go straight there now and we will see you tomorrow.' I could have jumped for joy and promised to give Monique a slobbery wet kiss on my arrival in Texel. But I'd sink the beer first in case she was pig ugly.

Tracking down the only two 24-hour party people in Den Helder, two men in their fifties walking home, I asked for directions and was told my destination was next to the water tower in the centre of town.

'Where was that?' I asked like a blindman. 'Right behind you,' they pointed, as I turned to see the largest landmark in the whole place just 200 metres away.

Arriving at a house in a quiet road with a natural garden fence of loved up twig like trees standing in a row holding branches, I rang the bell. An elderly lady answered the door with understandable apprehension at finding a stubble-stained, sweat-stinking, long-haired English oik on her porch.

Putting the lady of the house at ease with a bum-licking charm offensive she showed me up a pair of ladder-like wooden stairs and disappeared to fetch some milk for my sleeping quarters' complimentary coffee. It was just like staying at your nan's house. The bedside table was dressed in a flower patterned cloth, pot plants filled the window ledge and hand-stitched tapestries of windmills, lock bridges and traditional Dutch clothing, clogs and curvy hats hung on the walls.

My host reappeared with the milk and remembering I had rudely forgotten the courtesy of asking the miracle worker's name she told me: 'My name is Barend. Barend Bethlehem, just like in the Bible.' I was gobsmacked. Hallelujah!

8   Cycling in a Wadden Wonderland

Sailing across the Wadden Sea for a free pint was taking things to new extremes even by my ridiculous standards. Declining the breakfast table offer of toast covered in pink and yellow packet candy sprinkles, it was bon voyage from the Bethlehems and room left at the inn for the next weary traveller. Not a single drop of alcohol had touched my lips since leaving England and taking in Texel couldn't come quick enough (I hadn't sunk the kindly Germans' beer in Zandvoort just in case they had done something to it. Don't you know me by now?).

Idyllic Texel, pronounced *Tessel*, is the largest and most populated of the Dutch Frisian Islands, the western border of a Wadden Sea archipelago which hovers above the top of Germany and extends as far as Denmark. Originally two islands, Texel to the south and Eierland to the northwest, the two separate bodies were poldered together by those clever Dutchmen in the 17th century.

The Wadden Sea stretches some 500 kilometres from Den Helder to its northern boundary at Skallingen, north of Esbjerg in Denmark. This North Sea belt contains a highly dynamic ecosystem through its tidal channels, mud flats and salt marshes. The Wadden Sea is an important habitat for birds, seals, shellfish and other fish species due to high growth rates of algae. This is because the nutrient rich waters are shallow, allowing sufficient light to reach the 'green sea lettuce' and accelerate its expansion.

Around 50 species of northern hemisphere originating birds, many of which are on the threatened existence list, drop in to make a vital pit-stop. As many as 12 million of our feathered friends pass through every year on their migration route from breeding grounds in Siberia, Iceland, Greenland and north east Canada, to their winter retreats in Europe and

Africa. Just like parking up for a quick worm McMuffin at a drive-through McDonald's. Well the birds are peck-ish. I'll get my coat.

More than 10,000 common seals are believed to be living in the Wadden Sea, representing a remarkable recovery during the last 40 years. Less than 4,000 of the marine mammals were left swimming around these waters in the 60s, but numbers increased over the next decade following a ban on hunting the creatures for their prized coats and oil. After escaping a nasty clubbing to death in these parts, they found themselves up against a new adversary, the immune system attacking *Phocine* distemper virus. By 1988 the killer disease had wiped out half of the luckless creatures' population in western Europe. But you can't keep a good seal down and the hardy blighters have fought back to thrive once more after suckling up to the bosom of the Wadden Sea. The virus has recently struck again however, claiming casualties from the coasts of Denmark and Sweden. But if seal history has taught us anything, it is that these born survivors will pass this latest perilous test with flying colours.

The fertile arms of the salty Wadden Sea have also worked their magic across land and in the freshwater environment. Home to another exceptional richness of species, some 2,000 spiders, insects and other invertebrates flourish around these life-giving waters. Exceptional flora and fauna have also dug in, with the high biological productivity of the tidal flats comparable with tropical rain forests. It comes as no major surprise then that the governments of the Netherlands, Germany and Denmark have joined forces to safeguard the Wadden Sea zone and the wildlife which depends upon it.

Plonked right at the beginning of this unique strip of water, modern day Texel is a haven for outdoor lovers and stressed out southerners helplessly tractor beamed towards its natural charms. Cyclists, walkers and bird watchers flock here all year round, hoping to catch a glimpse of a wonderfully named spoonbill or pied flycatcher flapping around the untouched beaches and dunes. With the fishing industry long dead, tourism is the life blood of Texel now, sucking in as much as 70 per cent of its income. This is never more evident than during June's catamaran race around the island, which is the largest of its kind in the world and attracts 600 boats. But equally important is the careful guardianship of the surrounding nature. A seal hospital helps sick and undernourished pups get back on their flippers and sea birds discovered on the shore with disabling sticky oil-polluted plumage are given a miraculous makeover spin in a special washing machine.

But it all meant nothing to me. Texel was just one of a group of little blobs above the Netherlands in my road atlas. I'd wager my left buttock that nobody at home could point it out on the map. But that was the attraction of the North Sea Cycle Route, visiting obscure places that your friends had never heard of, where you had never been and would probably never visit ever again. Just what happened in these places? Why would anybody want to live a boat ride from the mainland and were their children all born with six fingers? These are the sort of questions my cycling investigations would answer and after boarding the centenary celebrating *Teso* ferry at Den Helder for the short hop to Texel other concerns began to creep forward.

Flashbacks of cult horror movie *The Wicker Man* began to fly around my mind, when an unhinged rabble of incestuous island dwelling pagans took out some vegetable crop insurance by sacrificing a virgin Christian policeman under a blazing sunset. Now, an adequate CV of sexual experience should exempt me from being burnt alive inside an enormous wooden effigy, while receiving a golden shower from petrified goats perched above my head on the same ritualistic ride. And on the upside, I was keen to take my chances if it meant cracking on with this outpost's very own answer to the film's Swedish siren Britt Ekland, whose mesmerising naked pub dancing was enough to start a fire inside anyone. There was no turning back now.

The packed observation deck was full of cooing Pac-a-Macs and binoculars as our transport was gently scooped out of the Wadden Sea and cradled by the Frisian Island's sun burnt arms. It was like heading towards a Caribbean paradise. But instead of being greeted by Bob Marley and copious amounts of jerk chicken, all there was to see were weather-worn brick outhouses, snoozing cows and rabbits making smoke clouds as they kicked their hind legs playfully in the bone dry fields. Oh and sheep, sheep and more sheep. In Wales the men would call it heaven.

It was only six kilometres from the port to the largest village on the island, Den Burg, which is home to more than half of Texel's 14,000 inhabitants. But keeping the chain circling effectively was taking a gargantuan effort. The legs were still smarting from the ill-fated race against the clock to Den Helder and the wind had definitely picked up a notch or two. Then there was the welcoming pungent stench of 'the country', as my father would have politely put it, before rapidly winding up the car window. The sweet smell of manure filled the air as I continued pedalling past the flat farming lands, which were all squared off by agricultural stream moats known as *sloots*. Sheep were definitely king here. They even had their own houses. The walking jumpers were trotting in and out of what resembled a thatched cottage chopped in two. I'd have been happy with that myself.

'Would you like that beer now?' The woman was obsessed, but I liked her style. I almost rode straight into Monique after rolling up at the StayOkay youth hostel. With short dark hair sitting above tiny glasses she was sunning herself on a bench underneath the impressive frontage of this ultra modern stopover point. Opened in 2006 and sleeping 200 people, the hostel was shaped like a massive tent with a glass facade supported by steel supported ropes pegged into the patio floor outside.

'It is more like a hotel than a hostel, or maybe somewhere in between, but we like it,' said Monique. 'It is a paradise for backpackers who are used to staying in more basic accommodation. Each room has its own toilet and shower. Not many hostels can say that as you usually have to share with everybody else. Travellers are spoilt here.' Any prospective room mates better be heavy sleepers as the stink of my ceremonial early morning number two was the only thing on Earth that could shift a blocked hooter quicker than a vicious stab of a menthol Vicks stick.

Monique was right about the beer, it was refreshingly cold and well worth the wait as it trickled gleefully down my grateful throat. Then she really hit me below the belt by waving a packet of 'smoke us, smoke us' screaming cigarettes in my face. Smoking was another catalyst for my episodes of paranoia. It was something I only did socially and sparingly with a weekend puff down the pub, but never at home. The first few ciggies would be wonderful. It doesn't matter how filthy a habit it is condemned to be, the taste of those first few deep inhalations were always gloriously sweet. But it wouldn't be long before the ecstasy vanished, replaced by crunching chest pains and breathing difficulties which left me sucking for oxygen through a straw thin airway.

It was all psychosomatic of course, created by a malevolent mental force trying to persuade me that lung cancer and heart disease were both knocking on the door at the same time. Funnily enough, this would make me pack up smoking forever yet again and in a few days' time calm would cover my body and physical well being would reign supreme. But all that did was give me the confidence to spark up the next time I was out with a smouldering drinking partner (social smokers never buy their own). Of course, the vicious circle would be doing the rounds again and I would be back at square one on Sunday morning.

Knowing my full energy reserves and best free breathing skills were compulsory components in completing this cycling mission, I promised my body a smoke-free trip. This was a giant enough step as it was, leaving home and going it alone. What I really didn't need was to add any further complications to the equation, possibly tipping me over the edge headlong into the chasm of insanity.

'But you're alright,' whispered the glowing red nicotine demon. 'This whole thing has been a breeze so far. You made such a fuss about leaving and it's been a complete doddle. Why are you always so hard on yourself? Give yourself a little treat. It's only one cigarette. Then you can stop again can't you?' Three days and no anxiety attacks, sleep choking or dizzy spells. I did deserve a reward. Just one lovely smoke wasn't going to splinter my current state of tranquillity. Besides, how can you make contingency plans for fending off evil cigarette-waving harpies such as Monique. I was soon lighting up again.

Taking time to finish my (second) beer I rose tentatively after chain-smoking three cigs and receiving the mother of all nicotine head-spinning rushes on my first stumbling attempt to get up. Floating across the tiled floor of reception underneath the futuristic metal piped ceiling decorations, I deducted the presence of a Japanese person in my room. It was the 20 Fuji camera film pods on the table which gave it away.

Yoshi, named after the goofy green dragon in Super Mario, was from Hiroshima and was backpacking around Europe solo. In his mid-twenties and with black bushy curtains covering his cheekbones, he had been in Texel two days. Catching a train from Amsterdam, Yoshi had escaped the stress of the city and made the pilgrimage north, adding some relaxing atmosphere and visual stimulation to his dope smoking holiday (not all the capsules contained film unless those innovative Jap scientists have invented a new hemp-based surround smell picture product).

Ripping a train timetable and blue pen from the zip pocket of his black Parker jacket, Yoshi asked which European cities were a must visit in his three month quest to absorb the continent's history, art and culture. Happy to help (I'd read a lot of books remember), I reeled off the bog-standard answers – Paris, Rome, Barcelona and London. Feeling duty bound to throw in a couple of my own top tips, Hull and Middlesbrough were both marked down with an appreciative: 'Oh really, thank you.' I'm sure Yoshi would be grateful when he was flicking through the magazines in those filthy Humberside sex shops, drinking flat slops at £1 a pint and sobering up with a chemical fume inhalation down by the river bank on Teesside.

It was time for an afternoon joint ahead of crashing out in the middle of the nearest random field for Yoshi, who skinned up and left the room. A few minutes later the key turned in the lock again and he was back. 'Excuse me. May I take your picture?' Of course, he was Japanese, a nation of photographic addicts who have to click everything at least once for the record. And how could I refuse him such an honour? Adopting my best Grattan's catalogue model pout (my hand would have been delicately placed in a front pocket if I'd been wearing a long cream cardy), I put on my best pose and let him snap away, three times. Well he had a bit of trouble finding my best side.

Texel was granted city rights in 1415 and is dubbed 'Little Holland' because the islanders believe you can find anything and everything from the mainland here. A Utopian feeling flowed around the place and everybody walked about wearing standard issue broad smiles as if they had been pumped full of cheerful pills. I wasn't used to such overwhelming friendliness and it was odd to be greeted so enthusiastically by complete strangers at the turn of every street corner. Den Burg could have been a testing station for a top secret happy gas mixed up in experimental government laboratories. God, it was so much simpler at home being miserable and glum, plodding the roads with your head down as if you were the only person alive. It was hard work moulding my face into a convincing smile and returning complimentaries every few minutes. People weren't this nice at home. What was going on?

Texel's happiness patrol is born out of healthy living, relaxing countryside and an infectious community spirit where neighbours really do become good friends. Eat your heart out Ramsay Street! The crime rate on the island is zilch. It only soars to the heights of a microscopic pimple on the redundant police graph sheet if some dodgy tourist rips through the harmony barrier by stuffing a carrot or radish in their pocket. And in winter, front doors are left wide open for other islanders to walk in off the street and make themselves a warming cup of coffee. People have been shot for asking for a cup of sugar in Moss Side or South London.

The island claims to have the cleanest air in the Netherlands, as well as attracting the most hours of sun. It has always drawn in working artists and writers spellbound by its natural charms. The chilled out atmosphere was also popular with hippy communes in the 60s, who came here to get spaced out of their minds in peace. And it must have filtered down the generations through the genes as the class of 2007 children readily admit they enjoy going to school without any form of financial bribe engineering such an outrageous statement.

Den Burg itself was an attractive village of two-storey thatched, flat fronted houses (the conservation friendly council won't rubberstamp anything higher) and cobbled streets that encircle the surprisingly hectic shopping lanes. These narrow streets lean right over, nearly high fiving each other, with the stores below stocking everything from pink Converse trainers to plastic sheep (really not needed here) and rolls of thick carpet. There was even a cinema cramped in somewhere.

The focal point of Den Burg was the *Hervormoe Kerk* church, which was visible from miles outside of the village, despite nestling snugly right at its heart. But it was pottering around the small hemmed-in stores, bakeries and grocers which drew in the punters and kept their euros on the island. Boxes of bright, pumped-up fruit and vegetables brimmed over everywhere. And there were all shapes and sizes of hams, sausages and salamis, plus wooden racks of rounded cheese slabs which wouldn't have been out of place flying down an Olympic curling lane.

The nostril seeking smells of cakes, pastries and warm breads breaking free from the bakeries is enough to drive you mad and the multiple choice of beer on offer could turn the most tea-total disciple into a taste-testing alcoholic. But good old England still had an ace up its sleeve and a poke in the eye for these island dwelling infidels. When it came to crisps we were still well on top. Forget your model fruit and veg, cracking cheeses and super salamis Texel, because when it comes to savoury snacks you were just downright rubbish. Row upon row of paprika, salted and cheese flavoured crisps just wasn't good enough. It didn't matter that some of them were cone shaped, like chip sticks or waffles. Where was prawn cocktail, Worcester sauce and smoky bacon on the menu? You didn't even have a box of salt and vinegar Pringles. Bloody amateurs!

After a couple of warm-up beers at the hostel, Monique dragged me off to Den Burg's brown bar. This is the name of a traditional Dutch drinking establishment and partly gets its title from the earthy hue clinging to every timber, wall and ceiling from years of cigarette tar going up in smoke. And this place did exactly what it said on the tin. The floors, bar and even the toilets were all dark brown, with the only break in the dinginess provided by old tin advertising boards for teas and beers plastered here and there.

Even the food and beer was brown. Monique introduced me to a glass of grog brewed on the island. The murky *Skuumkoppe* beer came in a (you guessed it) brown bottle with a red lighthouse shining out from its label. It should have come with a health warning too as it slid effortlessly into my system like honey, inspiring a heavy drinking session I could do without ahead of hitting the road again.

Tucking into a succulent brown bowl of tender Texel lamb goulash at the bar, Monique began to give me her life story. She was a keen traveller and had backpacked around Australia, New Zealand and Ecuador during her 32 years on the planet. As the effect of the beers began to take a grip, Monique opened up about her future plans to own a pesticide-free smallholding, after becoming sceptical of her country's farming methods.

'There is a milk lake in the Netherlands and when we were younger the government urged us to drink three glasses of milk a day to keep us healthy. We later learned that all the cows had been injected with antibiotics to artificially boost milk production and now it is causing us health problems. I have built up an immunity to antibiotics through drinking the milk and they are useless to me now if I get a cold or sore throat. This is not right and I want to get my own piece of land so I can control what food and drink is going inside my body.'

Monique wasn't a great lover of men. She wasn't ready to settle down, which she punctuated by pointing at her neck growling: 'No male stranglehold for me.' Always thinking of the bigger picture, this industrious lady had also taken out some baby insurance by lining up a gay sperm donor. I offered to be a godparent.

We shared a love of reading magazines and books on the toilet and she asked me if I had heard of the cycling term 'dead box syndrome?', which being a complete novice I hadn't. 'It relates to here.' She pointed down past the edge of the dark brown stool to what I guessed by the colour of her hair were dark brown lady parts.

'If you go out and cycle around the whole island the movement of blood around the body when you finally stop gives women the same sensation as having an orgasm. It is because your vagina feels dead after rubbing against the saddle for so long, but the relief of getting off the bike is just amazing. It is all about negative and positive blood flow. Who needs men?'

How would she define the typical Netherlander I wondered? From what I had witnessed so far, everybody seemed to have a fairly laid-back approach and decent quality of life. 'This is true,' she said. 'The Dutch tend to strike a harmonious life balance between work and recreation. As a race we like to be open minded and enjoy our freedom. But for all the easy going lifestyle we don't like people putting up boundaries. If you tell a Dutchman he cannot do something or take something it will all change. He will just go and do it anyway to prove a point.'

And then we got on to the Germans. Monique said there was still a lot of resentment among the older generation towards Germany following their occupation of a neutral Netherlands during the Second World War. The only time she didn't like the Germans was during sports events, like the World Cup, when the entire orange nation were desperate to dent the pride of their east border neighbours.

'It may have been 60 years ago, but it is still difficult for the older people to forget,' Monique explained. 'There were such difficult hardships, particularly during the hunger winter at the end of the war when my grandfather was forced to eat tulip bulbs to survive. When I was a little girl he would eat a loaf of mouldy bread and my nan would take used tea bags home. This is how they had to live during the war and they learnt not to waste anything. Everything was valuable and couldn't be thrown out. We live in a very luxurious world in contrast to those dark times.'

Grandma Kool was now in her eighties and had turned to something more herbal than tea to help cure the aches and pains of old age. 'Nan would hobble into a pot café in Delft with her walking stick and sit their surrounded by youngsters smoking away the soreness. You may think this sounds very Dutch. But it was just to help her. I do not smoke dope. Sure I tried it when I was younger, but because the laws are so relaxed here it is no big deal. When something is so easily available you soon become bored of it.'

And what about life in general, or even death. 'I don't think about it. I'm not a big believer in heaven, but we may be reincarnated. You should just enjoy life. You don't know and won't know when it is going to finish, so there is no point in worrying about death.'

Feeling a complete wimp next to this strong minded woman, I confessed that dying was my greatest fear. 'Then you are doing the right thing on this crazy cycle ride of yours,' she said. 'Sometimes people need to give themselves a big kick up the backside to realise what they want out of life and stop worrying about the things they have no control over. And I think that is what you are doing right now. Drink up, I have to work in the morning.'

It was still only six kilometres back to the port, but it wasn't easy clawing my way back to the Den Helder bound ship with a stinking hangover. And then there were the piercing daggers arrowing my way from fields on both sides of the road. The disgusted screams of 'Baa-d… baa-d… baa-d', were ringing out in woolly stereo. That was the problem with small island life. Nobody could keep a secret and gossip spread as quickly as foot and mouth disease. The Texel lambs knew I had gorged myself on their cousins the previous night and were trying to make me repent for my carnivorous sins. But there were no pangs of guilt in my stomach. You tasted great, boys, and this was the first place on tour which ticked the 'I'm definitely coming back one day' box. I couldn't wait to return and feel the juice of that tender meat dribbling down my chin again. I might even pack a jar of mint sauce!

9 Big Dike

Friday morning and Den Helder was still struggling to shake itself out of a coma. It would have been simpler cycling to the top of Texel and hopping across to the neighbouring Frisian Island of Vlieland, before taking another ferry to the yachting oasis of mainland Harlingen on the coast.

A black belt 10th dan master in the art of doing things arse-over-tit, I opted to cover the same journey by land. Retracing my path through the maze of lighthouse leering dunes and back to Callantsoog, Erika would pick up the LF10 Waddenzee Route across the roof of the Netherlands to the German border. Between here and Harlingen were nearly 100 kilometres of farming polders and a dual carriageway which walked on water, the *Afsluitdijk,* which bridged the gap between the provinces of Noord Holland and Friesland (no, this wasn't where chips came from).

So it was farewell to Den Helder after another thankfully brief shunt into the town centre. It was difficult not to have any sympathy for the place and it was desperately trying to modernise its face. But time had not been kind to the port which had shrunk in importance during the last five centuries. More than 400 years ago, during the Dutch Golden Age, ships assembled here ahead of setting sail across the world's oceans on exciting voyages of discovery. At this time the trade, art and science of the Netherlands was highly acclaimed to be top dog around the globe.

Den Helder evolved into an important naval base at the start of the 1800s thanks to the French. Conquest crazy frog emperor Napoleon was the first to realise its strategic sea value (Duh! It was surrounded on water by three sides), ordering the construction of a fort and naval dockyards. But the end of the same century sunk the dwindling numbers of merchant navy ships which passed through to sea, now offered a more direct passage by the Noordzeekanaal. Since 1947, the Royal Netherlands Navy have had their official base here, but even sailors are feeling the pinch. The end of the Cold War with Russia signalled a cut-back in the defence budget and the consequential loss of thousands of jobs. With fishing also declining over the last few decades, Den Helder hopes to stop the rot by concentrating on tourism. The old naval dockyards of Willemsoord now house restaurants, a cinema and other recreational facilities. But a complete overhaul is required to help this tired old town find its independence away from the waters which have always shaped its past.

Just falling short of stacking my bike, I wrestled the attention seeking phone from a bed of pens, notebooks and batteries in my front box to answer the call. It was an automated message from British Gas, which was very annoying as I'm not even one of their customers. But this was nothing in comparison to how I would feel in a few more weeks' time when, steam blowing out of my ears, they would still be getting their irritating computerised female voice to check up on me twice a day. Touched, I wasn't.

When I tried to ring British Gas back and get this all too regular intrusion cancelled the number didn't accept incoming calls. But it gets better as we travel forward in time briefly. On returning home I discovered the equally incompetent berks at my mobile phone provider hadn't bothered to switch off my roaming voice mail, despite only making this most basic of requests to their telephone chimps three times prior to setting off. When you contact these people, do they actually listen or do anything? I used to imagine them wearing headphones in a flashy call centre, facing hi-tech computers, fingers itching to eagerly punch the information you have kindly bothered to ring over into their keyboard. Nowadays I wonder if they are sharing a battered old phone in a flea bitten factory lock-up thinking 'blardy... blardy... blar' as they have no way or intention of addressing your problems whatsoever. That must be the explanation as nobody employable is surely thick enough to consistently score 100 per cent in the getting it stupidly wrong test. I was charged about £1 for every phone call received from British Gas, which I shouldn't have even been getting. So that's £1 multiplied by twice a day, multiplied again by a couple of months. I'll let you do the maths! And then maybe you can work out how to get these clowns to admit their failures and rectify their mistakes. The customer is always right – don't make me laugh.

Rant over and feeling a lot better for that outburst. Anyway back on the track and having kept my balance I swept into Callantsoog, hooking up with the LF10 Waddenzee Route. Plunging headlong into the heartland of Dutch agriculture the path ran parallel to reedy bedded canals. Residents were filling deckchairs in their front gardens and other people were just plonked by the waterways eating fruit or nibbling on a roll watching the ducks. All of them had a wave and a 'hi' for me and it was great to be back on the road. I don't know if it was the fallout from the lamb goulash, but I was definitely benefiting from my own special brand of wind assistance. The canals blinked past and headed right out into the sticks.

Erika was purring and the boys were still holding firm. This was another affectionate term reserved for my rear wheel packs, sleeping bag and tent, uttered every time I stretched an arm behind me in full cycling mode to pat them both and make sure they were still on board.

The village of Oudesluis, if you could call it that (well there was a derelict shed), was home to a magnificent octagonal thatched polder windmill. Built in the 15th century this green wooden panelled gem was still lived in today. These stunning works of farming art used a wind-powered paddle wheel to pump out the excess water from the surrounding reclaimed lands. This was revolutionary state of the art machinery during its heyday – the Concord, Vic 20 (minus the 16k ram pack) or gramophone of its time. Windmills were so efficient that the blueprint was cloned throughout Europe, where their brothers and sisters can still be found today resting long retired sails at the centre of dried out towns and villages. This particular beauty even had an intact emergency break rope running from its head down to the ground. Replaced by an electronic pumping station in 1950, the windmill is still going strong and this specimen is now back in full working order.

Next to the side door lay three sets of hand carved light wooden clogs and a pumpkin horror mask of wicked eyes and jagged shrieking teeth. It was only April, far too early for Halloween celebrations, and I would see plenty more of these spooky sculptures peering out from farms and barns between here and the *Afsluitdijk*. Certain it was some superstitious ploy to ward off evil crop spirits and protect the harvest, I pedalled a little harder, not wanting to discover a more sinister reason for their unsettling presence after dark.

Gliding past giant squares of flat cultivation, being drip-fed by the criss-cross of liquid manure filled *sloot* streams, groaning tractors were returning to base with potatoes spilling off the top of their trailers. And what a lorded manner these farmers were accustomed to. My perception of an agricultural worker had always been a leathery faced old git, with gnarled weather-eaten hands struggling to make ends meet. But these boys lived like millionaire rock stars once the muddy overalls and wellies had been discarded in the cupboard. The farmhouses resembled eight-bedroom English mansions and I bet they had heated swimming pools round the back. All of them were in perfect nick, with bright flower beds and not a single chip or peel tarnishing the immaculate paintwork. The finishing touch was a moat dug around the grounds and small wooden bridges crossing back on to the road. How the other half live.

This leg of the journey was becoming monotonous and the weather conditions were equally grim. After the first couple of hours, endless scabby fields begin to lose their shine. This really wasn't scenic eye candy. Seen one lifeless field, seen them all. Even the dunes were varied and sloped about in different patterns, bustling with wildlife, fitness fanatics and oh yeah, Nordic walkers. But this place was dead. I hadn't seen anyone or been greeted for ages. This area was low down and wide open, providing no protection from the elements. My growing grumpiness wasn't being improved by winds which blew straight through my bony body, seriously hampering any progress. It wasn't a bad day at all, still in the low 20s, but I was getting buffeted about all over the place like an empty crisp packet.

Slowing right down was the only way I could bat on, but that didn't help with the smell. The relentless air shelling had also increased the nauseating stench of animal poo, which filled the rivers, fields and was even rolling about joyfully in the roads. It really wasn't funny when you had cavernous nostrils like mine. Sunglasses were also a must to keep the squadrons of kamikaze shit flies out of my eyes. For the first time I'd really had enough and began questioning my actions during what was an agonisingly slow grind. The comforts of home, a nice bath, cup of real tea and cuddle-wuddle with the missus seemed a million miles away.

Music was doing nothing to lift my sullen mood either. One of my 'friends' Keith put together a couple of CD compilations, the 'Ping-Pong Mixes', allegedly designed to keep me going. The name was a tribute to his father who took great delight in treating us to a terrible 'One of our Dinosaurs is Missing' Chinese accent as we sat playing crude, but revolutionary TV table tennis as nippers, with two blurry white sticks and a dot on a Binatone games system. But instead of recording a series of uplifting tunes to put some positive wind in my pedals, the bastard cooked up a play-list of songs specifically designed to make me homesick.

Alison Moyet was wailing on about trying to reach her far away baby by phone, U2 tried to give me a quick rendition of 'With or Without You' and there was even that bloody Tripods song with the heart-string pulling chorus, 'But you're not here'. The lumbering alien camera stands could have conquered the entire world during the last few hours and I would have been completely oblivious, trundling through the bleak and deathly silent polder lands.

Then it happened. Day four on the road without any real disasters. But that was before the Flaming Lips' 'Do you Realize' burst open the floodgates. In that one moment, the dark, crushing lyrics brought everything back to me about mum dying. She was really gone forever and never coming back.

'Do you realize that you have the most beautiful face? Do you realize we're floating in space? Do you realize that happiness makes you cry? Do you realize that everyone you know someday will die? And instead of saying all of your last goodbyes – let them know. You realize that life goes fast. It's hard to make the good things last.'

Sobbing my eyes out uncontrollably for a good 15 minutes I pushed on, blinded by tears which were soaking my soggy reddened face. Those words touched a tender nerve. But maybe I needed to let it out once more away from the safety boundaries of home. It goes without saying that losing mum and dad so early and so close together had been as rough as it comes. But things can always be worse. I wasn't a young child riddled with terminal cancer who would never have the opportunity to gorge itself on life's many treats, or a fly-encrusted kid scrambling around for a bowl of rice in Africa.

Realising you are still lucky in a lot of ways doesn't make things any easier. I've always plodded my way pretty aimlessly through the weeks, months and years of my existence. It's like being in an epic film, a personal drama or soap with muggins here in the lead role. None of it ever feels real. Even when my folks breathed their last it was hard to accept it had actually happened. Maybe, it was some sort of protective mental block. I was numbed to the core, but you can't fully accept the frightening finality of it all.

Right now reality was giving me a real kick in the teeth. I'd shed oceans of tears since mum passed. But being out here, on my Jack in the hushed polder lands, with the words of that song ripping through the centre of my heart had left a sense of rawness. They weren't coming back and I had to make the most of this life they had given me, which meant getting on with things and kicking the negative vibe to the kerb. Fortunately, I had armed myself with a few of my own CDs and was able to swap discs for one of the most influential groups to ever sound a note in music history, Chas 'N' Dave. The mockney duo soon lifted my deflated spirits. Grinning like a hyena, new slants were put on their masterpieces, with 'All Down to Harlingen' and 'You've got more rabbit than Aldi' pumping urgency back into the wheels. Bollocks to going home, you loser. You're a long time dead (sorry folks) and I was here for the duration.

With all the poise of a circus wire balancing act, Erika lifted me across the thin gravel path summit of the green dike as frantically flapping ducks used the adjacent stream as a wet runway for take-off. Then it was down the other side of the bank and a slide back into civilisation at the wonderfully named Hippolytushoef. I half expected to find all the locals laughing out loud and having nude mud slinging fights in a communal town watering hole. But it wasn't to be and there was no point wallowing (ouch!) in my disappointment.

In neighbouring Den Oever an old windmill was busy demonstrating its staying power. Sailing blades cut the air in two above a brave family of diners tucking into a front garden evening meal and risking a decapitated head or two landing in the salad bowl. Stopping for a quick litre of water (my urine was still permanently carrot-coloured which meant I wasn't drinking enough) the greatest challenge yet lay straight ahead – the sea splitting *Afsluitdijk*. My school boy excitement would soon turn into leg-killing frustration.

The *Afsluitdijk* is a miracle of modern engineering. A 32 kilometre barrier dam or closure dike, whatever you want to call it, this man made marvel provides a short-cut between the provinces of Noord Holland and Friesland, straight across the middle of the Wadden Sea and Ijsselmeer lake. When it comes to compiling a list of Europe's most breathtaking constructions, it is up there with Paris' Eiffel Tower, St Peter's Basilica, Rome, and Gnome World, Buckland Brewer, in my book.

Taking six painstaking years to build and completed in 1933 some 5,000 workers were needed to piece this monster together. *Afsluitdijk* sounded the death knell of the Zuiderzee, a salt water inlet of the North Sea, which was blocked off and transformed into the fresh water Ijsselmeer lake. There were also the added complexities of including shipping locks and discharge sluices at both ends, which are needed to control the volume of water in the lake which is continually fed by rivers and streams.

Standing 7.25 metres above sea level and 90 metres wide, *Afsluitdijk* became a battle zone during the Second World War. In May 1940 the heavily outnumbered and ill-equipped Dutch put up a heroic scrap against the Germans, throwing everything they had at the invading forces and causing them to retreat both stunned and wounded. Afterwards the sour Krauts referred to *Afsluitdijk* as 'the dam of death'.

Much later, in 2006, racing driver Robert Doornbos hammered his Red Bull Formula One car over the dam at a speed of 326 kilometres (204 miles) per hour just to prove how flash and fast he was. Now, not quite as brave as the weapon less Dutch resistance repelling an army of ugly Square Heads with a wooden clog missile launch (well, they could hardly miss those beacon shaped bonces) it was time for another chapter to be written on this famous landmark. Me crossing it.

There she was, stretching between Den Oever at my feet and the out of sight village of Zurich on the other side. It really was an awesome spectacle standing here looking straight ahead. You couldn't see the end of the dam through the bright haze. It was a dual carriageway which disappeared into the sea on the horizon. The cars and trucks zooming past could have been on a one way ticket to their doom, failing to hit the breaks hard enough in the middle and falling into the watery depths below.

This was the most traffic I had seen in days after being spoilt by the car-free dunes, deserted islands and abandoned farming roads. I'd completely forgotten how much noise petrol guzzling engines and tyres flying across tarmac generated. It was hectic by Dutch standards, but this number of vehicles wouldn't have even touched the sides on the M25. At least I didn't have to use the road, a separate fenced off cycle path ran in tandem. With only water as far as the eye could see on both flanks the long concrete platform had a definite floating sensation. The endless blue of the Wadden Sea to my left and the tiny single-sail boats breaking up the glinting diamond surface of the Ijsselmeer's wide expanses to the right were both stunning and therapeutic visually. Rubbing my handlebar grips expectantly and all set-up for a nice leisurely ride, I would be in Harlingen and camped up for the night in no time. How wrong can you be?

No more than 10 turns of the wheels and my old mate the wind decided to put in a gusty appearance. Funny that, being surrounded by two colossal bodies of water without any form of shielding at all. Turning into my alter-ego of Sloth Man (maybe a cape, but not the rubber pants, might have helped me move quicker) the sluggish slog was underway and it took 45 gruelling minutes to reach the visitors' centre a third of the way along. Deciding to take a premature coffee break and hopping across the pedestrian bridge to the café, I almost choked on the prices and decided to stick to Erika's water reserves. These thieves of the catering cosmos wanted £2 for a small cup of the stuff. My disgusted walking off in a huff may have been hasty though as I could have upgraded to a *Koffie Slagroom* for another few pence. Who am I kidding? I didn't have the energy!

Paying my respects at the stone monument to a working gang of brave muscular men who built the dam and were throwing around heavy hammers, it was back on the saddle. The conditions were still tough and the end of the road wasn't getting any nearer. A few anglers were beach casting on the downward slanting sea wall next to me, but the only catches circling their feet were plastic bottles, old tangled fishing nets and cardboard containers washed up by the Wadden tide.

Respite finally arrived in the most unlikely shape of a Texaco garage. God bless those red letters. I was soon plonked up on a wooden bench supping a cheaper cup of coffee. It was a great garage to be fair, a refuge for the budget traveller. They sold just about everything from hot *broodjes* (which I passed on this time) to a comprehensive selection of porn mags, with free DVDs attached, for any truck driver needing a bit of company as he bunked up in the car park for another lonely night. Next to the garage was a reclusive trailer park, nestled in a small armpit of the Ijsselmeer. What a strange place to live. But what an excellent strategic point to dump all your country's trailer trash, who will probably bite the bullet first when the next killer flood hits these shores. On the other hand, they could have been truck spotters or simple odd bods who just fancied a holiday next to a motorway. They all deserved to drown as well.

Nearing the end of a two-and-a-half hour trudge, the tall silhouettes of buildings finally began to rise out of the sunny fuzz ahead just like the opening credits of the *A-Team*. One last push past the cardboard army green soldier on duty outside the *Kazematten* war museum and its bunkers half hidden by undergrowth and the end was in sight. I'd done it and I was knackered. With only a tiny drip of leg petrol left, not even able to muster a slosh in the bottom of the tank, I couldn't reach Harlingen fast enough.

Following another grassy green sea dike, happy spring lambs on the other side of the fence escorted me along the final leg, running and calling after me with high-pitched bleats. They obviously hadn't got word from their Texel cousins that the Butcher of Baa-Baa was in town. After another marathon nine-hour day turning the pedals it was a relief to see the signs for Camp Tightwad right outside Harlingen's centre. Of course that wasn't really the name, but I take it personally when somebody charges me £10 to put up the world's smallest tent, doesn't provide toilet paper and then wants to charge me 50p to clean my arse afterwards in the shower.

Crossing the train track that cuts through town, I walked into Harlingen by torch light. It was Friday night, wahey! Fatigue was setting in fast, but I wanted to briefly sample the night life. Low canals and white painted locks broke up the first silent brick floored street, with a small quay full of cramped unlit yachts the dominant centrepiece. This was meant to be a haven for British boat enthusiasts. But there wasn't a single white-bearded wannabe captain downing a jug of Pimms with his jolly crew members to be seen anywhere. I'd seen more life in a library. I don't know why, but I had a strong urge to yell a frustrated 'Fish Fingers' at the top of my voice. I kept it plugged. Nobody would have understood me anyway.

It was only 10pm and everyone was tucked up in bed. The thin side roads gave you a doll's house view of their owners through grand rectangular windows, who were offered no protection at all from prying outside goggles by nets or curtains. All the houses looked cosy, with comfortable furniture illuminated by the soothing glow of table lamps. But they were all just watching telly. It was Friday night. What was wrong with these people? I wanted some human contact. They should be out on the razzle making outsiders welcome in their town, not vegetating in front of the box watching *Van der Valk* solving another Beverwijk tulip robbery.

Harlingen had a long fishing and shipping history and was also the birth place of Simon Vestdijk, one of the most important 20th-century Dutch writers. But its last taste of proper excitement flew past 10 years ago when Henk Angenent crossed the finishing line first in the Eleven Cities Tour, Friesland's answer to the *Wacky Races*.

Elfstedentocht as it is known in the native tongue is an irregular speed skating competition over a distance of 200 kilometres. The outside track is made up from frozen canals, rivers and lakes linking the 11 Frisian cities of Leeuwarden, Sneek, Ijilst, Sloten Stavoren, Hindeloopen, Workum, Bolsward, Franeker, Dokkum and of course Harlingen. The first race was won in 1909 by Minne Hoekstra in 13 hours and 50 minutes, with Angenent taking the last crown 88 years later, shaving off half the time and rocketing home in 6 hours and 49 minutes. Some 15,000 amateur skaters also take part and even the Dutch Crown Prince, Willem-Alexander, got bitten by the bug in 1986, putting in a sneaky appearance under the alias of WA van Buren. He obviously didn't want to show himself up. There have been 15 races since its inauguration, with Coen de Koning and Evert van Benthem sharing top spot twice. A national obsession, the whole country tunes into TV and radio for extensive coverage which refuses to switch off until the last racer has limped over the course with hypothermia.

A whole new generation of Dutch Dastardly and Muttleys have been waiting more than a decade to get their skates back on. There hasn't been a race this century due to thin ice and mild winters, which are only expected to get warmer and may have sadly called time on this amazing natural circuit once and for all.

Using my vibrancy detecting kit, I finally tracked down two very different groups of people who had escaped their living rooms for some Friday night fun. Opposite ends of one street divided the generation gap in Harlingen's social calendar.

All the young beautiful things (I blended straight in, believe me) were in the *Palm Bar*. Pretty girls were leaning against the bar or practising their pole dancing skills on two silver chrome posts much to the delight of a panting group of teenage boys. While they were wriggling up and down to the beat of squeaky Dutch techno, the rest of the sisters were at the bar dribbling over a couple of black-shirted, open-buttoned bucks doing their best *Cocktail* impressions. The ladies were lapping it up and by the cheesy 'I'm going to get laid' smirk on their faces, the glass juggling duo knew it only too well.

Leaving the thumping electro pop to the Tom Cruise brothers and ignoring the temptation of taking a seat in the multicolour lighted floating drinking booth in the canal opposite, I moved on to *Skutsje* at the other end of the scale. A dingy nautical themed venue, with lobster pots, lanterns and ship wheels sprouting out of the walls and ceiling, this was definitely a bit of me.

Perched next to a smelly sea dog in blue-stained dungarees I ordered up a cold one and had a lustful stare at his thick, bristling, open pouch of… rolling tobacco. I hadn't smoked since leaving Monique and really did love a ciggie with a drink. The beer over here made the craving even greater. It was chilled to perfection and crammed full of life, making the inside of your mouth tingle with every gulp. It was a refreshing change from the flat crap you get served up at home. I've had to try and revive the beer in my local with a defibrillating smash of the glass down on the table, without even stirring a single pulse of climbing bubbles.

Plucking up the courage to approach my new drinking buddy (who I had a strong suspicion communicated by grunting) for a sprinkle of tobacco and a rolling paper, a four-fingered dirty talon slipped into the open pouch. The idea didn't seem so attractive after all and I couldn't possibly ponce a smoke off a man without a thumb. He probably didn't even wash his four fingers after having a wee. This beer didn't need a smoking chaperone after all.

Getting quite claustrophobic now, a mature crowd (older than me) had packed the place out to shake their stuff to boy band Kevin's Crew. A group of lads stood nervously behind their instruments before breaking into a cracking Radiohead cover with all the words grunted perfectly by Four-Fingered Freddy. Kevin's Crew were on a promotional tour and I was gobsmacked when their front man addressed the crowd in Dutch between songs as they had sounded so English. They still looked a bit shaky as they strummed their instruments, but it was nothing to do with their musical talent as they were pretty decent.

It was the lynch mob of women in their mid-fifties, poking out in all the wrong places through tight fitting cat suits and licking their lips which was worrying them. These predators wouldn't be satisfied until they had tasted young flesh. Hard dance floor stares a few inches away from the boys' terrified faces, betrayed their intention to chew up the band before spitting them out one at a time – pants, guitar strings, drum sticks and all. I had some sympathy for them because these girls looked like they could go on all night. But that's show business.

10   The ten Healthies

Two German kids decided to entertain themselves by terrorising an early morning dumper just trying to mind his own business. The little shits ran riot around the toilet block banging on my door and screaming while I tried to squeeze one out in peace. Ignoring them was the wrong tactic as that just made the brother and sister combo even more determined to ruin my morning ritual. They came back tooled up and hit me with a rapid double whammy, shoving wooden shower brushes under the door and smashing them into my feet.

I seriously considered jumping off the can and pissing all over the bastards or chasing after them, pants around ankles and toilet paper hanging out of my arse, which I would delight in smearing across their snivelling faces. Not up for spending the next three years as a regularly walked prison bitch for a tattoo covered Dutch sex case or being extradited to Germany to face a firing squad, I refrained. Clamping a foot down on each brush they soon fucked off once they realised they couldn't pull them back out and launch another attack. Play time was over.

I'd endured a difficult night and didn't need special attention. Sleep interrupted choking panic spasms came within a millimetre of installing an unwanted sun roof in my miniature canvas cabin as a disorientated daze sent my head thrusting just short of the stars. This was my first taste of anxiety on tour, but what triggered it? The only thing I could nail it down to was the previous day's upset when I'd had a long wail. Chas 'N' Dave may have rescued me from drowning in tears on the road, but these emotional events have a nasty habit of quietly curling up in the subconscious and biting back hard when you're not expecting it.

On a positive note, I dealt with the palpitations in record time and calmly breathed my way back to the land of nod. There were no hours of worried wide awake analysis or a terrified sprint over the campsite, wearing my tent as a mini-skirt with decorative pegs hanging off ropes and sounding out a 'madman coming through' warning to fellow campers as they scraped the floor. I'd passed this test with flying colours and felt really proud of myself for keeping my shit together on foreign soil.

Getting back to sleep so easily may have had something to do with the physical exertions of completing the *Afsluitdijk* challenge. I was seriously expecting to find my nose rubbing the tent roof on opening my eyes in the morning. The thigh and calf muscles were aching so much my body felt like it was levitating above the floor. I was having an out of sleeping bag experience.

I needed to take it easier and the headaches clustering across the top of my forehead were signalling a hydration alarm. More water consumption was required. Drinking a litre of fluid was nowhere near adequate enough to keep the cooling system ticking over for up to nine hours a day. I would have to double my H2O guzzling efforts.

Harlingen was a buzzing hive of Saturday morning activity. Maybe I should try turning up in places during daylight hours before writing them all off as zombie towns. The sun had got its hat on and the quayside bars were full of skippers slouched at tables admiring their gleaming parked up fibreglass boats. But it wasn't all about the yachting crew stopping off for a snifter after exiting the Wadden Sea. Long barges were gliding up the town's water vein past resting double sail vessels with mighty beams and an old bearded captain, complete with ship wheel printed cap, gently steered a motorised dinghy around the congested docking bay with his trusty sheepdog for company. Industrial fishing craft lay waiting for work at empty wharfs which were bizarrely being overlooked by a group of tied up camels. Now that's what I call an impressive catch!

It was back into the sheeping lanes alongside the great hump bank of the sea defence. The yellow ear tagged woolly wonders weren't fenced in here, but free to roam around and take on the mantle of unpredictable moving obstacles. There were hundreds of the bumbling blighters everywhere munching the day away. The baby lambs made me go a bit soppy as they sat all cutesy-wutesy in the short grass, crying out for a quick cuddle. But they didn't stick around long enough, taking evasive action as soon as I got within cradling range. Word must have finally filtered through from Texel. The temperature was rising again and the ragged adult sheep were having a torrid old time as we hit the high 20s. Their bodies were shaking and they seemed to be gasping for breath just trying to stand up. Others had given up the ghost, sprawled out in the recovery position or downed by a crack shot dike sniper, hitting the deck with a stiff leg poking out at one side.

The wind was on my side, acting as a cooling face fan, but the desolate farm road was covered in rock hard fists of mud, which made Erika wince as they crunched under her tyres. Crystal blue solar panel squares covered the roofs of farm houses and there were more barefooted reed dwellers reading books by the river bank, abandoning an engrossing chapter momentarily to call out a friendly 'hello'. A labyrinth of alleyways were my guide around the outskirts of the Italian dessert sounding town Tzummarum, before another spell in the speechless meadows led into Sint Jacobiparochie, which is a right mouthful.

The white town hall with domed bell tower held up by four straining steel arms may have dominated the town square, but it wasn't what caught my eye. A stone's throw away was a little piece of England, the East End Cafeteria to be precise. But there were no cockney expats cooking up pie, mash and liquor much to my ravenous regret. It was just a burger joint named after the road it stood on and I drowned my sorrows in a 'big coffee' served up in a plastic striped fizzy drinks cup.

It was El Scorchio and three skimpily clad female lobsters were soaking up the sun on a table outside and chain-smoking in equal measure. It was alright for some, but I had to get back on. Running my spurs down the side of the pedals, I mounted Erika and headed back into the Dutch prairies serenaded by Johnny Cash, whose unique railroad melodies kept me chugging all the way to Holwerd.

Mud walking, or *Wadlopen* as it is correctly known, was Holwerd's favourite pastime. The small village of less than 2,000 inhabitants would be invaded every summer by outdoor extremists who literally wanted to do a Jesus and walk on water. But the warm Sea of Galilee this most definitely was not, making these wadlopers an even crazier bunch.

Wadlopen is the art of crossing the Wadden Sea at low tide by tramping across the shallows and squelching mud flats from the main land to the Frisian Islands. With no mountains to climb or white rapids to shoot, the Dutch have adopted this bizarre pursuit to get their injection of natural adrenalin. Some 30,000 of them Wadlope every year and they seldom get bored of this off the wall hobby as there are a variety of routes. The islands of Terschelling, Engelsmanplaat, Schiermonnikoog, Simonszand, Rottumeroog and, in Holwerd's case, Ameland are all just a stinky, dirty plod from the coast.

Light canvas shoes are the desired footwear to protect the soles of the feet from any sharp objects hiding in the gunk. But whatever is worn, Wadlopers delight in reaching shore with a decent foot to knee covering of smelly grey mud. I'm not going to dismiss its moisturising possibilities, but I wasn't prepared to try a face pack to get rid of my expanding crow's feet.

You have to sign up as long as a month in advance to take part in *Wadlopen,* which was a genuine disappointment as I was well up for it.

This is because parties must be escorted by a qualified guide to counter the danger of miscalculating the tide and getting drowned at the halfway point. Another problem are the confusing sea fogs which can roll in out of nowhere and swallow participants whole. This is when the *Wadlopen* chief earns his corn, plotting a compass path through the ooze and leading a bewildered band of muck rakers back to the safety of dry land.

Holwerd was 12 kilometres from Ameland and the Wadlopers would have a last supper style jolly up in the village before making the crossing the next day. It usually took three hours to reach the island, which would again be celebrated by another hearty fresh fish feast and booze up ahead of catching the ferry back to Holwerd. Very social indeed.

Holwerd's past was heavily linked to the buying and selling business. Mercury, the God of Trade, stood tall on the yellow and blue village flag, colours symbolising wheat and the sea, the two main providers of produce at that time. Holwerd was the carbon copy of a classic English countryside village. I half expected to bump into John Nettles pondering his latest murder case on the single main street, which climbed up slowly, before descending to the grave stone toenails of the church below. The terp structure was built in the 13th century and had an important role in Holwerd's trading past, acting as a coastal bearing beacon for shipping. Standing 52 metres it is one of the highest churches in the whole of Friesland and can be seen clearly from Ameland.

The small enclosed field at the foot of the church used to be a watering hole for cattle, until it was drained, and now it was a pitch for caravans and tents. Freewheeling downhill into the campsite the well tanned warden's huge clogs had swallowed the pedals. 'I made them myself,' he proudly declared after clocking my gawping stare at the wooden monsters holding his feet captive.

Pitching my tent up next to the church's barbed wire fence, I set about squeezing my tube of travel wash into a sink and releasing the sweaty pong stained clothes from the 'worn' carrier bag. I even had a sniff of the padded crutch of the pants which had protected my backside for the first few days. Well, you have to check, don't you!

Scrubbing away merrily, after finally conjuring some soap suds from emptying half the contents of the tube, this was actually enjoyable. I never went anywhere near the washing machine at home. I couldn't tell you how to reduce my carbon sock print with a 30 degree wash. Just thinking about it put me in a spin (oh, that's bad). But here I was friction washing the brownish yellow saddle rubbing stains (not skid marks) off my pants and giving the socks and T-shirts a Chinese burn style freshen up. After re-engaging with my feminine side, all smalls and tops were delicately placed on an improvised washing line of barbed wire, steering clear of any bird shit, which separated my tent from the graveyard. Ah, I was loving the outdoor life.

The cycling clog carver pointed me in the direction of the campsite boss' bar, *De Steeg*, which was attached to the take-away he also owned (this was a powerful man) and hidden down one of the leg like alleys which kicked out of the main road. It was another hectic Saturday night in Holwerd as two men perched on stools mumbled to the barman. Parking my hungry arse on a table with a thick carpet style cloth, I ordered one of the strangest meal mixtures ever.

Asking for cod and chips was about as basic as it got. It's not the most glamorous food serving in the world, but it tastes good and does the job of filling your belly. What arrived at my table took this personal culinary delight to a whole new eating level. Not only was there a slab of cod and felled forest of chips on my overflowing plate, it was chaperoned by pineapple, baby pickled onions, cucumber, tomato, shredded carrot, boiled egg, gherkin, red cabbage, hot runner beans and a dash of soy sauce to top it off. I didn't know whether to laugh or get stuck in with my shaking fork and knife. It may have been an odd jumble of grub, but was absolutely scrumptious and all those healthy extras would give my legs the same power reserves as a hyperactive Duracell bunny.

A Dutch version of the happy wandering tune 'Val-deri Val-dera' was playing, in my honour obviously, as I rolled a cigarette from the blue pouch of *Shag* tobacco purchased in Harlingen, but not yet broken into. It was the only illicit wrongdoing I was allowed to get involved in on this trip.

One of the two bar flies had been twitching during my fish topped vegetable banquet. Having a quick glance over his shoulder he was itching to come over and open the lines of communication. It didn't bother me as long as he didn't want to vomit on my plate or rub recycled dog's crap on the cutlery. Edu, 'yes, just like the Brazilian footballer', eventually plucked up the courage for a chin-wag and what a genial gent he was.

Another perfectly sun burnt specimen, with the rouge complexion deepened by the love of a wee nip here and there, the white shaven headed local beckoned me to join him at the counter. Edu was intrigued by my journey and told me he too liked to travel and spent a lot of time in the French vineyards (now there's a surprise) when he wasn't fixing the roof of his 250-year-old thatched cottage. I imagined Edu standing in his living room watching the stars through a frayed gaping hole in the ceiling with a handful of long straw, forever leaving it until tomorrow and trotting down to *De Steeg* before closing.

He'd led an interesting life and was a bit of a Del Boy. Edu had been a wine seller, cook, chauffeur and boat seller, among other things, and now he claimed to be retired. He had friends near the Isle of Wight who post him English newspapers and he expressed his shock at the rising house prices in England. Tell me about it, mate.

More regulars had started to mill around the bar and Edu was determined to extend Holwerd's hospitality by buying me four or five shot glasses of the native tipple. *Berenburg* was a syrupy liquor which warmed your insides and containing 35 per cent alcohol could be used to launch space missions to Mars. But the ingredients of this Frisian speciality were a closely guarded secret. 'It is full of secret herbs gathered from the Frisian fields,' chuckled Edu. 'It won't make you fly, but it will help you sleep.'

Declining yet another freebie while I could still walk straight, I wobbled back to my chair and prepared one last smoke. There were about 20 people in for the night now and they were all very much at home. A couple of old timers were regularly letting rip across their acoustic friendly stools in a proficient manner which made the flatulent cowboys in *Blazing Saddles* seem rank amateurs. Another group of lads were smashing their cards on the table like hammers as they punctuated a friendly game of poker with a choir of loud belches. This was my kind of place.

Shag was jilted after one date. It was never going to work. Another poor night in the sack convinced me I was suffering from an appendicitis because of slight discomfort along the right side of my stomach, which was probably no more than trapped wind. I should have gone back to *De Steeg* for some releasing lessons from the pros.

The pain got worse the more I stressed about it, flowering into fears about my geographical location being nowhere near civilisation and a hospital in case of emergency. The appendix could burst at any time and there was no way I would find a surgeon out here before the poisonous bacteria swimming around my body finished me off. And why was I getting these twinges? Because I'd had a couple of roll-ups and God was displeased. So I went down the usual lifesaving route of making a panic pact with the Lord, promising to give smoking the chop once and for all in return for another morning still breathing. I think this was pact number 10,756, but who's counting?

I was up early, thanks to the church clock (which was five minutes slow and in urgent need of its 800 year service) ringing every half-an-hour, but I was still here. Thank you, Lord. It was turning into the hottest day yet, creeping up towards the 30s. Tucking T-shirt arms under the armpits to make a DIY vest and tying my beautiful mane back into a *My Little Pony* masterpiece I was ready to trot. But this horse had no water and not even a slim hope of survival without any. Holwerd was closed to the world on Sunday (just like the rest of the week I expect) and I had to resort to using my basic Dutch to communicate my precious needs to an elderly couple deck chaired out in their front garden.

What I meant was I said 'hi', held up my bike bottle and stuck a finger on my lips. Fortunately, they understood the universal language of pointing, filled the bottle from a hose (you can drink any tap water in the Netherlands) and invited their next door neighbour over for a 10 minute poke at my map while they tried to talk to me in Dutch.

Escaping my kindly benefactors, I went past the Ameland ferry point, which was already knee high in mud, fought my way through a stubborn farming spring gate and picked up the sheep highway. They were still shaking from dehydration under all that insulation, a white, black, brown and bearded herd wilting in the sun. Following the shoreline and the sea gazing resting place of the Wierum war graves, the landscape opened up into a wide open space of greenery embracing the west bank of the Lauwersmeer lake. Sun worshippers were out in their droves, tuning their bodies in to the browning rays across the shoulders of the swardy sea embankment, while binocular clad parties strode off into the bird reserves below hoping to spot a rare breed.

The route ahead and surrounding lands were a down sized, but much more attractive version of the *Afsluitdijk*, this time making the county water crossing from Friesland to Groningen. The Lauwersmeer had once been a bay at the top of the Netherlands, the Lauwerzee, which was blocked off by a 13 kilometre sluice and lock supported dike following the tragic floods of 1953. Renamed the Lauwersmeer, natural filtration turned the newly created lake into a body of fresh water, just like the Ijsselmeer, attracting an abundance of flora and fauna which resulted in the area becoming a national park.

Crossing over the Lauwerssluizen dike, the diamond strewn Lauwersmeer glittered brilliantly as the sleek white hulls of sailboats lazily rippled the waters. This was the Groningen province and the sun felt even more stifling on this side of the lake. But the Dutch weren't complaining, making the most of their Sunday and basking in the heat. Camping grounds spread out around the edge of the lake, with tents, caravans and cabins littered everywhere. Parents were splashing around in the water with their armband-wearing offspring, while other families hid behind sunglasses and wrapped their dry tongues around cool ice creams and lollies.

The route pulled me off road on to a thick sand path opposite a field full of frustrated kite boarders disabled by the lack of breeze. There was no way Erika could carry me through this, although she did try bless her and ended up sinking to a standstill after a couple of metres. 'Do you need any help?' came a well timed call bang on cue. The offer of salvation was voiced by a gangly smiling cyclist who was making the most of the fine weather with his wife. 'Our map shows the same way, but none of us will get through here,' he continued. 'You must take this route at the side of the main road to Vierhuizen, then you will be back on track.'

Jan and Antje ten Harkel were in their forties, both lean and fit looking with huge teethy grins which instantly put you at ease. Antje had been for a dip in the lake and Jan, who was well over six foot in height and didn't have an inch of fat anywhere, had probably spent a few hours on the stretching rack. Dutch people are among the tallest in the world, with the average male six foot and women clocking in at five foot seven inches. Keen cyclists, they were both interested in my journey and found it hard to fathom that such a novice was prepared to take on such a challenge. The ten Harkels led the way to the diversion, but we soon stopped again when one of the boys bounced off the back of Erika and they helped to capture and secure the absconding sleeping bag.

Waving a second farewell, I bumped into Jan and Antje again a few kilometres up the road in Vierhuizen. The bloody cheats were loading their bicycles on to the back of a people carrier and driving the 40 kilometres back home to Roodeschool. 'Where are you staying tonight?' enquired Jan as I stopped for another chat with my new comrades. I was still 100 kilometres from the German border and, using his local knowledge, a concerned Jan informed me that tonight's planned destination, a campsite on the halfway mark, was no longer open.

'That's OK,' I joked. 'I'll just come and stick my tent up in your back garden.'

'For sure,' replied Jan, which was a completely unexpected answer. 'You are more than welcome. We have a big garden.' That will be where you bury the bodies then, I thought. Jotting down the ten Harkels' address and promising to rendezvous at their place as soon as possible, I texted the details to Katie, so she would know where to send the murder squad if it all went quiet for a few days.

But my fears were horrendously misplaced. You couldn't have met a more considerate couple than Jan and Antje, who treated me like royalty on arriving at their house after another four hour cycle over the potato bearing farming polders. It's quite shameful to label a couple of strangers as potential lone cyclist hunting serial killers when they are genuinely showing kindness above and beyond the call of duty. This is what my experience was meant to be all about, hooking up with random people and making the most of any offers which came my way. I had to put complete faith in any new found friends and the ten Harkels were the perfect guinea pigs for a trusting test. Knocking on the welcoming coloured yellow front door of their detached residence, my suspicions were allayed by the sight of three blond lads huddled around a TV watching football and the lack of freshly dug earth out on the lawn.

Jan was a primary school teacher and still played football as a goalkeeper for the vets after injuries had forced him to work his way back down the team from his glory days as a striker. Antje was a housewife, devoted to her three teenage boys and daughter, and not fulfilled by her swim and cycle earlier had popped out for a mini shoreline *Wadlopen* session on the Roodeschool mudflats. A keen photographer, Antje gave me a quick exhibition of the dramatic landscapes and sunsets she'd clicked for the local rag. This remarkably resourceful woman was also a top notch volleyball player, but was recovering from an arm injury.

All the kids were sports nuts too and one of the lads had even built his own set of wooden goalposts (which Antje had snapped for the newspaper) in the back garden. And they all cycled everywhere. Jan pedalled to work and the children would make the 40 kilometre round trip to school in the city of Delfzijl every day without fail, come rain or shine. I wondered how that schedule would go down with the pampered brats of England who gave birth to the road congesting 'school run'. The lazy little shits can't even walk a few hundred metres to the playground gates, taxied to the classroom and back by over protective mothers in tank sized jeeps blocking up both the roads and environment. The ten Healthies couldn't believe it when I painted that little picture for them. It was unheard of in the Netherlands.

After rustling up a feast of mince like meat in burger baps and fields of salad, washed down by 10 glasses of hydrating tap water, Jan and Antje got the maps out over a pot of coffee and started tracing my route to their doorstep. They were so interested in me and enjoying my company as much as I valued their hospitality. It was a fair exchange and I took great pleasure from being the guest of honour, happy to answer all their questions and mesmerised by the duos' joint hands flicking across the pages of the map all the way up to Norway. They had a lovely house which was kitted out like an English home, the usual spread of sofa, armchairs and TV plonked in the middle of the living room. A family of Ajax supporters, all the children had been perfectly planned, purposefully staggered two years apart between 13 and 19 years of age, so 'they could share interests', Antje told me.

Jan was deeply troubled by global warming and the threat of rising tides washing over the barriers again with disastrous consequences. He believed the Netherlands could take a lead in cutting fuel emissions by converting cars to run on biodiesel using rapeseed oil. The yellow plant grew in abundance here, but the cost of turning rapeseed into fuel keeps its market value higher than standard diesel. 'It always comes down to money,' sighed Jan. 'But we must forget about cost and think about making sure there is a future for our children and their childrens' children.'

Changing the subject, I cheekily enquired about house prices in the Netherlands as the country seemed to enjoy a high standard of living. I hadn't see too many shacks or grotty falling apart council estates. Even the farmhouses were made out of gold. The answer pushed my jaw on to the kitchen table. The ten Harkels lived in a five bedroom detached house with a spacious garden. Price £180,000, which was less than my two bedroom flat at home. Absolutely criminal. I would be moving next door when it was time to breed with Katie.

The ten Harkels seemed to have an almost sickly perfect family life. But the husband and wife team had plans to spread their wings once their fledglings had left the nest. The couple were itching to get back out on their adventure bikes. Before getting married they had cycled across Indonesia and also pedalled around Austria with their daughter sleeping in a basket before the boys came along. 'I would like to follow you one day on the North Sea Cycle Route,' said Jan. 'I am jealous of you.'

'Well you can when the kids are grown up,' (hopefully I'll be home by then). 'You are both young and have plenty of time ahead of you.'

Jan agreed that there was plenty of time and while we were on the subject of the price of living I asked him if he would consider holidaying in my country. 'Would you bring Antje and the kids to England for a break?' I said.

'No, no, we couldn't. England is far too expensive and we could never afford to go there with the children. We have taken them to Denmark cycling, which is very nice and much cheaper.'

'Well that's strange as the people at home think of Scandinavia as being much more expensive than England.'

'That is not true,' said Jan. 'A lot more people here are put off visiting England for the very same reason.'

Wanting to educate me about Roodeschool, which was pretty much just one long road with houses on each side, Jan told me the village's biggest claim to fame was being the end of the line. It had the most northern train station in the country. How very exciting.

I was interested in how all the farmers seemed to be living a life of lavish luxury in their polder mansions. 'The farmers made a lot of money from potatoes in this area, but it is all changing,' Jan explained. 'Now they are having to do the work themselves, instead of standing holding their shirt lapels and paying field workers a pittance to do the job for them. People will not work for nothing anymore and the good old days for farmers are over. They must get their own hands dirty now which isn't as quick or profitable.'

And on that note I retired to the garden. The tent was up and I crawled inside. This would be my last night in the Netherlands before sneaking over the border to Germany and I felt privileged to have spent it in such a loving family environment. I was tempted to get out the adoption papers. You don't know what goes on behind closed doors, but Jan and Antje were very open people and obviously happy together. I could have given them a big squeeze myself. Realising I would probably never see them ever again after leaving in the morning made me feel quite sad.

When you are looked after so well by such wonderful people appearing out of nowhere on the side of a road, it does make you wonder whether the big man upstairs is pulling a few strings. What were the odds of bumping into a Jan and Antje out of all those hundreds of people who were milling around the Lauwersmeer, let alone being fed, watered and given somewhere to stay? If this was you working your magic, oh so mysterious moving one, then take a big cheers from this disciple and keep 'em rolling in. They don't come much better than the ten Harkels and this *Littlest Hobo* can vouch for them being the absolute dog's bollocks.

11   Downer in Deutschland

There was shear joy in sheep central as the rolled up rugs with heads finally got some help coping with the intense heat. Hung upside down in a harness, stumpy legs pointing upwards, I'm sure I heard a sigh of relief above the buzzing as a clipper handed out another short back and sides. The unshaved sheep pressed their woolly hides up against drinking troughs, fences and gates, anything which offered a shady retreat, preventing them from cooking in the merciless glare of the sun as they waited their turn.

Antje had seen me off with a motherly kiss on each cheek and an exclusive photo shoot standing next to the back garden tent. Bless her, she'd even given me a health conscious packed lunch, including a hydration aid – the biggest lump of polythene wrapped cucumber I had ever seen. Following the sloping eastern 'school run' down the side of the River Ems, which provides a natural border between the Netherlands and Germany on the opposite coast, the sea port of Delfzijl drew nearer. The pale blue horizon was broken by hideous tower block apartments rising above the mess of construction works around their feet. Retired German fortifications squatted along the banks of the industrial water course. The simple message 'We Don't Care' had been sprayed across one of the graffiti decorated concrete boxes, accompanied by a set of smiley yellow faces riding magic mushrooms. Whether this was a message of defiance or acceptance to their former German invaders I didn't know, but it certainly brightened up the place.

One thing the citizens of Delfzijl certainly did do was 'care'. The city was a political powder keg with the populace renowned for making their elected representatives' terms in office a living hell. A mayor of the city recently jetted out to America, which the disgruntled voters viewed as an unnecessary council funded jolly-up, only to return home and find her entire staff had been sacked. The people are strong minded in these parts and not afraid to make their feelings clear. A couple of years ago only 47.3 per cent of them bothered visiting the ballot box. Nearly 25 per cent of the city's votes were returned blank in protest against alleged political mismanagement. The electorate crack the whip in Delfzijl and a recent mayor branded it the 'Sicily of the North' after being run out of town in a hurry. Maybe she'd found a sheared sheep's head in her bed.

It was lunchtime and the sun was chucking rays down the middle of the pedestrianised city centre, which was dead. Shops were only just opening for business and the few people who were lumbering around aimlessly had all the vigour of an extra from *Shaun of the Dead*. It was hard to believe this was the nerve centre of a political war zone. It was more like a leper colony on day release.

Quickly grabbing some long overdue sun cream to massage into my bacon-coloured face, arms and legs, the white Eems Hotel waded into the still river on its stilted legs, before I crossed a suspension bridge and more locks than a Chub convention to get out of town. The outskirts of Delfzijl were an industrial eyesore. The grey smoke of metal plant chimneys stained the sky above, while tractors threw out choking dust clouds as they piled up chalky mounds for train carts which lurched in and out of factories across rusting tracks.

Delfzijl is home to a thriving aluminium plant and is also the Netherlands' second biggest exporter of industrial chemicals (after Rotterdam) such as chlorine. Back towards the coast, long pipes and chutes climbed out of filthy warehouses ready to feed boats on the Ems. I didn't like it and tried to hold my breath as long as possible before wandering back out into the sticks.

An upturned stone hand surrounded by skinny grave pillars paid tribute to the lost village of Oosterhorn (chemically evaporated?) before the growling industrial ogre was replaced by peaceful, lush meadows. Completely deserted yet again, the only other company I had was a tractor driver with crying steel wings watering thirsty crops. Waving away as I passed, the lonely farmer was obviously relieved to see me. Not another person blipped into sight for 90 long minutes of still feverish temperatures. Even the wind farms had packed it in for the day with their heads dropping motionless. The big yella fella was having a field day, permanently hovering above my head, trying to zap me with a collapsing dose of sun stroke. Keeling over here would be a nightmare. I wouldn't be found for days or weeks even, probably with wheat growing out of my nostrils.

The border town of Nieuweschans is the most eastern point of the Netherlands and was a lot cooler than the exposed farming lands. With a couple of cafes and general store all there was to get excited about, it was easy to understand why it was dead as a dodo. A hibernation party was taking place in one darkened bar where a handful of drinkers mumbled their orders to the grizzly plump owner. He had shoehorned himself into a *Von Dutch* vest to ensure any neighbouring German visitors were well aware this establishment was on passionately patriotic foreign soil.

Slowly sipping an ice cube packed lemonade under a sun repelling umbrella outside, the phone whined into action. It was 3pm in the afternoon and the computerised chick at British Gas was long overdue a check in. 'Hello,' I grunted in disgust. 'You alright, mate – you don't sound too happy,' came the cheerful reply.

It was Rhys, a friend from home, who had achieved number one fan status with my Sunday football team SORT FC because he always had a full packet of Malboro Lights and a flask of hot chocolate on the touchline. 'I'm going to parachute into Germany and keep you company for a couple of weeks if that's OK?' he informed me. 'Yeah fine,' I said. 'But how are you going to push your bike through a letterbox?'

Like me, Rhys had a few mental issues. Over the last year he had become a recluse and was rarely seen outside of his flat. I hadn't thought about anybody saddling up with me for this crusade. The original plan had been to do the whole thing solo. But no man should be an island and I was more than happy for Rhys to take on the mantle of Man Friday. I'd survived seven days without being properly tempted to turn back home, which was one tick on the achieved list. And why not share this cycling therapy with somebody else? If I was still mentally stable after a week and obviously reaping the benefits of the experience, then who's to say it couldn't do the same trick with curing Rhys' agoraphobia? Who was I to hog this remedy all to myself?

It was agreed then. Rhys would fly into Bremen in a few days' time and seek his own salvation. I was looking forward to him coming now, but still had plenty of kilometres to cover ahead of our meeting, which started with country number two – Germany. Edging alongside a train track joining the two nations, long stretches of bright yellow rapeseed were gently combed by a light breeze. I was going to miss the Netherlands. The immaculate signposted route across the slanting dunes and silent farming flat lands had almost been fool-proof (I'd concluded the Bergen bypass was born out of my stupidity). It had been a perfect place for a trainee cyclist to find his pedals. The Dutch had been an extremely hospitable bunch and I would have no problem singing their praises to anybody who had the ears for it. I really didn't have a bad word to say about my first country on the route – all 450 kilometres of it – and was optimistically looking forward to seeing how the Germans matched up to their neighbours.

There would be mouth-watering sausages to taste-test, dipped in multiple sauces and mustards, and washed down by a variety of frothy moustache making ales swimming in giant tankards. Maybe there would be an opportunity to knock back a few special Kaiser brews before swinging my pants to the adopted German royalty, David Hasselhoff and Bonnie Tyler, whose eternal popularity kept the populace trapped in an 80s time-warp of musical backwardness. And let's not forget those Kevin Keegan style mullets patented during a love affair with Hamburg FC. It wouldn't take me long to discover that the people next door were a different breed altogether however.

OK, so I'd lied about the optimism part. As I neared the German border town of Bunde a strong sense of trepidation filled my body. I don't know why, but there was an underlying feeling of unease about entering the land of our old sparring partners. I'm not Germanist, if that's what you can call it. After all we are all friends now and the last thing I wanted to do was open old wounds. It just felt weird, an Englishman cycling freely into a land which so many of his countrymen had given up their lives fighting against all those years ago to stop the Nazi nightmare reaching out across Europe.

I'm certainly not proud of the way I felt, but maybe it is something which is built into us, certainly in my case, as a reminder of the misery which poured out of Germany during the two horrific World Wars of the last century. These hardships are drummed into us in school history lessons and in much lighter hearted ways. Who hasn't laughed out loud at the unforgettable *Fawlty Towers* sketch when John Cleese throws his lanky legs around the breakfast room and embarrasses his German guests with silly walk lunacy. I hoped this deeply engrained blast from the past wasn't going to affect my judgement of the Germans and I certainly wasn't going to mention the 'War'.

Following the mainly car-free serene cycling haven of the Netherlands, making my way into Germany was a culture shock. Bunde was about as contrasting to napping Nieuweschans on the other side of the fence as it gets. The deserted streets were replaced by stomping muscular tank-like jeeps and wall to wall Aldi and Lidl supermarkets. Big shops made their presence felt with window dummies displaying the latest in 70s and 80s fashion and there were no friendly 'hellos' from passers-by, just odd stares at the long-haired freak with all the big packs. I checked my head for horns – there weren't any.

The tranquillity mustered by the Netherlands was draining away and adding to the gloom the North Sea Cycle Route directions, which were now marked by green lettering on a white post, were pants. There wasn't one single path to follow here, there were numerous destinations and cycle trails spiralling out everywhere. It was a case of heading for the next place on my map – Weener – which was easier said than done. Climbing up and over heaving highway bridges, I was being pushed around in a loop by the signs which I couldn't get off, much to the amusement of an old couple who popped up three times in a half hour stint of frustration. Exacting revenge, I crept up behind two Nordic walkers and made them jump out of their skins with a ring of my bike bell, before stopping and asking for directions. They didn't ask me for my papers!

Weener was a large town in Lower Saxony, one of 16 German states. It had definitely seen better days with rundown houses chewing the kerb and a lick of paint in desperate need. Everything seemed a lot grubbier than the Netherlands, even the grass took on a more darker ominous shade. But one thing Weener did have going for it was sharing its name with the American slang for a small penis. The moody expressions on the cigarette puffing men ambling around town may have had something to do with an inferiority complex then. Proving I was an outsider would be simple, but not wanting to get lynched for both exposing myself and riling the chipolata crew, I concentrated on locating a campsite.

Weener Camping sat right next to a yachting quay and an industrial waste site. The owner was a cheery old soul, not interested in conversation as he didn't understand English. But he did know how to point at a price chart and hold out his hand for money. The campsite itself was cheap and cheerful. The showers were free, the toilet roll was rock hard, but in plentiful supply, and there was as much rabbit shit as you could want on the deck. The venue was packed full of resident caravans and I got my first lesson in how the Germans liked to do everything bigger and better than everybody else. These caravans were the same size as houses and many of them tried to grasp the best of both worlds by whacking whopping great canvas porches on the front of their holiday chambers. Nothing was done by halves here, which sort of took away some of the outdoor fun. But if it was good enough for Little Jimmy the Clown, whose business card filled an entire window and had a big top strapped to the front of his caravan, then it would do for me.

Banging in pegs and pulling out ropes, erecting the tent was getting much easier. Finding new hidden support clips every time I put the thing up, it was starting to actually take a tenty shape and managing to hang off the floor on all four sides. Trying to take some morale-boosting satisfaction from this I stood and admired my workmanship. But who was I kidding? I'd only been here a few hours and I didn't like Germany at all.

It was unfriendly, shabby and making me feel flappy. For the first time, I seriously pondered going home and being re-united with Katie. I just felt fed-up and couldn't shake off my defeatist attitude. If I bailed out now I would let so many people down and the ridicule would be unbearable. It wasn't a realistic option and I was still holding it together upstairs which was a bonus. But at this stage I wasn't even prepared to give Germany a sporting chance to prove me wrong. An inner sense of dread kept cajoling me, things would only get worse tomorrow. It kept poking away at me, but I was determined to sleep on it and not do anything rash. Rhys couldn't get here quick enough!

12   Heaven knows I'm miserable Now

The most obscure things can lift your dampened spirits. A dull grey discharge hung in the morning air and packing up for home was becoming increasingly appealing. What about Rhys? He'd be here in a few days. But I really couldn't be bothered to hang on and if he moaned I'd just chuck him some money for his air fare to ease the guilt.

That's it, I was heading back. Back to my flat, back to my bed and back to a missus who would never give her cherished failure another relationship sabbatical to resurrect any similar future disasters. If I gave up now I would never have this opportunity again. But home was only a day's train ride away and everyone would understand. Wouldn't they?

God this place was depressing. Even the black stained orangey brick council flats opposite the camp were bringing me down. I just wanted to get out of this shit-hole at light warp speed. Then I saw it. My salvation appeared right out of nowhere in the shape of an old rust bucket which couldn't have possibly left its oil soaked drive in years. Emblazoned across the top of the windscreen in large white capital letters were the names Danielle and Thomas, the German equivalent of Trevor and Sharon, or Brian and Maureen. This was tackiness personified and an uplifting reminder of the Essex Boys and Girls who spend their evenings lapping Southend seafront at five miles an hour in a fifth hand Ford XR3I.

I'd needed a dose of divine inspiration to keep me on track, but I never expected a white car sticker to tickle me stupid. Breaking into a giggling fit of Stan Laurel proportions made me realise what a Grinch I had been. I was here to delight in the quirky and unexpected, that's what made me tick, not to throw in the towel. I had to stop being such a killjoy and get on with this. If only I could have bought Danielle and Thomas a brand new set of pink furry dice as a thank you for saving my mission.

Two salty sea hag statues were having a staring contest over a basket of fish on the outskirts of Weener. Not wanting the Medusa treatment myself, I ducked around the tattered cubes of wastepaper shedding bundles stacked outside a factory unit, which were doubling up as lofty penthouses for the local stray cat population.

It was back up along the banks of the River Ems now, heading north, opposite the Dutch coast I had already descended. The weather was stubbornly refusing to improve and the wind was awful, the worst yet by a long shot. Just moving required every sinew of my body's strength. It felt like I was dragging a blue whale along behind me. The waterproof jacket was on for the first time since leaving home, helping to build up some meagre resistance against the bruising elemental battering. Hood up and draw strings pulled tight, it was a futile attempt to counter the torrent of leaking tears and bubbling snot forced out of my face by the buffeting.

I really wasn't enjoying this and the surrounding wildlife hardly put a spring in my pedals. All around me were gathered the wicked farming herds of Satan. The field animals wore evil dark masks and started to give me the willies. Gone were the timid white shaking sheep I'd grown accustomed too, replaced by sturdy black headed bastards with matted grey coats. Lucifer's lambs refused to budge out the way of gates without being manhandled, just stubbornly standing their ground and staring. I couldn't believe I escaped without a biting incident. The cows were even more intimidating. Bulky white and black patched muscular lumps of beef and milk, bogging from behind barbed wire through dark undead eyes, with ugly troll like heads tracking my struggle down the lane. Their miserable mugs were a reflection of the farms here, cutting a depressing figure. Gone were the well kept pastures and glamorous abodes of the Dutch agricultural hierarchy, replaced by rickety houses with lemming like slates queuing up to dive off the roof. Overgrown blackened grass strangled the meadows, with huge tractor tyre mounds suffocating hay under protective plastic coverings.

The sluggish crawl after the river followed tiny farming settlements, complete with their own bolt on church and bell towers. It was all the ums as the upward slog continued, Bingum, Jemgum, Midlum, Critzum, Hatzum and finally Ditzum, where a boat would carry me to, wait for it, Petkum. I must have missed Rectum. Most of these ruralities had a cigarette vending machine welded against the side of a barn, some keeping a rusting bubblegum machine company. The kids obviously start puffing early in these parts. I'm sure Danny, whose 18th birthday party poster campaign was promising the most exciting social event in Jerryville for more than a decade, was already a hardened 20-a-day veteran. There didn't seem to be much else to do.

The scattered inhabitants of these barren backwaters were following the lead of the animals when it came to the friendly stakes. The stoat like children kept a beady set of eyes on me, while po-faced old women with faces like thunder limped up and down the gravel scattered roads. The few adult male specimens to go under the cycling microscope had uncannily similar features. I didn't stop to count any fingers, but inbreeding was obviously still alive and well. On the evidence of what I had witnessed a young farmer didn't have a lot of choice when it came to finding a partner. Nobody would have the bottle to slip the hind legs of a moody sheep into the front of their wellies. It was shag your sister or a take a lifelong vow of celibacy.

Boatyard workers hammered away at small craft suspended on wooden legs around Ditzum's concrete wharf. Mucky cold brown water licked the banks of the Ems as a fragile vessel just about big enough to take me, Erika and a space cruiser family to Petkum bobbed about waiting for last minute passengers who were never coming. Everybody else had seen sense and decided to gatecrash Danny's birthday bash. Ruffled ducks sheltered from the chill in the river's reedy beds and a first German wave came from an oily faced barge gang who had brought a JCB along with them for an underwater treasure hunt. A rosy cheeked lad net fishing by the side of the Petkum landing was having more luck after braving the weather for a bucket full of tiddlers.

It was 15 minutes to the opposite shore and the weather was still glum. The sky had frothed into a cloudy white, without a hint of leaking blue, and the temperature had dropped into single figures. Then the signs went AWOL again. I was trying to pursue the river course to Emden, but there wasn't a North Sea Cycle Route pointer anywhere. Instead of breezing along a straight line all the way to the city, it was time to play random cycle path roulette again. The blind detour meandered across scrub land and awkward gravel trails before finally reuniting with the North Sea Cycle Route at a map marked train line crossing. A barricade of plastic cones and red tape blocking off the track entrance snuffed out any short-lived elation. What was wrong with this wretched country? Bloody Germans! They weren't even carrying out any repairs. There was no fucker anywhere to be seen down either end of a lifeless track. In England, the orange coated layabouts would at least be leaning on their shovels pretending to do something constructive. Like drinking mugs of tea. Stress pains stabbed away at the side of my head as the anger gauge threatened to burst above the scale.

But there was someone here. I definitely saw minimal movement. A rail worker was slouched in the front seat of a maintenance van reading a newspaper on the other side of the crossing. 'Hey,' I shouted with a finger prodded towards where I wanted to go. 'Can I cross?' Not even bothering to break off from reading, Van Man issued a lazy affirmative signal and switched back off again. Clambering over the robust tracks after limbo dancing Erika under the tape was a task in itself. The rails sat on top of steep banks and the carcass heavy bike had to be half lifted, half dragged to the other side. Throw in the possibility that a speeding inter-city train could have chopped me in two at any minute and you can picture the fun I was having. After eventually conquering the track challenge, I tapped on the window of the van and shouted 'thank you' as loudly and sarcastically as my breathlessness would allow. Van Man just turned the page.

Emden had a proud industrial heritage and was formerly one of Germany's key northern sea ports. Coal would be shipped in and iron ore was another chief import, but the glory days of sea freight transportation died out 20 years ago. Ship building is still a vital source of income, with the *Nordseewerke* (North Sea Works) still tirelessly knocking out cargo boats and icebreakers more than 100 years after it opened up for business. Submarines are also welded together here and were the inspiration for one of Emden's most famous sons, film director Wolfgang Petersen, best known for his underwater war epic *Das Boot*, which even spawned a pub fruit machine. But the city's major employer uses dry land these days, with more than 10,000 workers on the Volkswagen payroll, producing the family friendly VW Passat car.

The past is not such a prosperous tale as Emden suffered terribly during the Second World War. The main city was almost completely destroyed by Allied bombing raids, annihilating most of the area's historic structures. The worst airborne attack on September 6, 1944, was horrendous and wiped out 80 per cent of inner city homes. This date will never be forgotten in Emden as the shipyard escaped unscathed. The citizens believe this was a tit-for-tat bombing following a similar Nazi obliteration of an English city. It took 18 years to rebuild the worst hit areas.

Emden was by far the biggest municipality on tour so far. Shame I didn't get to see much of it. After squeezing through a combination of lock bridges, with metal railings at either end, specially designed to painfully clip cyclists, the route arched a beautiful wooded area. The crunchy twig covered path skirted around the outside of town under a light green roof of gangly trees, completely concealing the sky above. Unexpected historical artefacts – cannons, windmills and thatched buildings – poked their noses into the shady trail from secret gardens branching away from the sheltered foliage, resting by the side of peaceful lakes.

Exiting the tiny forest on the outskirts of the city, Emden had given me the slip. Leaning on my handlebars bewildered at the station, an old black steam train was taking a well earned retirement outside the front doors. It was mid afternoon and the roads and walkways were crammed with cars and people splitting off in multiple directions. After so much time in solitary, it always felt strange, kind of claustrophobic, when you were plunged back into a hectic slice of civilisation again. This was the biggest dose since Bunde and on a much larger scale. It did my head in and got the alarm bells ringing. I had to get out of here as quickly as possible. Desperate to escape the cluttered madness of carrier bag hauling shoppers, students babbling into mobile phones at the top of their voices and coughing exhaust fumes, I followed the exodus of two wheelers using a steep flyover as an emergency escape route out of town.

A budget friendly Lidl supermarket sign beckoned me to sample its dirt cheap wares on the other side of salvation. These places were Godsends for backpackers and cycling idiots. You could get enough bread, meat, cheese and bottled water to stretch over two sittings for about £2. It really was a poor man's paradise. Head health freak, Jan ten Harkel, who I trusted completely on such matters, informed me that a recent survey proved the meat at Lidl was of higher quality than some of the big name brands in more upmarket chains. We can all be snobby when it comes to where we shop. I'm a strict Sainsbury's man myself and would never touch a slice of Lidl or Aldi ham back home. Mother used to go there every now and then and I would turn my nose up: 'I'm not eating that pikey crap.' The dejected ham would always end up in the bin and she wouldn't go there again for another month. But she was having the last laugh now as I ravenously tucked into another butty of cheese and unidentified pink meat stuffed with peppers. It tasted good enough!

I still wasn't convinced by Germany and there was a definite language barrier. The Germans either didn't understand me or just refused to undermine themselves by conversing in the Queen's English. Wasn't she a closet Kraut anyway? It wasn't their fault and rude on my part in all honesty. Why should I visit a foreign country and expect them to address me in my own native tongue? Who was I to expect such luxury? The truth of the matter is, the English don't bother learning other languages and go abroad expecting the natives to be fluent in our lingo. It's an arrogant attitude and one I'm completely guilty of having quit French at school as a 13-year-old in favour of the less demanding 'European Studies', which was a course for linguistic dunces. I failed that too.

So many countries are strong English speakers and it inspires us to be lazy at languages. In many places they are better at it than us. I had been spoilt rotten by the Dutch, who were most happy to entertain my inadequacies. Bless them, they even apologised for their 'poor English' when we were talking, despite my failure to know a single word of their gobbledygook. It really was embarrassing, but made life much simpler out in the field. I was learning the hard way.

I'd had the bare minimum of human contact since leaving the Netherlands. The longest dialogue I had managed with my new German friends was 'thank you' after paying for something. The lack of banter was really getting to me. A chat with somebody in a bar, at a campsite or just on the road, really helped to keep you going. Even Erika was quiet and had rolled along kilometre after kilometre in silence. I felt so alone and was starting to get dragged down again. Not having any idea where to pitch my mobile home for the night, I decided to push on as long as my body would carry me. It was late afternoon, but if it was physically possible I would have kept pedalling all the way to the Danish border (which was about 750 kilometres away) to get this country out of my system.

Mischievous cycle path gremlins were up to their old tricks again at Larrelt, sending me down a dead end alley where a windmill loomed over a broad canal. Four baseball cap wearing moustached men dropped a gazebo on its side as they stared at my bike and bulging packs in astonishment. I had this effect on people and after sitting under the idle sails for a brief, but disgusted tut-tut-tut session, I cranked Erika into reverse. They don't see many strangers in these parts.

It was all up coast from here. The progress disabling wind had behaved itself since the early morning grind to Ditzum, but returned for a late encore as dusk threatened. Straining alongside the sea wall's high grass bank, the route ascended the Wattenmeer National Park, set up to protect these unique life giving coastal Wadden Sea wetlands all the way up to Denmark. It was certainly popular with the birds. The feathered kind that is. Hundreds, no thousands, of black necks with tiny white masks were pecking away in the marshy fields which extended forever. The chorus of their high pitched chatter over dinner was the only sound to be heard out here in the Wadden wilderness. There were no houses or cars in this barren landscape. It was just me, the bike, the birds and a loving couple wearing his and her's stonewashed denim jackets, inspecting the graffiti scrawl covered *Pilsumer* lighthouse, resembling a red and yellow striped packet of Refreshers tailor-made for a Balrog with a sweet tooth. That was as exciting as it got for the best part of 40 kilometres.

I wasn't a big fan of beaked birds. I could watch wildlife programmes about whales playing volleyball with dead bloody seals or poison tipped scorpions hiding in bedroom slippers and giving irritating Australians a nasty wake-up call. But the fascination with all things feathered didn't do a thing for me – until now. Watching these worm hunting hoodies had taken my mind off the wind. It was all quite comforting and I was determined to find out who my distracting allies were. They must have been part of the goose family, or a breed of greedy obese ducks. Stopping at an information point, I made the nearest match – white head, black neck, greyish undercarriage – on a board full of bird drawings. It was called a *Nonnengans*, which didn't really help. But I would make it a personal quest to unmask this breed's real identity. All these mute hours of loneliness were finally nudging me over the edge.

It was gone 8pm and a desolate outpost finally popped into view. I'd been on the go for 10 hours and tallied up 120 kilometres, which, when I analysed it, was the same as cycling from my flat in Leigh to Northampton. What an amazing feat – I felt like Lee Majors. But I didn't have bionic legs and it was time for a hard earned rest. Greetsiel didn't appear to have the low finance solution however. The edge of this lonely town was as bleak as it came. A fire station and hotel faced each other uneasily across a deserted road, an eternal stand-off surrounded by yellowy scrub land.

It made sense to give the hotel a crack first. The well drilled staff would have a basic spattering of English at their disposal, having dealt with guests of my kind in the past. I approached the waist coated male receptionist with a winning smile. 'Do you speak English?' I pleaded.

'Of course. Vow can we help you, sir?'

'I'm looking for somewhere cheap to sleep tonight. Is there a campsite or youth hostel here?'

'You would like to stay here? Of course. We can give you a womb.'

'No. You don't understand. I am on a bicycle tour from England and I need cheap accommodation. Is there a campsite or youth hostel here?'

'You vant a bicycle? You are needing a bicycle now? But it is night time.'

'No I have a bicycle. I need somewhere to sleep that will not cost me much money. Campsite? Hostel?'

'You vould like to borrow my bicycle? Is that what you vould like? My bicycle?'

It was a generous offer, but wasn't going to keep me dry if the heavens broke open. So I said cheerio and made a bee-line for the faded brick work of the neighbouring fire station. I knocked on the door and was quickly surrounded by a huddle of middle and old aged men. Hardly the muscle ripped fantasy figures of hose waving calendars which had a habit of making women wet. They were voluntary officers from the Twin

Windmill Association and had been using the fire station as a meeting point for a complex festival summit.

'We have a special celebration on the first day of May in Greetsiel. I do not know what you would call it in England,' delivered the grey fluffy-haired leader in exemplary English.

'May Day?' I took a wild stab in the dark.

'Yes that is it. We are meeting to discuss our plans to erect a big pole, which everybody will dance around. What is it you call it?'

'A May Pole?' I intervened.

'Yes. Right again. You are good at this. This celebration has happened here for hundreds of years. We must all decide who will sell what on the night. The beer, the wine and the sausages are very important.'

And let's not forget, who's going to sacrifice all those untouched pure village virgins? I knew their wicked game, Pagan worshippers up to no good in the middle of nowhere. But they were kindly, as well as being a backward breed. After interrogating me about my journey to Greetsiel, soon realising I wasn't of good sacrificial stock, the band of do-gooders stuffed euro notes into my bike box to boost my charity fund. Bloody love the Germans. The cream of European civilisation they are. Could kiss every damn one of the bastards. But there was no breaking news on the lodgings front and I would have to battle on to the next village, Norddeich, to get some shut-eye.

The virgin slayer jumped on his own saddle and guided me through the village towards the correct path. I think he was trying to get rid of me as fast as possible. After a fleeting glimpse, I could fully understand why they wouldn't want a coasting scruff bag polluting such an enchanting spot. Boat masts poked out of a tiny harbour resting on the River Leybucht, which drained into a street splitting water feature. Immaculate red brick restaurants were lit by hanging golden lanterns with an orange shimmering outline acting as a homing beacon for any fairies playing in the nearby fields. Flat cheeseboard shaped shops were hidden behind spotlessly painted blue and black wooden shutters. Most of them were in the antiquity trade. And hidden somewhere in town was a ship in a bottle museum. Sod it!

Departing my chaperone, who was off to sharpen his wench slicing knives, I saluted Greetsiel's symbolic silent sentinels, the twin green and red windmills staring down at the village. It was less than an hour's shuffle up to Norddeich and a rest was long overdue after setting a record 130 kilometre total for the day. Back on the northern tip of the coast facing the German Frisian islands, this was my first proper flash of the sea for days. But it was a grim, soulless place buried in the sand and barely qualified as an oasis. There were a couple of empty bars, a gloomily lit guesthouse, plus a token souvenir shop for ferry hoppers travelling to Juist and Norderney, two of the seven inhabited East Frisian Islands. A dusty dump, with all the sparkle and charisma of a single workaholic accountant, Norddeich had that stranded at the end of the universe feel about it.

It did have a mammoth campsite. But don't ask me why. I could have spent days scratching all the hair off my head trying to suss out a decent reason for spending more than a single night of enforced necessity here. The campsite office was closed so I hunted out the tent pitches. A petite one man affair was erected on top of a raised mound surrounded on three sides by hedge windbreakers. I decided to set up in the natural booth next door until a rethink was enforced by the rising male cry of: 'Oh Ja. Oh Ja. Oh Jaaaaaaaa.' I really didn't want to listen to Norbet does Norddeich all night. This loud and proud chap had either banged one out and was mopping up with postage stamps, or had defied the laws of geometry by squeezing a playmate into his pegged out thimble. There certainly wouldn't be any room for positional manoeuvre.

My remaining choice was to camp up against one hedge in the space next to the road, minus any other barriers. Big mistake. Once I was all erected (the tent that is) I paid a visit to the camp master, who had opened up shop at 10pm. With a tiny moustache, short blond curls and blue dungarees pulled over a radiant yellow T-shirt, he could have been Rod, Jane and Freddy's missing link. But he didn't know the words to my tune.

He struggled to grasp I had 'put up a tent' or the word 'camping'. Grabbing a pen and scrap of paper, I scribbled down the universal picture for tents – a crude triangle. An artistic inability to recreate basic shapes – I can't even draw a circle properly – left two points sticking out the roof of the triangle. The confused camp operator was beginning to think I might have brought a wig-wam. But he didn't charge me for extra Indians.

The camp site had plenty of facilities. There was a shop, restaurant and bar with live entertainment – but it wasn't officially summer yet and they were closed. The shower block however was magnificent. This wasn't becoming an obsession and I wasn't running my fingers along walls inspecting for dust or checking the levels of the soap dispensers. I just appreciated a decent facility for my money and this white and yellow tiled palace left me drooling all the way to the hot tap. The single (free) shower cubicles were pumping out hard skin massaging water and there was bum friendly soft toilet roll in every chrome throne room. There was even a pubic hair-free bidet, which was bizarrely situated in full view of the front door. It was nearly 11pm and everyone was in bed so I gave my sack and crack a quick splash just to make it count.

Feasting on mouthfuls of Lidl Gouda cheese, pink peppery meat stuff and crusty bread under torch light, the weather was deteriorating horrendously. I'm sure I was taking the brunt of it on behalf of the whole camp. Literally spitting distance from the sea, strong gales were ripping through the skinny trees and shaking the walls of my tent. Flapping about ferociously, take-off would have been possible if I hadn't been carrying adequate cycling bag ballast onboard. Then the sky caved in and the rain poured down. I was going to be washed away for sure. There's no way this flimsy shelter could take such a vicious pummelling. It was going to collapse any minute and drench me to death.

The temperature had dropped fast. Lying low shivering and watching the raging tent dance violently to the beat of the wind, I was in Scott of the Antarctic's sleeping bag. An heroic explorer, I was all alone braving brutal elements deep in the heart of unforgiving terrain – not just a buffoon on a bike in Norddeich for the night. Inevitably, doubt kicked in again. Just what the bloody hell was I doing here? It was time to accept that you can't force feed some things in life. I'm not the outdoors type and would be far better off at home tucked under the covers with a book, dunking a Chocolate Digestive into a warm cup of sweet tea. You'd had a good go at it, mate, but this shit wasn't for you. Leave the adventure stuff to people who can handle it and stop fooling yourself you are a contender. I fastened the sleeping bag hood protectively around my head so that only my eyes could peep out. Consciousness slipped away as the storm screamed overhead.

13   At home with the Radmers

Punch and Judy were still going at it hammer and tong next door but one.

I bet they'd bonked their way obliviously right through the storm. Their howls of sexual ecstasy were a welcome alarm call. If the midget shagging marathon was still in full swing I obviously hadn't been scooped up by angry winds and tossed in the direction of Iceland. It didn't feel like I was bobbing about or getting wet. I was dry and still alive. My pathetic little tent had passed the acid test, firmly standing its ground against all the odds. Size really wasn't everything.

Cruel black clouds were still hanging over Norddeich as I made a hasty retreat. Bold wind surfers were making the most of the blustery conditions as dark waves washed up yellowy foam on the rocky shoreline. As Norddeich trailed into the distance the weather picked up and even the cows were standing up for the occasion. One ginger specimen bore an uncanny resemblance to German international goalkeeper Oliver Kahn, including his big flat square head and miserable expression.

The coastal communities of Bensersiel, Neuharlingersiel and Harlesiel were all small ports, serving the German Frisian Islands of Langeoog, Spiekeroog and Wangerooge. Much more attractive than neighbouring Norddeich, they reminded me of the Cornish fishing villages nan and granddad would drag me around by hand on school holidays. Day-trippers waltzed past the plastic floats and green draping nets hanging from small fishing vessels, while I had a quick map check outside the Minger Café, whose waitresses weren't unattractive. It was 60 kilometres to the city of Wilhelmshaven and the promise of a warm bed with the Radmers (in my own room). Head of the household, Horst Radmer, was a North Sea Cycle Route legend having road-tested the route on its inaugural ride in 2001. He had offered to put me up for a few days and I was hoping to re-assess my stubborn negative view of the German race.

Passing the village of Carolinensiel and its miniature Tom Sawyer style steam boat which lay idle on the banks of the river, I was hailed by a couple of Chuckle Brothers lookalike competition winners. These were real professional cycling tourists, kitted out in top quality gear and proving again that Germans have to do everything on a grand scale. I certainly felt inferior in my shorts and T-shirt compared to these guys, who were decked out in thermal padded head-to-toe covering body suits and even had satellite navigation systems screwed into their handlebars. Tossers. I pretended not to hear them and let them disappear down the road.

Heading cross-country on crude bone-shaking paths over grazing land, the legs were full of gas and Erika was galloping through the distance at great pace. Jever, a town which gave its name up for beer, was the main port of call ahead of Wilhelmshaven. Having been a famous maker of Pilsners since 1900, the polished futuristic glass towers of the Frisian Brewhouse were the town's tallest structures. Over the last few hundred years, a topsy-turvy past has seen the town ruled by Russia and the Napoleonic inspired Kingdom of Holland. The Ruskies handed it back to Germany in 1818 and today it is a pleasant place, with shopping lanes leading to the extraordinary Jever Castle. This four winged pink structure dates back to the 14th century and is surrounded by beautiful gardens and lakes. Originally built as a fortification, the castle is in remarkable condition and visitors can get a bird's eye view of the coast from the summit of the 67 metre high spherical baroque tower during the summer months.

Thundering down a path hugging a dual carriageway all the way to Wilhelmshaven (or so I thought), supermarkets and VW dealerships sprung up everywhere and a giant inflatable tiger growled at the traffic from his perch on top of an Esso Garage. The cycle signs had thrown up another red herring and I found myself facing a dead end next to a rail track. Scanning the map with Nicholas Crane accuracy, I soon traced an alternative route along the banks of the Ems-Jade Canal, which had started life back in Emden and reached the end of the line at Wilhelmshaven.

Rowers were out practising for an upcoming race on the still blue water, while catamarans twitched ever so slightly as they rested in their berths. The road was quiet and wound through an industrial estate on the outer crust of what was looking like another rundown broken town. With a population of nearly 100,000, the city of Wilhelmshaven was now officially the biggest place I had visited. And, unlike Emden, I was actually going to see some of it. But it really wasn't shaping up too well. The streets were grubby with litter blowing around my wheels and tatty discoloured flats were just about keeping themselves above the grime on tip-toe.

Wilhelmshaven was another prime target of the Allied bombing raids during the Second World War and on initial impressions was still struggling to recover. A garrison base and the main North Sea port for the German navy, two thirds of all buildings were destroyed during the attacks. Snuffing out the threat of German war ships and submarines was the main target, with Wilhelmshaven's docks completely wrecked during the air strikes.

And here I was lost in another key enemy stronghold with the Radmers' address jotted down on a wrinkled piece of paper. Their apartment wasn't on my town plan, it had slid just off the edge of the map, and everyone I approached, including an ambulance driver, didn't have a clue where it was. Hope nobody from that part of town needs to get to hospital in a hurry. But help was just around the corner and I was saved by a couple of middle-aged florists who were closing up for the night, barely spoke a word of English, but could decipher my hand writing. My map had fallen well short and so had their instructions, which I pretended to understand by smiling and head nodding a lot, before fighting my way out of their overgrown jungle with a machete.

There's something very unsettling about cycling down an unfamiliar street, in a strange city, as night closes in, not sure if you are going the right way or not. The florists had said something about a sports stadium, which I had passed ages ago, and after 10 minutes pedalling I was convinced my path finding skills had let me down again. I was going to have to collar someone else, but this was the other side of town and there wasn't a soul to be seen. Beep... beep... beep. I couldn't believe it. The flower lady had tracked me down in her white delivery van and was now giving me a slow escort all the way to Camp Radmer. After another 10 minutes of playing follow the leader, I arrived at the road matching the name on my piece of paper with Flower Lilly waiting by the kerb with her hazard lights flashing. Popping my head through the passenger window I expressed my overwhelming gratitude and relief by grabbing the street guide's arm and planting a wet kiss on her hand. That was obviously thanks enough and she did an 11-point turn before sounding a final beep of the horn and disappearing. What a good girl!

The Radmers lived in a quiet suburb with all the apartments linked by an off road concrete pathway. Leaning Erika at the bottom of concrete steps which led up to their front door, I pressed the buzzer. A well tanned man with an important face and shock of white hair answered, hardly able to contain his excitement. 'Hello, hello, you must be Bernie, come inside, come inside,' ushered Horst.

Taking my bags inside he told me to take the bike down into the basement, before introducing his wife Ursula, who peered out of the kitchen through small round glasses balanced under a white bobbed haircut. She was a real mummsy character who began every sentence with a heavily pronounced 'so', would not stop fussing and was on a mission to fatten me up during my two night stopover. But what shocked me most was that they were both in their seventies. Horst was a cycling marvel who had covered most of Europe on two wheels. When he contacted me via email, I pictured this super-fit middle-aged man bursting out of his shorts, who feasted on nothing but bananas, nuts and wild berries. Not the sprightly pensioner standing in front of me in blue jeans and a white shirt.

Showing me into a first floor bedroom in their four-storey apartment, I showered up and joined them at the dining room table. All meals would be eaten together, which I liked, and more than filled up the human conversation tank. Both Horst and Ursula spoke excellent English and made me feel right at home straight away. You couldn't have met a more hospitable double act. This trip was certainly a learning curve. I'd lost the fear of being bludgeoned in my sleep by hosts with evil intentions. Although, a pitch black eyed Victorian style doll with Princess Leia headphone shaped buns in a red dress on my bed side table was quite scary. I didn't even want to touch it, so I couldn't move it away. I kept the mallet under the pillow as insurance, just in case this ghoulish figurine decided to creak into life in the dead of night.

Horst and Ursula had been married 43 years and had three children, who had spread their wings across Europe. Ursula spent most of her time in the kitchen conjuring wonderful smells, sitting on a stool reading while various saucepans bubbled. A professional housewife, a role she readily admitted loving, the basement under the kitchen doubled up as a huge parlour spread over a couple of concrete chambers. This area was originally designed to double up as a bomb shelter, which surprised me in such a modern building. If war did break out again there was no chance that the Radmers would starve to death. There were hundreds of pots, jars and tins everywhere – enough grub to last another 10 years. Mrs Radmer could solve third world famine from her parlour and she'd be happy to do all the cooking.

Horst had been an engineer for the German government, but, now retired, was involved in local politics. Most of the important decisions seemed to be made over a sauna and few beers on a Friday night, but Horst was very serious about serving and improving Wilhelmshaven. The council had no financial muscle and the investment of new business was desperately needed to regenerate Wilhelmshaven, which had fallen into a poor state of repair. The great white hope was the construction of a new deep water container wharf – the Jade Weser Port – at the Jadebusen, a dent like inlet of the North Sea. It will have a natural water depth in excess of 18 metres and be able to accommodate giant vessels some 430 metres in length. Most importantly it will provide the easternmost deep water point in northern Europe for cargo loaders, attracting ships from Scandinavia and Russia, and should finally bring Wilhelmshaven on to a level footing with rivals Bremen and Hamburg, the two busiest ports in Germany.

The Jade Weser Port should be open for business in 2010, but Horst was more concerned that he was going lose 'his private beach' as part of the deal. 'There is a little quiet strip of beach that I like to visit, but it will sink under the new cargo terminal,' he said, pointing to his sun bronzed features. 'I like to go and sit there by the sea, but I suppose it is a small price to pay for the billions of euros, jobs and prosperity the new terminal will bring Wilhelmshaven.'

Horst had been a core rider on the first ever circumnavigation of the North Sea Cycle Route in 2001. Part of a hand picked group who set off from Hamburg, Horst had clocked up all 6,000 kilometres and seven countries on the route, but that only told half the story. He was an even later starter than me, putting my efforts into a pitiful shade. Horst woke up one morning with the urge to take up cycling at the tender age of 65 and since then has embarked on a monster cycling marathon every year.

'Taking part in the first North Sea Cycle Route journey was a great experience and really whet my appetite for cycling,' he explained. 'I had never been to Norway and Scotland before, which are two of the best countries I have ever visited. The natural beauty really was something else, as were the people. Long cycling tours allow you to understand people from different countries by immersing yourselves in their culture. Some of them are rich, some are poor, but they are all trying to get on and live their lives in the best possible way. It is very important to see this with your own eyes.' One thing was for certain, Horst was hardcore (he had packs on the front and back of his bike) and didn't muck about hitting the ground running in his new hobby. He took five months out to bike it from above the frozen Arctic Circle at Norway's North Cape, virtually mainland Europe's most northern point, all the way down to the sun cream shores of the Med and Greece. He pedalled over the Pyrenees to meet his shell-shocked son in Spain and made a 'shorter' trip to Italy. His next big push was to reach Istanbul in Turkey, before maybe hanging up his cycling vest for good. But there is still the strong temptation to go out in a blaze of two wheeled glory with one last trip to Beijing, China, for the 2008 Olympics.

'I keep getting hassled by the Baltic Cycling Club to go to Beijing,' added Horst. 'I cycled the North Cape to Greece route with them, Lithuanians and Poles, and they are amazing people. When we set off from the North Cape it was freezing and I was having difficulty holding on to my handlebars because of the cold. Norway is very expensive, but I was fortunate to have enough money to stay in hotels and get out of the cold. They couldn't afford to do this and had to put up tents and make fires outside to keep warm. They all have good jobs in their countries, some are scientists and professors, but they earn small wages compared to western European salaries. I would like to join them again, but I am an elected councillor now who must serve his people and it is impossible to spend long periods away from home.'

That sounded rough, certainly not my cup of tea, and I wondered if Horst had encountered any real danger, especially ducking behind the crumbling crime rife outposts of former Iron Curtain countries. 'I have never been worried for my life or anything like that, but there have been some peculiar incidents,' he chuckled. 'We was in Belarus once and had to bribe guards with cash who were blocking our route and there was another time in Kosovo when my camera was snatched away by a soldier. They thought I was a spy and after holding me for three hours the solider told me "this is a free country" before giving me my camera back. I just laughed at the hypocrisy.

'Another time in the Ukraine we were camped one evening on private ground next to the Black Sea and five of my companions had their bikes stolen by thieves on boats. I suppose you could call them pirates. But I was OK. I always take a big tent with me so I can lock my bike up inside with me at night.' You probably give it a cuddle as well, Horst, you big German softie.

And what of Ursula? Did she mind her husband gallivanting across Europe for months at a time? 'We have been married a long time now, so I do not miss him too much,' she said. 'I do not sit around worrying as I know he is coming home sooner or later.' What most men would give for a marriage like that.

Horst was keen to give me a whistle-stop tour of Wilhelmshaven. First up was a salute to the city's founder, Kaiser Wilhelm I, who was immortalised in a green statue, wearing the full medal splattered royal regalia and sporting a magnificent moustache which sprouted across both cheeks. The Prussian king kindly lent his name to the city in 1869 and its most important landmark, the 20ft blue swing bridge which climbs above an inlet of the Jadebusen and was once the greatest of its kind in all Europe.

The city centre was surrounded by parks and old war bunkers sitting on the middle of roundabouts had been strangled by green foliage. Light brown sculptures of flat fish swam across the floor of the modern pedestrianised streets. A multi-storey shopping centre was the focal point, with bars, café houses and pretty much anything else you could need from bread sticks to luminous tracksuit bottoms spiralling out everywhere else. They loved a lumberjack top here. Most of the men, who were part of a Heir Flick cloning programme, complete with tiny round metal glasses, lumbered around with jeans tucked into their logging shirts at armpit level.

You couldn't escape the seafaring life here – it had a hand in everything. Horst revelled in these links to the past and future and felt compelled to drive me down to the navy warship base. Our progress was abruptly ended by a high metal fence and barbed wire topping which restricted all views. But at least I knew where it was now which made Horst happy. Passing the long stretch of blue water on Wilhelmshaven's outskirts, Horst pointed out the old English school houses which the occupying Allied forces had introduced after the Second World War. This Jadebusen inlet had also been the site of a German shipyard where battle cruisers and U-boats were constructed ahead of unleashing terror on the seas. Sitting here now it was hard to comprehend that such devastating nautical weapons of human suffering had been spawned at this spot. Not one scrap of machinery, rusting warehouses or ageing wharfs still existed. There wasn't a single sign of the death and destruction which had poured out of this place.

The only surviving relics of war were kept in the impressive marine museum which sat by the waterside in the shadow of the Kaiser Wilhelm Bridge. Rows of glass cases containing pristine German uniforms taken from the backs of petty officers and U-boat commanders stood sentry around the downstairs reception. Old pictures led visitors through the historical time line of the navy from 1905 to present day, with old radios, Nazi flags, ship logs, medals and even the captain's china beefing up the exhibition. A large section focused on the use of mines in sea warfare – with one bomb covered in cartoons of Allied leaders Churchill (chomping on a cigar of course), Roosevelt and Stalin – and how the navy are now concentrating their efforts on removing the underwater menaces which still lay dormant, ready to explode.

The upstairs display was dominated by a 3-D rotating viewing booth, which plunged you head first into black and white battles on the high seas aboard the SMS *Hegoland*. You could almost smell the smoke of the torpedoed ships and feel the spray of the waves splashing you in the face. At one point I was standing on deck with the Kaiser, whose highly technical naval role seemed to revolve around scratching his bushy beard a lot while getting away with wearing the most outrageous feathered headwear. But the ladies obviously loved it. The show ended with an obscure selection of frilly dressed women sitting in a rowing boat twiddling parasols and giggling to themselves. Maybe I'll get myself some feathered headgear after all.

Resisting the temptation to buy myself a model battle cruiser or captain's hat on the way out of the museum, it was time to play with the big toys outside. Old jetfighters, boats, subs and anti-aircraft guns rested in the courtyard. But the most impressive exhibits were a retired rusty brown submarine, suspended in the air above the concrete, and a muscular grey blue destroyer which puffed out its chest in the adjacent river. Squeezing through the opening hatch of the submarine, my thoughts turned back to the three grubby faced submariners pictured in the museum smoking on top of a surfaced U-boat. They looked so relieved to have come up for air and as I descended into the claustrophobic, cramped body of the vessel, it was impossible to fathom being stuck down here for months on end, skulking around the ocean's darkest depths.

Just pulling my body across the narrow corridor – jammed between fold-away tables and couches, bunks and banks of switches, wheels, dials, pressure gauges and red diving lights – for a few short minutes was nauseating enough. There really was no room to fart down here. Every millimetre had been utilised in a suffocating space no more than one-and-a-half metres wide and seven foot high. I had a quick nose at the radar room, well it was more of a cubby hole, before staring down the empty cold torpedo bays at the front of the ship. Ten minutes was all I could take before getting out of the bloody thing almost gasping for breath. It was a very uncomfortable experience for somebody who can't even handle tube trains.

Walking slowly across a metal gangplank, creaking in the strong winds blowing down river, I boarded the bulky destroyer *Mölders*, with its communication tower and 40 foot mast almost touching the sky. This nautical beast was pensioned off in 2003 and looked deathly bored as it stood motionless, a million miles away from the excitement of chasing across the North and Baltic Seas on NATO peacekeeping duties. I felt sorry for the old girl whose enforced retirement marked the end of an era in steam driven ships. Built in America during the 60s, she was once the pride of the navy, but had now been downgraded to a giant climbing frame for adults who had outgrown their Airfix kits. This was the first German ship to be equipped with guided missiles and computer aided command weapons, but she never fired a live shot in anger in almost 34 years of service. Guided by arrows, I took a brisk walk around the main deck, under the missile launchers and satellite dishes, before ducking into the navigation room. Standing there surrounded by all the controls and computers, staring ahead through square windows, you could understand

113

the thrill of heading towards new, but invisible horizons hidden by the sea. I still wouldn't swap Erika for anything though.

Climbing down through the internal organs of the ship was a stark contrast to the poky conditions of the submarine. These sailors certainly had it cushy. There were stacks of evenly spaced bed bunks and a large eating mess specially designed for manoeuvring your elbows to shovel in a mouthful of grub without hitting the grizzly ship mate next to you. They also had a beautiful line in silver shining showers and urinals, plus a gleaming set of washing machines on the way out. How the other half live!

The last exhibit was the tiny camouflage boat, *Tirpitz*, which was German for 'small pain in the asshole'. This vessel was deployed to the Norwegian fjords in 1942 and became a right nuisance, using double steel wire netting and firepower to prevent Allied ships landing in Scandinavia or British convoys making Russian shores. But the little fucker was put out of action in 1943, when two British mini subs breached *Tirpitz's* barrier netting and gifted her a quartet of two tonne explosives. Now that's what I call a rocket up the arse.

My tour ended on a sombre note at the altar of the Lutherean *Christus und Garnisonkirche* church. A place of worship for navy crews seeking a protective blessing across dicey waters, bright stained glass windows shot rays of light across the pews. A memorial chapel decorated with old ship wheels and a register of those lost at sea highlighted the dangers of this hazardous occupation. But the most poignant symbol was the painting hanging over the altar of a glowing crucifix hovering above a calm sea. The message was that faith in God can steer you through even the roughest waters. With plenty of boat trips ahead I didn't want to be tested.

What appeared to be a plate of vomit awaited me at Ursula's dining room table. This culinary delight was called *labskaus* and was usually served up on High Street pavements on Saturday nights. It really did resemble sick, in both colour and texture, but actually tasted quite good. This was a meal favoured by sailors, made from corned beef, onion and potato, which was simple and cheap to make and cooked up in a boiling hot galley cauldron. Ursula's brand was accompanied by fried eggs and gherkins and went down well enough, but I had to turn my head away from the plate as I forked this gunk down as quickly as possible. Looking at what I was eating actually made me gag. It did the job as I felt well stuffed afterwards. No wonder this grub was the staple diet of Wilhelmshaven's mariners on long distance sea voyages. It filled you to the brim, but you certainly wouldn't deplete the stores by rushing back for more.

Horst had popped out for a serious networking session with his council chums, which allowed me to prise Ursula out of the kitchen for 10 minutes. She was a lovely lady and reminded me of my mum in a lot of ways. Here I was a complete stranger and she couldn't do enough for me. I'd only been inside her home a few minutes when she had insisted on unpacking all my bags and washing everything straight away. 'So! We will dry them on the line outside as it always smells better and fresher. It is no problem. My pleasure.'

Ursula had a kind rounded face, but behind all the goodness there was a lifetime of sadness and hard knocks. Stranded in communist East Germany after the war she had to wait until 1948 to make a break for freedom over the Iron Curtain by motorbike. Steve McQueen would have been proud. She was desperate to escape. Her grandfather had died in a concentration camp controlled by the Russians after the conflict had finished and her grandmother had been run over and hospitalised by a Red Army truck driver. She never fully recovered. But an even bigger tragedy shrouded in mystery had taken away Ursula's mother during the fighting. The last message was that her mother was boarding a boat to visit her, but she was never seen or heard of again. Ursula believes her mother was condemned to a watery grave by a torpedo attack on what she led me to believe was a passenger ship. I didn't know if this was an accidental sinking or something more sinister.

Her father had been a German navy officer, who was captured by the Allies and made a prisoner of war. His smartly dressed picture hung inside an oval frame on the wall outside my temporary bedroom door and he was certainly a handsome chap. Once the war was over he helped out in the clean up exercise, dismantling bombs and German sea defences on the North Sea island fortification of Hegoland.

Ursula can still remember her risky dash over the closed border to escape the 'cruelty' of the Russians. 'There were certain times when you had a chance to make it into West Germany, when there maybe weren't border guards about,' she explained. 'I got a phone call telling me it was my time to go. It was my only chance and it was very scary as I could have been shot if I had been seen. I paid a man to take me on his motorbike over the border as fast as he could and I escaped. Others weren't so lucky. I made my way to Emden and knocked on my father's door. He went white. He couldn't believe I was standing there in front of him. It was a great day.'

Horst had returned at this point and pushed a tall long glass in front of me, plus an accompanying cool green bottle of Jever to toast the next stage of my journey. I thanked the couple for their hospitality and complimented them on their excellent English.

'It has been so nice talking to you as I have had a lot of language problems since I arrived in Germany,' I said.

'Really?' replied Horst. 'This is unusual and would certainly not be a problem in the big cities. But we are in the middle of nowhere here, right off the beaten track. No main roads pass through this part of Germany, so we don't get many foreign visitors. There is no reason for people to come to Wilhelmshaven, but that will all change once the new deep water cargo terminal is built. Cheers.'

We all raised our glasses and as I sat there with mein perfect hosts huge pangs of guilt vibrated through my body. I'd been far too quick to write off the Germans and felt quite bad about it. The Radmers had taken me in off the street and treated me like their own son. It had proved once and for all that Germans were human after all. Thanks to the kindness of the Radmers I would stop being so judgemental and share this new love with every single one of their rude, robotic, money orientated and stubborn non-English speaking countrymen.

14   Friends Reunited

The spectral shape of the *Arngast* lighthouse led a lonely existence at the centre of the mist shrouded Jadebusen. It was easy to sympathise with the red and white structure after abandoning the warmth of Hotel Radmer to begin circumnavigating this cold bowl of grey mudflats. Ursula had bear-hugged me tightly to her more than ample bosom before letting me disappear, probably forever. It was the sort of cuddle that only a mother can dish out and was the first time I had been gripped that way since my own dear mum left this mortal plain. But I didn't get upset. It was appreciated and the affection most definitely reciprocal.

Horst had promised me a sunny day with 'only a 20 per cent chance of rain' after consulting the weather oracle on his laptop. Predictably, the clouds grew blacker and every cow was pinned stomach down to the floor. Fine drizzle began to filter through from up high as I began circling the Jadebusen to make my rendezvous with Rhys somewhere over the other side at Bremerhaven. Having a cycling buddy would be good. I really didn't want to fly solo again after snuggling up with the Radmers for the last couple of days.

The route ahead looped a nature reserve linked by multiple spring gates to keep roaming animals in check. Seagulls were patrolling the shore for breakfast titbits left behind by the retreating tide. Lone ramblers wrapped up tightly from head to toe were being shoved around by furious winds whipped up at the heart of the Jadebusen cauldron. This was still part of the Wattenmeer Park and a series of bizarre sculptures were dotted around the clock face of the basin. A stone man with his winkle hanging out was diving backwards at one point, closely followed by a giant mussel and a disturbing red foetus with octopus tentacles sprouting out its body. My favourite was a gigantic Frosty the Snowman, complete with a concrete carrot nose.

Skidding into Dangast, the small seaside village was slowly blinking into life. It was too nippy for visitors brave enough to snap up the inflatable orange rubber dinghies and paddling pools tied down outside the front of beach shops. And there were no takers for Germany's answer to the simple deckchair, which they'd attempted to get all superior about yet again. It was a two seated design, which sat in a wooden box and was covered by an arched roof. Similar to a genetically modified mutant sea shell. Row upon row of the things stood in line on the beach facing Wilhelmshaven, which was now on the opposite side of the mud splodged horizon behind the always dead central *Arngast.* But you couldn't knock the Germans for industry as no light fingered Franz was going to take one of those sturdy buggers home with him at the end of the day.

The mudflats vanished behind the powerfully built frame of a green dike and it was temporarily back into the sheep lanes. Grinding my way through pebble sized gravel required far too much effort as the forces of nature tried to put the brakes on Erika's advances. Hoofing out of the stones we dashed down a tractor trail and linked up with the main road running parallel with the mapped route. Erika's powdery dust stained tyres dispatched a turning pitch of relief as her wheels hit smooth path heaven. But the comfort zone was interrupted by the radar blip of a cyclist hungry dog licking its lips, sprawled across the centre of the path on sentry duty outside a farmhouse.

I don't know if it smelt the fear or viewed me as a tasty morsel after a fattening up session with the Radmers. But the German Shepherd rose to full extension, tilting its big bad black head to one side after spotting me. It didn't look like it wanted to play. When I got within belly tickling distance the hell hound issued a savage bark and sprung towards me. It actually flew through the air with two outstretched front paws like a canine Superman. I took evasive action and bashed over the kerb on to the empty road. It would have been Scooby Snack time for sure if I'd stacked it.

Panting away as all energy reserves were emptied putting breathing space between my bodily menu and the rabid attentions of the slavering mutt, a Labrador scrambled out of nowhere for a piece of the action. That was the last time I threw a 12 pack of Andrex in my supermarket trolley. And that wasn't the end of it. A snorting bull with bloodshot eyes identified me as fair game at the end of this animal version of Tunnel of Death. It was actually contemplating hurdling the low wire fence keeping us apart, even stepping back to take a run-up. The bull was going to strike a blow for farmland kind and do more than just gouge a hole in my tyres. Then as if by magic, the horny devil's pink lipstick suddenly popped out of brown fur, and he decided to mount Ermintrude instead.

All the houses on this stretch loved a garden ornament. There were all different sized replicas of the *Arngast* lighthouse. One of them was so impressive it was topped off by Captain Birdseye, chuffing on a pipe in a crane lowered lifeboat. Other lawn decorations included gnomes, long whiskered seals, a red-faced drunk accordion player and an old couple sitting knitting on a bench. There were also German flags hoisted up high everywhere on whitewashed poles. This blatant show of nationalism had been on display throughout the country and they were obviously a very proud people.

After completing a three quarter navigation of the Jadebusen, it was time to capitalise on a shortcut passed on by cycling high master Horst. Rhys had touched down in Bremen and was preparing to catch a train to meet me after ripping free his dismantled bike from the air regulation bubble wrap packaging and clicking everything back together. Horst had told me to cut across country to Mitteldeich, which coincidentally was in the middle of where I was, instead of wasting time following the longer route around the entire coast to the Blexen ferry point.

Horst might have been a black belt sixth dan in long distance cycling, but it didn't mean his directions were RAC route planner standard. Inevitably, the cheat turned out to be more time consuming than following the North Sea Cycle Route. Two frustrating hours getting blown around barren country lanes, completely devoid of life, inspired screams of 'wankers' at the top of my voice when mischievous German cycle signs enforced 30 minutes of backtracking. It was only 17 kilometres to Blexen after the first hour's push. Ten minutes later there was only another 12 to go, before the ferry landing decided to sink without trace. Breaking off to tuck into Ursula's packed lunch (the picnic hamper had been politely declined for cycling weight considerations), the bread tasted soggy as tears of frustration rolled into my gob. It was time to start again, consult the map and pick out the nearest coastal point still clinging to the signposts.

Burhave was a carbon copy of Dangast and only a 15 kilometre slide down the sea wall to Blexen. The even path was an effortless express way and it took no time at all to gobble up the distance in perfect harmony with my CD walkman. There just had to be a sting in the tail. Pacing past a whimsical village church, soured by a smoking industrial chimney pulling rank above its steeple, Erika galloped through an allotment and swerved to a halt at the isolated ferry landing.

It had started to brighten up this side of the River Weser, but the featureless apartment blocks and weatherworn communications tower of Bremerhaven on the opposite bank cut a grim figure. A handful of cars eventually signed up for the short ferry crossing as a feeling of childlike excitement shot through my body knowing Rhys was holed up in a bar on the other side. Patting the back of my bike, my hand grasped at a space which shouldn't have been there. Sting in the tail. My sleeping bag and flip-flops had decided to bail out while pelting along the home straight singing the 'You're the man' lyric of the Happy Mondays anthem 'Step On'. I blatantly wasn't.

Despair soon turned to joy as an advertising poster pasted across one side of the ferry turned the smile switch on again. A toddler with a painful expression on his chubby little face was struggling to keep hold of a giant slippery sausage between his legs with two hands. The caption next to his mouth read: 'Mmh – Lecker'. Now that was funny and rude, but wrong for so many reasons. I could buy another sleeping bag no trouble, but this kid was mentally scarred and faced the torment of recurring king size frankfurter nightmares for life.

Rhys was camped out in a watering-hole slap bang opposite the ferry port and was sipping a cool one when I walked into the bar. An England Cricket baseball cap covered black hair, sitting above piercing bug-like blue eyes. Milky white legs hung out of a pair of blue shorts and the bastard had a ciggie on the go as he tilted his throat back to receive another stream of German heaven in a glass.

'Have you got a quarantine licence for those horrible things dangling down there,' I pointed at the visually offensive pale limbs, which were enough to put a man off his beer.

'Yeah. I got it from the same place you got all badged up for that big sunburnt hooter of yours,' he replied. Only a matter of seconds together and it had already started.

Rhys was a sight for sore eyes and after a quick man hug, cigarette and cup of warming coffee we headed off into the icy drizzle of Bremerhaven. It was freezing here next to the docks. He filled me in with all the gossip from home (which took about two minutes) and it was a touch surreal having a familiar grinning face alongside me. Rhys was a little bit of home, a place which had felt years away, and it was a relief to rekindle the link to familiarity. Don't get me wrong, I had relished the daily challenge of being on my tod and trundling through alien backdrops. It was a notion which filled me with dread before setting off, but was now being conquered. I'd managed to stick at it by myself, despite the temptation to pack it all in on a number of occasions. And anxious episodes had been few and far between.

This may not seem a landmark achievement to 'normal' people, but in my wacky world it was as big an accomplishment as a vertigo sufferer hauling himself three quarters of the way up Mount Everest. I was quite rightly feeling proud of myself as I headed down strange streets. Yes, me, the travel phobic hypochondriac, taking the lead and making decisions which only a few weeks ago seemed like impossible fantasy. But I was glad Rhys was here now. It would be rewarding to share this experience with a sidekick – he would be the Robin to my Batman – and I convinced myself this was company well earned. Rhys was itching to release the brakes, hit the road and clock up some virgin kilometres. But the weather was deteriorating badly and I was forced to put on the baby restrainers of collaring a hostel for his first night on tour. Rhys in his usual laid-back style was happy to play ball: 'It's your trip, mate. I'm just glad to be here. Whatever you say.'

Bremerhaven had new town stamped all over it after losing most of its buildings in war time bombing blasts. Most of the Weser harbour had been spared by the Allies, wanting to utilise this landing point once the fighting had ceased. And that strategic decision has helped the city thrive as a bustling centre of sea trade, shipping more than 3.5 million containers every year and exporting 1.4 million cars. But one thing they certainly didn't get the hang of was architecture. I could have been tripping on recycled memories of home, brought on by Rhys' arrival, after parking up in the shopping square. It was a carbon-copy of Basildon High Street. But I wasn't hallucinating. Some other visionary had got away with pushing such an uninspiring mish-mash of concrete slabs, token water features and rubbish shops through the planning process. Add a giant cemetery of dull faded stone apartment blocks around the perimeter (there wasn't a house in sight) and you've just nudged Milton Keynes a step closer to residential paradise. Well at least they've got concrete cows.

One thing Bremerhaven High Street did have however was a camping shop which didn't sell tents or sleeping bags. But you could purchase a bullet-proof jacket with COMBAT printed on the front in huge white letters, meaty jagged knives which would make Crocodile Dundee wince and a selection of BB guns. I was tempted to get kitted up for the next roadside dog attack. I'd show those pesky mutts who was boss.

After being identified as English we were ordered to produce all of 'our papers' by the elderly cardigan-wearing hostel receptionist, whose previous job was bellboy at Colditz. Placing a loving arm around Rhys and demanding a 'room for two' probably didn't help. He obviously thought we were gay and, looking at my nose, probably Jewish into the bargain. Ejecting our baggage we finally escaped the white pimply corridors and security buzzer partition doors of the hostel, which had all the ambience and decorative charm of a prison wing.

Free at last, we whizzed through the streets on packless bikes like the BMX Bandits. It was Friday night in Bremerhaven and time to seal our unification deal with a few beverages. The contract of comradeship was drunk in a peculiar bar opposite a fishermen flanked statue of the city's 17th-century political founder Johann Smidt. Three-pronged street lamps sprouted out of tables and cardboard pop-up figures screamed at the open windows of paper houses burning bright orange across the back wall. It could have been the film model of Rainbow's opening titles, except 'up above the streets and houses bombs were dropping from on high'. Boney M were playing in the background and a limp string puppet of Adolf Hitler wearing Bavarian green lederhosen hung above the beer pump. With his Nazi saluting hand forced down by his side the tyrant was about as menacing as John Inman.

The pub was run by a middle-aged couple who must have cashed in their pensions early and got out of the porn trade. The talkative artist formerly known as Candy had a cheeky expression and wore sunglasses on top of thick black hair which fell down above a finely shaped posterior. She was in good nick for her age, which was more than could be said for playmate Dirk, who possibly poured the slowest and headiest beer in northern Europe. He never said a word all night. Leaning with one arm against the bar, with legs crossed at the bottom, he was failing miserably in an attempt to come over all mean and moody. It had something to do with the black Primark suit jacket and trousers, Bundesliga mullet and gingery brown stubble. 'He likes the blues,' whispered Candy. You don't say!

It was getting on for 10pm and there were only a handful of punters in the Twin Peaks saloon, mostly just staring into space as if on some sort of medication. Rhys randomly started moaning about a scab on his hand, which attracted the gaze of a Lurch like individual on the next stool, supping a misty brown liquid in a large laboratory test tube glass. He watched Rhys picking away without once batting an eyelid, before cranking his neck round with a jerk to meet my stare and uttered: 'Life is so strange.' With a crazed roll of the eyes and maniacal smile he turned back the other way in creepy slow motion. Rhys didn't know whether to laugh or make a lightning bolt out of the bar, while Candy was making small talk about Bremerhaven's booming Fish Finger empire. We didn't want to overstay our welcome.

15   Happy Town Beach Club

Rhys was chomping at the bit. He'd got up at the crack of dawn, raided the hostel's breakfast buffet and filled up extra cheese and salami rolls for lunchtime. Good work my young Padawan. The day's itinerary was to continue north to Cuxhaven, hop over the congested River Elbe shipping lane to Brunsbüttel and close the gap on the Danish border. We could have hugged the North Sea Cycle Route along the Elbe all the way inland to Hamburg, Germany's principal port and second largest city, before crossing a bridge somewhere and following the other side of the bank to Brunsbüttel. But catching the Cuxhaven ferry was a 230 kilometre short-cut, so it was agreed to skip the bright lights of Hamburg in favour of following the natural shoreline curvature of the North Sea. After all, it wasn't the River Elbe Cycle Route. We wanted to plunge headlong back into random, obscure adventures by the seaside. Hamburg could keep its lavish theatres, historic museums and wonderful architecture. We'd even sacrifice the prostitutes and sex shows of the *Reeperbahn*, every sailor, cyclist and male tourist's favourite haunt.

The Bremerhaven exit door was blocked by a man dishing out flyers on his Saturday morning to earn extra beer money. Respecting anyone who puts so much dedication into drinking, I took one of the glossy leaflets for all it was worth. I couldn't even tell you what was on it. Flyer bloke was under the impression that most of England lived in or around Sherwood Forest and was hoping to make a pilgrimage very soon. I warned him to watch out for arrows. Gliding past the rockery style zoo, the port was a hive of activity as dock working drones carried out their duties. Metal tracks spiralled off in all areas to double-decker car carriers, shipping cargo containers and a long line of banana trains, with the peeling yellow paint of ripe bunches branding every carriage. Spanking new cars, caravans, tractors, diggers, speedboats and lifeboats waited for boarding passes which would whisk them off to the far flung corners of the earth. Shrinking in size with every spin of the pedal, the gleaming washed down gargantuan hulls of long distance freighters sat parked up, exposed in the shallower waters. These superboats had sailed in from all over the globe, China, India and Japan, but the most impressive specimen was getting the full beauty makeover treatment in dry dock.

The *Al Salamah* was a multi million pound mega yacht, which had more in common with an ocean liner. This sparkling white catwalk model of the seas had eight decks, 82 rooms, 8,000 square metres of living space, a crew of 96 and a helicopter pad thrown in. It belonged to Prince Sultan bin Abdul Aziz, the Saudi Arabian defence minister and son of the late King Fahd. Who needs an arsenal of nuclear weapons anyway? Spunk it all on a big boat and sail the seven seas on a non stop partython. He would get my vote!

Rhys was like an excited puppy chasing a well chewed ball. He was pumping those spindly legs hard, desperate to christen his start to the expedition in style. The shirt was already off, stuffed down the front of surfing boardies, in a desperate bid to attract some colour to his snow white chest and back from the midday sunshine. Ten years my younger, he shouted out: 'Keep up, old man.' Bloody cheek. Rhys' puny bike packs were a third of the size of mine and his legs were being powered by raw adrenalin. This was my 12th day on the road and I knew only too well this was a marathon not a sprint. Keep goading, keep pedalling ahead of me. Cycle for your life, matey. Let's see how far you can get during the course of the whole day, not a 30 minute stint. I'm going to break you into Ivan Drago style pieces, my apprentice. Rest assured the last laugh will belong to the master!

The sea was still hidden by an enormous grassy bank, which doubled up as a mountain range for the inhabitants of tiny Hobbit houses outside Cappel-Neufeld. Holiday homes for dwarves, the orange-tiled roofs were only two foot off the ground and had cute dinky chimneys. Cappel-Neufeld was a remote elevated outpost with a scattering of burger bars and beach chair boxes, brightened up with starfish and coral interiors. We'd missed the sea ascending the hill, the tide was out, and were greeted instead by a dour dark gothic lighthouse. But there was plenty going on. Kids were pelting across the empty roads in windsurfing buggies and a suited and booted wedding crowd were gathering on another green embankment. Rhys wanted to check out the bride and gatecrash the ceremony, but we pushed on.

The word England sinking under a ferry, with a thick red line crossing its road sign bows, was a bad omen. Cuxhaven sits at the mouth of the River Elbe, one of the busiest freight highways in Europe. More than 1,000 kilometres in length, cargo vessels nip out of the North Sea and head along the river to Hamburg and as far inland as Prague in the Czech Republic. But our ship wasn't sailing and I didn't fancy our chances of thumbing a lift with the traffic. Even Rhys dangling out one of those girly thin legs by the harbour was unlikely to catch the eye of a sexually starved sea dog.

Circling around the docks, finally asking for advice at a warehouse converted pet shop, we were informed ailing ferry crossings to England had been put out of their misery last year. On the positive front there was still a boat to Brunsbüttel. The bad news was it started on May 1 and we were nine days too early. But it's good to talk and a little bit of local knowledge unearthed another ferry crossing over the Elbe at Wischhafen. Kevin the Gerbil promised it was only 25 kilometres away, give or take another 30 clicks. Waving cheerio and buying a cuttlefish for politeness, the brooding green witch's hat water tower stared down as we beat a line along our new path through the docks. The rising hot air stank of fish food crumbles, or did Rhys just need a good hosing down? There were ginger rusting propellers and anchors abandoned everywhere, with many of the warehouses forced to adapt and survive by upgrading into restaurants serving fresh sea dinners.

One of the most stunning parts of the route awaited. A freshly drenched path teetered along the wide expanse of the Elbe, which slapped against a seaweed and barnacle covered rotting wooden fence. Carefree sheep roamed around marshy knolls, brushed by the moving shadows of turning wind farm blades. Tangled netting, rope and plastic fish boxes littered the floor and the spray of the river leaped across our spokes. Two young girls scooped a red bucket through shallow rock pools searching for tidal treasure. And a husband and wife took cycling in tandem, on two separate bikes, up another gear. The poor old git was sweating his bollocks off in the sunshine, towing the old bag along as she slumped, pedals motionless, down on her own handlebars, which had a piece of rope tied to them.

The most awesome sight was the hulking river traffic. Broad shouldered, long freighters, stacked to the max with different coloured rectangle cargo containers, gliding so close to the shoreline you could almost reach out and touch them. They may have been the ogres of the sea, a multi million dollars away from the *Al Salamah* playboy vessel, but they sailed down the Elbe with extreme grace. Despite cutting large creases into the surface water either side of a weighted down hull, these ships hardly made a sound. Imagine a mute elephant performing ballet in cotton wool booties and you'll get the picture.

The quest for Wischhafen took us away from the Elbe and back into the rich agricultural lands prospering by its banks. Delicate pink and white apple blossoms coloured the branches of orchards on both sides of our handlebars. It was a tranquil setting, making for a relaxing ride as the late afternoon sunshine warmed our backs nicely. The lethargic backdrop was momentarily disturbed by the strained mooing of a death row cow in one of the slaughterhouses. There were also Rhys' intermittent groans about the monotonous mirage teased road in front of us, which had followed a boring straight line for what seemed an eternity. But we weren't the only ones looking for hope on the never-ending highway. Alerted by a clunk of pedals, a teenage boy peered out from the gloomy interior of a wooden hut bus stop. He could well have been there for donkey's years, abandoned as a blanket wrapped baby to grow up as a child of the shelter. There had been no sign of a bus over the past couple of hours, we hadn't seen so much as a squirrel or rabid dog, and as bus stop boy shrunk into the distance I wondered whether I should have attempted a saddler back to civilisation. Maybe he's still there right now, just watching and waiting patiently, hoping to purchase a Day Rover and end his exile.

My upbeat travelling companion was still moaning, questioning whether the mystical Wischhafen ferry crossing existed outside the litter tray and goldfish fuddled brain of a distance miscalculating pet shop owner. Kevin the Gerbil wouldn't have liked it here that's for sure. Posters of giant white rats auditioning for a part in Germany's remake of *The Goodies* hung off lamp posts in the villages of Horne and Frieburg. Equally large tailed eels, drawings this time, were splashed across wooden signs hammered into front gardens. We decided not to stop for coffee.

The Wischhafen ferry point finally materialised down a scrubby side road at 9pm. Greeted by a welcoming parade of waiting cars, motorbikes and a trailer light truck, dusk set in and a chill gripped the air, calling for waterproof trousers to be hoisted over shorts. Rhys had collapsed in a broken heap next to his bike. We'd clocked up 100 kilometres, a harsh baptism of fire for my novice sidekick, whose earlier tauntings and excited racing ahead were long forgotten. Old man eh? I wasn't the one looking pale, gaunt and clammy, desperately draining the last vestiges of recycled wash back from the bottom of a plastic water bottle. No, I still felt just fine and dandy. That was, apart from losing the feeling in both little fingers, because holding the handle grips for hours on end in one position was slowing the blood flow. But I could deal with that and decided to celebrate by snuggling up with my latest *Shag*. Mind games had tempted me to give our on and off relationship another go. It meant breaking another health pact with the Lord, but there was no bolt of lightning, so maybe he'd let me off, AGAIN. This concoction of woody tobacco came in the same slender, blue packaging as my old *Shag*, but had changed sex to Nelson. It certainly had a more pungent flavour, but in Rhys' current demolished state, smoked as sweetly as a victory cigar. It was a definite Hamlet moment.

Darkness clung to the fragile crate of a craft as it hobbled slowly towards the orange lights hovering above the cloaked town of Glückstadt. It was nippy on the square shaped open deck, which was heaving under an impressive weight of vehicles. There must have been 16 cars cramped in for the 30 minute ride, sniffing each other's bumpers, with a naked goods truck cab squeezed in at the front. No wonder this box felt lopsided as its loud engines strained to reach the other bank in one piece. The lorry must have been too heavy, surely breaking some sort of nautical balancing act rules by just being shoved on the end of the boat, on the right hand side. I'm sure the German crew thought: 'It's OK. If we stick the truck in the corner nobody will notice. I'm sure we'll get away with it.' All I knew was that my body was leaning downstream to Hamburg, not standing straight with a cool breeze flicking past both ears in readiness to embrace Glückstadt. Visibility was zero in a 360 degree arc as blackness pushed against the ferry. If this thing sunk the journey was over – for everyone.

Rhys limped down stairs to find a food and water pump for his fuel drained frame. Figuring drowning would be quicker at the bottom of the boat, unless I was really unlucky and it flipped right over, I followed suit. But there was no feeding frenzy to be found in the bowels of the ferry as the bar shutters were firmly locked down. Rhys was now getting feverish, even mumbling to himself, as he slumped on to a wall-bolted couchette. He convinced himself the catering boys would be opening up shop soon, as Holmesesque powers of deduction (and finger tips) located peanuts and discarded drinking straws in the table ashtrays. 'Someone's been eating and drinking here, so where's mine?' he grumbled.

A gorilla of a ticket inspector scraped his knuckles across the floor as he searched relentlessly for fare evaders. Memory monkey checked our tickets, which he had sold us 10 minutes earlier, before interrogating the chain smoking family. Dad, mum, granny and daughter, aged at the most 14, were all puffing away merrily on long cigarettes. I couldn't believe this little girl's parents were encouraging their daughter to poison her body without so much as batting an eyelid. Wearing a baseball cap and matching pink towling tracksuit top and bottoms, she was for all the world a very young girl, far too immature to realise the potential risk of her actions. She should have been chewing a Curly-Wurly. But her red-faced, smoke haggard guardians were waving the snouts around as if they were sweets. It seemed so irresponsible, but was something which became more and more the norm in Germany. Smoking was up there with PlayStation games, Harry Potter and bonking with the impressionable teenage Deutschlanders.

The ferry docked with a shudder just after 10pm, spitting us out shattered, cold and starving, with no sleeping reservation, on a concrete platform. The final car brake light winked goodbye, a red speck swallowed up by the hungry all consuming black abyss ahead. This really was the arsehole end of nowhere. Tired pupils started adjusting to the gloom and then we spotted it. There was a square shimmer of yellow and faint music filtered downwind. Dragging worn out wheels, legs and lungs closer, the sound grew clearer as recognisable words teamed up with an audible tune.

I couldn't believe my ears. The song was 'Don't pay the Ferryman' and was emitting from an old Portakabin struggling to illuminate this deathly quiet corner of the Elbe's murky banks. Pretty sure we hadn't stumbled across Chris De Burgh performing an intimate secret gig for burly ticket inspectors, we stared up at the sign of a ship leaving a desert island above the door. We had stumbled across The Happy Town Beach Club, a rickety shack of an oasis surrounded by a wasteland of blinding blackness, but promising warmth, food and hot coffee by the smell of things.

It was a right Aladdin's cave inside and so claustrophobic it could have been used for submarine training. Every spare millimetre of space had been utilised. Stacks of red and green plastic beer and fizzy drinks crates were lined up against the wall at face height, under shelves supporting model trawlers, fishermen and pipes, plus a seven inch set of the Kaiser (with full beard) and his chiefs. It was probably some sort of breakfast cereal collect and keep giveaway. Two long wall sofas were shoe-horned under a table and there were more big bottles of alcohol stuffed under the saddle. A handful of locals had beaten us to the sanctuary of the bar, where the slight owner, a dead ringer for Ian Rush, was taking orders while poking a pan full of watery frankfurters with a fork, in a space too small to swing a stickleback.

Rhys returned to the table with the most sickly hot dogs ever to slide down into my usually unfussy gullet. Covered in dried onions and some sort of congealed sweet pickle, mayo and mustard hybrid, with a few slices of gherkin for good measure, the rolls were falling to pieces on the plate ahead of contact with human hands. They were disgusting. Rhys only managed one before turning visibly green, but I destroyed both with the help of three cups of coffee. Trying to keep the nauseating feeling at the pit of my stomach, I scanned the array of psychedelic artwork adorning the walls. The stuff of 70s rock album covers, these visions of the sea were definitely aided by some sort of illegal substance and brushed by a user definitely coming down on the side of nature. Giant serpents coiled their bodies around wooden ship masts and attacked the terrified crewmen on deck, while big blue whales got their own back on harpoon carrying hunters by swallowing splintered ships in one large gulp. More disturbing was a smiling tuna returning from a shopping trip with a tin under his fin. I'm sure it said 'human chunks in tap water' on the side, but

I could have been hallucinating on all those E additives in the hot dog sauce mix.

White stars pulsed overhead in the clear night sky and there was a feeling of magic in the air. Forget being tired, ready to vomit and desperate to get some kip in, there was something special about the glow of the moon leading our bike lights to cut a path through the black blanket around us. Here we were, getting on for midnight, pedalling through the middle of nowhere, not knowing where we were or exactly where we were going to stay. Glückstadt didn't have camping facilities, so it was a 15 kilometre ride to the next best thing at Kollmar. The weariness began to drain away as we relished the excitement of our first night ride. Being sensible and sticking to the cycle paths, I nearly nosedived into a roadside ditch when the full beam of an approaching car completely blurted out my vision and any hope of keeping a straight line. Rhys found it hysterical of course, but almost found his own boggy hole soon after.

Then, leaving the main road, it was down a field crossing alley and along deserted village roads. There wasn't a sound to be heard apart from the cranking of pedals, turning of wheels and the occasional ruffling of leaves on the gentle evening breeze. Hogging the tarmac all to ourselves, we ruled the roads and had huge grins on our faces. Finding a second wind, we even contemplated popping into a party going on late at a farmhouse. There were at least 20 bikes parked outside and I'm sure we would be welcome. I hope they weren't drinking and cycling.

Picking up the signs as we zoomed under a bridge, past sparse houses barely revealed by garden lamps hidden behind tree guarded drives, we rolled quietly into the campsite. The bewitching hour was well upon us and the other guests were long tucked up in bed. Without a soul to be seen or heard, we quickly built tents, without torches, under the watchful stare of the wise old moon and a bright playground of stars. Sucking on a nightcap chocolate chunk, I snuggled into the sleeping bag with a huge beam spreading across both cheeks. What a day. Another 120 kilometre slog, but I'd got through it and, more importantly, so had Rhys. I was getting used to this adventure lark and actually really enjoying it. Relishing the challenge each new day would bring was a far cry from the Essex boy petrified to leave the safety of his county's borders less than two weeks ago. It was the little things which had changed me. The natural stuff, which comes free of charge, like the hushed tones of sheep staying up late in the next field singing me a bleated lullaby. The North Sea Cycle Route had cast me under its spell.

16 North Sea Wife

Struggling to squeeze through Glückstadt's narrow quayside market was like wading through thick human porridge. Hundreds of legs dragged slowly along the cobbled conveyor belt of drainpipe jeans, luminous tracksuit tops, ancient video games, Samurai swords, fresh vegetables and sausages of all shapes and sizes. Bargain hunters embraced the Sunday morning sunshine hoping to pick up a Bobby Dazzler from the vociferous traders luring their prey towards cheaply labelled wares by the water's edge. The collective swarm of stuffed carrier bags probably contained more bodies than I had seen on the whole trip so far, which was killing any hopes of making a quick getaway. Attempting to steer two overloaded bikes through the crowd without knee-capping innocent casualties was proving near impossible. A paraplegic tortoise would have made quicker progress. But no matter how many leg and thigh obstacles got bashed by pannier bags, we didn't attract one dirty stare or unintelligible insult. No wonder Glückstadt means 'Happy Town' in German.

Getting nowhere fast, we took a break from battling against the tide of limbs, hemming ourselves in against a fresh fish stall. Using our bodies as cycle racks, one hand was now free to drain the ritualistic morning cup of sweet, mud coloured coffee, while taking care of a chunky pickled herring roll with the other. Fish for breakfast failed to improve a bad case of stagnant early morning breath, but made a pleasant change from rolls, cheese and ham. It took another half-an-hour to escape the throng of the market and pick up the cycle route, following the sheep dotted banks of the Elbe. Our late night ferry ride had delivered us into Schleswig-Holstein, the most northerly state in Germany. The trail now flowed west along the opposite bank of the river, before arrowing straight up to Denmark. It was certainly a picturesque and popular path. Husbands and wives wheeled their way along the copse bordered tarmac (they didn't go for towing on this side of the river), while an inquisitive toddler on a parental guided stroll found himself bottom down on the turf after losing balance trying to grasp a hand full of moving wool.

'Fucking morons,' cursed Rhys.

'That's a bit strong, mate,' I replied, wondering just what could have possibly inspired such an angry outburst.

'Straight ahead. Look at the floor. Watch out!'

Slamming on the anchors, Erika's front tyre came within a whisker of puckering up to a carpet of broken glass expertly laid by German lager louts. Rhys was stressing about the unprotected feet of the sheep, who were fortunately street wise and sticking to the safety of the soft grass. I, however, was more worried about my companion. Back on home soil, Rhys was a prolific puncture magnet. He could get deflated cycling through blancmange and didn't have the luxury of ringing mummy for motorised back-up right now. But practice supposedly makes perfect and Rhys assured me he had the puncture repair speed of a Formula One pit-stop grease monkey these days. I didn't want to put his skills to the test and suggested a short bone-shaker over the grazing lands instead.

Sturdy green roofed farmhouses peered out from adjacent fields. They were vastly superior to the ramshackle, depressing abodes of struggling agricultural workers between Weener and Ditzum witnessed earlier on my travels. Those poor buggers always seemed to be hunting two potatoes to rub together, but the farmers here were saved by sparklers from an old German colony on the other side of the globe. Namibian diamond miners had invested their African treasure in finishing these homes when the farmers' dosh had run out, literally keeping a roof above their former masters' heads.

They loved a thatch in these parts. There was hardly a roof slate to be seen and it wasn't just the houses and cottages staring down at the Elbe which benefited from a securely weaved straw syrup, but garden umbrellas and conservatories too. The weather was kind again and this really was turning into an agreeable stretch of the route. Our legs felt full of power, despite the overnight operation to Kollmar, and the added bonus of natural eye candy definitely distracted the mind enough to lighten the load. Tall trees blocking a clear view of the Elbe fell away to uncover flat sandbanks and a cargo container chaperone, whose giant frame was put into scale by two speck like single sail boats sliding past its brawny starboard shoulder.

But there was one blot on the landscape. A huge oval white egg of a power station pierced the horizon and grew increasingly unattractive as its nuclear boiled shell drew closer. High metal fences and barbed wire clung to the ugly carbuncle, surrounded by a brooding moat which probably contained man eating alligators and radioactive eels. We got the hint, they didn't want unexpected guests dropping in for tea.

Brunsbüttel was a mirror reflection of Cuxhaven, a small port resting close to the North Sea, but a far more valuable co-ordinate on the captain's chart than its cousin across the Elbe. The importance of the town stemmed from its role as gateway to a cheeky shortcut between the North and Baltic Seas – the Kiel Canal. This man-made construction is the world's busiest artificial waterway and not only acts as a time saver, but allows boats to avoid tackling the alternative route of the hazardous storm prone seas which rage around Denmark's Jutland peninsula. At just 98 kilometres in length the Kiel Canal stretches between Brunsbüttel and Kiel-Holtenau, cutting a route straight through the middle of Schleswig-Holstein. The canal can swallow vessels as big as warships whole, chopping 280 nautical miles (519 kilometres) off their journey. It took 9,000 workers eight years to build and officially opened on June 21, 1895. And guess who took the credit? Another celebrity hungry Kaiser, but this time mark two. Not content with stealing everybody's thunder laying the final stone, old royal weirdy beardy continued the family obsession by originally naming the canal after himself.

The white-knuckle Brunsbüttel ferry ride was not for the faint hearted. Transporting foot passengers and cars across the bustling water course, width ways, it was like playing Kiel Canal chicken. The crazed controller seemed to be enjoying himself though and ploughed straight through the centre of the traffic, while a fleet of enormous ships headed towards us on a crash course from both directions. It only took 10 minutes to reach the other side, but the best was saved until last with the delicate vessel ramming the opposite bank with a violent jolt forward.

Having unfurled ourselves from crash-safety impact body balls it was time to turn inland on a northern route along silent country roads following reed strangled rivers. The attractive backdrop of Meldorf spun around a web of quaint buildings, circling a white oval church which sat at the raised centre of town like a patiently waiting spider. Not wanting to get stuck, a maze of brick streets slid away into a yellow rapeseed canvas, framed by a North Sea border. It felt good to have ditched the Elbe after a two-day flirtation, returning to the arms of my true cycling mistress, who was still playing the big tease. A familiar hardened green hump of sea fortification put the block on satisfying my craving to gaze straight into the blue complexion of her face again.

A proper reunion was just around the corner at Büsum, a seaside hot-spot for day-trippers, resting its pretty chin right on the coast. Originally an island, a dam built in 1585 allowed this sun-trap to stretch its neck out to the mainland. A popular spa town since 1818, tens of thousands of visitors flock here every summer seeking relaxation and revitalisation from the surrounding saltwater and mudflats.

Büsum has always provided sanctuary for people trying to escape the stress and rigours of their jobs. Notorious pirate Cord Widderich decided to settle down in the town, making the backwards career jump from scourge of the seas to Mr Normal as a trader in 1412, which must have been a boring transition. Widderich and his gang of booty hunters had previously hoisted the Jolly Roger above the church tower of the North Frisian Island of Pellworm, looting the surrounding villages and tricking passing ships into wrecking on the rocks. God obviously took a dim view of his holy house being abused by a gallery of rouges and dished out a stormy retribution, which threatened to topple the church to the ground. Widderich heeded this most heinous warning and retreated to Büsum, prising away the bronze baptismal font for a keepsake. The wily old sea snake won over the understandably cautious locals by giving up the 13th-century font as a consecration gift to Büsum's newly built Saint Clemens church, where it can still be seen today, and they all lived happily ever after. We soon discovered this hospitality was extended to out-of-town cyclists too, as Büsum gave up its biggest secret – the North Sea Wife.

Christina found us. The slightly built, impish faced girl with light brown curly hair tied back above her shoulders was serving late night ice creams in a parlour on the car-free main street. It also sold cold spaghetti bolognese in a cone, but couldn't whip me up a lasagne 99 with a flake. They obviously had a thing for Italian food in these parts. We hoovered up a tomato and mozzarella cheese covered plate of fish and fries in Dyson fashion at a nearby restaurant, which Rhys admitted hadn't even touched the sides after another 90 kilometres at the handlebars.

'I didn't even taste that,' said my famished colleague as he rolled his ladle of a tongue around a plate tipped at a tactical angle. 'My muscles and brain have just soaked up every single nutrient from that food. It never had a chance of hitting my stomach.' So we took advantage of three huge dollops of cheaply priced ice cream to even things up. Standing there with strawberry, chocolate and bubblegum flavoured goo, topped off with whipped cream, covering our slavering jaws, Christina was drawn in by a tractor beam of male attractiveness.

'I notice you. You are maybe from London. Why you come Büsum?' giggled the inquisitive ice cream vendor in broken English. Chin mopping with the back of the hand, I slowly attempted to explain about the North Sea Cycle Route and raising money for charity. Her English was patchy (but still far superior to my German) and I'm not sure how much she understood, but a big smile and repeated nods of the head seemed to confirm she had the general gist of things.

'Maybe we go and drink a beer and try to speak more?' she replied. 'There is bar. Jolly Joker. Meet me soon.' And with that she jumped on her bike and pedalled off into the fading daylight towards the red and white lighthouse and beach at the end of the parade. We were both gobsmacked. 'That was odd,' I said.

'Yeah. But how friendly was she? What a good girl!' Rhys chipped in.

'The snotty birds at home would never come up to a couple of strangers in the street and just talk to them like that.'

'That is so different from England, mate. Talk about refreshing. Do you want to go and meet her for a drink or six?'

'Why not. It's only 9.30pm and I don't fancy the tent just yet. She probably won't show anyway. Let's go and sink a couple.'

Nobody was laughing at the Jolly Joker. It was dead and Christina was nowhere to be seen. Rhys shouted up a couple of beers and dealt out the bar mats before spilling out his heart. 'I'm so pleased to be here,' he confided. 'I've been stuck in a rut at home and being here with you is making me feel so much better. Even after just a couple of days. Thanks for letting me come.'

Rhys had become a loner, stubbornly unwilling to break free from the confines of his High Street flat's prison bars. Degenerating into a reclusive misery guts, he preferred to shut himself away and smoke his way through life. What a dope! I first noticed his problems taking shape on a mutual friend's stag party a few years ago. Rhys refused to leave the London hotel all weekend while we went out on the lash mob handed. But that was one of his better days. You couldn't prise Rhys out of his own front door now and most people had given up trying. I was probably guilty of throwing in the towel, despite having enough of my own shit to deal with. It was such a waste, as Rhys was one of the most laid-back and nicest fellas you could wish to meet. I hadn't seen him for months before linking up out here. He'd even stopped bringing the Thermos to football on a Sunday morning. The guy was on a downward spiral. We made a great pair – the hypochondriac and the hermit.

As we sat there wondering whether Christina would show, Rhys admitted he had been suffering from depression. You don't say! Numerous surgery summits at the doctors had failed to shift the problem and he knew his love affair with the green wasn't helping matters. But he'd knocked the puff on the head and was determined to tap into some mobile medicine by cycling his way to a remedy for his own brand of madness. It was doing the trick for me and as I got into first gear about my own closely guarded secrets, laughter punctured the background silence and Christina burst through the doors squeaking to the barman.

Blagging a free beer, the mystery girl wiggled a finger and indicated she wanted us to follow upstairs. The top floor was an empty nightclub, complete with tacky rotating disco ball, but Christina didn't have dancing in mind. 'You like to play?' she asked, pointing towards the table football game standing lonely in the middle of a back room. Mentally, I rubbed my hands in glee, thinking this would be easy. How wrong can you be? Continuing an English tradition of coming second best to the Germans on the football pitch, apart from a linesman assisted victory of some importance in 1966, she beat us both. It wasn't so much of a thrashing, more of a massacre, heightened by her cocky offer to take us both on at the same time. We'd get revenge for sure. Rhys and I had all four rotating handles on the table covered. I had the goalkeeper and line of plastic defenders, he took control of midfield and attack. It was simple. I'd keep her out and he'd smash them in. But these things never go to plan and it was more like Torquay United taking on Real Madrid. Christina commanded the quartet of controls in devastating fashion, with a combination of neat footwork and superiorly dainty dexterous hands serving up the biggest humiliation of the lot.

This whole episode was so surreal. Standing in a closed nightclub, getting hammered at table football and drinking beer like old friends with a random girl who we had met just an hour ago and only spoke pigeon English. After finally scoring a solo victory at the sixth attempt (she must have played the reserves for sympathy), the forever smiling Christina asked: 'Where do you sleep? You must come to my apartment.'

'Are you sure? You don't know us very well,' I replied.

'It is OK. You nice men, I know this. You come and sleep. You can eat, drink and watch English news. I have CNN.' I didn't have the heart to tell her it was an American channel.

The communal cycle shed was packed full of bikes. Murder again came to mind. Could these be the lost relics of the sweet and innocent appearing Büsum banshee's past victims? Christina led us through a security door and up to her second floor flat in a modern apartment block. I couldn't believe this was happening and was still pinching myself walking through the door. Just how could this girl take the massive risk of inviting two complete strangers, who she could barely communicate with, back to her home? The risks were so high. We could have been a tag-team of wrong-uns, with less than honourable intentions, plotting to force ourselves on our new found host, with or without her consent.

As Christina emptied the entire contents of her fridge on to a coffee table, I just couldn't get my head around how trusting she was. This was a whole new mindset to me. I'd never met anybody quite like her before. At home these actions would be dismissed as naïve. It would have been 'her fault' if something had gone wrong. But out here, in another alien town by the sea, it was a miracle of human kindness. She really couldn't do enough for us. Me and Rhys just stared at each other in amazement as she started singing to herself, merrily slapping butter on bread and filling sandwiches, before sloshing about beakers full of fizzy orange pop. Convinced we were fully fed and watered, Christina leapt across the room to examine a small CD collection. Her favourite bands were all German, the Beat Steaks and Weft, who sounded like American guitar rock wannabes, were given a whirl. Another group was Diesterne, dooplegangers with Inspiral Carpets bobbed fringes who ripped off everything from early Pink Floyd to plagiarising The Animals' version of House of the Rising Sun. Pretty much just howling over the original riffs.

We'd already erected tents among the mini canyons of Camp Mole Hill, slap bang next to the sea wall, making the alternative of topping-and-tailing on a sofa bed next to Rhys' mature odour eaters a luxurious proposal. But our hostess with the mostess had that base covered too, returning to the living room with a bowl of scented oils and massaging Rhys' smelly, hard-skinned soles. Unashamed groans of multiple pleasure followed as Christina prodded, pushed and rubbed with her fingers and hands. I think Rhys was getting into it too.

I couldn't believe this. I was going to wake up in a minute, rolling over in my sleeping bag to scrum a hard clump of earth poking through the tent floor. But this was reality. An angel had flown down to care for our every whim. Christina wanted to be our slave for the night, which was a little bit embarrassing because I didn't want to take the piss, but she was relishing every moment. What she couldn't spit out in English, Christina attempted to explain through laughter, theatrical arm waving and facial expressions, always lit by that beautiful big smile. She was just happy to have us for company and plug the gap of what I guessed must have been a sometimes lonely existence.

Christina was only 25 and her parents lived in town, but all her school chums had ditched Büsum in search of high paid jobs under the bright lights. Our guardian was left behind and didn't seem to have been anywhere else, content to serve up ice cream, listen to crap bands and eat salami in her ivory tower. Her nan lived in France and she had an aunt in Mexico, but didn't like boats or planes. The furthest Christina had spread her wings was the grubby Danish port of Esbjerg, which was only a couple of hundred kilometres away. But she hated abandoning Büsum and its sunshine, which she punctuated with a circling of her hands and a sad down-turned lip. So to recap, Christina didn't like travelling or leaving home. No wonder the three of us stumbled across each other. This strange little girl could have been a long lost sister.

'Why did you go to the beach after work?' I asked.

'To offer pray to the spirits of the sea. This I do on all night times. It is very important to me.'

'So you say prayers to the North Sea God. That must make you the North Sea Wife.

'Yes, I like. I am your North Sea Wife for tonight. I look after you. You are my new friends.'

The most special thing about this touching chance encounter was a complete lack of sexual agenda. Neither of us were planning to crack on with Christina. It was a forging of instant friendships and mutual benefits, which made me feel all warm and girly inside, as well as restoring some faith in the humanity of an increasingly unfriendly world. But, as always, there was a sting in the tail. And this time it came with a lingering ouch! Christina shoved a yellow leaflet in my hand. A picture of a well groomed, dark haired young man and a crucifix sat above a wad of German print. Not getting it at first, I thought this confirmed my hunch that Christina was part of some fanatical bible-bashing circle. Only religious nutters would pity a couple of scallywags such as Mr Chisam and myself by scooping us off the street. And then I twigged. Oh no! It was a funeral notice and a picture of Christina's boyfriend Nathaneal. She told me he died three years ago from a 'broken' heart. He was only 23 and they were very much in love when what must have been an undetected major organ defect turned into a fatal attack. It obviously still hurt Christina, but that infectious smile never wavered as she struggled to find the right words to explain.

'Now you see why I make pray,' said Christina, pushing the flats of her hands together. 'To speak to Nathaneal, for protection from the sea spirits and for beautiful Büsum sunshine. Our meeting was not chance. The North Sea God brought you to me so I could look after you and have company. I will now pray they protect you on your journey. Come see.'

Christina grabbed my hand and led me to the bathroom. Flabbergasted eyes nearly popped out of my head on stalks. The back wall of the room was a shrine to the 'North Sea God', who was a woman, which will please that irritating mike for a mouth bore of a lesbian in the Scissor Sisters. Blue netting cradling shells and starfish draped from one corner of the room to the other, like a flowing cape hanging from the shapely shoulders of the painted wooden figurine nailed to its centre. She was a Goddess in every sense of the word, a stunning olive skinned brunette with deep red pouting lips and a set of heavenly curving breasts. Blue seaweed clung around the exposed bosom, above a tight velvet skirt and large pink shrimp buckle covering up her lady bits. Feelings of puberty left long undisturbed began to stir. It was like the first time I realised it was Betty I wanted to Bedrock more than Wilma from the *Flintstones* given half-a-chance. I know, I know. Once you get more worldly wise you realise Fred's red head is more of a filthy dirt bag and you don't give sweet and innocent Betty a second glance. How I ever made the schoolboy error of overlooking Wilma's slutty torn dress still haunts me now.

Snapping out of my fetish for wooden women and cartoon characters it was time to get closely acquainted with Rhys' newly perfumed toes and ankles. Sinking deeper into a fluffy cushion, hypnotised by the dreamy whispers of Jim Morrison's stereo poetry, the opium scented vapour of joss sticks forced my heavy eyelids towards surrender. The North Sea Wife blew out the candles, flickering on stands around the room, and in a hushed voice as soft as silk wished 'sweetest dreams' upon us. I didn't even make a count of ten.

17 Birds and Snails

Sliding up and down the smoothly arched concrete back of a soaring sea wall with barely a care in the world. What a turnaround! My head felt straight. There were no palpitations or panic, no heart rate finger tests and the dizzy spells had been ditched hundreds of kilometres away. It finally felt like I was breaking free, switching my attention away from worrying about the unknown and embracing the adventure of the unexpected. The physical and mental demands of hauling my carcass further up northern Europe didn't afford the luxury of dwelling on any weaknesses. Mind and body were totally focused on completing energy sapping, long daily cycling shifts, and there was no spare room for entertaining fearful time wasters.

This wasn't a magical cure. It had taken buckets of guts and willpower to haul my sorry arse out here in the first place. But confidence was on the climb and I was cashing in on the benefits. Paranoia about ditching the safety zone of home had been beaten into submission. Every day of this trip was approached with renewed relish, wondering just what each new town or village would cough up into my path. It was all so unpredictable and exciting, certainly not something to be petrified of. I was finally living the dream.

Demonstrating tunnel of death riding bravado, we hitched a lift to the *Eidersperrwerk* dam along the top of the wall. A merciless port side splosh into the North Sea didn't deter the daredevil combination of the Great Friendino and his loyal assistant from zig-zagging their way to the coastal fed River Eider crossing. The current bun was straining every sinew above our heads and with shirts already discarded (Rhys had finally pinkened slightly in an undercooked chicken kind of way), we were warming up for a corker.

Behind the excited giggles of pulling off another top-bottom-top freewheeling loop, the rewind switch returned to Christina. It had been painful abandoning her. She wanted to be our serving wench for another day and a crushing goodbye cuddle at the front door only increased the sadness of our departure. Finally wrenching free to pedal away from our frantically waving saviour and snapping a final mental picture of that non-stop smiling face was a killer. It had been a night never to forget which would be remembered fondly from time to time. And there were lessons to be learnt from Christina's selfless generosity. This unique act of kindness would domino for sure, pushing me to help somebody out in a reversal of roles. Especially if it meant sharing my bed with two attractive, bi-sexual female travellers. I hoped, but doubted, we would encounter anymore North Sea Wives on the way.

Continuing along the coast, hopping over the dam and wall, we expected to be guided by glittering waves creeping up on our pedals. But the North Sea had gone all shy again and done another runner. Shrinking away to a barely visible twinkle, a poor substitute of bird print criss-crossed mudflats greeted our arrival. Cycling the wrong side of the hill defence to gain protection, a harsh vacuum flew in from the bare horizon and slowed us down to a torturous 20 kilometre grind. The compulsory sprinkling of sheep were as happy as Larry (the Lamb), tucking in to a dry straw buffet dished up along the path. Rhys took his mind off battling the gusty head and cross winds by taking on the mantle of Dr Dolittle. His initial strained 'baas' sent adult sheep scurrying to safety, in slow motion, to the hill's summit. The scared nippers darted off to headbutt the swollen udders of mothers and suck in some comfort liquid refreshment. But Rhys was in determined mood. Continuing to tinker with the strangled vocal pitch of his tortured farm noises, he eventually came up trumps when an inquisitive youngster, with a kazoo jammed in his throat, responded. Contact with sheep kind had been made and Rhys had cracked the ancient code of woolly wordsmiths. Give the man a Blue Peter badge.

Tactically, I had snuck in behind Rhys, holding a perfect line with his rear and using him as a wind shield to ease the burden. But I got too close. Erika gave into temptation and displayed her opening sign of affection by planting a flirty kiss on the back tyre of Rhys' Globe bike. The loser in this love match, I toppled towards the deck. A keen viewer of the *Fall Guy*, I slapped out an arm for a perfectly orchestrated Colt Seavers break-fall on the grass, with my flat palm slamming down inches away from a huge dollop of poo. Rhys escaped unscathed and as I lay there, Erika pinned on top of me, he decided to point, laugh and 'baa', rather than lend his chum a hand. He'd been on to me all the time, slowly pulling the brakes back to send me flying. Did this fool not realise I was a universal champion in patient grudge bearing? Big mistake, buddy!

A red-hot sun continued to doff its cap our way, paying a fitting tribute to the dazzling coastline ahead. The five kilometre stretch of pure white sands between St Peter Ording and its originally named neighbour, Ording, were a summer pilgrimage post for kite and windsurfers. These spectacular beaches were the most popular in Germany and on this evidence I wasn't going to argue. St Peter Ording's suspended surf shack restaurants lifted themselves proudly on wooden legs above a woven mixture of sand and scrub, staring out towards the distant sea melting under a mirage.

A quick shunt along a dusty path unearthed the real daddy of all German beaches at Ording. It was the finest specimen of bucket friendly sand I had seen since exiting Zandvoort on day two. And here I was, exactly two weeks down the track, having just broken the landmark 1,000 kilometres barrier, standing awe struck at the twin towers of a beach bum's paradise. A parched sun bleached surface blazed out a water-seeking trail, ducking between two huge sand dune toes, guarding a secret entrance to distant waves wearing diamond necklaces. The drink was a long gulp away, but the Germans didn't let minor details bother them. They just drove their cars and jeeps across the compacted sand and parked up in their tight thongs and bulging Speedos. It was just how they did things here, even if it did seem environmentally unethical. There weren't any tell-tale pollution signs. No oil leaked moats surrounding sand castles or jagged pieces of discarded exhaust pipe sticking out of the top turret. The whole area was unspoilt apart from a steady stream of ghostly tyre tracks, which were swept away by sand particles shifted by a gentle breeze.

Hopping back on the four legged freeway soon wiped the sun bathing haven from our minds, replaced by unattractive gnarled grazing pastures. Steering a twisting path, 30 kilometres of empty wilderness lay between us and the harbour town of Husum. The orange hot rock was still on fire and the sweat pores were recording increasingly uncomfortable levels of stickiness. Shit stinking black flies buzzed around everywhere, trying to scratch their hairy-legs up your nose, deliver nasty germs to the mouth and nosedive through eyeballs. Release shades from top of the head, check, stuff tissue in nostrils, check, close gob, check. Breath as little as possible. The cretinous swarm of irritants were lapping up a sheep shit fest and wanted to invite us to the party by smearing their booty across our faces. A mine field of crunchy rock hard crap, which failed to crumble under the tread of a weighty passing tyre, coated the entire path. We were trying to steer a safe passage through an asteroid belt of thousands of sun baked turds. But what did these sheep eat to squeeze them out so big and strong? Concrete pine cones!

It must have been a long, hard winter in Bleaksville for the shepherds who ate and slept in lifeless one-storey brick houses. Cold, unfeeling structures, falling apart at the seams, they were scattered few and far between. Sure, you had all the wool and lamp chops you could need, there was no chance of freezing or starving to death, but it was a 10 mile walk to borrow a pot of mint sauce from the nearest neighbour. Motorised transport links came down to a couple of crude gravel roads. I wouldn't fancy being the postman. Dirty great flies, sheep and their armoured shit were all we saw for two hours, until human life finally stirred outside a collection of paint peeling barns selling hanging woollen garments. The sound of a powerful car engine offered a surprising alternative to the silent monotony. A handsome black Jag was bumping and grinding an awkward route across the uneven meadows. Spotting us the car jerked to a halt and a brown goatee bearded driver poked his head out grinning. 'Hey. Off-road guys. Yeah,' he yelled, before punching a fist in the air and smashing his foot back on the accelerator. Completely bonkers!

'By the grey shore, by the grey sea, close by lies the town. The fog rests heavy round the roofs and through the silence roars the sea, monotonously round the town.' The dreary words of novelist Theodor Storm, labelling his 1817 birthplace Husum in a poem as 'the grey town by the sea'. A touch harsh it must be said. This wasn't the most electrifying place in the world, but Theodor's cheery epithet was hardly doing the local tourist board any favours. Husum's inland harbour was carved out by a catastrophic storm tide in 1362. Such floods are a severe danger to coastal populations here, just as they are in the Netherlands, with a ferocious sea storm capable of lifting water levels five metres above the normal tide line. In other words, squeaky bum time.

A gateway to the North Frisian Islands, visiting pleasure skippers were an important source of income for the modern day town and the usual throng of café bars jostled for space along chunky cobbled roads and squares. Forget depressing dittys and Pimms O'Clock on a private yacht, taking nest with a family of bird twitchers had seen us swoop into town at the invitation of Dr Barbara Ganter. An active member of the German Bike Federation, Husum branch, the red cheeked anthropologist lived in a detached house perched at the end of a quiet cul-de-sac. The 42-year-old was a cycling nut and had completed small sections of the North Sea Cycle Route from Hamburg to the Danish border. She opened the door accompanied by a couple of perfect blond Arian boys, Robert, eight, and Richard, five, who demonstrated immaculate manners by bowing and shaking our hands as Barbara took care of the introductions. It was her dream to complete the entire 6,000 kilometres of the North Sea Cycle

Route with her children, but she was 'waiting for their legs to grow longer'.

Throwing our gear into a children's guestroom, I claimed the bed with smiley face sheets and matching pillow, while Rhys would be folding his legs into a mattress squeezed on to a wooden shelf. A picture of a rainbow coloured *Inuit* deer, Tuktu, hung above my pillow and a bedside globe lamp put my cycling progress into inferior perspective. I may have pedalled a healthy distance over the last few weeks, but it was a speck in comparison to the joined might of all the continents.

As we spooned pasta on to our plates from a metal dish plonked on the middle of a square wooden kitchen table, Barbara was keen to extract information about the places we had visited. But our host's life was a far more interesting topic than a leisurely lurch across the Netherlands and Germany, quickly becoming the subject of our interrogations. Barbara loved birds. They were her whole life (apart from cycling). After acquiring a PHD in Canada, she had travelled to some of the world's most inhospitable and raw, but awe-inspiring destinations to study our feathered friends. Barbara had taken part in scientific expeditions to the frozen icy wastes of Greenland, Siberia and Norway's North Cape, using different bird species in tests to gauge the effects of climate change on the planet. The most difficult part of her job had been gaining access to the barren places favoured by the birds, far out of reach from mankind. On one thumb-twiddling nine week visit to Siberia, Barbara only managed to get out into the field for four days, because of a lack of helicopters to transport her party.

But I felt she was more frustrated now than ever. Barbara had given up her career to raise two beautiful children and was blatantly bored of the housewife set-up. Her kids were a testament to her parenting skills. Impeccably polite, they spoke excellent English, which their school started drumming into them from the age of three through brainwashing nursery rhymes. I was more amazed to learn the horrific atrocities of their Nazi ancestors were made clear to them at such an impressionable stage too. 'Our children are taught that this period of our history was very wrong and must not be allowed to happen ever again,' said Barbara sternly. 'Their teachers tell them everything about the Second World War at an early age. And I mean everything, including the terrible treatment of the Jews in the concentration camps.' I was gobsmacked. I don't remember being told about deadly gas chambers and the genocide of millions of Jews and other races whose frightened faces didn't fit the crazed criteria of the Nazi master plan. It was a grim history lesson, self taught by delving into TV documentaries and newspaper articles. But they were nipping it in the bud in Husum, serving up shock tactic classes to kids not much older than toddlers, just in case this powerful nation of 80 million people was tempted to throw its weight behind an illegitimate, failed Austrian artist's deranged vision again.

During my punt across Germany, mostly south of the Elbe, much of the country had been ailing, tatty and rundown. I wondered whether Barbara agreed her country, despite its industrial wealth, was in a state of poor repair. 'There is still a struggle and much has been left undone following the damage of war 60 years ago,' she added. 'We are supposed to be a strong, united nation again after the reunification of East and West Germany in the 90s. But the old Iron Curtain is still there, even if it is not visible. Our former chancellor Kohl promised us "fields of flowers" across the whole of Germany once the Berlin Wall was knocked down. But the country is still run down and resources are not being used properly to repair the damage.'

The man of the house, Hans-Ulrich, who was a big cheese in bird circles, joined us at 10pm. Now I don't know if he was unhappy to find his wife breaking bread with two odd Englishmen, but he never removed his black body warmer, eyeing us closely and making a huge racket smashing his fork into abused pasta shells on a plate. The spectacle wearing hubby worked for the World Wildlife Fund and was another bird geek. It was his job to monitor all the species which visited the important wetlands and marshes cradled around this part of the North Sea coast. He was flying off to Hamburg in the morning for an important conference to decide whether a planned wind farm's underground cables risked harming this special bird sanctuary.

Happy Hans eventually mellowed after tiring of battering his poor plate and even managed to crack a smile at one point. Not wanting to outstay our welcome, I tactfully kicked Rhys in the shin under the table and announced our retirement. Just before vanishing upstairs, it was time for Barbara to prove her knowledge as a fully fledged bird nerd. 'I don't suppose you know what *Nonnengans* are?' I quizzed. Barbara didn't even flinch. The fat hooded birds hogging the coast outside Greetsiel were her specialised *Mastermind* subject, known in the trade as Barnacle Geese. They breed on top of the world at the Russian archipelago of Novaya Zemlya and westwards along the Arctic Ocean. Migrating down the Baltic to the Netherlands in winter, the geese spend spring time in Germany stuffing their podgey little faces in preparation for migration. Too much information, Barbara, a simple name would have sufficed.

A partially shrouded giant black snail rose above the far-away surface of the North Sea. Poking out of the mist was a shell-like mound, hanging on to the back of a flat pencil strip of land, which could have trailed off into a thin neck and head. This was a Hallig, one of 10 tiny islets embedded in intertidal flats, scattered between the four bigger and better defended

North Frisian Islands of Amrum, Föhr, Pellworm and Sylt. Pellworm and the Halligen are the remains of a much larger west coast island, Strand, which was totally submerged by a vicious storm tide, the Burchardi Flood of 1634. There were once hundreds of Hallig, but without any protective dikes to keep them afloat, the majority have submitted to consistent drowning over the past 400 years. Others have opted for a safety in numbers approach, welding themselves together through sediment deposition to improve strength and posterity. Langeness, for example, includes a former islet by the same name and two others, Nordmarsch and Butwehl.

Nobody in their right mind would live on a Hallig. Wearing a life jacket on the toilet and raiding the wardrobe for a pair of clean brown trousers every time a spot of rain flicked against the kitchen window didn't sound much fun. But nearly 350 people have settled here, happily setting up sticks amongst the mud in almost total isolation. The snail shell protruding from the fog was a *warften*, a man-made hill built a metre above sea level. When storm tides consume the area, the *warften* are the only part of the islets to keep their necks above water, keeping dry both the houses on top and the residents' lungs. The artificial mounds have done their jobs well so far. A freak windstorm, peaking at 200 kilometres per hour, caused the North Sea flood of 1962. More than 300 Germans died and 60,000 homes were obliterated as the banks of the Elbe and Weser rivers burst, carrying the destruction 100 kilometres inland to the doorstep of a hard hit Hamburg. But the puny Halligen, standing like sitting ducks straight in the wrath path of Mother Nature's relentless fury, didn't suffer a single casualty.

Most of the lunatic population of this death dicing backwater were employed in coastal defence (surprise, surprise) or farming. But consistent flooding put the kybosh on arable agriculture, with salt poisoning the soil and turning the land into cattle grazing ground. I really hope that cows can swim. Or buy a train ticket. That's because some bright spark had the brainwave to connect two of the Hallig, Oland and Langeness, to the mainland by a narrow gauge railway, running across a fragile causeway straight through the middle of the sea. This was the pure masturbation fantasy of a 40-year-old Hornby enthusiast still living with his mum.

A weather bitten track, rusted red by sea salt, disappeared into the haze outside the teeny-weeny village of Dagebüll. It was a sunny, well lit early evening, but there wasn't a Hallig to be seen from this corner of the shoreline. The spindly, single arm of railway was right at my feet, heading off across the sticky mud towards the sea, before vanishing into thin air behind a curtain of smog. It would have been easy to cycle across and investigate, if there wasn't a risk of meeting the ghostly Oland express head-on. This bizarre episode soon took another turn towards the Twilight

Zone. A sample of the trains, strictly only for the use of Halligen residents stocking up on supplies, rested against each other on a track with grass growing between its teeth. They were like open top coal mining carts, with green plastic floats dangling around the skirt and bike lights attached to long poles in each corner. Did this mean they clanked across the pitch black abyss, under a shower of sea spray, on these things at night? That beat any scary ride Alton Towers' technical drawing team could muster. The head engine, a primitive wooden box tacked on top of another square rust bucket with a splintered hole for a window, was even more hi-tech. A lanky metal control lever sprouted from the middle of an uneven floor and a squeamish inspection under the bonnet revealed a lawn mower engine had been cannibalised to provide a source of power. Prepared for just about anything now, I half-expected to see a train load of carrier bag clutching, blue faced Oompa-Loompas, chugging across to Dagebüll on a shopping spree.

Dagebüll was about as basic as it came. A no thrills coastal community which had grown stumped around a small harbour port serving Amrum and Föhr. Apart from an occasional train load of hermits with a watery death wish (Rhys was seriously considering finding himself a Hallig wife and emigrating), there were two hotels, a car mechanic and a battered fresh fish caravan. A square of rough turf doubled up as Camp Moin-Moin, a traditional north German gesture which translated as Camp Hello-Hello. In a tumbleweed jungle, offering minimal human contact, it was probably worth greeting anybody you were lucky enough to bump into twice.

'We've got no chance of the seeing the footie,' was my gloomy prediction. Manchester United were going head-to-head with Italian aristocrats AC Milan in the first leg of their Champions League semi-final at Old Trafford in a few hours and I wasn't confident of finding a TV set anywhere in this dump. 'Have confidence my friend. Everyone watches the Champions League at this stage of the competition. They must have a box in the hotel bar,' said Rhys, a keen United fan, trying to convince himself as much as me.

After tempting a plump seagull, wearing a black and white Mikado mask, into dancing nervously around a trestle table for a hurried peck at a tossed breadcrumb supper, we made for the Strand Hotel. Half-an-hour until kick-off and the ground floor, boat shaped bar was as lively as the Mary Celeste. But there were two televisions bolted to the wall. Ingrid, the white haired barmaid, didn't speak any English, but understood Manchester United and tracked down the big match on her remote control. Chink of beer glasses – game on!

A familiar nautical theme of ship dials, netting, portholes and knot racks adorned the sides of this watering-hole. The wise old barmaid filled empty half pint glasses with salty, thirst generating pretzels, which were tactically placed by beer pumps. As soon as we polished off one batch of the crunchy sticks, Ingrid replaced it with another. We'd finished off the remnants of our Aldi bread and salami for dinner, sharing our meagre rations with a Japanese sea bird, so we shouldn't have felt guilty about downing eight pints of pretzels. The bar gradually filled up with a coach load of pensioners. Old men in shiny white trousers and pastel coloured jumpers creaked on to stools, accompanied by wives in matching outfits.

Joined by an overfriendly drunk, I missed most of the game, but sitting in the middle shielded Rhys, who was glued to the screen for 90 minutes. The denim clad spitting image of Paul Hogan to my left was in his early forties and absolutely pickled. He had made eye contact on numerous occasions and I wasn't sure whether he wanted to have a natter or just fuck me senseless. He plucked up the courage to speak at half-time following four pints and brandy chasers.

'Where are you from?' was the slurred opening gambit.

'Near London,' was the most uncomplicated reply I could offer my new buddy, whose alcohol stinking spittle was firing straight into my face as he snuggled up closer. But never judge a book by its cover. He had my best interests at heart.

'Ah. Englander. What are you doing in Dagebüll? You must go to the island of Sylt,' he continued.

'We plan to head there tomorrow.'

'Good, good,' he continued excitedly. 'You must go there. You can have lots of girls. Many pretty, sexy girls. One, two, three, four or five, all in the same night. I know zis as I lived there 35 years.'

Hogan slapped a flat hand on top of his fist to highlight the rumpy-pumpy potential of Sylt, before continuing his sales pitch with a finger under his eyelid. I couldn't get a word in edgeways. 'Go and see the girls. You must go to the Wunderbar and the chief Susi. She will look after you. I have been on Sylt 35 years and had lots of girls. Many, many girls. You must have some too.'

Hand on fist, finger under eye, grab of his groin and it all started again. 'The Sylt girls, they love you. You don't need money. They are great girls. I know zis. I have had small girls, tight little girls.' His hands curved up and down. 'They are like models and stewardesses and they all want sexy time. Two, three, four all in the same night. I live there 35 years. I know zis.'

I was getting the hint. I think he was trying to tip us off about Sylt's thriving meat market. But just in case I hadn't got it the first 10 or 15 times. 'Please go to Sylt. See Susi. Tell her Money sent you. Lots of girls. You will lose your friend for days. He will be with girls. You tell me how many you have. You must tell me about the girls.' Money eh! He even had a porn star name and now wanted a shag report, as he scribbled down his mobile number for me.

And his prolific pulling technique all came down to nuts, of the eating variety, apparently. 'When you see the girl you like, you must take a big peanut out of a glass and throw it at the one you want,' added Money, with a huge grin on his face. 'She will come to you. She will not be able to resist. Remember, throw the peanuts.' Money was 41 years old and lived in the other hotel, working in the restaurant by day, getting blitzed and handing out fuck tactics to random Englishmen by night. 'I have no wife,' said the long blond-haired Love God. 'I live alone. Too many women in Germany to get married. It is very crazy, but I like girls.' This was a lie as Money later confessed he resided with a goldfish. I hoped it wasn't female as he began letching over two unimpressed young waitresses who had come down to the bar for a nightcap after clocking off upstairs in the bistro. This man would try anything for a drunken thrill. Even a Fish Finger.

Getting nowhere with the ladies, Money started screaming at Ingrid, who was more his own age. 'Ingrid, Ingrid. Where are my car keys?' Surely, he wasn't going to drive home in such a drunken mess, but he nodded affirmatively and pointed to an old black VW Golf parked outside the window. His keys were under his stool, attached to a long, fat chord. 'It is OK,' Money reassured me. 'The hotel is only 300 metres away. My car knows the way home.' We were in the middle of nowhere, again, and I'm sure he would get away with it, but why bother bringing the car when his sleeping quarters were only a short stride away. The rozzers must still do their rounds every now and then. 'Do not worry. I know the police. They come at 8pm, 10pm and midnight. It is 10.30pm. I will be OK.' Money stumbled out the door with a wink and a last hand on fist action, before nearly tripping over the step. 'Remember me to Susi and the girls. I know zis.'

Wayne Rooney's late goal handed the Red Devils a precarious 3-2 first leg advantage over Milan ahead of the return at the San Siro. And out in the watery black hole, inside a Hallig house balanced on top of a *warften,* a big fat German couch potato wearing a Manchester United shirt spilt beer all over himself, cheering as the England hitman's all important strike hit the back of the net. From Guilford to Tokyo, those bloody United supporters get everywhere.

18 Wunderbar

Sylt hung at the top of Germany's west coast like a wonky star on a Christmas tree. The wishbone shaped island was a summer tourist trap for a diverse cross-section of sun worshippers. Casual holiday makers, nudists seeking refuge and a top heavy clientele of turned-up nose snobsters were all sucked on to these party friendly shores. Sylt had something special to share with everybody, rich, naked or poor.

The largest of the North Frisian Islands, with a thriving population of 21,000 inhabitants, was just a few kilometres shy of Denmark. This closeness led to an indigenous dialect, *Söl'ring*, a mixture of German and Danish, with a dusting of Dutch and English thrown in for good measure. But I very much doubted the Hooray-Hermann brigade, who snapped up Sylt's immaculate thatched cottages as vacation homes, while tearing around an island only 35 kilometres long in a mega bucks Mercedes, had any smattering of the lingo. But that was Sylt. White gloss beaches caressed by clear blue water, mountain clean air and huge hideaway dunes (for people desperate to strip their clothes off) which could be enjoyed by anyone, despite its reputation as an exclusive meeting point for the jet-set crowd. It had a pay and display private jet park, an airport outside the central main town Westerland, which is where we were heading.

Sylt was reachable in three ways, by plane, boat, or in our case, a leisurely scenic rail ride across the *Hindenburgdamm* causeway. The passenger train departed from the town of Niebüll, a mere 15 kilometres from Dagebüll. As the riff-raff (us) sipped coffees on the station platform, drivers sat patiently at the wheels of flashy sports cars and top of the range four wheel drives, waiting to be towed by a double decker carriage to the same destination. Our train left first (1-0 to the cycling paupers), racing over the stony embankment which bridged the sea. The sun had beaten us to the opposite side of the track and was already smothering the island in its browning glow. It was only the end of April, hardly a calendar circle for soaring temperatures, but the freak wave continued.

Sylt's welcoming committee was provided by the Jolly Green Giant's family, who appeared to be leaving town under protest. The suitcase carrying statues of a nine foot tall mum and dad were ushering forward a sulking son and daughter, who had twisted their disgruntled heads upside down to highlight their unhappiness. Westerland was a vibrant place. A maze of wide shopping boulevards climbing up to the beach steps were brimming over with well dressed, fairly good looking patrons, poking their noses into window displays, relaxing with a glass of wine or tucking into a plate of top notch grub at numerous fancy restaurants.

The nearest campsite was a short walk from the centre, a stone's throw from the sea and surrounded by wind-breaking sand peaks. Perfect. Leaving our dusty baggage in tent storage, we were off to explore, pedalling seven kilometres up coast to Kampen, the summer village of Germany's stinking rich elite. Millionaires row was a scattered community of raised, flood protected, thatched cottages, complete with dangling satellite dish earrings. There wasn't a roof twig out of place, complimenting spotless manicured lawns, bordered off by round stone walls of perfect symmetrical construction. Hundreds of thousands of euros lay on the driveways, idle Chryslers and Porsches, but there was also the option of stretching one's legs. Bikes could be strapped to the rear racks of buses calling at Kampen, allowing one to go out for a ride without straining too much. But only if one could stomach public transport.

Expensive jewellers and boutiques, displaying the latest in sports casual blazer fashion and Ralph Lauren jumpers, attracted bulging wallets and purses. Despite the intensity of the weather, it was obviously compulsory among Kampen's posh fraternity to keep up appearances by draping a boiling hot cardigan or jumper over your shoulders on outdoor parade. Dishevelled and smelling of sweating buckets, we stuck out like a sore thumb. One perfume soaked old trout sneered and tutted as our greasy bare torsos cycled past, snatching her phone from a tiny handbag. Beam me up Snotty! She was probably ringing pest control. The pampered pussies even had electric button operated towel dispensers in a coffee stop café, which, making a strike for all commoners, I managed to empty into a sink in just 16 seconds. That'll show 'em.

It was Champions League part two, The Battle of Britain, as Chelsea and Liverpool locked horns in their semi-final, first leg clash. Rhys was right to believe Westerland's *Compass Bar* would point us in the right direction of a TV set and we got nice and comfy, served beers by a barmaid who bore an uncanny resemblance to Tom Hanks' bird in *Big*. It couldn't have been her though, as she had no idea where Sylt's nearest Zoltar machine was despite repeated requests. The game was pretty tame in comparison to the previous evening's five goal fiesta at Old Trafford. Biggest cheers of the night were sarcastic and reserved for Liverpool's beanpole striker Peter Crouch, the subject of intense finger pointing and laughter from a group of cravat-wearing middle-aged Germans standing north-west of the bar. Fair enough, Crouch does not possess the football genius of Pele. His embarrassing attempts to run with the ball emulate the stumbling motion of a baby giraffe taking its first tentative steps. But Crouch has a prolific scoring record for England and didn't deserve this blatant disrespect. As his fellow countryman, it was my duty to stick up for him by calling out two words, 'Carsten Jancker'.

Magnetic north cracked, the Compass needle swung lifelessly south and the hecklers fell silent. Boris Karloff clone Jancker must have been the most ugliest, baldest and ungifted player to represent a footballing nation as proud as the Krauts, spearheading the impotent attack of a mediocre German side famously tonked 5-1 in Munich by England in 2001. 'Good point, well made Englander,' admitted one of the neck-covered clan, raising his glass with a cheeky smirk. I returned the gesture and Crouch was allowed to play in plasma screen peace, as the Scousers slumped to a dull 1-0 defeat at Stamford Bridge.

Luminous yellow writing, sliding along a curving song sheet accompanied by dancing semiquavers told us this was the place. We had tracked down the *Wunderbar*. At just gone 11.30pm, it would have been rude not to call up one for the road in Money's honour at his favourite haunt before turning in. There was no escape until 4am.

The drunken old dog of Dagebüll had stitched us right up. There was no tribe of sex hungry vixens under the control of seductor in chief Susi. It was a dingy sweat box full of horny blokes. 'That piss head's done us up like a kipper. This is a gay bar,' deduced Rhys anxiously, as we sheepishly hid behind our drinks on a table, somewhat fittingly, at the rear of the establishment. We were cornered by wall-to-wall testosterone and had nowhere to run. Trying hard not to make eye contact with any interested men, who were kitted out in the same denim uniform as Money, a quick scan located only two bona fide holders of vaginas. They were both behind the bar and shot us with sympathetic looks, specially reserved for the fresh meat in town. We were going to get buggered black and blue for sure.

Then a tall athletic blonde pushed her way through the cock heavy crowd. 'Hi,' she said. 'I saw you on the train today with the bikes. You are from England?' Evon had too many well tanned assets to be a transvestite and our deafening sighs of relief interrupted a delicately poised floodlit croquet match in Kampen. An architect from Bremen, with crystal clear English, Evon reassured us the *Wunderbar* was a venue for all sexual orientations. 'It is not a gay bar,' she added. 'It is only early. There will be lots of girls here later. You will see.' Evon had driven up to see a friend, who was having an affair with an islander. They soon joined us, getting right in our faces with a constant open mouthed tongue fandango and twanging each other's knicker elastic at every giggling opportunity. Evon's main topic of conversation revolved around the fact she was all alone in her hotel room for the night. At the tenth mention, I let Evon down gently by informing her we had an early start ahead of us tomorrow and needed to keep every drop of energy safely in the tank. The *Wunderbar* girls were as bad as the boys.

Evon eventually got the hint and slopped off with her slobbering companions, probably for a hotel threesome. Euro techno filled the air, followed by a German version of *Saturday Night Fever* and dance mixes of traditional oompah songs. Attractive pockets of females had finally materialised, but all the men seemed interested in was bonding to the music. They were jumping up and down, crashing chairs on the floor, slapping high fives and forming circles for a group hug. The *Wunderbar* regulars sure knew how to let themselves go and the place was buzzing. Plastic palm trees sprouted from the walls and a painted lizard crawled across a surf board attached to the ceiling. And then I tried to inspect the floor, but it was hidden under an avalanche of peanut shells. They were scattered everywhere and as if by magic one of the barmaids pushed a glass full of monkey nuts in front of me. I was tempted to test Money's pulling theory by launching one at her, but I'm a taken man.

The staff treated us like royalty. We never left our table all night, making a fishing rod casting action towards the bar every time we wanted to reel a drink in. They probably would have gone to the toilet for us too if we had asked them. Little thank you notes in English were glued to our glasses and they dished out more than a couple of complimentary toxic sour apple shots, the straws which broke these camels' backs. Staggering back to the tents, arm-in-arm, was an admirable achievement. It was a balmy early morning and the temptation to collapse in the dunes, listening to the waves lashing against the beach, was difficult to resist.

Nursing stinking hangovers, we still got the tents down and scarpered off without paying. It was our silent rule that if wardens couldn't be bothered to be on duty when we either set-up or struck camp, then it wasn't our place to chase after them and hand over the little money we had. It also helped compensate for a late night drinking session eating into the budget. Despite draining copious amounts of water, dehydration was kicking in with a vengeance aided by a merciless sun. With bare backs burning to pork crackling, it was tough under pedal too. We could have been struggling through the unforgiving terrain of the Nevada desert, climbing steep, crude gravel paths hemmed in by mountainous dunes, which occasionally offered snatched glimpses of the beaches far beyond and blue strips of sea.

It was 17 kilometres to List, Germany's most northern point, and a short ferry ride across the border to the Danish island of Rømø. As the top arm of Sylt bent around the vista in front of us, an overheating Rhys decided to take drastic cooling action. 'That's it. I've had enough. I'm so hot and we're surrounded by water. I'm going for a dip.' Ditching his bike at the side of the road and running barefooted over the cooked sand, Rhys waded out about 50 yards and threw himself into the water. His head hit rock bottom straight away. 'Fuck, it's shallow!'

List had a Scandinavian feel about it, with the thatched quarter making way for brightly painted wooden houses, yellows, reds and blues. The diminutive ferry port presided over a calm sea, encircled by timber-built restaurants serving up fish with just about everything, including the village's speciality, locally caught oysters. Locking our bikes to the car deck, we settled into an outside seat on the ferry and waited for Denmark to show its rosy cheeks on the horizon. It was *auf wiedersehen* Germany and I was relieved to feel a tinge of sadness at leaving. We'd got off on the wrong foot and I'd been tempted to pack it all in before barely getting started. I'd been so lonely. The country was grubby, the people unfriendly and even the wildlife did its best to make me unwelcome. But I'd stuck to my guns through gritted teeth and come out the other side. An immense test of mental strength, which would have ended in failure not so long ago, I had hung on for the morale boosting arrival of Rhys and conquered my negativity. A trouble shared and all that. The reward of batting on was finally unearthing some generous Germans, displaying acts of kindness which will live inside me forever. As will some of the weird and wonderful places visited on this 11-day jaunt. Germany had undoubtedly played a prominent role in the healing process and the not so travel phobic passenger gliding over a still sea towards Denmark couldn't wait to see what country number three had in store. Mum would have been proud.

19 Denmark's best kept Secret

Convinced I had been abducted by a Scandinavian stork and dropped off with a nasty bump, face down on my parents' doorstep, the northern lands had always captivated me. My one prominent facial feature, which I believed to be kind of sexy and distinguished in certain lights (like pitch black darkness), shared common ground with the magical big nosed trolls of Norse mythology. Sporting long curly locks and usually some sort of lazy facial hair, this rugged refugee had more than a slight touch of the Nordic Gods about him. I could have been swimming around the loins of the mighty Odin himself, before being ejaculated into the blood-thirsty line of the Vikings. Those fearsome marauders first sailed across the North Sea in their longships to terrorise English shores in 793, building up their fragile confidence by attacking a defenceless group of monks at Lindisfarne on the north-east coast. Thank heathen for small mercies, at least they were saved from the even crueller torture of hearing footballer Paul Gascoigne's painful recorded collaboration with a future band stealing the ransacked monastery's name.

An early Saxon chronicle described the opening assault as 'the pagans of the north coming to Britain like stinging hornets'. The swarm continued for nearly 300 more years as invaders, with fantastical names like Erik Bloodaxe, Ragnar Hairy-Breeches and Ivar the Boneless, claimed large chunks of the British Isles, forcing three kings on to the English throne in the process. But all good things come to an end and the Vikings were finally banished for good in 1066 when Norwegian king Harald Hardrada was killed at the battle of Stamford Bridge. But as one door closes, another usually opens, and the English soon had more unwanted guests to contend with as the Normans landed on their doorstep at Hastings.

Ravaging horny hordes of Vikings would float their boats along the River Blackwater for a spot of rape, pillage and murder just down the road from my gaff at Maldon. Again, like me, they obviously loved a good party and I wanted to meet their tangled bearded ancestors and see, no stroke, retired longships in museum moorings. With any luck, I'd get a 1,000-year-old splinter stuck in my thumb, which I could pluck out with a pair of tweezers for the *Antiques Road Show* next time it hit town.

Refuelled by gherkin swamped hot-dogs, served with a smile, we were ready to roll across Rømø. This unstaple diet had been a bitter pill to swallow as the grumpy girl in the ferry kiosk actually looked like a pig. She was so miserable it wouldn't have surprised me if she had murdered her own mother for sausage meat.

Rømø was one of Denmark's four Wadden Sea Islands, taking over as the most southern of the quartet after the uninhabited Jordsand sank in 1999. Speeding coloured triangles darting over golden sands grew into kite boarders as we came into land. Rømø was the favourite summer destination of German tourists too poor for Sylt, packing a suitcase and hopping just over the border in their droves for the next best thing. There were a lot of similarities with Sylt, the endless beautiful beaches and purifying air, but Rømø was more tranquil than its noisy German neighbour. There were no jeeps ripping up the roads and extrovert thatched holiday mansions were replaced by modest wooden houses flashing vivid colours, poking shy triangular rooftops through the dark pine trees taking root around them.

A causeway led to the Danish mainland and the Jutland peninsula. Sticking out like a huge wrist and hand pointing towards its Scandinavian cousins, Norway and Sweden, Jutland was Denmark's biggest land mass. The rest of the country was a plumbing job of bridge connected smaller islands and hundreds of minor sea settlements, christened Denmark's archipelago to avoid confusion. Our Danish task was another slogathon. Getting jiggy with Jutland, we would clock-up an intimate 800 kilometres of coastline, completing 75 per cent of the peninsula by pedal power. The opening sortie followed Cycle Route One way up west, ahead of a dizzy climb to the country's summit. Picking up Cycle Route Five, a simple slide back down the east side booked us in for a restful boat trip over the Kattegat sea to Sweden, which felt forever away.

The sun was having a blast, but the sea had done its usual disappearing act, leaving Barbara's geese to stalk easy pickings of worms marooned on mudflats. Distressed sheep clung to the slanted banks of the causeway, shaking like a washing machine in the desperate hunt for an inch of shaded salvation. The herd's struggle got to Rhys. He jumped off his bike to aid the disciples of his language barrier triumphs, showering water from a carrier bottle on the poor creatures wilting visibly over the metal fence. Exiting the causeway and hitting the main road, it was our troubles which took precedence. The gentle trot across Rømø turned into an impossible grind through the North Sea Cycle Rocks, as the guiding white bike on a blue background led us into impassable farming roads. 'What bright spark qualified this as a cycle path? You'd have your work cut out driving a tank through here,' I grunted at Rhys, who nodded in sweaty agreement.

If we hadn't been surrounded by idyllic pastures, it wouldn't have been a major surprise skidding to a dusty halt next to the edge of a crumbling quarry cliff top. It was so hard to push on, as a montage of jagged stones and knuckley fist shaped rocks tried to pull you off balance into the chasm below. Foolishly, we attempted to keep going for the best part of an hour, making just two kilometres, without amazingly picking up any punctures or buckled wheels. Cursing the official route and wondering if the guardians of its paths had actually trod here, we cut our losses and picked up the main road. A black painted bike held captive inside an angry red road triangle warned cyclists not to go this way, but the sign next to it tempted us with a smooth 10 kilometre ride all the way to destination Ribe. Sold to the two pissed-off cyclists!

It was love at first sight. Ribe stabbed its head above a flat plain as the majestic spires and towers of its focal cathedral penetrated an untainted sky of perfect blue. Heath, marsh and reedy fields banked the remnants of a once important trade river sharing the town's name, spiralling a protective moat of an arm around a cluster of orange tiled roof tops and red brick chimneys. A gentle breeze sent a shiver to my body's core as a spooky feeling of something ancient rattled my bones. Little did I realise on approaching this magical, but minuscule town, it would be a living library of so many wonderful stories from forgotten ages, as well as being Denmark's best kept secret.

Passing over wooden bridges, straddling small canals feeding off the River Ribe, a mothballed inner sanctum of crooked cobbled streets and 16th-century half-timber framed houses was revealed. History was oozing out of every doorway and lump of brickwork. 'I've never seen anything like this. It's just so old, but still looks so good,' I dribbled. Rhys was open mouthed and speechless. Ribe is the oldest preserved medieval town in Scandinavia and we could so easily have been travelling back in time cycling along those bumpy roads. The peppermint green sloping roofs of the robust cathedral dominated the centre of town, *Torvet*, with tightly hemmed in lanes and shadowy hidden alleys twisting off at every opportunity from a spacious high street. Feeling like an excited young boy hunting out adventure, I couldn't wait to start exploring all the nooks and crannies of this unique antiquity.

Ribe's residents were rightly proud of their heritage and one of the kindly natives had offered us a bed for two nights at the immaculate Danhostel. The ultra modern guesthouse sits on a quiet meadow overlooking the river, just a short stride from the breathing museum outside. In a place where being so up-to-date makes you the odd one out, the hostel is an environmentally friendly Green Key establishment, translated as having everything from water-saving taps, toilets and showers to a strict waste recycling programme. Luckily for me, a highly infectious middle-aged lady, Gudrun Rishede, was married to Jens, the man in charge. A historical nut with a healthy complexion and winning smile, she was desperate to give me the grand tour free of charge, promising mesmerising tales of Vikings, witches curses, headless pirates, fairytale queens and returning storks.

Gudrun was so in love with Ribe, you couldn't help become instantly smitten too. She was bursting to show off her knowledge and revelled in the role of ambassador for this sparse, but privileged community of only 8,000 people. Dragging me up and down wonky well worn roads, dashing in and out of crumbling 600-year-old basements and decoding Danish texts, Gudrun's whistle-stop tour was conducted with feverish fanaticism.

Ribe is split between the Viking and medieval quarters. The ascending *Sct Nicolaj Gade* is the oldest pedestrian street in Scandinavia, which Vikings stretched their legs along to visit the town's bustling market on the way to the river. Its grand old age is highlighted by a 20 foot excavation display at the post office, dating back to the beginning of the 8th century. Vikings are believed to have ruled the roost here between 700 and 1100, with an unearthed wooden well dated as far back as 704 by archaeologists. Ribe was Denmark's most prominent port to the west, attracting immense wealth from the Viking age right up until the 18th century, using the river link to launch expeditions out into the North Sea and beyond. Sadly, the present day river has been sand filled and is too shallow for anything more than pleasure sailing boats.

The best way to trace the evolution of this former trading hub was to visit the excellent Ribe Viking Museum. Glass cases hold thousands of treasures given up from deep beneath the town's foundations, which have stood up well against the test of time. Keys, pots, gold coins and even shoes have been found in recent years, with amber stones and pearls used for trade with visiting merchants also liberated from the soil. My favourite was a small Odin amulet, capturing the crazy wild features of the most revered Viking God. Two mad swirling eyes, maybe under the influence of more than a horn or two of mead, sat sandwiched between a propeller moustache and a striking winged raven battle helmet. More than enough to put the wind up your average superstitious pagan. Following the change from living in tents to crofted homes, the museum contains a recreated 9th-century Viking market, with workers using a furnace and bellows to create jewellery for sale across the seas. Opposite the mock-up market rests a full-scale replica longship. Laden with furs and trademark war axes under a single square white sail, slabs of smooth rock are carefully positioned along the floor to balance out the boat for its difficult journey.

The second part of the exhibition takes a trip to the town's medieval era between 1050 and 1536. Brick buildings have started to appear and a hooded monk signals the birth of Christianity in Denmark. A freshly dug grave and the sinister figure of a black rat sniffing the air signifies the spread of the Black Death pandemic which wiped out a large portion of Denmark's 14th-century population. Finally, the museum moves on to the town's religious development. Vikings would traditionally be given a heathen internment alongside prized possessions, as well as sacrificed favourite slaves and horses. Convinced they could force a camel through the eye of a needle, these accompaniments were expected to join them on their voyage to the eternal afterlife feast in Valhalla. It could be a long ride and all that gold was going to be heavy, so the horse and slave was probably not a bad shout. But things were certainly getting a lot more civilised earlier than expected in these parts as two perfectly preserved specimens entombed in glass floor cases confirmed. The exhumed yellowy skeletons of a man and young boy, clutching a crude set of rosary beads in a bony hand, represent the first Christian burials dating back to 900.

The German priest Ansgar, dubbed the 'North Apostle', was the first missionary charged with bringing Christianity to these savage shores in 855. Trying to set new trends, King Horik of Denmark gifted Ansgar a piece of land in Ribe to build a church and spread the good word, which caused outrage among the locals who stubbornly refused to give up the old Gods of Norse mythology. But the Danes eventually adopted the new religious path and another of their kings, Harald Bluetooth, took the credit for converting his people to the light in a touching tribute to his father Gorm the Old and mother Thyra. Good old Bluey parked a massive carved rune stone, next to one his old man had prepared earlier, but an even bigger and better boulder, at Jelling, on the other side of Jutland. The 10th-century tribute pretty much read: 'Miss you mum and dad, but you'll be glad to know Denmark's still ours and I've also beaten the crap out of Norway. Oh, and by the way, I've made everyone go to church on a Sunday'. But old habits die hard and evidence of heathen Viking burials have been found as late as 1030. Ansgar had the last laugh though, despite his frustrations, and was eventually made the patron Saint of Denmark.

Ribe revels unashamedly in its Viking past. And if you want to get a bit more hands on, then the Viking Centre is well worth a visit. A reconstructed outside living area allows you to take a nostalgic dip into the past as Icelandic horses graze by the long house and hot sparks fly around the forge. You can even parley with the chieftain and have a stroke of his animals. Hundreds of modern day warriors descend on the town for the country's biggest Viking market at the beginning of May each year. Shit! I was a week early and would be long gone, missing the opportunity of stroking a few grog moistened beards. Discovering the Viking mead on sale had a mind blowing alcoholic content of 39 per cent softened the blow. I didn't fancy an axe wound to the back tyre.

Ribe had been a strict town to live and work in during medieval times, with money mad kings coming down hard on people who didn't toe the line or failed to follow an absurd set of rules. Trade traffic had to wait in a queue at the *Arda Gate*, which stood as a barrier until it was demolished in 1843, waiting to cough up over-inflated taxes to bring their goods and livestock into market. But a crafty landlord cashed in on the reluctance to pay, smuggling merchants through his pub, the *Det Lille Ølhus* (the small beer house), for a much more pocket-friendly entry fee. He was a brave man, for the penalties for breaking the law were severe. You could be executed for something as trivial as making a pot of honey the wrong way in the 13th century, with women buried alive upright and men hanged. Thieves were looked upon more leniently though you'll be pleased to know, branded on the head for a first offence and killed for the second. Two strikes and you're out! With a thriving port, Ribe was one of the richest settlements in Denmark during the 1500s, which attracted a lot of attention from gold hungry pirates. But they preyed on the prosperity of these shores at great risk, as seafaring brigands were dealt with ruthlessly. Hanged and then decapitated, the pirates' heads would be shoved on stakes at the Meadow of Heads next to the river, which now sits at the feet of the modern day Danhostel.

The 16th century opened another macabre chapter in Ribe's blood-stained past. The 1536 Protestant Reformation swept across the country, sparking witch hunts ending in a painful death on a burning stake for the unfortunate souls who fitted the crime. In many cases the victims came from poor backgrounds and acted as scapegoats for desperate neighbours trying to save their own skins. People had been able to buy themselves absolution from the Catholic church, but this was not possible under the long winded Reformation. The only option was to pass the buck. Argue you were bewitched into sin by dropping somebody else in the shit and they would take your place on the fire. Women took the brunt of the blame. More than 50,000 condemned witches met a fiery end across Europe during the Reformation, with Denmark leading the way in the death toll. Between 1572 and 1652, starting with Johanne Rygge and ending with Anna Bruds, 12 women were trialled for witchcraft in Ribe, all ending up as smouldering ashes.

The most famous of them all is Maren Splids, whose terrifying ordeal is remembered on a memorial plaque outside the site of her house in *Sønderportsgade*. Maren didn't fit the profile of a normal witch as she had both wealth and respect in the town. Her husband was a renowned tailor, Lauritz, and she was an equally successful landlady. But some of the Splids' green-eyed rivals felt Maren was getting too big for her boots and needed taking down a peg or two. One of the jealous crowd, a struggling tailor, Didrik Skrædder, went the whole hog and accused Maren of being a witch in 1637. The incompetent Skrædder had been ill and blamed his sickness on Maren, claiming she had entered his house at the dead of night and breathed into his throat while two faceless hags forced his mouth open. The alleged victim of bad magic, Skrædder told anyone that would listen he had vomited a strange lump of living matter, which moved of its own accord, into a bedside cup. He turned the stomachs of the town's authorities, priests and bishop by ferrying the cup of sick around to them. They all agreed it was the foul work of a witch's hand, probably just to get rid of the little weasel.

Maren was put on trial, much to the disgust of Ribe's townsfolk, but her husband succeeded in springing her free from the kangaroo court. Snivelling Skrædder wasn't easily beaten and turned the heat up even higher by snitching to King Christian IV in 1639. Christian was a superstitious man and well known woman hater, who was convinced the cursing words of witches had harmed him on the battlefield in past wars. The trial was rescheduled, but this dilemma still had more twists and turns than a Monday night double bill of *Coronation Street*. Maren was found guilty, but was once more acquitted in Ribe, before the king took it upon himself to preside over the case as judge at the Supreme Court of Denmark. Maren was imprisoned in the Danish capital of Copenhagen in a tower and horribly tortured until she confessed to being a witch, despite this woeful treatment being prohibited against prisoners who hadn't been found guilty.

Maren was finally barbecued on November 9, 1641, at Galgebakken, Ribe, in front of a sympathetic crowd so huge the priest struggled to get through to her. She was granted half-a-pint of beer to drink as a last request and had gunpowder loaded to her back to speed up her death. Maren was then tied to a ladder and cooked in the flames. To this day, many houses in Ribe still have iron crosses nailed to their houses to ward off evil witches.

There were plenty of other strange little quirks to be found around these meticulously preserved streets. Long before television was invented, the residents made the most of their window seats by attaching two-way mirrors to the outside of their houses in the 1800s, allowing nosy parkers to take a peep at what was going on at both ends of the road from the comfort of the living room. Narrow alleys, known as *slippes*, leading down to the waterways cutting through the town had a duel purpose. The women washed clothes on the side of the river heading towards them, while others would squat over the downstream flow to relieve themselves. Also known as not mixing your colours. There were also segregated bathing sheds built on the water, but these were later phased out after randy chaps kept invading the women's washroom to instigate an orgy while they powdered their noses.

There are still fire ladders attached to the gutter-less *slippes,* allowing rainfall to roll back into the river and prevent flooding. The ladders are a reminder of one of Ribe's blackest nights in 1580 when 11 streets were wiped out by fire. Every fifth house in the town, 110 in total, is now preserved by the Danish Trust. Keeping an eye out for fire and flood was the job of the night watchmen, who began patrolling Ribe after dark, carrying lanterns and maces topped with a crude rounded head of spikes during the 14th century. Also charged with making sure children were tucked up in bed and kicking crime off the streets, the nocturnal guardians would sing a song every hour between 8pm and 5am to warn off wrong doers.

'Master, maid and boy, would you the hour know? It is the time that you to rest should go. Trust in the lord with faith and careful be of fire and light, for 10 o'clock has struck.'

The night watchmen had their own shed, but were caught napping on the job when the river's burst banks flooded the town, drowning visiting merchants' cattle. As a punishment, this perk was taken away forever, forcing the night watchmen to continue their ghoulish walk on foot. They hung up their lamps in 1902, with police taking over the responsibility, but the tradition was re-born for tourists in 1932 and they can still be heard pounding the beat between May and October every year.

Ribe's creaking houses arched the pedestrian streets in a rainbow brushed mix of radiant yellow, green, red and purple. One of the best examples of medieval architecture was the Gable House in *Sortebrodgade* which resembled an old world galley ship sinking slowly into the pavement. V-shaped wooden oak beams criss-crossed intricate triangular brickwork around rows of tiny squared glass windows. The two-storey house belonged to a wealthy merchant, Ebbe Mogensen, who allowed travelling tradesman to rough it downstairs with their animals, while business was conducted in front of the luxury of a warm glowing fire in the penthouse. Attempting to rest my brain from absorbing more information than it was ever intended to digest, Gudrun ambushed me with two fellow Ribephiles who joined us for coffee in the enclosed courtyard of the adjoining Quedens Gaard café. Poul, a big friendly giant with a bushy white beard, was keen to know when he could set sail to England and honour the memory of his Viking forefathers by ransacking a coastal village. His sidekick, Børge, a pair of spectacles hidden underneath a safari style hat, was more interested in letting me in on a 'secret'. Apparently, medieval builders also liked to pull a fast one with the council's planning chiefs and he pointed out an odd tower-like wall jutting out the back end of the Gable House. This was in fact a service shaft for old Ebbe's number twos if he couldn't make the bathroom following a hefty drinking session with his business buddies. A secret shitter!

The tour continued with a quick skip around the impressive Kunstmuseum art gallery, which was exhibiting the paintings of women from the 19th and early 20th centuries. Female art was frowned upon at the time of its inception, they should have been washing clothes down river and avoiding fast moving poo sticks. But it is appreciated now and going through something of a renaissance. Pride of place went to Anna Ancher, whose husband Michael was one of the great Skagen society painters. This group captured Danish hearts with their golden age luminescent interpretations of the furrowed weather-worn landscapes and fishermen of the northern town. Huge canvases covered entire walls, bringing to life toiling field workers, packed christenings and dirty old cattle houses from back in the day. Girl power was the gallery's theme however and Anna Ancher's 1912 painting *Bedstemor Underholdes* took pride of place as a young girl, with a red flower tied in beautiful blonde bunches, watched intently as her bonneted grandmother patiently sewed a dress by her side.

Gatecrashing a wedding witnessed by portraits of stuffy vassals and councillors dating back to 1600 at the old town hall, Gudrun revealed a new chamber of horrors. The building opened its doors in 1496, but retired just before my arrival, and any adulterous minded brides or grooms could easily be deterred from breaking their vows in its torture room. The former debtors' prison was crammed full of manacles, cuffs and painful persuasion devices such as thumb screws and a ghastly executioner's sword, sending shivers down my spine. The town hall is also one of the perching points for Ribe's returning storks. Round, twig-covered landing nests sit on roof tops around town, awaiting the harbingers of spring who are worshipped here. Storks are rare in Denmark (so they could be related to my kidnappers) and their arrival in March sparks frenzied celebrations. A red carpet welcoming committee is held for the birds outside the old town hall and chocolate frogs and spring water are handed out. There is also a reward for the first person who spots the stork's arrival.

Exhausted and heading for meltdown, we finally arrived at the doorway of the magnificent Romanesque Ribe Cathedral. Finished in the middle of the 1200s, Gothic architectural ideals have also crept in to the façade. The ribbed vaults and Commoner's Tower, built in red brick, plus the remains of the vaulted ambulatory have all succumbed to the Gothic touch. Two kings are buried inside the cathedral alongside a carved pompous burial slab, picturing the eternal rounded features of Ivar Munk, a 16th-century Catholic bishop whose fingers are encrusted in gold rings. Renowned for keeping a low profile with parishioners, he was believed to be too busy to make speeches as he was counting his money.

Most striking was the fusion of old and new high above an altar basking in multicolour pixels of light sieved through a ring of stained glass windows. Artist Carl Henning Pedersen only died in February 2007, but his imaginative ceiling display will fuel heated debate for many more years to come. Like Michael Ancher before him, Pedersen was part of an exclusive group of Nordic painters, Cobra, who had the courage to make the break from the traditional school of naturalistic painting in the 1930s and create revolutionary expressionistic imagery. Towering fantasy figures of bright colours painstakingly constructed from tiny mosaic stones and christened with Bible themes, 'Heaven's Gate' and 'Jacob's Ladder', were slapped up high. They looked as if they would have been more at home in a Disc World novel than the pages of the Old Testament. Despite her devotion to all things archaic, Gudrun was also a future thinker and held spellbound by Pedersen's legacy. But I would soon learn that Ribe wasn't just concerned about holding on to the past, as the town's next generation came out to play after dark.

20   Skål to Queen Dagmar

Just gone 7pm on a Friday night and Ribe was fast asleep. Crowds of sightseers had been whisked away by coaches or returned to hotel banquets. Sitting in an empty bar, bored out of my brains, I couldn't get my head around it. English pubs would be brimming over with punters desperate to kick-start the weekend by chucking beers down their necks at light speed. 'Where is everyone? It's Friday night. Where's the party?' I asked Rhys.

'It is early yet,' butted in the barman. Again, in exceptional English. 'People do not leave home until very late in Denmark. They have parties indoors before coming out to socialise. Believe me, come back at midnight and we will be very busy.' Thomas was as tall as a tree and the perfect host, offering us a beer each on the house, which was gratefully accepted. He ran the *Peppers* bar, just around the corner from the cathedral, and was the youngest of four family generations living and working in Ribe. He said he will never leave. I didn't blame him.

You don't see many low budget backpackers in Scandinavia because it has earned the whispered reputation of being a rapid wallet emptier, particularly if you fancy a few sherbets. But this is a complete myth. Drinking alcohol in Denmark is no more pricey than England, cheaper even than London or other big cities. When we first arrived in Ribe, it did seem expensive at first, but that was more to do with getting our heads around a new currency, the Danish krone. The euro calculation is very compatible to the pound and provides excellent value for money in the Netherlands and Germany. The krone, meanwhile, is a completely different ball park and there is a lot more of it, with another zero added to the end of anything the euro or pound purchased. It felt very strange pulling a 100 krone note out of my pocket, which was just under a tenner at home. Mind-boggling for a mathematical retard like myself.

Our favourite tipple was a crisp green bottle of Tuborg, which, brewed in Copenhagen by Carlsberg, claims to, probably, be the number one beer in Denmark. This beverage has been knocking around since 1880, but we'd never heard of it, and is apparently the favourite brew of Eastern Europe too. At £1.50 a bottle it did the job for us and we would become close friends during the weeks ahead. But there's nothing worse than drinking alone and after burning poor Thomas' reddened ears for the best part of three-and-a-half hours we headed down town. 'Make sure you make it back for midnight,' he called after us raising a cheesy thumbs up.

It was getting on for 11pm and there was a gentle stirring of young blood outside, but nothing to get excited about just yet. Our next stop was the *Café Valdemar*, which was of course a pub, and named after the 13th-century king, whose horse riding frame was plastered across the ceiling. The painting was uncanny as he was a dead-ringer for Liverpool's Spanish manager Rafa Benitez, complete with the new season black goatee beard. A past life maybe? It soon got weirder. This establishment prided itself on having Ribe's only beach, an amusing boast in itself as we were a good few kilometres from the coast. But there it was, a sandy pit, surrounded by thatched Caribbean style umbrellas and palm trees, slap bang in the middle of a beautiful pub river garden. Sadly, it was too cold to sunbathe and the cloud of midges circling around the banks were, in perfect Ribe tradition, angling for a blood-sucking.

It had just gone 11.30pm and the place was heaving under the weight of Ribe's youth club. God, I felt old. Apart from us, nobody sinking drinks at the wooden tables and stools could have been over the age of 16. I'm surprised we hadn't been asked to wave our furry club wallets on the way in. *Café Valdemar* was an underage drinking den rife for a police raid. But it was the parents who were to blame. All the bright young things of Ribe, who were holding their drink very well it must be said, there wasn't a splodge of sick in sight, had got tanked up at a 'private party' at the town's gymnasium. The Danish equivalent of a school disco was for under-18s, who were supposed to be too young to go to the pub, but having a few bevies under adult supervision was obviously tolerated. The problem is, once you start you just can't stop, and here they all were topping up in their flashy ball gowns and tight fitting suits, with the odd sprinkle of T-shirt wearers in knee-high shorts. A mascara smudged Gothic girl, no more than 15, clutched my hand firmly between her black painted finger nails, with a wanton look in her spiralling eyes. This teenage vampire was ready to bite. She wanted to crack on with me. I was old enough to be her daddy, it was terrifying. Counter affectionately grabbing Rhys' hand and running out the door we beat a hasty retreat to *Peppers*.

You're having a laugh! There was a queue, 15 bodies long and four people thick, to get back into *Peppers* just before the chimes of midnight. Ear deafening music pumped out of the previously morgue like venue, which was now threatening to split at the seams. After hacking our way through the crowd, we were cheered by Thomas, who had transformed into a bar tending superhero. The mild mannered alter-ego and dark drab shirt from earlier had been ripped off, replaced by a dazzling white number, a gleaming twang of a smile and plenty of small talk with the adoring Danish ladies hitting their tongues on the bar. Nonchalantly ignoring his harem, Thomas ushered us straight over: 'Hi guys. I told you not to miss out. Have these on me.' We quickly downed the sticky shot tumblers of alcohol Fishermen's Friend, sending the room spinning and nearly burning a menthol hole through the centre of my chest on its way down. Forget those packets of hot fish-shaped lozenges, this was the stuff to keep you warm on a long trawl across the North Sea for cod.

Trying to focus on one thing and stop my head crashing around in circles, I noticed the ceiling was covered in English newspapers, The *Sun*, *Mirror* and *Times*, rolled around networks of tubing. Seeing only two of everything which moved now, my attention turned back to how many more free drinks we could milk. At that point, Thomas pointed out a group of middle-aged men, finally knocking me off pole position in the adult stakes, who were farmers. 'We don't close until 5am. The farmers come in to party until 4.30am, before returning home to milk the cows and climb into bed with their warm wives,' he grinned, with a knowing wink.

A staggering ascent to the upstairs disco uncovered a world of steaming drunken harmony and politeness. The average age had increased to mid twenties with smartly dressed girls swaying around next to blokes wearing a strange combination of hoodies, with either ties or scarves, on a square dance floor blinking under the DJ stand's lights. Everyone was pretty stewed with three or four members of the drunken disco rollers stacking it on the carpet after flying blindly into a pillar or somebody standing at the bar. But there was no hint of aggression, they were hauled straight back up by the nearest set of helping hands and released on a wibbly-wobbly path again.

Back downstairs, a sozzled girl fell into the bar, clutched the back of a chair to keep balance and, while looking in the completely opposite direction, slurred: 'Have you seen my friend? She has hair in blonde plats and has huge boobies.' Unfortunately, we hadn't made this lost acquaintance, but begged the well lashed young lady to return on finding her companion and introduce us. Fed-up waiting for a mammoth pair of breasts to squeeze themselves through the doorway, we teamed up with a trio of trainee nurses from the Faroe Islands. They obviously didn't suffer from home sickness. Having ditched their remote North Atlantic outpost, which was 1,200 kilometres away, they were studying just up the road at Esbjerg. Like the Arctic sprawl of Greenland, the Faroes is an independent nation, but is part of the Kingdom of Denmark. The Danes' equivalent of our Falkland Islands.

Eighteen islands make up the scattered jigsaw pieces of the Faroes, with a population of a mere 47,000 hardy souls battling harsh elements in the middle of nowhere. It rains 280 days a year there and being shut inside for weeks on end obviously leads to plenty of alcohol training, concentrating on drinking Englishmen under the table. The pale girls all had blowing-a-gale chapped faces and pointed little fish-like snouts. They came from a mist-shrouded island of just 250 inhabitants and must have got through a shot of lime and Southern Comfort for everyone of them, accompanied by a saluting chorus of *'Skål'* to their homeland. We were well out of our league, but Rhys, the idiot, encouraged them further by ordering an extra two rounds of firewater. I couldn't drink anymore. I felt ready to chunder and was trying to piece together just what I was doing here, while endless giggled shouts of *'Skål'* revolved around a disorientated mind drowning in booze. I didn't know what time it was, I couldn't focus on the 12 hands on my watch, but it was the early hours as dots of daylight peeled holes in the darkness outside. Getting to bed was a mystery, solved by waking up at the Danhostel fully clothed and drenched in sweat. My battered body was crying out for the uplifting scent of soap and hot water. Leaning against the wall, under the shower, a final memory whacked me around a fuzzled head like a plank of wood. One of the nurses was staring at me with evil eyes and warning me in a stern voice: 'Beware of Danish fish. It is bad. Faroes fish is best. Eat Danish fish and you will be sorry!' It was a strict beef, chicken and pig diet all the way to Sweden now.

Holding a lonely vigil on the windswept moated mound remains of *Riberhus* castle, stands a statue of Ribe's much loved Danish Queen Dagmar. With a hand cupped just below her crown, sitting above long strands of hair curling down to her royal robed breast, she watches over the town for eternity. Margaret Dragomir was the daughter of the Bohemian King, Premysl Ottokar I. In 1205 she was shipped to Ribe in great splendour to be married to the Danish King, Valdemar the Victorious. One of his country's most famous medieval sovereigns, Valdemar, according to legend, gave Denmark its national flag after a red cloth with a white cross fell from the heavens during the 1219 Battle of Lyndanisse (Tallinn) in Estonia. The royal bride was christened Dagmar by the Danes and a posh hotel named after her faces Ribe cathedral (although, as Thomas tipped us, the poorer diners ate down below in the cellar restaurant, *Vægterkælderen*, converted from old kitchens). A queen of the people, numerous ballads and myths honour her popularity and great beauty, remembering many good deeds she did for the Danes. *'She came without burden, she came with peace. She came the good peasant to cheer.'*

But it is in Ribe where she is held with the highest esteem through a tale of truly heart-rending tragedy and romance. In 1212, just seven years after her arrival in Denmark, Dagmar died. As she lay on her sickbed, Valdemar charged back 120 kilometres from Skanderborg to be by his cherished wife's side, riding so fast he left behind 100 accompanying men staring at the dust of his horse's hooves. When Valdemar arrived Dagmar was already dead, but magically woke up and made three last requests of her husband: To release all prisoners, not to marry Princess Berengaria of Portugal and to make sure their youngest son, Knud, was crowned King of Denmark. He immediately obeyed two of his wife's final wishes, but did the typical bloke thing and went against her will two years later, marrying the daughter of Portuguese King Sancho I.

Ribe Cathedral's bells still pay homage to the town's favourite adopted daughter, chiming out the ballad 'Queen Dagmar lies ill in Ribe', on a daily basis at noon and 3pm. She was buried in St Bendts Church, Ringsted, on the island province of Zealand, and a Byzantine cross taken from her grave, picturing Christ on the crucifix, has inspired a modern day tradition. The 'Dagmar Cross', made in silver, is a christening gift for girls in Denmark.

21　Howling Sands

After being spoilt rotten by enchanting Ribe, the drab port of Esbjerg cut an uninspiring silhouette. Smoking metal industrial chimneys and filthy warehouses were no reward after paying for our drinking crimes with a painful 26 kilometre morning ride up coast. The harbour was Esbjerg's main economic driving force and one of my pre-trip designated bail out points. A simple ferry ride away from my starting point at Harwich, this was the last chance to take advantage, before trundling on to Sweden and getting another opportunity at Gothenburg much later on. But I wasn't even mildly tempted to accept the offer.

Once Denmark's largest fishing base, the docks are now the headquarters for the country's offshore North Sea oil activities. Granted, my watery eyes were still partially blinded by alcohol poisoning, but I couldn't fathom just how it had been crowned Danish City of the Year in 2006. The award was in recognition of the hard work and support of the area's young talent. They must have beaten the stopwatch by crushed-ice packing a hell of a lot of fish in record time. In Esbjerg's defence, the North Sea Cycle Route hardly showed its best face. If it had one. Taking you on a back-street detour of dour dual carriageways, with the main highlight a dashed water break at Aldi or Netto, completely bypassing the city centre, it was as if Esbjerg was trying to save itself further embarrassment.

Esbjerg was partially redeemed by two finely sculpted works of art on the other side of its hiding place. Four speckless white seated giants stared out to sea through immortal bulging eyes as families played on a discoloured beach below the shadow of their awesome six-packs. Across the road, in contrast to this powerful quartet, a memorial to dead fishermen underlined man's fragility at the other end of the scale. The semi circle of carved bricks listing the names of those lost at sea between 1901 and 1992 was a poignant reminder of how dangerous an occupation it was, risking your life on a daily basis to earn a crust in perilous waters. Something you take for granted demolishing a plate of cod and chips.

Leaving behind Esbjerg's mucky industrial towers, the shoreline cleaned itself up approaching the pleasant village of Hjerting. Our great luck with the weather was continuing and the locals were cashing in too, cruising lazily down the road in old roofless sports cars waxed to perfection, while youngsters took motorised mini-bikes out for a spin. The sea was sparkling and one lucky passenger was yelling excitedly as he was pulled along in a rubber-ring on the back of a speedboat. Another exceptional piece of scenery was the native females, which had failed to avoid Rhys' wandering eyes. 'Oh my God. It's wall-to-wall babe heaven. Just look at them all. They're so sexy. So perfect. Not a minger in sight. I really need a wank. Hmmm.' Crude, but true my dear Rhys, the women here were approaching Goddess level, with nobody scraping below a 9 out of 10. Tall, well toned, slender brunettes, with model qualifying features and all the other important stuff sticking out in the right places. The boulders of our nut covered ice creams were obviously feeling the heat too and had already melted beaten down the cones' rimmed shoulders. It was hard jumping back on to the saddle with a raging boner, energised by three weeks of womanly drought. I really missed Katie. Just how was I going to stay on the straight and narrow with all this top quality temptation hanging around everywhere? I was starting to feel sympathy for Rhys. If I couldn't conjure a cure for this sexual frustration there was a slight chance he was going to get tent ambushed on our next drunken night in the middle of nowhere and ripped to pieces where nobody could hear his screams. I haven't got any leanings towards men in that way, but I convinced myself that jumping on Rhys wouldn't technically count as being unfaithful to Katie. It wasn't the same as bedding another woman. I gave Rhys' body a lust packed look up and down inspection. Snap out of it! Things hadn't got that desperate yet. Had they?

Cooled down by another 20 clicks on country roads, shrinking back to an acorn nestling comfortably on the saddle, we soon arrived in the sleepy suburb of Oksbøl, which acted as clever camouflage cover for a military training base. I didn't even realise Denmark had an army. I thought all the fighting had finished with the Vikings. Another 20 kilometres of deep woodland followed completely deserted roads. Innovative metal skewers were hammered into the ground and pierced by discarded fizzy drinks cans. God knows who had come out here for a drink. Thirsty soldiers? The forests were black as night, with only the occasional squeak of illumination managing to break through the thickset branches, throwing light on the pine cone rug below. They had an ominous look about them and you really wouldn't fancy taking a walk under the canopy, just in case you disturbed a trigger happy crack Danish commando covered in leaves underfoot. Tank signs stood at the side of the road and the chunky tyre tracks left behind from military exercises disappeared into the bush. Exhausted red ammunition cartridges popped up intermittently, which a wide-eyed Rhys decided to pocket for some obscure collection back home, before we escaped into Henne Strand without coming under friendly fire.

Henne Strand was a drowsy seaside strip nurtured by dunes. The shifting sands had half buried oak trees, suffocating their multitude of arms deep below. It was also close to the largest dune in Denmark, the 64 metre high 'Blue Mountain', which gives off an eerie blueish glow. Red wooden houses with grass roofs rested in the sand. They were the homes of yesteryear fishermen who would have to go through the frustrating ordeal of catching herring first to use as bait for their main catch of cod and haddock. It was a family affair with the wives backing their men to the hilt. The 'Ese Girls' would remove old bait and untangle fishing lines at home, while setting up as many as 200 lines with 2,400 hooks in preparation for their husbands' next day at the office. When did the cooking, cleaning and ironing get done?

An athletic blond Nordic God of a man, Peter, who was the most gut-wrenching picture of perfect health, took pity on the wandering weaklings in his campsite office, handing over a one night only complimentary lump of grass for our tents. 'Why do you come from England to Henne Strand?' It was a pertinent question. He also warned us about the dreaded Dancard, which was chargeable on all sites for putting up a tent and compulsory practice. The Scamcard was an additional insurance payment of an extra few quid, supposedly safeguarding the campsite owners from any damage you may incur during your stay. Like what? Making too big a hole in the floor with your tent pegs. What a rip-off! Peter turned a blind eye for us.

Our host ran a tight ship and a facility packed venue, complete with swimming pool, water tubes, sauna (very good for calming sexual frustration), bubbly hot-tub and best of all a spider's web shaped climbing frame. It also introduced us to the luxury of family rooms, which meant you could illegally hog both a toilet and shower all to yourself. In typical polite Scandinavian style, Peter also warned guests to beware of potential thieves in the camp brochure. 'Remember, there are people who are more weak minded than us.'

It was Saturday night, but Henne Strand was lifeless. Apparently the holiday season didn't pick up for two weeks. A short plod down the single main street, past a selection of tall windowed flamboyant designer gear shops, revealed a cutting through the scrubby grass infested dunes. A breath-taking panoramic red sunset awaited on the other side, splashing a rosy tint over the empty beach and endless pile of the North Sea below. It was a romantic setting and just maybe, this could be Rhys' lucky night. But he missed the chance to take my hand in his and we retired to the nearest pub (I was sulking a little bit). Three other people, all men, had social lives in Henne Strand, but only just. Two sat on stools chuckling through an obscure game of smashing dice on the bar from a brown plastic cup. Saddo number three chucked electronic darts in solitary confinement. Two Tuborgs and it was time to retire early, winning back a few of those forgotten drunken hours lost in Ribe.

A manageable gravel trail led the way through the heart of another dense pine plantation. Knobbly wounded stubs and high stacks of felled trees were scattered around and a redundant train track charged out of a clearing at Nymindegab. I prayed it was definitely out of working order because the unsuspecting kids working their way along the rails on wheeled carts could have been in for a high speed squishing. Bridges traversed transparent fresh angling lakes full of dark swimming fish schools, before the peculiar sight of a burnt-out knackered tank guarding the gateway to another range of dunes nudged us back into the army training core.

A yellow sign with a rifle-holding sniper kneeling down under a Danish crown read: 'It is forbidden and dangerous to touch any objects found here.' Before continuing more worryingly: 'NO ADMITTANCE when the ball is hoisted or red light is on.' Fearing a spell in the brig, or an exploding cycle bag, Rhys emptied his spent cartridge collection in a nearby dustbin. A short trot forward and a second sign jumped to attention: 'It is quite safe here. If at any time it is not, the area will be closed for 10 minutes.' Well that was a relief. But we still made a mental note to duck for cover if any gunfire broke out or incoming tank shells whizzed overhead. All men and bikes for themselves. Reassured to find all orange plastic balls sitting undisturbed at the foot of their posts, we defeated the army dunes in one piece. But another threat soon promised to shoot us down, as a blue sky broke out in front and a gathering of timid clouds were blown over our shoulders by whistling head winds.

The route now chased a 45 kilometre trail of howling sands, completely exposed to a bruising buffeting. A yellow strip of anorexic ink, which hardly seemed worth marking on the map, swam between the North Sea and ruffled crest of the Ringkøbing Fjord. Two wide open masses of water, but obviously not the best of neighbours, and we were caught in the middle of their furious exchange of roaring arguments. A sympathetic sun tried to offer support up above, with the temperature still clinging on to the 20s. But with little natural protection offered from the stunted terrain, we were treated to a first taste of coastal wind chill, signalling the clarion call for waterproof trousers and jackets. Proving things usually happen in threes, the gradient of the sand-sugared path started to lift itself higher. Not a problem on a calm day, but in these conditions it was hell on two wheels. The route continued throwing up varied tests of difficulty, with harsher gravel replacing the tarmac beneath our tyres and short, steep, sometimes almost vertical hills, becoming regular pains in the saddle. Booby-trapped by the firm grip of sand cake covered climbs and straining against the gales, the bikes were paralysed before reaching the top, forcing a falling, sliding dismount, pick-up and wheezing push to the other side. Brief respite came in the shape of hidden Hobbit holiday communities, whose wooden homes, porches and avenues filtered out a fraction of the storms blowing through this barren Danish desert. Children left behind sunken footprints as they trudged to the summit of miniature dunes, before rolling their turning bodies back down the soft cushioned slope. Towering steel skeletons of triangular viewing posts clambered upright and snakes, black and brown adders with white tattooed diamond backs, sat coiled by the path like a Cumberland Sausage cooking in the sun.

Freezing cold and just about breathing out of our backsides, it had taken three hours to make 25 kilometres and the halfway stage of this laboured grind against the elements at Hvide Sande. The sparse inhabitants are scattered either side of a large canal driving straight through the centre of the small fishing town, linking the North Sea with the inland Ringkøbing Fjord. Nursing a wind battered aching neck and ears, gripping shaking hands around a steaming cup of coffee, the resilient short and T-shirt wearing Hvideians stared at our head-to-toe covered bodies as if we were mad. Rhys' wet nose had been whistling in tune with our blustery foe and he was tempted to funnel the contents of a hot drink into his sock to revive worryingly numb feet. Sheltered inside a take-away facing the canal bridge joining Hvide Sande's opposite cheeks we ravenously tucked into a plate of *pølsemix*, chopped-up frankfurters, fries and onion drenched in tomato sauce. But we were still shivering with an added sweat. How was it possible to work so hard getting here and not physically generate any bodily central heating? The diner was run by two plump girls no older than 12 and 15. They obviously gorged themselves on the leftovers (but got no food tip from us) and were also qualified to serve lager as well as fizzy drinks, offering an explanation for their over developed beer bellies.

Begrudgingly returning to our arduous path we crossed the bridge as stocky seagulls were hopelessly smashed from left to right attempting to climb above the atmospheric block on their flight path. A claustrophobic crowd of anglers rubbed shoulders on the harbour wall, without any hint of a punch-up brewing over crossed fishing lines, and two brave windsurfers made the most of the perfect conditions for a whipped ride across the surface of the fjord. Peculiar 'No Rocket Signs' took off at the roadside, convincing me this natural wind tunnel was the perfect aid for Denmark's secret plans to join the space race.

We had another 20 kilometres in front us, but I was already spent, falling asleep at my handlebars. Exhaustion turned into despair and for the first time since Norddeich I questioned my presence here, not helped at all by Rhys' decision to start singing 'Show me the way to go Home'. But we crawled on hands and wheels through more goading lumps of hill, sinking sand-traps and breaking gravel, before limping, not galloping, to the peak of our torment, the one-horse town of Søndervig. Closed bars, restaurants and ice cream joints with security grills shut tight wasn't the welcome we had hoped for. But Søndervig, like everywhere else north of Ribe so far, was two weeks away from opening up for summer. Another desolate destination powdered by dancing grains of sand, Søndervig had only two things to offer. A bowling alley at the edge of town, where a lane side quarter of a litre of beer cost £3, allowing the expensive Scandinavian drinking myth to launch a vengeful comeback. But the laddish local Kingpin, who had honed his technique by letting cloth hungry pants suck his shirt inside skinny jeans, seemed to be in his element. Bowling champ printed off his winning scorecard and rubbed it in the face of a defeated girlfriend, who was demoralised further by an obese clapping and cheering pal with nacho crumbs guacamole gunge glued to all three chins. A sign for a candle shop called Hand-Ys provided the other minor attraction. The red company logo could have been a hand holding an upside down, sperm-filled, used strawberry flavoured condom. Oh, how we chortled! But it was just too much excitement to handle after a cycling shift of such hard graft. Making the most of campsite sandwiches, the day's accumulated filth was hosed off a gratefully sighing Erika, Globe and packs, before raising the white flag.

22   No Defence for St George

Rusty coloured fields gave way to a rife nostril full of dung streams intensified by a gentle warm breeze. Pungent liquid brown treacle flowed around the drinking feet of heaving pines, parted only slightly by the chopping of a gale-free cycle path. Animated hefty mounds of fallen brown needles, fading fast under the sun's glare, teemed with life as the sturdy plate armour of inch-long wood ants went about their daily business. Rhys, unbelievably, had failed to pick up the strong whiff of manure and began waxing lyrical about the soothing smell of the trees.

'Wow, man. That pine is so fresh.' Rhys must have possessed some genetically inherited nose filtration system, as all I could smell was shit, shit and even more shit. 'It's never smelt that good before. Just goes to show you how much of a rip-off those pine toilet cleaners and little magic trees you hang up in your car are. They never smell as refreshing as this.' Rhys was obviously suffering dope withdrawal and was getting high on the next best thing as he started going all philosophical on me. 'You know what, Bern, cycling out here in the sticks is great for spring dusting the brain. It gives you room and time to think. What's life all about? Is there a God or flying saucers? How did man suddenly evolve from scrabbling around for a bit of flint and making a fire to lashing a load of wires together for a TV set? Did the information just suddenly pop into his head or is it something to do with alien intelligence?' Too shattered to indulge in an intellectual debate, the best I could muster was an occasional 'ummm' or nod of acknowledgement. Rhys, however, was just getting into his stride and happy to do enough talking for the both of us. 'Did you ever wonder who was the first person to say fuck? And then classify it as a universally accepted swear word which spread around the world. And if there is a God why did he invent the daddy-long-legs? It's got to be the most useless insect ever. Apparently it's got a deadly poison trapped inside its body, but can't use it. What's the point in that?' Great! My cycling partner was tripping on pine cone fragrances and adding to the shit around here with a dribbling mess of his own verbal diarrhoea. Mustering the strength with a wince, I pushed on and pulled away to rest my battered ears.

A single duckling-shaped cloud flapped around ahead. We were back balancing on a pencil of land between the North Sea and the Nissum Fjord's bluey hue, offering a much smaller and easier going border than its growling predecessor at Ringkøbing. Another harbour clinging population, Thorsminde, acted as a half-way coffee stop. Freshly caught flat fish hung out to dry on back garden washing lines and a waterfront museum café presented a curious jumble of ancient propellers, anchors, cannons and heavy splintered timber remains of the British Royal Navy vessel *St George*. England was at loggerheads with the Danes between 1807–14 and in order to protect trade routes to the Baltic against Danish privateers and cannon boats, nearly 100 warships were committed to a North Sea safety convoy.

Many merchants were still captured and rough weather off the unpredictable Jutland peninsula inflicted considerable losses on the navy. The sneaky Danish bastards even turned off the lighthouses to make life more difficult. *St George* had been disabled by previous sea damage and was crawling back home under escort from the *Defence*. The cursed warship was wrecked in a violent storm two kilometres from Thorsminde on a grim Christmas Eve in 1811. Just six men from *St George's* 850 strong crew escaped a watery grave and survived to see Boxing Day. The *Defence* was wrecked slightly further north up coast. Nearly two centuries later, diving teams have braved these unpredictable waters, hauling back a treasure trove of lost items. Lumps of wreckage, wine bottles, octants, tools and weapons salvaged from *St George* have been brought back to the surface and are now on display at Thorsminde's *Strandingsmuseum*. Sinking warships, Dutch sea battles and North Atlantic Walls. Was I getting paranoid again or had my country blemished most of the foreign shorelines on this trip with a connection to varied past hostilities? All I wanted to do was have a cup of coffee in peace without being reminded.

A spectacular sweep along an elevated coastline bridged the villages of Fjaltring and Ferring. Ice Age sculpted cliffs of fragmented orange sand rose high above the beach and the rocky groynes below casting an arm into the sea. It really was a long way down. Cycling carefully along the edge of a jagged grass-topped periphery, it was a strain on the eyes to make out breaking waves kissing the shore at the feet of faint human specks moving slowly along its lips. We were definitely climbing now. Right from day one, most of this journey had pursued flattened cycle friendly trails, invaded for the first time by the dusty hills of Ringkøbing.

But the big boys had certainly hit town. The prominent stack of coast ahead, which followed a downward freewheeling heaven, for the next few kilometres at least, could have had irregular chunks bitten out of its sandy face by a famished giant. Purring contentedly, the North Sea fell backwards in an endless calm expanse of grey-tinged blue and white wooden pencil box churches, stapled with metal crosses, concealed shrunken passing villages on our blind side. It was an incredible view from all angles.

The serenity was shattered by a descending bug swarm. Our heads, legs, arms and bike packs were covered in hundreds of the black critters, parachuting in from up above for a nibble. The sturdy shits had a firm grip too, clinging on tightly for more than a single frantic swipe of a rolled-up town guide. Ploughing forward as quickly as possible we managed to shake off the unwanted attention and slide parasite free up to the red stack of the *Bovbjerg* lighthouse. Its lamp tower is 62 metres above sea level, offering a 35 kilometre observation of your immediate surroundings and 18 different churches at the last count. Next door, tiny Ferring was a collection of one-storey red tiled roofs, with strings of polished beach pebbles dropping down from front doors and porches. A rough, lumpy concrete man with folded arms stands on the cliff top overlooking the sea. His creator was expressionist artist Jens Søndergaard, who, fascinated by the powerful nature of Denmark's west coast, had a summer house studio here until his death in 1957. It is now a museum of his work.

Brown cows sat on a lawn outside a Vejlby farm house, crowding around a window for a peek at the phosphorus glow of a TV set inside. A boring background of bumpy marshy fields bordered by wooden posts and barbed wire was momentarily saved by a curious picture of a cape wearing, high-kicking musical icon. 'Elvis Museum – 700 metres' directed the sign. The universal appeal of The King never seizes to amaze me. Apart from a couple of movie soundtracks, Elvis never recorded songs in other languages, and the only time he performed outside his United States home was five concerts in three Canadian cities during 1957. And here we were again, in the arsehole end of a Danish nowhere, 30 years after Elvis' untimely death, and they had a permanent tribute going on.

It reminded me of a bar I visited on my short-lived camper van tour of the Netherlands, which reached its pinnacle at the northern village of Haren, just outside Groningen. The thirty something owner of the pub, hidden behind a quiet suburb chip shop, had only left the building once in his whole life. Where did he go? Over the North Sea to London? Across the border to Hamburg or even down south and west a bit to visit Brussels? No, he put his mum on a plane and made his one and only flight out of the Netherlands to Elvis' Graceland home in Memphis. The back room of his joint had been transformed into a shrine to his hero, with blown-up pictures of the Graceland pilgrimage surrounded by the various guises of Elvis, in both handsome chappy and fat pill-popping karate suit mode. The bar owner even had a chunky gold TCB ring, which stands for Mr Presley's favourite catchphrase, 'Taking Care of Business.' It was much more unhealthy than my own Dr Who obsession.

More animals greeted us at the gateway to Langerhuse. Two horses scraped their heads along the metal wire of a rounded enclosure, trying to find a weak link to an escape route. It was a sign we should have heeded. A bleak outpost, Langerhuse's only campsite rested on a wide open strip of field and couldn't have been refurbished since the 1950s. It was Butlins' worst nightmare. Bent nails held fragile door locks together and it was easy to get an unwanted mucky finger, pushing a hole straight through the middle of tracing paper toilet roll generously supplied for guests. Dim light bulbs made hard work of sorting yourself out down below as it was and the lukewarm showers dribbled out weakly at an additional coin operated expense. Worst of all, the whole shower block stank of vinegar drowned chips. It was rank! Attempting to convince us to stay (we had little choice), the German Shepherd guarded mumbling old man in the camp office said hot food was available at caravan 49. Maybe he had trouble counting, because they only numbered up to 39, or Alzheimer's. Either way, I gave him the benefit of the doubt. The only other eating option on site were three bruised, black pudding bananas, which you would struggle to give away in Ethiopia.

Pedalling hungry bellies into a desolate village, it soon became clear that Langerhuse was now top of the charts in the grime ball stakes. Teenage delinquents sat on a wall outside the Spar supermarket, which doubled up as a youth club, drinking bottled beer, smoking themselves to death and scooting around the empty street on mopeds. Filthy houses were brick chipped and in desperate need of decorative TLC and the incoming station platform, a grandiose term for a 10 metre long bank, conveyed a general lack of out of town visitors. It was the village Denmark had forgotten (or was bloody trying hard to). Langer-shit-huse's bright spots were few and even fewer. There was an army surplus store, closed of course, with a window display of plastic duck and pigeon decoys, plus various military jackets and webbing (camouflaging an underground X-rated hardcore porn superstore I suspected. There had to be something to do here). A depressed ramshackle pub falling to bits slumped an aching wall of ribs against a car park entrance. It appeared that a person of charitable conscience had attempted to put the broken boozer out its misery by gutting it with fire. But it was still in business, only opening at weekends.

Luckily, the Pizza Shed was open. An olive skinned owner with bushy dark eyebrows awaited our order as flies buzzed around his grease splattered, previously white apron, which had more than one set of grubby fingerprints down its front. Stavros never uttered a word as he prepared our meal. I felt slightly put out that he hadn't shown a touch more excited appreciation for our custom. After all, four glasses and ten plates stacked on a wonky shelf were hardly the catering tools of a man spoilt for choice with punters. Did he not realise how far we had come for this feast! It was probably the only business he would get all week in this dive. Very much doubting that Danish Health and Safety officials had visited this neck of the barrenlands recently, I prayed Stavros had washed his germ festering mitts. The wall tiles were covered in a thick film of dirt and as the pizza and charcoaled chips were thumped down in front of us, I wondered how many flies had crawled into the oven and congealed with the herbs sprinkled over six cheapskate circles of gammy pepperoni. The phone buzzed into life and Stavros finally bellowed a deep tone into the receiver. I hope it wasn't the kids at the Spar making a crank call on behalf of the next village, as with no logo emblazoned delivery van outside or special heat retaining bag our host was going to struggle keeping a pizza warm on a 10-mile hike. He really couldn't afford to lose any more customers. We weren't coming back. Ever!

23 Shaggy

At the earliest invitation of a meek sun losing a chilly dawn battle against grey clouds and a moist overhang, we beat a hasty retreat out of Langerhuse. It was a miserable May 1st and I couldn't even be bothered to offer Rhys a pinch and a punch for the first day of the month. It was day 22 in the grand scheme of things and it began with a fully clothed, silent trudge through misty marshes and lakes. Not even attempting to locate kick-starting morning coffee juice in our bid to escape Langerhuse, we sulked as we cycled. A mother swan hadn't plucked up the courage to face another gloomy day. Curling a majestic long slender neck around a crown shaped nest of straw supporting a noble white plumage, she let her old man do the rounds, gracefully gliding around the ringed enclosure of reeds encircling his missus. An alarming oily green substance began spreading tendrils over the surface of the lake. I hoped it had nothing to do with the smog exhaling chimneys of Thyborøn straight ahead.

Another trawling community, the rocky headland of Thyborøn was the North Sea entrance to the Limfjord, an irregular shaped sound, twisting and turning around 180 kilometres of bays, narrowings and islands, before exiting on to the Kattegat at Hals on Jutland's east coast. This was a sheltered route for bottle-job boat skippers targeting a smooth passage to Sweden, lacking the balls to take on the stormy point of the peninsula. And who could blame them! The whole place stunk. A disgusting concoction of raw fish and rubber inner tubes filled the air. It was an awful pong generated by the town's dominant feature, the three-pronged blue arrow painted smokestack of the Triple 999 fish processing plant. A useful number to remember when a blaring ambulance is urgently required to whisk you to a hospital emergency room for a nose transplant. The few pasty people ambling around the roads didn't look well at all. There was definitely something more sinister to this atmospheric pollution. The unclean handful were a bit scabby, spotty and greasy-haired. I was seriously waiting for diseased limbs to fall off at the road side. Even the coffee, finally percolated at a Super Spar, had a briny taste to it. Uggh!

A nearby sculpture was carved into the shape of a giant Jenga stack. A game nobody had finished (probably because their mutating arms had dropped out of sockets leaking green chemical gunk as they attempted to gain the upper hand). Temporary sanctuary was provided by the *Sneglehuset*, or Snail House, a Hansel and Gretel style building with the candy and chocolate pebble-dashing overhauled by mussel, oyster and snail shells from the nearby beach. Hand painted and arranged in colourful patterns of flowers and mermaids, the house had a large collection of sea shells from around the world. Desperate to make another speedy exit, while two sets of healthy enough legs remained free of airborne fish flu, we passed picturesque mounds of brown dirt, rolled timbers piles and the peeling hulls of land raised boats on route to another ferry ride. A small carrier boat, packed with the usual assortment of cars, trailers and heavy trucks, bobbed up and down across choppy waves. It was freezing outside. The weather was definitely taking a turn for the worst. Huddled up close to each other, shivering on a squeaky couchette in a small passenger room, we were greeted by one last fishy aroma, this time delightfully diluted by the stench of toilet piss. But neither of us moved as it still beat getting rinsed by the ice cold deck spray outside. Unfortunately, it was only a 15 minute crossing.

A long dreary road divided two channels of dapple-grey water leading upwards towards Agger. Swans getting bashed around by the wind skimmed surface were no mugs and kept their heads tucked inside a warm bed of floating feathers, while we plodded on, hoods up, under a growing drizzle. Turning away from the tall rock carved interior above the banks of the disappearing Limfjord, the route bridged two lakes and an old motor boat snucked into a reedy bed, before plunging back into serene country lanes. We both felt exhausted, but I couldn't work out why. With our immediate surroundings offering nothing better to do than sleep, we had treated ourselves to three ludicrously early nights since departing Ribe. We should have been full of beans. Rhys was feeling it the most, lagging a whole kilometre behind at times. After forcing a totally bushed body up another steep meadow bordered hill, or gratefully accepting a descending gift requiring no effort at all, I would glance over my shoulder to make sure the consistently receding dot was still tracking me. Sometimes my speck of a friend would blink off the radar, only to blip back on a few minutes later.

This game of sloth and mouse continued for the remainder of the morning, before Rhys pulled off a complete disappearing act. Having not seen so much as a gravy granule in my rear mirror for the last 20 minutes,

I made an emergency stop. Concern for my chum's welfare was partially distracted by a fascination with a front garden penned baby goat training its horns by viciously headbutting an antler shaped set of branches. Deciding it was sensible to wait in the same spot, while keeping my fingers crossed that a bored, lonely farmer's wife would toss out a freshly washed bra and knickers to give Billy some chewing practice, I waited and waited a bit more. Where was he? I prayed he wasn't lying face and bike down in a ditch somewhere because I didn't have the energy and couldn't be bothered to launch a rescue mission, re-tracing the sharp hill raising its legs behind me. Another 10 minutes passed before Rhys loomed back into view, freewheeling back to my side. 'Where have you been. I was worried,' I blurted uncontrollably.

'Sorry, man. I found a dead white cat in the road and started knocking on peoples' doors to see if it belonged to anybody. I couldn't just leave it there. God knows how it got run over. We haven't seen a car all morning.'

We were back in the heart of Deadsville again, miles of drifting fields, houses scattered few and far between, and electricity lines running off little brick towers with wooden doors connecting them to the power grid. Spotting an oasis up ahead, a Merlo garage, we downed bikes and sniffed for coffee beans. Predictably, it sold everything but. We'd had enough now, Rhys was still in mourning and our spirits were flagging. It was vital we immersed ourselves back into any form of civilisation as fast as possible. Cutting back on to the main road north – the 181 – we continued our ascent along a ghostly single track of tarmac slicing through another hefty chunk of pine plantations. Twenty-five low-key kilometres lay between us and Klitmøller, the next decent sized village on the map and the hope of finally sipping something hot. Rhys had been given time to think again and had his entrepreneurial hat on. 'I'm coming back here with the contents of my piggy bank,' he vowed. 'All these miles of road and not one burger van selling coffee. I'm going to buy 50 of the bastards and set them up at every 10 kilometres. I'll clean up no problem.' Rhys was allowing a parched throat to rule his head. We saw no more than 20 cars in two hours. It really wasn't a viable foundation for a sound business.

Could we have stumbled across Shangri-La? I had cycled a fair distance over the past few weeks, but this plateau hamlet resting among mini peaks of rising dunes wasn't the mountainous spiritual haven of Tibet. It was the Danish surfing paradise of Klitmøller. The office at Nystrup Camping was more chilled out than the average freezer. An old curiosity shop of junk, vibrant oriental garden pictures hung from the walls and huge smiling bronze Buddha statues kneeled around a driftwood table supporting a chess board, scratched gold plated coffee pot (yippee) and an assortment

182

of lanterns. This hidden refuge also had its very own Dalai Lama, who eventually decided to give us a special audience after 10 minutes of ringing the counter desk bell.

But it was worth the wait. Long swishing curtains of grey hair, discoloured teeth and baggy hippy flares hovering above bare, hard skinned, feet added up to one person. It was that loveable coward Shaggy from Scooby-Do, who by the intoxicating smell of things had hit the bottle after hanging up his ghost hunting shoes.

'Ahh. Deutschlanders?' he asked tentatively.

'No!' we responded in stern perfect tandem.

'Ahh. Cockneys!' he replied excitedly.

'We're not Cockneys, we're Southenders,' I batted back.

'Apples and pears Guv,' he giggled. 'You are Cockneys. We do not see many of you here. You must be crazy to come to Klitmøller, but so am I and it is good to be this way. We get plenty of Danes and Germans, but not Cockneys. You will like it here, everybody makes friends, everybody talks, there is a good vibe.' I resisted the temptation to enquire if he had a talking dog with a soft spot for deep-filled French bread sticks. Shaggy ran a laid-back campsite with caravans and tents napping inside their own private fern clustered huddles. I'm sure I spotted the Mystery Machine's back bumper poking through a knot of branches.

Klitmøller is one of the top surfing spots in northern Europe, packed to the rafters with male sun-tanned torsos topping flowery patterned boardies and skimpy bikini clad honeys, who flock here for serious summer competition. But we were two weeks too early, again, and the wind-swept village was still hibernating. A single road trailed past small houses down to an exposed dead end strip of sand, fringed by rocks, sitting on the edge of a car park. White heads of surf were kicked up by aggressive wind swells, with waves breaking off at left and right tangents towards the shore. There were no dudes brave enough to conquer the sea on our fleeting visit.

A surf shack bar, shop and take-away combo faced the raging drink. Windsurfers and boarding fanatics broke numerous waves on a giant plasma screen, while colourful surfing uniforms and boards filled the walls, along with a framed collection of dead butterflies. A pink ring of Hawaiian flowers paid homage to the roots of surfing. Jackson Crane, an American serving under the explorer Captain Cook, was the first person to have witnessed boarding art on the Central Pacific volcanic archipelago in the 1700s. The Hawaiians were believed to have started surfing on logs and it was an important part of their culture, with the chief the most skilled wave rider in the community. He also had the advantage of whittling his board from the best tree. Commoners were not allowed on the same beaches, but they could climb the social ladder by demonstrating their ability to surf, handicapped by much heavier boards. Surfing is regarded as a way of life by many of its disciples and a marker pen scrawl across a white board hanging by the entrance preached a meaningful Gospel which certainly rang true with me. *'Don't let your biggest fears stand in the way of your dreams, even if your biggest dreams happen to be your biggest fears.'*

Two bald headed Mitchell brother lookalikes were holding a high level meeting with the only other people in the bar, the owner and his wife. Eavesdropping their discussions became increasingly frustrating as they chopped and changed between speaking Danish, and then English in a northern accent. One of the brothers, Tage, was in his early thirties and preparing to cash in on the hectic summer trade by opening a fresh fish buffet restaurant upstairs. His mother was Danish, from Ålborg, and his father from Leeds. The quietly spoken Manchester United fan had only spent a few months in England during his life, but still spoke in broad northern tones. Spending much of his adult years posted in the army in Germany, Tage was looking forward to escaping into a new business venture. 'I don't miss England that much, as I've hardly ever been there,' he admitted. 'The way of life here is more relaxed and the Danes are a very hospitable people. The only thing I miss about England is the pasties and sausage rolls. You can't get them anywhere here.' Tell us about it!

Retreating back to the TV room at Camp Shaggy and stretching tired legs across a long sofa in our sleeping bags, Liverpool knocked Chelsea out of the Champions League on penalties. With the temperature dropping around the tents and the central heating cranked up to sizzling inside, Rhys opted to stay put and kip in front of the television. 'It's not like Shaggy's going to come and chuck us out. He'll be rat-arsed by now,' was his argument for squatter's rights. Freaked out and woken for the last time by a demented coin hungry Paddington Bear kiddies car ride, which hunted money by rocking up and down, asking if you wanted a marmalade sandwich every 15 minutes, I ventured back out into the bitterly cold dark. It was 3am and peeling back the dew-soaked outside flap of my tent, I threw the sleeping bag inside and fell back to sleep. Rhys continued to snore obliviously in the TV room.

The next morning, Shaggy, still wearing the same clothes, was filling Shangri-La with mystic smoke as he chomped on a big fat cigar in his office. Gangly legs wide open, he sat on a red couch with two drinking buddies and shouted out: 'Hey! It is the Cockneys. Come and meet my friends.' It was 9am and all we wanted was a strong, hot coffee, poured from the gold plated pot. 'Have you any coffee?' I asked. 'No! But you can have some beer,' laughed Shaggy insanely through blackened teeth, swilling around the brown contents of a raised glass. We hit the road.

24   Sea fog vanishing Act

Hanstholm was the first step on a steep curvature of coastal staircase climbing to the top of Denmark. A former island raised out of the water and fused to the mainland by plate tectonics, it faced the mighty channel of the Skagerrak, a windstorm magnet separating the roof of Denmark from southern Norway. Back on the 181 approach to the harbour town, shivering dunes had sprouted raked back green hair, flecked with blonde highlights, to keep out the cold. Ghostly apparitions of fishing vessels faded in and out of focus on the horizon, picture framed by the burly backs of sand. Face wind was minimal, but the jerky sea made instant sense of a clutch of 'No Swimming' warnings hammered into the road side. Ominous concrete gun posts, relics from the Germans' occupation of Denmark during the Second World War, tracked us from the rising cliffs above and a well fed, brown hawk with a yellow beak perched on a post waiting patiently for its next meal.

Shaggy had a promotional video in his shop, entitled 'What made Hanstholm Great?' We didn't watch it. The bizarre sleeve design was self-explanatory; fishing trawlers, ferries, goods lorries, a woman welder and two dead pigs hung up behind a smiling slaughterhouse worker wearing a bloody apron with a knife in his hand. The town itself rested on a raised mound circled by dockyards and ferry terminals, whisking passengers off for a bumpy ride to Norway, the Shetland and Faroes Islands. Forklift trucks carrying plastic boxes full of ice-packed freshly caught fish clunked in and out of warehouses. Green fishing nets sat slumped in wooden chests outside rickety sheds waiting for untangled employment. The sky above was fuzzy and the freezing breath of the Skagerrak was a bone chiller. Rhys wasn't happy. 'When are they going to turn the lights back on?' he demanded. 'We haven't seen the sun for two days now. I've had enough of these damp, miserable starts already.' I tried to feign sympathy. Where was he in Norddeich?

Ducking into an industrial estate to take shelter from the Skagerrak's fierce temper, a graffiti sprayed alley of pink stick men, aliens wearing berets, jellyfish and slimy green eels led to a hefty downward slope back into farming country. A Doberman pup, still bigger than the average dog, sprung up alertly from his front garden chair, giving me nightmare flashbacks of the attempted Jadebusen mauling. But it only wanted to play and chased us all dopey pawed for a good half-a-kilometre, huge balls swinging from side to side, before finally surrendering to watch us vanish, all slobbery mouthed and burnt out with a trailing tongue scraping the floor.

The sun finally put in a decent appearance outside the village of Vigsø, which filed awkwardly into a crunchy path of gravel, heading deep into quarry flanked dunes. 'This couldn't be the right way,' I warned Rhys and he agreed, but with no North Sea Cycle Route marker offering an alternative we persevered. The conditions continued to deteriorate and a carpet of thick non-cycle friendly sand forced us into an uncomfortable saddle convulsion across a lumpy strip of grass bordering the path. Growing doubts about our current route were fuelled by no other signs of life for 30 minutes, before passing a lonely parked car unveiled a red faced owner's head popping out of a scrubby thicket. 'Did you see that? He was just lying there stark bollock naked,' I called to Rhys.

'I saved you there. If you were cycling alone he would have shot you in the bum with a tranquillising gun, leaving you to come round tied up in a barn with a sore arse,' he laughed. The sun had obviously cheered Rhys up.

Neither of us were laughing after another 15 minutes of cycling vibrations, which were anything but good. The trail went cold at a dead end of sand, barred by a huge impassable dune. 'Fuck it. I knew it was the wrong way. We'll have to go all the way back to Vigsø. What a waste of fucking time.' I could have cried. Lifting our spirits with a wave and cheer to nudist man, we struggled back to the starting point. There was a North Sea Cycle Route sign all along, but it was purposefully turned to face the wrong way. It must have been twisted around by a horrible troll as our embarrassing efforts weren't enough to bend back the post. There could be hundreds of cyclists lost in the dunes, gravel and sand right now, but at least we tried to put things right. The official route wasn't much better. It was more like an assault course. A slight indent in a field of rock hard mud and grass, drooping tree branches provided an overhead hazard, calling for two or three delicate limbos on the move.

Restored to the luxury of a flat main road, a cycling couple decked out in identical red waterproofs hailed us as they passed. The oxygen required to say hello nearly finished off the puffing woman at the front, who was lugging four heavy bike packs and had a complexion to match her jacket. The relaxed male partner taking up the rear was pannier free and gave us a nod and a wink translated as: 'Yep. I'm the man.' Acres of green pasture padded out the background and a herd of black cows gathered around a runt of a calf drew a typical Rhysinism: 'You see that one. His mum was raped by a goat.' He then went on to broaden my horizons further by informing me the strongest brand of mind-altering magic mushrooms were the ones hand picked from cow pats. 'That's right. The cows eat the mushrooms in the grass and shit them out. Just brush them down and swallow. They're right mind blowers. It won't do you any harm.' Of course not Rhys, ever heard of mad cow disease? The people out here lived in complete isolation, you didn't see a house for miles and then they would pop up in all sorts of strange places, in the middles of bushes, surrounded by dunes or hanging on the edge of a cliff. It must have been sub-zero here in winter as tiny sheds were crammed full of neatly chopped firewood and big pyres were stacked up in front gardens. One rare abode, laying way back in a field, was named 'Klitgaarden'. I wondered if this was Danish for brothel. I should have read that phrase book.

Well made roads whizzed past the large water body of the Lund Fjord, before clicking into the lowest gears possible to stave off a heart attack, a killer of a hill lifted us panting to the summit of the gargantuan *Bulbjerg*. The 47 metre high limestone cliff stares boldly into the face of the Skagerrak. For centuries chalk blocks were sawed from its body and used as building material. Visitors have carved their names into the limestone, which also includes the signature of a 19th-century king. The all consuming power of the Skagerrak was made blatantly obvious by the sad vestiges of the once proud 18 metre tall ***Skarreklit***. The old limestone and flint rock broke away in a brutal storm in 1978, but the wave lashed remains can still be spotted by a keen pair of eyes 100 metres out to sea. *Bulbjerg* is the only bird cliff in Denmark. The steep face is home to a colony of 4,000 breeding pairs of Kittiwakes, a pelagic gull from the North Atlantic. A much rarer breed, the Fulmar, has also been known to put in an appearance. The stunning view from the top tower is something else, offering a bird's eye sweep along miles of Denmark's best beaches. During the Second World War this all seeing vantage point was utilised by the Germans and two concrete forts still remain. The pillbox next to the sandy car park has been put to good use, transformed into an underground toilet block for visitors. The other bunker, a former radar and gun post, is now plastered in educational bird pictures and accompanying texts. You can still peer out into the dark blue and turquoise patched Skagerrak through the narrow weapon slit and imagine snipers keeping a deadly vigil for enemy boats. The stink of skunk smoke filled the air. A greened out Rhys staggered into the gun room all marble eyed from a quick puff nicked off a group of young lads in the adjacent concrete chamber. 'I haven't had a spliff for so long and that has knocked my socks right off,' he wobbled. 'I couldn't help myself. I just had to have a smoke in this amazing place. This is better than any Amsterdam café and I bet the police never come up here. It would have been rude to say no.'

Another 15 kilometres of ancient pine forests and scurrying red squirrels brought us to an early evening stop at Klim Strand. Yet another back of beyond hemmed in by fields, it possessed a five star campsite swarming with builders busily refurbishing the facilities. It didn't look open and we had another big game on our minds, Manchester United's Champions League return match at AC Milan. Entering camp reception, our expectations of tuning in had dropped even lower than the first leg in Dagebüll. We cornered the girl behind the desk. 'Three questions. Can we stay here? Have you got a TV room? And is it showing the football?'

'Yes, no and yes,' was the mixed reply.

There was no TV room, but the amused camp lady told us we could hire a cabin, which was only going to cost us £5 more each than putting up tents, and she would give us a flat screen TV to watch in the comfort of our timber shelter. Smiling so hard it hurt, we snatched the TV, kept with the Milan theme by stocking up on pasta, cheese, mushrooms, salami and bread from the half constructed market (plus a few bottles of Tuborg) and retired to our own private theatre of dreams. The Alpine hut was like a grown-ups' Wendy House with curtains. Complete with its own porch to hang out the washing, it had running hot water, a stove and cooker, all the cutlery you could want, comfy beds and, most importantly, electricity and a sacred aerial socket. Equally impressive was the kids' wash block. I know that sounds a bit dodgy, but they were decorated with mosaics from the *Asterix the Gaul* cartoons and had tiny showers which would have been tempting to use if they had a lazy scrub seat underneath them. I reverted back to the family room.

Rhys took on the role of wife under protest and prepared dinner, while I promised to make left over salami and cheese sandwiches for the morning. The game was a massive disappointment as an inept United display led to a 3-0 drubbing in the San Siro, effortlessly wiping out their one goal Old Trafford advantage. The Italians would go on to gain revenge over Liverpool in the final, following the Scousers' shock victory in the previous Istanbul showpiece. After swigging the last of our beers and flicking one last desperate time through the channels for some late night European porn action, or even just a glimpse of nipple, we got under the covers. In separate beds. Cosy though it was, I managed to keep my hands off the makeshift wife.

The morning coffee trail was stone cold at Klim Strand so it was a case of plunging straight back into the deathly quiet pine laden wilderness. An effortless stretch of downward glee unmasked another campsite. Rhys banged on the front door: 'Coffee?' But the startled owner, scared to open up, snorted condensation marks on to the window calling back: 'Not today. No coffee for two more weeks!'

Salvation was just around the corner at the posh white wooden panelled *Svinkløv Badehotel*. And it had prices to match! Riding across a pebbled drive, we tallied up more than a few odd looks from guests sitting around tables overlooking the sea. Quickly returning to normality, they scanned the financial pages, forked their way through a bowl of steaming creamy mussels, while quaffing an early tipple. Ordering two coffees from an impeccably dressed waitress, we were stung with a £5 bill, including a 25 per cent service charge. With prior knowledge, I'd have offered to carry the tray myself. Rhys, falling under the influence of a sweet tooth, licked his lips observing the slices of chocolate and strawberry smothered cakes doing the rounds. I reminded my drooling companion he didn't own a house to remortgage and raise the necessary funds of purchase. Heeding my warning, he cracked open a packet of Danish cigarettes to stave off the desire for sugar-coated pastry. Rhys was carrying out extensive research into the curiously named, but cheap brands of Jutland tobacco. So far he had puffed his way through LA's, North State, Princes, and was now putting the 'sawdust, with a touch of pine' flavoured Corners under scrutiny. Getting our money's worth by draining every last vestige, we allowed a crowd of arrivals to disembark from a horse-drawn cart, before scrambling back across the shingle.

Intensified gravel strewn and pot-holed pine forests awaited. It was like bouncing across a moon crater. Every time Erika's wheel hit a rough edged rock, I could imagine jumping two kilometres ahead in ET fashion, which would have been a touch under the circumstances. Concerned feelings built up, as leaping stones twanged off bruised spokes and wheels slid uncontrollably in the pulling grit. Poor Erika was visibly rundown with spots of rust creeping along her brakes and chain. The old girl was taking a right battering and I couldn't believe she hadn't picked up a serious injury yet. But one thing we had learnt about these gravel obstacles was there was no point in pussy pedalling around. You had to hit them hard and get from one end to the other as soon as possible.

And this particular end came to a halt at Blokhus, a seaside resort popular with visiting American airmen, according to an ice cream vendor waving the stars and stripes outside his parlour, who were based inland at Ålborg. What we didn't expect to discover was the next instalment of the route followed a 15 kilometre trail across the beach in front of us. The compacted surface, flattened by cars using it as a motorway, was only a stone's throw from waves splashing against the shore and led to the neighbouring town of Løkken. Cycling on top of sand is hard enough, but doing it with heavily weighted packs was near impossible. Cars printed tyre tracks into the beach as they trundled past, while other drivers had parked their motors under dune cover for a picnic. Parental hand guided children jumped about screaming excitedly as the cold waves tickled their toes and one woman, harness strapped to a monster sized kite, was in danger of taking off as she got caught out by a strong gust of wind. It was a beautiful spot, especially being this close to the sea, but completely impractical for cyclists. Salt water streams leaking across the beach were poisonous for a bike's internal organs of cogs and chains. Erika was suffocating fast as splodges of unrelenting sand strangled her wheels and brake blocks. Enough was enough and we wimped out half-way through, taking a primitive wet dune path and reuniting grateful bikes with a real road. And they were quick to show their appreciation, galloping with increasing speed past valleys of rapeseed crops.

Løkken was another seaside retreat, renowned for its broad 10 kilometre pebble free strip of whitewashed sands and a village of 500 matching coloured beach huts placed along the high, sheltering dunes and lyme grass. Charming fishing houses are dotted around the old quarter and you can buy fresh catches – plaice is a speciality – from vessels drawn back up on to dry land after a shift at sea. The hulls of boats patiently waiting to return to work are half buried in sand, needing a winch or tractor to nudge them back into the Skagerrak. Houses were first built here in 1678 and most of the modern day dwellings had been swabbed with a few tins of deep yellow. Løkken had once been the most important sea trade link with Norway. Grain, butter and meat were swapped for timber and iron right up until the early 1900s and some of the large warehouses dating back to this period still defy time on creaking legs.

Løkken was half-way up the stairs to Denmark's summit and we had been promised a vibrant atmosphere. Getting bored with deserted dust-bowl outposts containing a meagre sprinkling of visible inhabitants, we wondered if the Danes were in hiding. The receptionist at Klim Strand had vouched for Løkken, guaranteeing a superior level of human contact: 'The next day is a Bank Holiday in Denmark so everybody will be out partying. It is a very young, lively place.' With a population of less than 1,500 people I had my doubts. They were proved true. The sun was still straining to make an impression on a clear blue sky as we pedalled into town, but it was definitely growing colder, with a clingy damp feeling attached. Then, in a matter of seconds, it all went grey. A blanket of moisture particles hung all around as a veil of mist swept in from the sea and swallowed Løkken whole. All the buildings vanished, but the rain held off. The air felt wet, you could have jabbed a piercing finger upwards and burst the precipitation bubble, but the atmospheric levers got jammed switching into downpour mode. Passing through the shroud to discover a town square, there were plenty of pubs, restaurants and banks (which looked like bars), but the walking only streets were empty. Maybe the sea fog had come in and swept everybody away, prompting a call for Mulder and Scully.

Erecting our tents at the camp site of a fat controller, with jam dribbles sliding down his shirt, we went hunting for food. With the Faroes fish wife's warning still ringing around my ears the plaice was off the menu. The town centre was still dead and there were more cats prowling the pavements than people. One moggy, with a bushy brush of tail, inspired another vulgar quip from Rhys: 'You see that cat? His mum was raped by a fox.' Examining every alley and street corner for a pulse beat led us to Murphy's bar. There wasn't an Irishman in sight, just a sprinkling of haggard inebriated men in dirty overalls slumped over the counter as they reached the peak of an all day session. The anything but Danish knick-knacks decorating the walls of these grubby watering holes never failed to surprise. Statues of Laurel and Hardy, photos of the indestructible Memphis Belle, plus two Elvis picture discs and a copycat Shakin' Stevens album were the latest offerings. My concentration levels were interrupted by a barely open-eyed wrinkled tramp, who launched into a violent coughing fit, threatening to chuck a tub of lung butter in our direction. His medicinal response was to light up another cigarette. The barmaid sounded the bell at 10pm, making a sleeping drunk jump up startled, before checking the coast was clear and laying a heavy head back down to snore. It was early for last orders, but there was no need to be alarmed, it was just a signal for the changing of the guard. The woman picked up her cigarettes and handbag, trading places with one of the male punters sitting on a stool. The relief staff, already well tanked up, was working the late shift and had hands like shovels, shrinking a pint glass into a thimble. I wondered if everybody here took turns, keeping the place open 24/7 and drinking their wages in beer. They would never leave. But maybe this was home.

Sweet Danish pastries had relegated bread rolls, with slices of cheese and ham, to the sick and tired breakfast division. A heavenly mixture of flour, yeast, milk, eggs, butter and sugar, with the end product filled with dollops of chocolate, marzipan, custard, fruit or jam. These flaky pastries came in all shapes and sizes, circles, figure-of-eights, spirals and even stodgy logs, making every selection a new eating experience. Tucking in on a table and chairs outside a Løkken bakery, two leather clad motorbikers, a pretty petite dark-haired girl and a young Arnold Schwarzenegger, joined us for coffee and cake. Touchy feely leather lady (the lump of a partner didn't seem to mind) had travelled as far afield as Africa, but was taking time out to do something she had never tried before, exploring her own country. The friendly couple were road-testing the bike ahead of scrambling off on two-wheeled adventures to foreign shores. She wanted to know if her arse could handle sitting on the back of a bike for days on end, which she demonstrated by patting a shapely behind. 'So what do you think of Denmark?' she asked.

It was looking much better now was my first thought, but, not wanting to get filled in by Lurch, I said: 'Beautiful countryside, nice people, but very quiet.'

'That is good. I like that. It is very important to the Danes that visitors enjoy our country. We are only a small nation and it makes us burst with pride.' She could rip apart in front of us any time she liked, but please let us finish off the pastries first. It could get messy.

25   Green Square Hooligans

Dunes sprouted mountainous mobile legs in this part of the world. Hulking great banks of sand, with calf muscles toned as big as bungalows, stomped clumsy footprints across the top of Denmark. Trampling down the coastline, aided by strong onshore winds, the shifting white giants mercilessly gobble up any obstacles on their migration path. Passing north between Løkken and Lønstrup, we spotted a half buried building, bearing witness to this awesome natural phenomena's untamed power.

The *Rubjerg Knude* lighthouse may be 60 metres above sea level, but its sad tower face is wedged between huge suffocating shoulders of sand, resigned to a conquered fate. A happier life started on December 27, 1900. Lighting and foghorn operations were fuelled by an independent gas works supply for the first eight years, before switching over to petroleum. Trouble with the neighbours rumbled on between 1910–20. Large amounts of melt water sand from the Ice Age, deposited in the surrounding cliffs, was blown around the area between the lighthouse and the sea, piling up against the tower, filling the well and ruining the kitchen gardens. To reduce movement, marram grass was planted on the dune, but with no success as the sand monster grew even higher. It was the beginning of the end and the lights were finally turned out forever on August 1, 1968. The lens apparatus was produced in Paris at a price equal to building and furnishing a quarter of the completed tower. To prevent an enemy from utilising the lighthouse during a future war, the expensive hand-ground lenses were thrown from the top of the lamp room and smashed. A museum and coffee shop remained, but the relentless build-up of sand and coastal erosion forced the doors closed forever in 2002.

Advancing sands have been a constant problem for the population of north Jutland since the 16th century. Enormous dunes stretched up to seven kilometres inland, driving people back from coastal areas. The Danish Government tried to find a solution with their *Sand Drift Act of 1857*. This allowed the state to buy or pinch whole areas of sand drift, while further legislation allowed them to purchase plots adjacent to their quandary. The thickset mountain pine plantations, which we were still cycling through, were the last lines of defence, ecological buffers seeded on the government gathered lands to keep wandering sands at bay. These forests were common by the end of the 19th century, but helped form barren dune zones, allowing only limited sheep farming and inshore fishing. But by the 1950s most of the migrating dunes were under control.

Hirtshals was harshly exposed to the elements and still struggling to shake off the final vestiges of winter in the middle of spring. A wind-swept town, hemmed in tightly by shivering dunes huddling close together to keep warm, the temperature was dropping into fluffy mitten wearing low single figures. Salty gusts of screaming winds whooshed down grey shopping lanes, hurdled empty benches in paving slabbed squares and danced their way mischievously around the creaking decks and shrieking masts of off duty ships trying to snooze in port. But the coldest and choppiest place, sitting on the edge of town, was the level camping ground. A wide open, sea spray speckled window, staring straight down the throat of the thunderous Skagerrak. The entire horizon was blotted out by the tempestuous shifting of a bluey green haze, broken only by the ragged manes of wild white horses galloping alongside its crashing waves.

Finding a row of splintered fencing to utilise as a crude wind break, we had to fight hard putting up flimsy tents, taking it in turns to stand weight on each other's carrier bag light canvas skins, while pegging foundations were hammered into the ground. It was only the middle of the afternoon, but some so and so obviously hadn't been slotting enough krone into the electricity meter as the daylight was already starting to dim. This inconsiderate individual also needed to keep up with their gas bill payments as it was growing rapidly colder. 'Definitely time to crawl inside our sleeping bags for a warmth conserving power nap,' I proposed. Rhys was already tucked in, the last inch of his closing tent zip sounding a full-stop for the suggestion. Before getting the opportunity to quickly follow suit, another cyclist joined us at the broken fence. With blowing red cheeks, a tangled mass of blonde ringlets and a stained sweat band slapped across a spotty spam, she almost fell off a bike groaning under a mass of baggage. Heidi couldn't have been much older than 20. She had pedalled all the way from home in Switzerland – an amazing 2,000 kilometres in 16 days – and was on her way to the frozen ends of the earth at Norway's North Cape. What was wrong with these people? That was a six-hour ferry ride across the Skagerrak to Norway and then another 2,500 kilometres of seriously deteriorating weather conditions, equalling superiorly colder climates. Heidi was either lacking Alpine friends, had bionic prosthetic joints, or was just a complete weirdo. Why else would you spend the hot summer weeks, hopefully not too far around the corner, getting somewhere so cold? My final question confirmed my final deduction: 'So once you reach the North Cape, just how are you going to get back home?'

'I'm not so sure,' she said with a nervous giggle, before unpacking an orange tent from a circus big-top sized bag, large enough to sleep in anyway. She was more cuckoo than one of her country's famous clocks. We were going to get slaughtered in our beds by a cow bell ringing, Toblerone munching mad woman, wielding with deadly skill the multiple folding arms of a Swiss Army Knife. Death by magnifying glass or toothpick. That sounded painful!

Repeated knockings from Rhys provided a 4pm alarm call and a startled jumping clutch of my throat. Phew! It hadn't been cut. 'Quick, quick. Come out here. We've got a visitor. And it's a girl,' he whispered carefully, so as not to wake his prey, breaking chip paper news. Heidi had decided to catch up on a few lost zeds too, but her slug-shaped tent seemed to have shrunk as two feet wearing white trainers poked through the front zip. Unconcerned about our fellow camper's potential future problems with frostbite, a Gollum like Rhys was dancing excitedly around Heidi's tent, examining the precious dripping items clinging to a rope hanging down from the door. 'Look, look. It's a washing line,' he pointed out with stunning accuracy. 'And there's knickers on it. I haven't seen a pair of knickers for ages. Oh, knickers, I've missed you. Do you think I'd get away with sniffing a pair?'

Dragging a frothing Rhys away from the wet underwear, it was time to check out the camping facilities. The other sprinkling of brainless holiday makers were busy gutting raw fish on special outside metal preparation sinks in their shorts. Shaking chilly heads in utter disbelief, we ducked into the TV room for the welcoming respite of warmth and entertainment. The heating was broken and the TV could only pick up a white dot on numerous channels (without any volume). Soon getting bored with spinning around the leaflet rack, we decided to pick up a few pamphlets and check out what was happening on the Hirtshals area social circuit. We weren't disappointed. Who needed football, bowls or croquet when there was a good old-fashioned knife throwing contest coming up in the neighbouring town? A flier proudly boasted that 'enthusiasts from all over Scandinavia' would be sharpening their blades to take part in this popular attraction for all the family. But live targets for the competition were obviously in short supply as 'people interested in nature were also welcome to attend'. And get hurt, probably. Another handbill advertised a 'New York Style Warehouse Rave' back down coast at Løkken on a Friday night, 'regularly attended by 1,000 people'. Now I knew that was a blatant lie as we'd struggled to tally up 10 people in Løkken. That included our reflections in a shoe shop window and a bushy tailed cat. What did the organisers do, kidnap anybody in a 50 mile radius under the age of 40?

Hirtshals is the Danish headquarters for the Norwegian ferry company Color Line. Thousands of day-trippers make crossings from Kristiansand, Larvik and Oslo all year round, taking respite from the super inflated prices of Norway, which can cost at least twice as much as Danish goods. It would be rude not to take advantage and many Hirtshals counters cater specifically for the fat wallets of loaded Norwegians, desperate to get their hands on cheap groceries, meat and booze. Straight lanes of shops and cafes trickle down to the prominent airy *Green Square* where, on a warmer day, you can sit and watch sturdy passenger ships lumbering in and out of the docks. But to discover Hirtshals' star attraction, you need to bypass the steep vehicle loading gangplanks of the ferry terminals, trawling wharfs and fish factory estates, and head to the opposite end of town. The ultra modern *Nordsømuseet* aquarium offers an enlightening underwater peek at how life ticks by in the North Sea. Claiming to have the largest oceanarium observation tank in the whole of Europe, 6,000 specimens and 70 different species of native marine life are on display here. Sea trout, conger eels and cod are just a few of the traditional population swimming around various tanks, all accompanied by educational English texts.

Some of the live exhibits offer a fascinating microscopic glance at North Sea existence. You can witness the birth of tiny lesser spotted dogfish, wriggling around in small transparent egg sacks, while another glass chamber houses a poisonous spiny weaver fish. The accompanying placard warns its venom strength is similar to a viper, but not fatal to healthy humans. I'd still double dare you to stand on one with bare feet! Other tanks contained slumbering hermit crabs, lugging their shell homes below alien eyes popping out of long stalks, while anchored Norwegian lobsters lazily sharpen their claws against rocks. Touch screen computers and cinema footage fills in the missing gaps about fish from all around the world, as well as the hard working life of North Sea fishermen. You can even turn your hand to a shift on a virtual trawler deck, making yourself sick in the process as the green screen horizon rocks up and down in dicey waters. Luckily a recovery room is available, a recreated slanted cabin, where fellow trawlermen recall tales of a harsh life spent at sea on a TV video loop, just next to the brandy. And if you survive that test, a ship to shop style IKEA kitchen show next door, explains just how all the favourite fish dishes swim from the sea on to a plate.

The most important display deals with the future and the fight to eradicate pollution. The label 'Blue Dump' has been given to the North Sea because of the harmful oil, chemicals and paints thoughtlessly emptied into her waters. This industrial litter is helping to decrease fish stocks, but an even bigger threat to the food source is the consistent rise in the world's population, with unclassifiable human consumption now crushing the maritime economy. Worrying red numbers continue to flicker upwards on a planet Earth computer population counter, hovering above a darkened picture of the globe. It had just reached 6,708,686,746 inhabitants on my visit and I could still hear it clicking away frantically as I walked away worried.

The jewel in the underwater crown was the oceanarium. A sound corridor of rolling wave claps and jellyfish holograms led to the giant four-storey tank, holding 4.5 million litres of liquid. The water is pumped in from a three kilometre long pipe running out into the North Sea, sucking in more than 600 tonnes of the stuff a day to provide the inmates with the most natural surroundings possible. An eerie green light illuminates the tope, mackerel and plaice gliding in slow motion around the rock piles and shipwrecks decorating the floor of their cylindrical prison. Circling this silent chamber, watching the soft bodies curving around their glass domain, was extremely relaxing. But it felt like a two-way mirror. It was impossible to ignore the likelihood that these rubbery emotionless masks were having a good gawp at you too, pushing an inquisitive snout up against their window or making return passes overhead. But keep your grand tanks and Hollywood lighting, I'm a sucker for a seal sanctuary and they also have a comfy retreat here. Walking along an underground corridor, dipping below the surface above, white seals with black spotted faces swam upside down and joyfully torpedoed through the water. You could almost make out a smile underneath those whiskers as they stretched blubbery bellies across stony resting islands upstairs, waving a wet flipper towards a captive audience. They are so cute and make me go all girly inside. But reaching a stroking hand over the slime stained pool wall is strictly prohibited. A cautionary sign reminds visitors that seals are wild animals and just as likely to bite a chunk out of a human hand, as a nice oily fish at meal time. The warning shattered the illusion, transforming me straight back into a suspicious, distrusting male again.

A pitch black Friday night arrived in Hirtshals far too early. It was 7pm and the only landmark of any significance, the 150-year-old *Hirtshals Fyr* lighthouse, was having difficulty flashing a ray of light across a starless sky from its 35 metre Dutch tiled neck. It really was brass monkeys outside and it had been democratically agreed to stay out for as long as possible. We would eat and drink at a painfully slow pace, taking only small bites and sips, keeping our bodies locked inside a heated room and staving off a teeth-chattering return to the tents for as long as possible. Settling into an over priced eatery next to the *Green Square* we called up the cheapest and smallest burgers on the menu. Bored kids with flicked gel fringes punched fruit machine buttons in a side room. They weren't eating, just gambling the value of an economy sized bun to try and generate the necessary funds required to purchase a substantial protein and vitamin friendly meal. We couldn't afford to take that risk. Steaming hot coffees soon arrived (the portly waitress nearly fainted when we declined her costly offer of a beer), ending a futile attempt to warm numb hands around the tiny tear of a table candle flame. Eating became a mental wrestling match. No matter how minuscule the portion of food forked into my mouth (I'd never used cutlery to eat a burger in my entire life), or how leisurely I tried to chew it, my primitive reaction was to rapidly wipe the plate clean. Dinner lasted five minutes and 23 seconds, hardly keeping within the pre-meal guidelines, which, thankfully, Rhys managed to obey with greater discipline, saving us both from a quickfire return to the refrigerator.

Stop two was the *Peder Most*, a fisherman's pub on the main street, packed with well oiled punters crushing themselves in the stampede to claim a front row seat around a circular wooden bar. It was only 8.30pm, early doors by previous Denmark drinking times, but the atmosphere was lively and they were well on their way already. It was 'Prayer Day', a Danish Bank Holiday with a double meaning, giving everybody a great excuse to get absolutely trolleyed off their nuts. Fundamentally a religious day of worship, held on the fourth Friday after Easter, the older generation also remember the unwanted wartime German occupation of their country. The Danes were forced to hide behind dark curtains during the Second World War blackouts, so they illuminate house windows with lit candles every year to signal the end of those bad times. A remembrance meal of a special oven cooked bread is also eaten with cheese or marmalade.

'I'm West Ham 'til I die. I'm West Ham 'til I die. I know I am, I'm sure I am, I'm West Ham 'til I die.' I couldn't believe my ears. I'd been stalked the best part of 1,700 kilometres by a tanked up East End Hamster from just down the A13, close to home sweet home. Or was he a Gooner? Or a Scouser? As the same terrace chant was repeated, with Arsenal and Liverpool taking pride of place, followed by Manchester United and then a rousing chorus of 'there's only one Dennis Bergkamp'. The noisy instigator was Daniel. The teenage delinquent possessed a higher volume than the all singing and Yamaha 9000 keyboard playing crooner belting out 'Mustang Sally' and 'Hotel California' with a Danish twang on the other side of the room. A mess of greasy curly hair and a bottle of Tuborg in both hands, Daniel was a student, who liked to drink a lot and loved watching English football on TV even more. He hadn't been able to pin his colours firmly to the mast of one team, but was obsessed with the cinematic take on West Ham hooligans, *Green Street*, starring Elijah Wood. Daniel didn't have an intimidating bone in his body, wrapping an arm around my shoulder and continually spitting: 'We are the Green Street hooligans!' I tried to convince him that Frodo Baggins wasn't the unscrupulous mastermind behind the Hammers' notorious Inter City Firm.

Daniel's fresh faced friend Jess was on the complete opposite end of the scale. Quietly spoken and well behaved, Jess was a carpenter who idolised Liverpool's Danish defender Daniel Agger and dreamed of watching a live Premiership match at Anfield. He even sported their colours, a red tint across a shaven head. Jess only stayed for two beers, as he needed to get up early for a morning football match, but boisterous Daniel was going nowhere. The loveable wannabe yob was just getting warmed up and, keen to look after his English guests, got in a double round of Tuborg. Daniel could knock them back too and was getting through a bottle every 15 or 20 minutes. It was all going to end in tears for sure. Eager to impress, Daniel wanted to demonstrate his might and admirable cockiness by challenging the other people at our table to an arm wrestling contest. Gripping a sweaty palm in one hand and drinking his beer with the other, he topped off the act with an arrogant stare away from his rival. Daniel put down three opponents in quick succession and I admired his technique. But, hoping to wipe the smug look off his face, I issued the next challenge. Now I'm no arm wrestling champ, there was no pedigree, and with arms not much thicker than the cardboard guts of a toilet roll, the young buck must have fancied his chances. But one thing I did have on my new friend was a wealth of conniving experience. Daniel was even drunker than when he had begun this show of strength and those arm muscles must be tiring. He tried all the tricks, sloshing the beer, looking away laughing and trying to put me down with a surprise attack. But I held on to crack it, slamming his hand into the wooden top after three minutes of wavering struggle. 'Denmark 0, England 1,' I chuckled, extremely pleased with my efforts.

I was the one smirking now. I don't think I've ever won an arm wrestle in my life. But the opportunity of bowing out at the top of my profession, with an undefeated record intact, was shattered by paternal revenge. 'Are you strong?' a deep voice bellowed. The gloating smile fell off my chin and went in hiding under the table as I gazed across an arena of moist cigarette ends and spilt slops straight into the lumpy Adam's Apple of a man mountain. 'No!' I squeaked. This was Søren, Daniel's dad. A moustached North Sea trawler fisherman, with granite shoulders threatening to rip open the top of a brown suit jacket begging for mercy. He grinned unnervingly, holding out a huge tanned Peter Schmeichel sized paw. But there was no epic fight. No head vein pumping, teeth grinding, straining side-to-side toing and throwing of tightly locked palms. It was all over in two seconds. I was just grateful to have an arm sitting comfortably in its socket, still in full working order.

Søren had been flinging his nets out into harsh waters for mackerel and herring for the best part of three decades. Taking his life into his own hands for 170 days a year, he would venture out of dock for two week tours at a time, chasing his quarry all the way to Lerwick on the Shetland Islands and Peterhead in Scotland. The North Sea fishing game sounded about as much fun as rubbing a stinging nettle across your bare bollocks without the relief of a dock leaf antidote anywhere in sight. 'The Scottish say fuck this and fuck that a lot. You speak much nicer in England,' he laughed. 'They also sell shit fish and chips. We don't like it, but when we are in dock we stuff it down inside our empty stomachs so we can drink.'

'It must be a very dangerous job and a hard life?' I asked.

'I have been working the sea since I was a young boy of 15 and I am used to it now,' Søren replied. 'But yes, you must be strong in the head to do this job as the days can be long, hard, cold and rough. I took Daniel once, but he was sick everywhere on the boat and never came again. Fishing is not for him. If he was strong enough to be a man, he would be able to get his whole hand around a beer bottle like me.' Søren's shovels could fit around a bottle with ease and manage a victory lap, while poor Daniel was wincing in pain as he tried to pull his thumb and forefinger together at the bottom of his Tuborg.

It must be hard for the wife, spending long nights in Hirtshals, cold and lonely under the covers, while her man was being buffeted around the North Sea sucking a Fisherman's Friend. 'Does you wife miss you?' I bravely ventured, taking another look at those massive clubs on the end of his wrists.

'You hope she does when you are at sea,' Søren shot back, with fire burning in his eyes. 'I am married for a second time now. My first wife was a bitch.' OK Søren, point well made, whoever did the dirty on you, mate, was either very brave or very stupid. Or probably just dead. I got the beers in. Søren was full of opinions about England and its leading figures. 'I don't like that Tony Blair. I do not trust him. He smiles too much. I was also unhappy to see Prince Harry dressed up as a Nazi at a party. That was very bad as we took your Princess Diana to our hearts and didn't like to see her son doing this.'

He also wanted my honest view of the Germans. 'They got better,' I said. 'Yes, but they still concern me,' mused Søren. 'We must watch them closely and carefully. We cannot let them occupy us again.' Sixty-two years down the line and the awful scars of the Second World War still cut deep, even with a generation not alive during the hostilities.

Daniel's uncle Brian joined us at the table. Another big suited and booted lump who loved Eric Clapton, demonstrated vigorously by playing an air guitar on one knee, and had spent a long time living in Australia. 'You two are poofs? Right!' asked Brian.

'Err... no!' I said.

Brian looked confused: 'But that's what they call you Englishmen in Australia.'

'No! That's Pommes,' Rhys butted in.

'Oh. Sorry!' giggled Brian, before getting up and dancing back to the bar with his hands in the air. Daniel was out of his skull and had crashed face first, snoring into a stack of beer bottles. Søren picked up his boy with a large mitt and dragged him across the floor, while waving goodbye with the other. 'I told you. Daniel is not strong enough yet to drink. We go home.'

It was 2am and, still aiming to keep the frost at bay, we popped in next door to the *Crazy Lady's* disco, a carbon copy of the *Peder Most*, except the windows were blacked out. It was mostly the same crowd filtering in for late drinking. A wrinkled drunken hag with a plaster cast on her arm (maybe Søren's ex wife?), who split the night between falling over for attention and then crying in her beer when the tactic failed. Two male fatties, with matching naval fluff hoarding belly buttons staring out from white boulders beneath ill-fitting shirts, wobbled into the room. And then there was Yamaha man, who had ditched the keyboards and was probably clocking on for a DJ shift. Paid in beer of course. The musical offerings were snatched from a time loop, warping us into school disco mode. The likes of Tina Turner, Chesney Hawkes and Cher all got their turn before Denmark's continuing infatuation with Shakin' Stevens really got the house rocking.

A mega-mix medley, from the great man who danced like he had a wasp in his shoe, contained all the big hits, except, disappointingly, my favourite, 'Green Door'. Indulging in a favourite pastime of people-watching there were some top specimens on the sticky black carpet dance floor. A group of girls were making a circle around their handbags, a ginger Shermanator was jerking around robotically and another couple used free flowing salsa moves to navigate one end of the room to the other. It was getting on for 4am when we threw in the towel, before munching on the biggest, cheapest pissed food pizza slices baked in the world ever (greedy Rhys wanted to smuggle the Turkish owner back through English immigration in his saddle bags after a second slice). Like a giant cinema usher, the guiding torch beams of *Hirtshals Fyr* showed us the way back to our tents. Blowing outwards I could see the cold air in front of my face. But I wasn't feeling it. I was centrally heated by beer and the big, warm hearts of the Danes, who had made us so welcome. This really was the stuff of sweet dreams, inspiring a solid unbroken drunken kip. Scumming it with all my clothes on.

26   Land of Light

'Get up. We're leaving this tight-arsed shit hole right now!' was Rhys' cheery early morning wake-up call. Mr Happy had jumped in the shower, before settling up the overnight camping bill. Both had turned into frustrating experiences. 'What's up?' I asked, chiselling away eye bogies with my fingers.

'What's up? I had to pay for a shower and it never got hot. That's what's fucking up!' fog horned Rhys. I really shouldn't have bothered asking. It only continued. 'I asked for my money back and the office bloke just laughed in my face. He said it was a complicated system and I hadn't worked it properly. It isn't complicated, it's a crappy old dial that turns between hot and cold. He wouldn't refund me and then stung us £5 for a bloody Dancard!'

'So what did you do?' Why was I pretending to be interested? All I wanted was an extra hour crunched up in my sleeping bag. It was only 8am for God's sake and faintly thudding hangover murmurings were stirring!

'What do you do?' Rhys ranted. 'I called him a wanker and he laughed at me again before leaving the office. He couldn't have understood me. He was a big geezer and I should be dead by now.' But Rhys did get revenge. Refusing to flush the toilet after a beer blender of a messy number two and bravely stuffing the entire contents of his pockets – crinkled sweet wrappers and creased cigarette packets – through the reception letter box on the way out. Bet they're gutted now! It was comforting to see the same old faces from the night before back drinking in a smoky packed *Peder Most* on our way out of town. The chalk board outside the door was advertising 'Happy Hour' between 10am and midday.

'Moin-moin!' came the bright and breezy German greeting from a cyclist sharing the last rung of the ladder to Denmark's northernmost point. The 60 kilometre track to Skagen, a mixture of gravel and roads, dividing more pine plantations and minor outbreaks of moss covered silver birches, had been typically deserted. Then all of a sudden Berlin's answer to the BFG (Big Friendly German) burst on to the scene. Dressed from helmet to boots in black, including a fetching cycling leotard, the BFG couldn't speak a word of English, but communicated by chuckle pointing his way through a set of laminated maps. This freak of human nature tied to two wheels was fast approaching seven foot in height and possessed the longest legs I've ever seen (No! Rhys didn't crack a joke about his mother being raped by a giraffe). His lofty saddle perch sat just below my shoulder line and a massive black waterproof bag, grip strapped to the back of the bike, could have contained an inflatable bouncy castle. The BFG remained with us for half-an-hour, smiling, pointing and laughing away, showering a mood lifting sprinkle of happiness over a sullen Rhys. Then the big man was gone as quickly as he had first appeared. Tiring of treading tarmac, the BFG opened up those elasticated legs and rocketed off into the distance. Boy could he move!

Something else was buried deep inside the pine forests. Blank faced metal doors, large and small, painted green to blend in with their surroundings, appeared at the front of grass covered hillocks. They were entrances to half concealed bunkers of some sort. But these hush-hush hidey-holes were a complete mystery. My mind cranked into overtime, wondering what top secrets were guarded by these secure silent sentinels. Were they the gateway to redundant tunnels, dug down below the roots of the trees to a communal survival burrow, offering shelter from a deadly Cold War nuclear attack? Or perhaps, this was the classified underground research facilities of Denmark's leading scientists, eggheads desperate to come up with an even tastier formula for smoked bacon. We would never know.

Climbing higher and higher, almost right to the very top of the Jutland peninsula, I was beginning to get altitude sickness. Or maybe it was just the ill effects of the day after the night before. Skagen wasn't far now, it would soon be time to rest and eat. Denmark's headland was sandwiched in between the unpredictable forces of the Skagerrak and Kattegat seas, the dramatic site of many a shipwreck over the last few centuries. It really was a unique location of untamed and unspoilt beauty, where all the elements, sea, light, air and sand, were truly inseparable. Hulsig Heath was a rugged 10 kilometre plain of natural barrier at Skagen's front door. Brown and red scrubby bush, mixed into the pallet with a splash of pointy yellow and green grasses swarming around kneeling dunes, crowned by another procession of dark mountain pine.

Close by were two imposingly powerful migrating dunes. The *Sandmilen* had stomped right across Skagen and is expected to blow into the Kattegat, while the *Råbjerg Mile* is only half way through its long journey. A two kilometre long mobile desert environment, it is the largest moving dune in northern Europe, extending to 40 metres at full height. The wind pushes the *Råbjerg Mile* in a north easterly direction up to 18 metres a year, leaving a low, moist snail trail of sand behind, stretching back westwards towards the Skagerrak where it originally formed more than 300 years ago. The *Råbjerg Mile*, which attracts 250,000 visitors every year, was never stabilised by plantation for educational purposes, a working model allowing future generations to understand the problem of sand dune drifts. But there have still been man-made casualties. Built in the 14th century and named after a seafaring guardian, *St Laurentii Church* is still hanging on, breathing through a straw like white stepped tower sticking out of a sand packed tomb. At the start of the 18th century, the loyal congregation would dig their way into the chapel to attend services, but the final death knell was sounded in 1795 by royal decree, condemning this house of God to a quirky tourist attraction.

Skagen prides itself on attracting the most sunny days in Denmark, including a strange, sometimes unsettling, glow of luminous evening light washing across its wild landscape. The town records nearly 2,000 hours of sunshine annually and is also blessed by one of the lowest rainfall counts, thanks to Norway's sheltering mountains homing in on showers with magnetic attraction, while a dry Skagen spends another day on the beach. I bet they clean up with umbrella sales in Hirtshals.

In a modern day world madly obsessed with technological forward strides, desperately close to losing touch with its human identity, it was a massive relief to find somewhere still clinging on to its well worn charms in the 21st century. Standing here now it was easy to understand just why the golden age of Danish painters packed up their city easels and rushed to this uncultivated northern outpost for time-testing inspiration. Every turn of a cycle path or street corner was worthy of a stroke from a Skagen master's brush. The quaint pointed roofs of former harbour side fishing warehouses with dark red wooden panels, complimented by gleaming white shutters were a picture themselves. Transformed into gourmet fish restaurants, offering the best of Skagen's speciality dishes, business was obviously booming as customers crammed thighs on to outside benches and filled every corner of a cramped lamp lit interior. There was also something extra for the purists. Nobody could ignore the rustic appeal of the old fisherman's cottages, with wood smoke rising slowly from wonky chimneys and the lingering smell of long eaten catches still milling around.

All of the cottages, like most of the houses hemmed into narrow roads here, were covered with the same deep coat of yellow we had first spotted blanketing numerous buildings in Løkken. But there was method behind this almost regimented madness of conformity. In days long gone by, the houses in Skagen were re-painted every year at Whitsuntide with a mixture of lime and ochre. A remote geographic position and the hindrance of a sometimes impassable coastal road, forced merchants to buy 250 kilos of ochre at a time from the town of Flade, south of Skagen. Safely delivered the ochre would be stored away until the walls needed a spruce up. But one year there was an almighty cock-up, when French golden ochre was mistakenly dropped off to one of the paint sellers. This ochre offered a much more intense yellow colouring, but the locals liked it and splashed it all over their walls, christening it 'Skagen Yellow', and it has stuck ever since. The other distinguishing housing features were to be found among the steeply slanted collection of orange tiled roofs. The edges are licked with a distinctive white border, a nod back to an era when the ends of thatched roofs were treated with protective lime, while the mortar of their slate topped neighbours were white-washed.

Funnily enough, one of the rare outsiders to rebel against the compulsory yellow colour code, was the former living quarters of revered Skagen painters Michael and Anna Ancher. They bought a long red, low house on the edge of town in 1884 and their daughter Helga, who successfully took up the artistic family trade, also lived there until her death in 1964. Sitting contentedly in peaceful gardens, the Ancher house has been painstakingly restored in an attempt to re-capture the working atmosphere of the resident greats whose canvases brought this far flung Danish outcrop to the attention of a wide-eyed world. The house is open to the public and a side annex, *Saxilds Gaard,* has staged changeable art exhibitions since 1990.

Just like your average elephant, Rhys had not forgotten his Hirtshals ordeal and stampeded straight into the reception of our latest camping rendezvous. Moving with such force that two leaflets dropped away scared from a shelf, he went straight for the jugular, not even bothering to offer the usual greeting niceties, just grilling the poor startled cow behind the desk.

'Do we have to pay for a shower?' he blasted through an angry trunk.

'No,' squeaked the female camp mouse.

'Is it hot?'

'Yes.'

'Do we have to buy a Dancard?'

'No.'

'And... er... have you got a swimming pool?'

'Yes. A big one,' she replied confidently, before moving in for the kill by pointing at the sea. 'It is out there. Can you see it?' Top marks love. You played a blinder. Rhys kept his trap shut.

Just a few kilometres' ride from the camp site was the landmark which made Skagen special for me. The sandy finger of Grenen, or Skagen Point, extends out a nail well polished by the buffeting of the seemingly endless Skagerrak and Kattegat seas, clashing head on at Denmark's most northerly tip. These channels act as dividers between the North Sea and Baltic, helping to give Grenen a standing on the edge of the world feeling. The Point is still growing after 8,000 years thanks to natural reclamation and the vast amounts of sand and gravel washed ashore here from other eroded coasts. Over the past 300 years the Point has annually stretched out another eight metres, continuing to move along an underwater reef which reaches out for four kilometres itself. Give it another 1,000 years and you should be able to walk across a sand bridge to Gothenburg on the opposite Swedish coast.

More than 50,000 visitors make the pilgrimage here every year, mainly to have a novelty photo taken of a foot plonked in both seas at the same time. The serving wench in the car park kiosk informed us about visitors from all over Europe; Sweden, Norway, Germany and Italy. A couple had even flown in from Ecuador once, but she'd never seen anybody from England here before. An interesting selection of postcards included an aerial shot of the Point's sandy fin, dividing the easily discernible blue and green shades of the neighbouring seas. There was also a mixture of well tanned breasts, a pink luminous thonged bum straddling a saddle and, something for the ladies, the well formed pecks and backsides of six grinning Danish body building brutes.

Lazy visitors could jump on a tractor-pulled carriage for the mile long journey to the Point, but we decided to freshen up with a gallant walk in the face of a double sea breeze. There were two German pillboxes here. Painted words across the first, half sunken in sand, welcomed you to a land of 360 sea birds. The other crumbling relic from darker times was being cleansed by the sea, just about keeping a concrete perch above water for greedy barking fat seagulls as big as small dogs.

Rhys couldn't throw his shoes and socks off quick enough, scrambling across the Point, dropping a skinny pair of anchors and turning his back on the turbulent shower of white strobes spraying around behind him. Just a few metres away, the inquisitive black heads of amused seals bobbed about carefree among the hilly waves of the Skagerrak. And the sun overhead burnt with the ferocity of an orange jet fighter engine, without ever reaching a sizzling take-off. Grenen had all the ingredients for a remarkable setting rubber stamp. Fine white sands, exclusive different coloured seas, an army of well fed wildlife and an intimate relationship with an amazing sun window, deservedly earning Skagen the nickname 'Land of Light'.

Skagen was a tourist trap, with inflated food and drink prices to match, but well worth a visit. It was the biggest overnight habitat of our Danish tour, but still only accommodated 11,000 people. There was something very comforting about its predominantly yellow canvas, washing over your senses and sucking away the stress and tribulations of everyday life. The bars offered a friendly welcome to outsiders, with great attention taken to cosy lighting and decoration. Just off the town centre, the *Skaw Pubben* was such an establishment. White candles warmed glass table jars, pushing their bodies away from a bed of grey sand and sea shells combed from the nearby beach. Regular past drinkers were obviously highly thought of as their brown tobacco stained caricatures filled a series of tiles lining the walls. Flicking across the bearded, pipe smoking and fishing cap wearing faces was similar to playing 'Guess Who.' The barman informed us most of the old boys had long since passed on.

Artistic renaissance made Skagen famous and tourism might be its bread and butter now, but fishing has always been the real lifeblood of this town. The hectic harbour has just celebrated its first centenary, backing up statistics that Danes catch more fish and shellfish than anybody else in Europe. Denmark is the world's sixth largest exporter of fish and related products, netting nearly 20 milliard krone every year. And Skagen plays a key role in generating such a colossal figure, as far as size and value of catches are concerned, operating arguably the most successful port in the country.

There could only be one choice for the evening meal then. I had to exorcise the cauldron of tauntings from the Faroes Islands' witches, Esbjerg branch, by tucking into a free range feast scooped from the well watered fields of the sea garden. And I was going to eat it with bread. A *smørrebrød*, or traditional Danish open sandwich, sort of does what it says on the tin. That's if one slice of bread equals a sandwich. I always find a solid top and bottom, securing the middle content, makes for a much tidier munch.

But the Danish equivalent consists of one piece of buttered *rugbrød* – a hard, whole-grain rye bread – topped with various meats, fish or pate, a further vegetable layer of tomato, cucumber or beetroot, topped off with a mayonnaise condiment or toasted onion sprinkles. And no, you don't try and pick it up. Use a knife and fork you animals. My cut of loaf was heaving under a pile of hot breaded fish, prawns, herring, mussels and black specks of caviar served on a green salad lining and soaked in freshly squeezed lemon. And guess what women of the Faroes? It didn't 'arf taste good!

208

27   Happiness is Skin Deep

The annoying buzzing of an irritated fly with a headache, ramming the sunshine infiltrated inside of the blue tent canvas, finally got me moving.

It was time to head south along the inwardly curving temple of the Jutland peninsula. The 10-day climb north from our Danish starting point at Rømø had tallied up nearly 560 wheel burning kilometres. The best part of 250 more awaited on the east coast slide down Cycle Route Five, all the way to Grenå and a ship shunt over the Kattegat to Sweden.

A main road cycle trail dissected sprawling farm lands, occasionally interrupted by a muck spreader cleaning family, children offering nervous handfuls of grass to a brown llama straining his chewing jaws over a barbed wire fence and the odd petrol station, all the way to Frederikshavn. The port was a large built-up sea settlement, with more than double the population of Skagen, but lagging far behind on the charm scorecard. In happier days it was the biggest ferry terminal in the country, before the construction of convenient road bridges, linking Jutland with the two main Danish islands of Funen and Zealand, triggered a vastly reduced need for passenger vessels. Unemployment has hit the town hard. The closure of the Danyard shipyard in the 1990s resulted in more than 2,000 workers getting their cards. The sense of gloom hanging over the deserted streets spelt out a slow recovery. A navy base presides here and ferry services still connect the town with Norway, Sweden and the major Kattegat island of Læsø. But it was an uninspiring setting. A fleeting pedal along wind-rushed streets opened out on to a featureless dockside tarnished by the soiled pillars of industry. The only splash of on-loan colour was supplied by a queue of goods lorry shells waiting at the spacious blustery dockyard car park for sea transit escape routes.

A short ride from Frederikshavn's glum face was the contrasting green leafy uplift of the *Bangsbo Museum*. This well maintained country estate spirals back 500 years and was the stimulation point for some of Denmark's most inspirational authors, inking their nibs around the same time Skagen's artists washed their brushes. Every building stores enough antiques to get David Dickinson rubbing his gleeful hands. The moat circled manor house holds a collection of ship figureheads, military documents and a display following the Danish resistance to the German occupation. But the most fascinating feature is the *Ellingå*, the reconstructed remains of a merchant Viking ship – dated 1163 – retrieved from a nearby stream bed. The outside of the museum is skirted by a tangle of botanical and herb gardens, including a bridal grove where newlyweds traditionally plant commemorative trees. A peaceful deer park invites visitors to sit on shaven log benches or pull up tree stump stools to observe fallow, red and roe breeds wandering around freely, nibbling the grass without fences or threat. Or so I thought until spotting a chubby kid pictured in the brochure, watching his father skewering a piece of suspicious looking meat over an open fire. Deer kebab anyone?

We had no idea our bikes were trotting along a mere kerb of Europe's answer to the American Route 66. The 5,000 kilometre E45 made a chilly start in Finland, heading south through Sweden, Denmark, Germany and Austria, before receiving the chequered flag on the sunny island of Sicily. That's the Mediterranean football at the end of Italy's shooting coastal boot and about 16 scrolling pages of your AA European Road Atlas. Concrete armour of ageing German gun turrets dug its way out of the hills above, training invisible weapons across an even older coastal skeleton of sharpened rocks, bullied by the colossal force of ice masses some 14,000 years ago. Filling round pools of jagged fossil teeth, the dull grey porridge of the Kattegat sloshed against stony groynes and the wind started misbehaving again. Grinding on weakly, grimacing above thighs ready to fall off, the backward pushing JCB bucket of nature was doing its best to put up a road block. We'd been spoilt over the last few days, loafing along on a gust-free run, and this was a shock to the system. Protesting against hard work, a struggling body close to strike action released a constant trickle of cold sickly sweet armpit juice dribbling down my sides. To make matters worse, the rock surrounded bowl of grumpy shifting cereal was sending a horrendous stare upwards, threatening to slice the darkening heavens in two. I really didn't need to get any wetter.

A leg destroying 50 kilometres since Skagen had sounded the brake or bust bell. It was only early afternoon, just short of the next town Sæby, but we had exhausted our storm fighting reserves and needed to regroup.

Thankfully, someone in the penthouse suite still loved us, as timely salvation materialised in a very real vision of three neighbouring camping grounds, squeezed closely around the Kattegat's murky banks. Hedebo had a trans-dimensionally engineered Tardis of a mini-market. The much bigger on the inside store's metal baskets and fridges stocked everything from pink fluffy slippers to bulging phallic salamis (with the appropriate bend) and an abundance of porn magazines to really get the flavour. Sold! Despite the restaurant being closed until summer. In another two weeks! Neat level camping lawns were named after American states by the Danish owner, who had even managed to adopt an accent from across the pond. Dane Wayne possessed the largest collection of classic motorbikes in Denmark. His son, Eric Christensen, beamed: 'This is my father's little hobby. He probably has the biggest private collection in the whole of Scandinavia. But there is another big collector in Sweden, who may have just as many.'

'So if the Swedish collector buys a bike, your dad goes out and gets two more?' I replied. Eric chuckled.

The bikes were parked in a glass fronted viewing cabinet outhouse. There were 80 in total, worth a towering stack of dollars. But the bikes didn't seem to be in any immediate danger, redundant headlights facing a deathly quiet stretch of the E45. Open to prying eyes at any time of day, this was surely easy pickings for a motor-minded rustler. I couldn't detect any security cameras, hi-tech electronic door locking devices or late night car park barriers. But Eric assured us his father's prize exhibits were safe and sound: 'We don't leave the keys in the ignition you know. And why would anybody want to steal my father's bikes?' How refreshingly naïve. How Danish! Dating back to the 1930s, many of the bikes were the pin-ups of their era, the heartily cheered mechanical heroes of exhaust fume engulfed race tracks. Heady days they obviously still yearned for as handlebars slumped depressingly to one side. The stunning models on the garage catwalk had been shipped in from all over the world. Beautiful BMW, Norton, BSA, Triumph and Harley Davidsons, all with immaculately polished curving bodies and gleaming eyelash spokes, specially loved and cared for. Christensen Senior had all the powder room accessories too, log books, gloves, helmets, goggles and racing plates, all within their rightful owners' reach. Pick of the bunch was a black and white Motto Guzzi police bike, complete with chunky blue siren. It took me back to nostalgic 80s' Saturdays nights in front of the box, watching officers Poncherello and Baker patrolling the Southern Californian freeways in cop motorcycle drama *Chips*. Apparently they hated each other in real life, which I could never understand as they did a great job on screen. More confusing were the 20-strong car pile-ups on their weekend adventures, with upside down and sideways tossed vehicles miraculously never picking up a scratched bonnet between them.

Hedebo was a pensioners' paradise with no expense spared on creature comforts. These old codgers could give the Germans a run for their money when it came to setting up a flamboyant home from home. When I was a kid, four of us crammed into a single sleeping compartment, behind a head stooping 'kitchen' chamber of wet uncovered grass housing a small gas stove that never lit as it wobbled about on a table with a lame leg. But Hedebo was in the Big League. Outrageous canvas front rooms were attached to caravans, housing everything from tall fridge freezer units to giant plasma screens and a workbench if you fancied knocking up another extension. There were rugs and carpets on the floor and outside the door they had sectioned the grass into gardens with a bordering green plastic trim. This luxurious twilight existence had tickled one of the ageing holiday community's regulars, Hilsen Bendt, who penned a humorous ditty, 'The Golden Years are Here at Last', for the reception window.

'I cannot see, I cannot pee. I cannot chew, I cannot screw. My memory shrinks, my hearing stinks. No sense of smell, I look like hell. The Golden Years are here at last, the Golden Years can kiss my arse!'

Staring out through the rain splattered double glazing of an elevated TV room towards the sea, bottom lip drooping, I feared for Rhys. Frowning drizzle clouds adopted the dark strip of the swill below, which was being engulfed by patches of thick rolling fog. 'This is a nightmare,' he said. 'My tent won't be able to handle much more rain.' With perfect twisted comedy timing, a coal tinged sky of evil exploded, hammering sharp penetrating nails around the flimsy flesh of Rhys' road home. It didn't stop pouring down for hours. After putting off the inevitable for as long as possible, watching a frustrated Jeremy Clarkson failing to drown, burn and crush an invincible red Toyota pick-up, we waded along the mushy grass banks of the newly formed Oklahoma River. Wailing tents were soaked through on the outside, not even dripping, just completely saturated. Moving inside quickly, relieved hands shuffled across a bone dry sleeping bag and floor. Safe, warm and snug as a bug, tuning into the pitter-patter of roof splatting droplets sent sensual shivers through my body, generating a comfortable state of bedtime stupor.

Not feeling the same wash of relaxation, Rhys rudely interrupted my perfectly sheltered gratification. 'This tent stitching is useless. My sleeping bag's soaked and I've got a swimming pool inside the front door. That's me and Argos finished forever. I paid them £7.98 for this tent and it doesn't work. I'm taking it back when I get home to demand a refund. Bloody cheapskates!' Shouting out goodnight and tramping off in a showery huff, Rhys was fast becoming a connoisseur of TV room floors, tonight's episode; sleeping next to radiators.

Sæby was another former Viking trading post, still clutching hold of a sprinkling of 'Skagen Yellow' half timbered buildings, feeding off a traditional market square. Well worth a look was the attractive 15th-century *Church of St Maria*, the final remains of a four-winged Carmelite monastery. The monks were devoted to the Virgin Mary, who is also the central figure on Sæby's coat of arms. The church is famous for its finely detailed medieval ceiling frescos and a Dutch 16th-century altar. Drawings of boats are still visible in the monks' benches and prayer stools, scratched by the attention wandering hands of 17th-century school children, bored with lessons and staring out the window at ships in the harbour, dreaming of exciting adventures at sea.

The love of a strong Sæby woman could melt the blackest of hearts. During the war against England, the town was a nest of privateers, notorious licensed pirates who risked their lives to plunder great fortunes from English vessels. Among them was a young Norwegian captain, Peter Jakob Larssøn, who fell head over heels for the parson's 17-year-old daughter. After a sink or swim ultimatum from the holy man, the dirty old sea dog proved leopards can change their spots, ditching his wicked ways and getting straight down to the nitty-gritty of knocking out 10 kids with a knackered Laurenze Marie. Building an honest life for himself as a merchant, the transformation was complete when Larssøn became the mayor. His grave still rests in the church yard. Another remarkable example of the fairer sex holds court at the small harbour. The towering 'Lady from the Sea' is a braided two-headed statue, half mermaid, half guardian angel. She is believed to shield the town and its residents with a great white cloak, covered in multi-coloured protection symbols made by 880 children.

The east coast of Denmark certainly wasn't as kind as the west. Paralysing winds were still creating havoc, hindering our hopes of completing a 100 kilometre daily target as quickly as possible. More farming lands filed backwards against the sea, with trees swaying their heads to one side above bending crops of yellow rapeseed. The dominant 'Skagen Yellow' was on the wane, with red and white foundation starting to creep into the tired complexions of dusty roadside houses. The tiny village of Asaa offered caffeine respite at a Shell petrol station. Behind the counter keys to a locked toilet revealed other secrets. Pulling the string chord of the grimy shoebox lavatory threw an unexpected light on Julie's Gallery. Casting a critical eye over musty paintings of beaming lighthouses, gliding seagulls and polished bowls of fruit was enough to take your mind off developments downstairs. Resisting the temptation to punish the trustworthy Danes by stealing the keys and pictures, before fleeing to Hals and escaping over the Kattegat back door of the Limfjord to Egense, I was rewarded with a first pig sighting. There are 20 million porkers in Denmark, the equivalent of four pigs for every human being and a lot of bacon to boot. We hadn't seen a grubby trotter anywhere until now, but here they were at last, four little fatties snuffling up a littered bed of old cabbage. The joy of a missing pig tick was interrupted by unwanted grumblings.

We'd been buffeted around like empty crisp packets all day, as head, cross, left, right, back, forward and diagonal winds queued up to lay one on us. Burly cracked trees spewed splintered innards over the floor, wonky tiles got ready to launch themselves from rickety roofs and steel supports gripped metal chimneys. Cold biting gusts of air chewed the skin around your trembling face, making so much noise I could barely make out a screamed sentence from Rhys. It wasn't all bad then. The bikes forgot their heavy cargos, banking from side to side, almost pushed backwards by the biggest and baddest blasts. If we capitulated now, I could spend my life in a muddy field foraging Ray Mears style, sharing a marital tent with Rhys and sprouting a toe tickling beard in zipped together sleeping bags. Ugggh! I had to keep those pedals turning, even at an agonising pace making geriatric Nordic walkers look like Speedy Gonzales. I couldn't risk seizing up. Dinner time was upon us again. Just another 15 kilometres to Hadsund, an hour's ride tops, if you discounted the set of steep climbs heading straight into the screeching mouth of the howling torment. How cruel can you be Lord? Remember Rhys picked up that dead cat. My knee was starting to hurt. Give us a break!

Hadsund stood on a hill of bubbling water courses swimming above and below its main slope. The 35 kilometre Mariager Fjord washed in from the Kattegat, removing the stormy sting with a cleansing brush along the feet of the town. Idyllic lazy meadows flourished next to broad lush banks, past the drooping sails of an old windmill and over a trim of dark tree tops stretching up to the skyline. Dancing fair-haired horses larked about carefree, safe in the knowledge this green and pleasant land was protected from development and preserved for future generations. Nestling under the snap of bird hopping twigs was a neat split of camp site and red wooden bunk huts. Maria Hürlimann was the proprietor and cherished this unspoilt spot the most. It was her little bit of paradise. The pink cardigan wearing middle-aged Swiss Miss blended naturally into her surroundings, with owl like features hatched straight out of the Sylvanian Families' mould. Maria had the dream job. Living at the office in a caravan, she enjoyed every working minute of every day, which seemed so unfair. My envy of her perfect utopia would grow increasingly.

This was all a far cry from Maria's former life at sea, working on banana containers, shipping fruit all over the world. 'It was a hard life, especially for a woman,' said the duchess of chill. 'It is a job mainly worked by men and the sea can be very rough. But you get used to it and I loved the job. It took me all over the world to places I would never have seen. And there is something very special about spending solitary thinking time at sea. It is good for the brain.' It was hard to picture this meek woman slipping across salt soaked decks on high seas, whacking rum down her neck and dropping anchor in an intimidating profession dominated by grizzly unshaven geezers. Not without getting tattooed or picking up a tricky spinach addiction along the way.

Maria spent the working day nattering away to guests and deliverymen ducking in and out of camp reception, as well as sneaking the odd look across her beloved countryside through a window telescope. It must have been amazing embracing such a high level of contentment, approaching each day with the same enthusiasm she obviously possessed in bags. I was ridiculously jealous. So many hours, months and years of my life had been wasted, wallowing in exhausting negative thoughts about unknown future pitfalls out of my control, or getting in a frustrated tizzy about unrealised plans, just like this trip. But I'd proved I could overcome that obstacle. Maybe there was a little Maria inside me somewhere too. An inner temple of peace which could be tempted out into the open.

Maria allowed us to hole up in a wooden chalet for a couple of nights. We'd been on the road for 10 successive days and were long overdue a break ahead of the final furlong to Grenå. Freshly hand washed clothes and wet tent shells thrown across every available hanger and wall hook added a jumble sale flavour to the digs. But there were people much worse off than us, with real, not self-imposed, hardships to deal with. A haggard cheap labour gang of undernourished Polish workers were busying themselves with pots and pans in the combined kitchen and TV room. Their far from culinary feast consisted of watery soup, tiny chopped frankfurters and a bowl of spring onions. An army marches on its stomach and this wasn't enough to feed a sparrow, let alone a group of men dragged around the Danish countryside by a stingy Swedish pay master to erect agricultural grain silos. Rhys whipped up another of his pasta specials and feelings of guilt filled our greasy mouths and bellies as their hungry faces watched us shovel it back like animals. Bursting point was successfully reached, with half a pan of steaming pasta to spare. Tentatively, I offered the remaining food to the proud Poles, hoping to cause no patronising offence. I didn't want them to think I felt sorry for them, I just wanted to help them out, trying to bridge the language barrier by explaining the food was destined for the pedal bin otherwise.

Commandeering the sofa and TV control, an after dinner flick through 1,000 satellite channels began. Maybe Maria hadn't been paying her bills because many were blocked, strangely including all the Nordic options, but there was an abundance of Spanish speaking South America programmes and dodgy flickering transmissions from Eastern European stations. The BBC was clear, but we weren't bothered about catching up on the misery and suffering at home. We finally agreed on a cabaret of thick lipstick smeared, suspender belt wearing German hags with huge hair, writhing about on yellow leather couches without so much as flashing a well chewed nipple above a long list of premium rate phone numbers on *Eurotic TV*.

Tangerine faced girls carrying shoulder bags waggled criminally snug rear fitting jeans in and out of clothes shops. They loved a sun bed here and numerous tanning salons hired space above ground floor stores. But some of these dark-haired teenagers weren't doing their young skin any long term favours. I could have been lost in the valley of Kat Slaters. 'If all the young girls in Denmark are so cute, where are all the older birds?' pondered Rhys. 'I haven't seen one bit of fit Milf.'

'What the bloody hell's a Milf?' I asked.

'You really don't know what a Milf is? It stands for mums I'd like to fuck.'

'Thanks for the education.'

'Seriously, Bern, there must be some sort of cruel Scandinavian curse? Do all the women get slapped across the face with an ugly stick at 30 and go into hiding. Where are they all?'

'Well, what about the blonde bird in Abba? She was a right sort.'

'Yeah, but has anybody seen her since the 70s? I don't think so.' The mature women were probably busy trying to Polyfilla dried-out skin cracks from 15 years of artificial sun ray abuse, only coming out when it was safe after dark.

Hadsund was another place only open for business at the weekend. OK. That's a slight exaggeration. There was a faint light bulb dying in one pub at the bottom of the hill. But an assortment of boiled and bleached deer skulls and antlers hanging from the walls failed to generate the required ambience for relaxation. Various stores huffed and puffed their way up the stairs of the town and a modern enclosed shopping centre was lulled into an empty coma by funnelled sleep inducing music, usually reserved for calming strapped-in mental ward patients. The 18th-century Rosendal Farm grounds housed the *Hadsund Egns* museum, a fleeting illustration of how this settlement, sandwiched between two slices of water, had developed from modest beginnings as a small ferry landing into an er… town with people living in it. This is the salt capital of Denmark and a wall mounted pot invites you to dab a moist finger and taste the area's greatest export. Don't worry about germs, it's all part of the history learning fun. Salt has been the trading mainstay here since the

1400s and boats still use the Kattegat to reach the Mariager Fjord and load up on the condiment, distributing to dinner tables and steamy kitchens across the whole of Denmark.

Maria tipped us off about a swimming pool and sauna in a sports centre hidden by trees on the other side of our hut. Swimming is a completely different ball game to cycling. I could just about fend off fearsome winds and struggle over energy zapping long distance gravel tracks, but chuck me in a pool with a pair of trunks on and you'll be lucky to get a couple of lengths out of me. Two up and down lane weaving splashes of chlorine nostril filled puppy paddling and I was finished, red faced and gasping for breath, before slowly sliding a rock hard nipple guidance system up and over freezing pool tiles. Rhys had doubled my efforts, but was quite happy to quit while he was ahead, joining me for a downstairs sauna.

Derived from Finland, a sauna is a closed heated wooden room where people sit with a towel, or in the buff, and sweat their tits off for 15 minutes, before finishing the torture with the opposite extreme of an ice cold shower. The latter part is hugely beneficial after staring through the steam to cop an eyeful in a naked mixed sex sauna, which is nothing out of the ordinary in Scandinavia. The release of perspiration is good for the skin and aids a healthy lifestyle, most significantly helping the body release toxin pollution. Regular saunas combined with exercise therapy can efficiently clear organic chemicals, solvents and drugs out of the system. Other proven benefits include easing the pain of rheumatoid arthritis sufferers, reduction in hypertension and improvement of blood flow to constricted areas. Scandinavians swear by this pastime, believing a sauna a day really can keep the doctor away. An old Finnish saying goes: 'If booze, tar or the sauna won't help, the illness is fatal.'

I was a big fan of sauna skulking, but always seemed to be surrounded by men and wasn't brave enough to peel my pants off yet. With heat singeing my nostrils' hairs and beads of sweat sliding down both arms and legs, I was transported back through the haze to Sweden and my first hot house experience in Malmö. Two big black guys without a stitch on between them, slung muscular walrus hides over wooden benches, blissfully fiddling away with their lower tusks. Another sauna colleague, an old bald-headed man, let it all hang out confidently, shrivelled and surrounded by white fluff, above my head. But as soon as he stood up, an inferiority complex kicked in, forcing a crabby sideways scuttle to the door with two flat palms shielding his raw pink cocktail sausage and cherry danglers.

What I found more therapeutic than anything else on this planet was channelling my energy into playing football. Physical exercise provides an amazing level of stress relief, allowing the mind to escape from life's troubles by placing full mental focus on the sporting field of combat. It was five weeks since I had wellied a ball and I was gagging for a kick about with the lads. Walking back wet haired across the sports ground, different groups of bib wearing teams were running around orange cones and gearing up for a training session. I had stumbled across the home of Hadsund FC. Feverishly following the diagonal lines of a football knocked around the feet of a passing circle of players was frustrating. Taking envious over the shoulder glances, greener than the grass, at shrinking boots scything through the turf, withdrawal spasms forced out a shouted playing request to a beanpole centre forward. The Danes looked stunned. It wasn't every night a random English stranger frothing at the mouth begged to join in their game. 'Of course,' called the tall guy, Christian, offering a hurried introduction to a bemused bunch of team mates stretching out their leg muscles.

A full scale match ensued and sliding about in bog standard trainers on damp grass was difficult, but I gave a decent account of the English game, even managing to notch a far post headed goal from a corner. I could tell my new comrades were impressed, displaying their affection by reserving the hardest crunching challenges for my legs. The girls' team joined in for a mixed match, a completely alien development for me. This wouldn't be tolerated at home. Everything was strictly segregated. Girls don't even play football! Blonde and brunette pony tails swished about, demonstrating a confident first touch. One of the girls was a ferocious midfield tackler and another young lady a penalty box predator, sticking the ball in the back of the onion bag with deadly accuracy. There was plenty of lively banter between both sexes (which they translated into English for my benefit), with the girls jeering loudly if they nutmegged the ball through one of the embarrassed boys' legs. It was a good-natured competitive edge, forged by two sets of players who socialised off the pitch. Maybe I was witnessing Hadsund FC's future footballing wives and husbands, ready to combine tactics in this small community and produce the next generation of players. That was the true secret of a club which had been fielding football teams since 1926. Christian extended the invitation of a boot room beer after the game, presenting me with a white and red trimmed club shirt to take on my travels. I think I might have blushed. Shaking my hand he said: 'You trained well and are now an honorary member of Hadsund FC. If you are ever here again for a weekend, you are more than welcome to wear this shirt and play a game for us.'

What another great night. The simple things in life didn't cost much, if anything at all, and were definitely the best. An unnatural glow illuminated the metal rim of Maria's glasses through the reception window. It was pitch black inside, but there she was, a shadow hovering above a stool watching a TV programme all alone. But she couldn't have been happier. There was no hustle or bustle, no worries or stress, just complete absorption in her own private bubble of tranquillity next to the restful silence of the Mariager Fjord. Maria may have been a long way from her native Switzerland and didn't have two krone to rub together as far as I could tell. But attaining such comfort in her own skin was a vast richness in itself, unable to be calculated by the most clever computer in the universe, making this lucky lady the wealthiest person I had ever met.

28   Sink or Swim

Katie was coming. To Sweden that was. A morning phone call from my much missed nearest and dearest confirmed a flying visit to Gothenburg for a two-night hotel rationing. She would touch down in five days. I couldn't wait. Neither could Rhys. Having escaped unwanted male sexual violation he released a deafening sigh of relief. What a start to the day (for both of us). And the positive theme continued. Evening prayers had obviously done the trick as we were blessed by sunshine and minimal wind. Our final day cycling across Danish soil to Grenå played out a medley of the Jutland scenery. Most roads were firm and the kilometres ticked by nicely, with a thrown in scattering of gravel, sand dunes, pine, birch and even a few new additions, the spiky balls of conkers hanging from branches and baby Christmas tree nurseries. We were making healthy progress.

A twin steel cable pulled bucket dragged us away from a lifeless bus shelter of a boat stop at Udbyhøj Vasehuse and over the Randers Fjord. Empty roads bent around miles of soundless fields, briefly interrupted by a rustling breeze caught head of rape, which had grown half a metre in height over the last few weeks, highlighting the strength and speed of mother nature. Butterflies fluttered around the crest of crops and bees were busy carrying out their nectar basket rounds. All was well with the world. And then it got effortlessly better. Car free tarmac rolled downwards for up to a kilometre at a time and upward nudging winds caught our bodies at boat sail angles, blowing us over sporadic gradients. Just over the half way point of an 80 kilometre ride we decided it was coffee break time. Vivild was another village teetering on the edge of oblivion and didn't look capable of brewing up any answers. The only thing open was a trusty Spar, but with no hot drinks machine down any one of 12 aisles, I approached a check-out seeking official confirmation of a coffee drought.

'Do you have any coffee?' I asked the mummsy lady sitting upright behind the till, illustrating my desire with a feeble attempt to make a cup out of my hand. It could have been worse. I could have tried to shake some imaginary beans in front of her face and got arrested. Murdering my last grains of hope she said: 'No. Sorry. You may be able to buy some at Fjellerup, but that is five kilometres away.' Then, as I trudged away with suicidal caffeine withdrawal, my love affair with Denmark was officially signed and sealed. 'But I have made a flask for myself and you are welcome to have it for free. Would you like cream and sugar?' Now that's what I call a cup of human kindness. What a country, what a race. Where are the immigration papers?

Refuelled we returned to a main road, tearing into the final leg of our Danish journey with heavy hearts. It was unanimously agreed we were going to miss this generous old lump of sand, rock and gravel. But not the wind. Realising every eaten kilometre brought us closer to the Danish exit door was tinged with sadness. A feeling quickly banished by a bike hungry car. 'That one was so close I could smell his breath,' Rhys called out after a close shave with an erratic steering wheel trembler. Danes really couldn't drive. Their road skills hadn't progressed much higher than a provisional licence holder. They lacked self-assurance and were scared to pass you on the road, but didn't mind edging their front bumpers within hazardous snorting distance of a back wheel. When they did overtake it was painfully slow. Starting to sympathise with the motorised morons, after being trailed for five minutes at a top speed of 'you'd be lucky to make a mile per hour, mate', a complete cycling halt was required, giving Mr Magoo and friends a wide berth to crawl past. It was time consuming, but beat reducing drivers to a pulled over bawling mess, confidence shot to pieces, in the next hard shoulder. Such road courtesy was only fair. It was good to give something back to Denmark for all its kindness.

The three pronged retail veins of Grenå pumped its citizens along paved shopping arteries to the central marketplace tower of the clock topped *Kirke Church*. The collective staggered red stones of the Gothic structure was the proud keeper of northern Europe's biggest organ and a glockenspiel set of 35 polished bronze bells. Equally impressive was the port's very own super hero, Søren Kanne, who posed robustly on a marble block next to the church, immortalised forever in stone. Kanne didn't appear to come from a rich background, sculpted wearing knee-length shorts and an old tatty waistcoat covering his shirt. But where was the flowing cape? He cemented his place in history on a stormy night in 1835, earning a medal from King Frederik VI for his act of bravery. According to local legend, Kanne's high-pitched ear antenna picked up the screams of a captain sinking on a wreck in the Kattegat. The lifeboat was unable to reach the stricken vessel, but Super Kanne rushed to the rescue with two of his father's horses, wading out into the treacherous sea and carrying the skipper and one of his sailors back to shore on the old nags' backs.

There would be no such pulse racing adventure for us in Grenå. Safely stored away out of sight, the camp site had been quarantined next to the dreary ferry terminal car park, at least three kilometres short of civilisation. Rhys was beavering away with a new tent acquired in Hadsund, pulling out ropes and banging in pegs with scouting fervour for an eagerly awaited dry debut. Ditching his single skinned one man interior water feature, Rhys had gone from one extreme to the other, lashing out on a circus big top, roomy enough for a clan of juggling clowns, flying trapeze double act and a ball balancing seal family. My Halfling habitat was already getting an inferiority complex. Food on the campsite? Guess what? Two weeks too early. But an excited receptionist relished informing us Grenå had enjoyed its hottest day of the year 24 hours previous to our arrival, as if it were some sort of consolation prize. Cheers luv! And that is supposed to make us feel better just how exactly? Wholesome sustenance was nowhere to be found, unless you were a glutton for daylight robbery, parting with £8 for a bowl of fish soup (not including bread dunking rolls) at a ridiculously overpriced hotel, barely upgraded from a Travel Inn. The only other option was a lorry drivers' greasy grub hut sat next to the brooding expression of the Kattegat. Cheap and cheerful on the wallet, two acne riddled teenage girls, splattered in cooking fat, served up just about anything ready to be fried or nuked in a microwave, ahead of a ketchup and mustard drenching. It wasn't ideal, but wouldn't hurt just this once. We had a four hour ferry journey to Sweden ahead of us at lunchtime tomorrow and wouldn't require anything more substantial to power our legs until we disembarked at Varberg. I just wanted to eat something fast and get in an early night, saving as much energy as possible for pouncing on Katie. Gothenburg was less than 100 kilometres from Varberg, a distance we could easily cover in one hit, offering a leisurely four day pedal up the west Swedish coast. A concoction of both lazy and naughty thoughts suppressed pangs of guilt as the warm juice of a pork crackling burger streamed down my chin. Always health conscious, I hadn't fallen into the squeezy tomato sauce tap trap, fending off ballooning into a pot-bellied roadster scoffing double dinners, while painfully balancing on a chrome pole supporting an invisible stool swallowed by a huge portion of lard arse.

Foulest weather stirred from the stagnant bowels of hell jeered our soaking arrival at the Stena ferry terminal. I may have started conquering travelling phobias and buried deep numerous fears from the past, but removing my feet from solid ground was still a huge concern. Without an instantly accessible run away get out clause, I couldn't deal with anything out of my control. And here I was, steadying my shaking body for the Beelzebub Death Cruise straight into the gargling mouth of Hades. Panic punched a reminder of tingling tremors across my chest, signalling dedicated intentions of an unwanted comeback. Draining a complimentary coffee jug, regularly freshened up by female waiting room attendants built like tug-boats, anxieties spiralled as spiteful wet flecks crashed against the shuddering window of the shelter. A miserable looking Erika and Globe were feeling it too, locked to a metal rail at the mercy of the elements, teardrops of rain diving off their shivering frames.

An internal silent vigil of desperation prayers pleaded for a miraculous change to the weather chart. It just got shoddier. Maybe this was pay-back for all those missed cigarette deadlines. The clouds just got blacker, pouring their heavy falling loads into hundreds of car park pot-hole buckets. A ripping wind revelled in its freedom, flying over the flat building obstacle free concrete, bending poles and sending red and white partition tape flapping in a loud spin between two trembling lamp posts. Hair blown back above a drenched facial, it was boarding time, offering a proper peek at the road ahead. Why did I bother? It would have made more sense imitating a blind man, keeping my eyes shut and holding on to Rhys for guidance to a comfy chair. Trying to get a grip and be a man, I stared straight into the terrifying highway of hurtling livid waves covering our way out of town. I squeaked like a mouse.

Reserving my usual sailing berth, a deserted corridor couch next to the toilet, the *Stena Nautica* suddenly lurched to one side, before pinging back up again. What the fuck was that? We were still in the harbour, the engines hadn't even started yet, but this crate was moving about like a giant see-saw. The movement continued, sending a fuzzy sinking sensation down the inside of my head and into a churning stomach. Sea sickness kicked in next to dry land. This was a ride I definitely wanted to get off. There was something critically wrong. We should have departed 30 minutes ago, but were still swaying around the dock. Ding-dong sounded the intercom. 'Hello. This is the captain speaking. We have a serious technical fault, but hope to be underway soon. Don't worry!' What? What? That was it. I couldn't handle this. Why did they even bother making those announcements in English. Say it in Danish, Swedish, German, French or even bloody Mongolian, but not in crystal clear words I didn't need to hear. My chest was tighter than a porn star's rear end and sucking in air without the aid of a hyper ventilator was approaching meltdown. I'd be using the brown bag handed out by a sliding steward for emergency breathing, not green vomit storage, any minute now. I curled up into a ball on the wall couch, seriously considering jumping ship. This was too much to take.

'Hey. Guess what?' grinned Rhys insanely as he threw out a hand against the wall to keep balance. 'The cabin crew have all got their life jackets on down there. They're handing them out at the end of the corridor just to keep on the safe side.'

'Are they?' I started to get up.

'Shut-up, you idiot.' Rhys sniggered. Old bug eyes was grasping the opportunity of turning the knife into my squirming body far too readily for my liking. 'I was talking to one of the staff and we've been delayed by a small problem with the front doors. It's nothing to worry about. They're jammed and they can't close them. A normal problem with ships that sink at sea.'

I jumped up white as a sheet. The ship jester burst into a laughing fit and I offered him a sincere 'ha-ha' applaud for his efforts. 'Did you know this was the oldest boat in the fleet?'

'Keep it buttoned now, Rhys.'

A whistling handyman in oily overalls tilted past holding a battered tool box containing primitive hammers, screwdrivers, chisels, nails and screws, shaking away to a metallic groove. This couldn't have been the engineer entrusted with fixing this half floating multi-storey block of junk and keeping us alive. Could it? The boat started to stagger uneasily out of the blowy harbour. The lifeboats clanged about on their rusted support chains, a sharp axe would be needed to cut them free, and I scanned the distance for support ships in close proximity, able to rush to our aid once we began drowning. There wasn't so much as a funnel to be seen through the fine mist. I'd reached the point of no return now, Rhys was already soundo, but my worrying mind wouldn't stop racing, hitting psychotic overdrive and projecting twisted cinematic scenarios around my broken brain box. The opening credits of the Poseidon Adventure rolled around my head, before a director's cut matinee of my own composition hit the mental screen. Water slowly leaked through a gap in the bulkheads, sloshing around our bikes, trucks and coaches on the car deck, rising higher and higher, while the unaware passengers joked about in the bar upstairs. The disaster movie was interrupted by a newsflash from Moira Stuart, announcing to the folks back home in perfectly executed received pronunciation (BBC English to you and me) that a passenger ferry had sunk in stormy seas off the coast of Denmark. 'Two Brits are believed to be on board. The search for survivors continues.'

I hadn't suffered like this for weeks. Putting my mind and body through such self-inflicted torment knocked the stuffing right out of me.

Waking up sprawled along the length of the double wall couch was a relief, only bettered by looking at my watch. Nearly three hours had evaporated folded up into a stress ball. *Nautica* was still having trouble standing straight, but the movement was ever so slight now. Peering outside, the Kattegat still wore a mean mask, but the fog had cleared and moody waves had receded to pinching surface ripples. What a difference a sleep makes. Stretching aching arms and legs, without needing to grip the walls, I distracted my mind by swotting up on a large Stena fact board plastered across a passageway. It was crammed full of life changing information. Did you know that Stena customers buy 250,000 kilograms of Bassett's Liquorice Allsorts and Wine Gums every year? It wasn't so reassuring to know the company had stepped up its safety procedures in 1994, only after one of their boats went down in the Baltic just shy of Estonia. Didn't need to read that.

Nautica was another ghost ship, there couldn't have been more than 40 passengers on board. The centrepiece was a carbon copy of a tacky shopping centre food court, complete with overhead sun seeking glass panels. Heads slept in folded arms on hard round table cushions, while other people forked unenthusiastically at stodgy meals or smoked away the end of the trip with a duty free can of Carlsberg. Rhys was at work in the market, spraying himself freely with deodorants and aftershaves, ahead of loading up on cheap chocolate and cigarettes, all bizarrely stored in a fridge.

Bald shoulders of rock guided *Nautica* into Sweden. It was still overcast outside, but that hadn't put off mini skippers of tiny single sail boats gliding along the Varberg canal, skirting bravely close to the ferry's powerful backwash. Cold vertical walls protected the stony keep of Varberg's 13th-century fortress high on the cliff. Shifting Scandinavian borders had seen the fortification under Norwegian and Danish ownership, until the Swedes took back control in 1647. Used as a prison during the last century, it now plays host to a youth hostel, café and museum. The remains of a medieval murder story are kept behind these foreboding ramparts. The Bocksten Man was found in a peat bog 15 miles east of Varberg, knocked to a lake bed death by two poles, one of oak to the heart and a beech blow to the back. One of the best finds of its kind in Europe, a woollen tunic, boots and leather sheaf, containing two knives, were all found magnificently preserved with the body. Inner organs were also intact, with parts of the lungs, liver, brain and cartilage, protected by nature's tomb for scientific examination.

A minuscule bullet exhibit is the centrepiece of another great Swedish mystery. King Charles (Carl) XII of Sweden was killed in 1718 during a siege on the Danish fortress of Fredriksten. Ever since that fateful day, historians have been unable to decide whether the king was taken out by friendly fire or an accurate enemy shot. Another theory, now believed more likely, is the blast of a political assassin's gun putting paid to the monarch. The debate continues. Sweden's down-scaled version of the Loch Ness Monster lurks in the dark waters of the fortresses' moat. A small lake creature has been spotted rising to the surface and devouring ducks in one fatal bite. Eye witnesses describe the furless beast as brown with a 40cm long tail. Sounds like a shaved London sewer rat to me.

Varberg conjured the usual hash of criss-crossing block stone roads, wonderful cooking smells released into the atmosphere by porched restaurants and the mandatory airy centrepiece of trees, benches and a grand town hall. Receiving a nose prodding whiff of pocket friendly hot dogs, we were drawn to the *Torggrillen*, a fast-food cubby-hole run by a typically blond Swedish lad drowning in a pair of pant flashing baggy knee shorts. It was a miserable evening and business was slow as we stood there gassing about our journey. Chatting away like old muckers, our new pal fetched a Swedish peace pipe out of his pocket, a blue and white shoe polish tin containing miniature tea bags. I didn't remember ordering a drink.

'Would you like one of these? It is *snus*. Very Swedish,' offered baggy burger boy.

I was completely puzzled now. 'What is it?' I asked.

'Tobacco,' he replied. 'You put it in your mouth. It is like smoking, but 10 times stronger. It can't give you cancer, but might make you feel sick.'

The pant flasher was never going to climb the corporate ladder from burger flipper to life of luxury with that sales pitch. But I was still curious. 'How does it taste?'

'Like little Christmas trees,' he grinned, before waving the open tin of pine scented shrunken tea bags under our noses. 'And this is even stronger.' He cracked open another pot containing a solid brown interior, which really did resemble a slab of boot shine. 'You sure you wouldn't like some?'

Snus is a moist powder of air-dried tobacco, pushed under the upper lip for an extended period. Originally developed from nostril inhaled snuff, *snus* comes in cake form, rolled into a ball before gum absorption, or the milder tea bag brand pushed under our noses. The potential health risks of *snus* have not been studied in great detail, but it isn't believed to present the same threat to the lungs as inhaled cigarettes. It does contain more nicotine than a pack of smokes, but people all over Scandinavia can't get enough of that sweet *snus* taste. The total Swedish production has rocketed to 300 million tins a year, influenced by the indoor smoking bans in Sweden and Norway. That's an impressive amount of gum rot when you consider the combined populations of Denmark, Norway and Sweden only adds up to 20 million potential tea bag suckers. I didn't want to become just another number.

29 Drunk on Nature

Sweden was another kettle of fish. Every country had been different so far in its own little way, but the drizzly trundle out of Varberg signalled a dramatic change. The flat and sandy Netherlands were animal bonkers, Germany, grubby and rundown as well as wondrous and weird, and pine planting crazy Denmark, the land of moving dune giants, cruelly exposed to a paralysing elemental buffeting. But they all shared rural similarities. Sweden on the other hand, had its own unique identity, a spectacular sweep of open nature reserve, complete with granite garden rockery, dark forest shrubs and passive pale blue sea inlet water features. Old rowing boats lay upturned on skerries and wooden houses were sparsely dotted across a fertile green floor, well out of earshot from the nearest neighbours. The fact that Sweden is the third largest country in western Europe, with one of the lowest population densities, explains this perfect isolation. Eighty-four per cent of the nine million population reside in urban areas, accounting for only 1.3 per cent of a whopping total land mass of 173,720 square miles, leaving plenty of room for the out of townies.

Moss covered rocks of varied dimensions and bulk burst randomly out of the stretch-marked soil. Jagged grey boulders and London Bus sized mounds were scattered around the ground like discarded broken teeth and bones, fallen down long ago from ancient craggy faces soaring up above. Human dwellings and raw earthly materials were inseparable. Painted timber walls were pushed against huge wind protecting humps, while others stole a solid base from the sturdy foundations beneath their feet. Sheltered homes rested on tree surrounded perches in hollows half way up cliffs, while some climbed even higher, lights blinking from the shadowy ridge. There wasn't a block of flats, multi-storey car park or smashed up phone box in sight and it was wonderful.

Sweden relished being close to nature and had brought the great outdoors to its front doorstep. We were keen to give it a go ourselves, erecting tents in an empty field next to a rocky copse of dripping trees at Kärradal, 12 kilometres from Varberg. Unlike Denmark, Sweden observes a right of public access, allowing anybody to walk, boat, swim, ski or camp for free anywhere outside the fenced borders of private property. Tents should be set up at least 50 metres from houses and fires safely made from fallen wood, away from bare rocks, are permitted. You are also free to pick wild berries and mushrooms. Leaving behind rubbish and taking living wood, bark, leaves, bushes and nuts is strictly prohibited. We soon got a fire started, combing the ground for strips of lichen invaded bark and small pieces of tinder, carefully stacked around a bed of scrunched up toilet paper. Damps logs and brown leafy branches were dried off by the darting lick of young flames as a wraithlike billow wafted up the granite staircase. A ballet of orange embers danced around gracefully in the moist night air as the hissing burning wood cracked underneath. Rhys feverishly scampered about, chucking on more splintered fuel, as a mad glow filled those big eyes. A teenage pyromaniac, Rhys nearly burnt down his dear old nanna's house after poking an inquisitive twig around her living room fire place, only to shove the smouldering stick under the couch when granny returned home unexpectedly. Boys will be boys after all, but Rhys was definitely re-forging his bond with man's oldest obsession. The fierce warming glow forced a backward step, scorched and blackened faces ready to crack and red-hot to the touch water-proofs well on their way to fabric meltdown.

Then, attracted by the flickering flames, something magical happened. Here we were standing on soggy turf in full sight of nearby houses, pitched against two empty main roads and a redundant railway line, without a single decibel of man-made noise. But there was a rustling in the bushes opposite our camp and the gentle sound of movement in the long grass. Turning slowly away from the fire we discovered with awe struck surprise we were being watched by Bambi mark one and two. It was an enchanting stand-off, unwashed Neanderthals and graceful beasts no more than 150 metres apart, staring straight into each other's eyes, without an ounce of threat or danger. Time stood still as the brown coated double act motionlessly held their ground in close proximity for a good couple of minutes, before, curiosity satisfied, the wild deer trotted off heads bowed towards the hills.

Retiring to our tents, with side flaps pulled back, we watched the fire die a slow death in a pile of ashes. Still only dusk dark at nearly 11pm, a white stripe tore through the sky line, separating blackening clouds above from the fading blue below. It was one of the most peaceful moments of my life, watching the heavens and blowing cigarette smoke out the doorway, head upwardly supported by a bulging bike pack and spongy grass below the tent floor cushioning my body. Rhys was in tune with the ambience too, opening up emotionally about his darkening mood at home, a complicated relationship with a much loved father exiled in Florida for legal reasons and a general loss of appetite for life. I was honest in return, for the first time giving Rhys an insight into my own personal issues, especially the fear of suffering a premature death born from the mental scarring of losing both my parents at such a young age.

'Thanks, Bern,' said Rhys.

'For what?' I replied, sparking up another cigarette.

'For helping to change my life. Coming out here to cycle through all these amazing places has made me realise there is much more to life than sitting indoors feeling sorry for myself. I was so depressed, but this experience has given me such a lift, better than any of the pills doctors have been trying to throw down my neck. Just getting up early every day and using my body, instead of lounging around watching TV all day, has given me a new lease of life. My hermit days are over!'

I knew exactly how Rhys felt as the North Sea Cycle Route's medicine had perked me up too. And lying here now in the recovery position, out in the sticks without a worry in the world, life really did feel better than it had done in a long time. 'Happy to oblige, mate. Never be afraid to bring your troubles to the door of Dr Bernard.'

The west coast Swedish part of the journey was 400 kilometres in length. There was no official route booklet, only outline maps in freely available tourist brochures prevented you from biking completely blind. The Halland trail, christened after one of the 25 Swedish land provinces it crossed, was fortunately well marked, with a white arrowed cycle on a black square sign edging north towards Gothenburg. A muggy start got underway with the pleasant job of peeling slimy sausage-sized slugs from the outside walls of a morning dew soaked tent. Packed up and ready to go, another country ramble of quiet roads, small bridge tunnels, stony bulges and rising tree-lined peaks awaited. But I felt like crap. Unable to distribute any power to a crumbling pair of weak legs. This was the curse of eating nothing but shit kicking in. Everything I had consumed since arriving in Grenå two days ago had been utter garbage. Greasy pork crackling in a bun, watery frankfurters and chewy hamburgers, all downed with a salty side portion of chips. None of these foods contained the staple requirement of proteins, vitamins and carbohydrates my body craved to fuel a daily grind of pedal turning. My only chance of a proper meal, stocking up on some of those recommended five-a-day fruit and vegetable portions, had been on the topsy-turvy boat to Sweden, but the fear of sickness stopped me digging in. I wasn't looking after myself and now I was paying the ultimate price, ready to keel over and spend the rest of my days in a roadside thicket. Rhys on the other hand was flying, still running off three well stacked plates of ferry buffet. Force feeding his two remaining lumps of chocolate into my mouth for emergency energy we crawled along for three hours and 20 kilometres to an exhausted collapse at Åsa.

The coastline had changed now, with the jumble of pointy rocks replaced by smooth sandy beaches. Ducking away from the shoreline, the village of Åsa kneeled on one side of a main road squeezing its fairly straight torso through woodland. After a night of roughing it in the outback, we were ready to take advantage of a free set of accommodation vouchers kindly donated to this expedition by the Swedish Tourist Association. The STF has a thorough countrywide network of 320 hostels and 10 mountain lodges, plus 40 lonely mountain huts in the road-less wilderness. Part of the Youth Hostel Federation, Hostelling International, all affiliated card holders are welcome to seek refuge at these well kept shelters. If you're not in the club, you can still stay, signing up on the night and earning future access to hostels all over the world. The STF offers clean, non-smoking, self-service bedrooms, bathrooms and kitchen facilities at a price low enough to fit in with most budgets. Breakfast, plates and cutlery are usually available, but bring your own bed sheets and pillow covers, which are compulsory for hygiene reasons. If you don't, an extra hire charge will be made.

The greatest thing about STF hostels is that they are like Garbage Pail Kids. No two are the same and you never quite know what you're going to get. Åsa's offering was a selection of blue wooden chalets, lifted up on ramps, cradled gently by a forest glade cutting next to the road. Claiming a bottom bunk and nodding off reading names scratched into the wood above my head (a lot of girls loved Christoffer), I dragged my smelly body to the shower on awakening, scrubbed a few pairs of padded pants in the soap suds and hung up a wet tent in the wardrobe. I was revitalised, able to walk again and ready for a thirst quencher. But there was no beer on sale at the driest wagon in town. The hostel doubled up as a meeting hall for the Swedish Temperance Organisation, IOGT, and operated a zero tolerance alcohol policy. Established in 1979, the action group combats increasing alcohol consumption and drug abuse, which they believe is having a detrimental nationwide affect on social society. IOGT has 60,000 members and 700 temperance halls, using sport and leisure activities to get through to kids before they pick up a glass, while attempting to change the attitudes of already pickled parents. They also try to influence the country's political agenda, lobbying the European Union to raise the legal drinking age in Sweden. The group is self-funded, raising money through a lottery system played by 140,000 Swedes every month. Gambling seemed to be tolerated then.

To buy strong alcohol in Sweden you must be aged 20 or over. But that's not enough for IOGT, which claims the EU's desire to relax drinking laws and lower alcohol tariffs will lead to more people picking up the bottle, comparable to the figures from Sweden's darkest drinking days 125 years ago. In the 1800s virtually every household made and sold their own hooch. Swedes were guzzling an average 45 litres of pure firewater from 175,000 distillers every year, using enormous amounts of grain and potatoes that could have been eaten as food. Sweden may have a universal reputation of being tall, blond, athletic, reserved and non-aggressive, but in fact it harbours a nation of thirsty pissheads who can't wait to get down the pub. Hefty rationing was introduced during the First World War, restricting a parched population with the shakes to just two litres of liquor every three months. The throat screws were tightened further by banning beer. This unpopular scheme wasn't abolished until 1955, replaced by the *Systembolaget*, a government run chain of alcohol stores. *Systembolaget* is the largest purchaser in the world of wine and spirits from around the globe. A cross between a pharmacy and a supermarket deli counter, customers take tickets from a wall dispenser and wait patiently to be sold bottles imprisoned in shackled glass viewing cabinets and beers stacked on hidden shelves behind tills. To this day it is the only place you can buy booze containing more than 3.5 per cent alcohol volume and opening is restricted to 6pm during the week and 1pm on a Saturday, with Sundays shut for hangovers. All profit margins are exactly the same, but all prices are based on alcohol content.

Hostel Åsa was run by a strict tea-totaller, Ann-Sofi, who was in favour of seeing the age limit for buying alcohol radically increased. I bet it wasn't much fun round her house at Christmas and birthdays. 'So how high should the drinking age be?' I asked.

'As high as possible. Up and up. Keep on going,' she hit back with fanatical zeal.

'Do you drink?'

'No.'

'What. Never?'

'No.'

'Have you ever?'

'No. Never since I was born. Not in my whole life. Not even a single sip of red wine with a meal.'

Whatever happened to don't knock it, until you've tried it? I didn't understand how somebody could be so passionately dismissive, without actually ever experiencing what they condemned. Ann-Sofi had never even been tipsy. As I watched her young kids joyfully running up and down the stairs, I wondered if they would be allowed to make their own minds up about the evils of alcohol, free from brainwashing. I hoped she would let them follow their own future paths.

A few hundred yards down the road, Friday evening was already in full swing as Åsa's cheering and screaming middle-aged chain-smokers piled into the bevvies. Two restaurants, Thai and Italian, doubled up as bars and the locals were already well oiled at 7pm. There didn't appear to be much temperance observed here and feelings of host projected guilt soon dissolved when I spotted the hostel cleaner swooping down on a few Falcon beers at the bar. A roof top pub with a wooden veranda offered an unfriendly nightcap, served up by a couple of sour-faced blonde glamour pussies, far too big for their bras, preening themselves at the bar. No wonder it was dead as a dinosaur. But there was plasma screen entertainment, of sorts, a time warped Swedish take on Britain's Got Talent. The cream of the country's backward acts had managed to make the grand final of Talang 2007, one of Sweden's top three TV shows. Rockingrings Maria twirled numerous hula hoops, Robotman, an anorexic Terminator, complete with sunglasses and black leather jacket, danced like a slow motion playground steam train, and a sickening little shit break danced and moon walked in a trilby, milking the elderly crowd with a helium powered 'I love you' at the end of his act. But move over Nookie Bear, the winner was Zillah and Totte, a pretty ventriloquist with her arm stuffed up a smiling puppet monkey's backside. A victory for precious young talent and nothing whatsoever to do with a nicely toned set of pins reaching out of a risqué short green skirt.

Chancing another stony Medusa stare from the miserable fake tanned fillies, I snatched a newspaper off the bar, *Aftonbladet*, one of Sweden's national rags. I nearly rubbed my eyes out of their sockets after reading the bold black capped front page headline, 'Piss Ocksa'. Translated as 'Piss Also' in English, a photograph, leaving nothing to the imagination, showed a woman pulling up a red dress and peeing in a cup. You could even see the urine dribbling down her legs. A special report inside revealed this was in fact a work of abstract living art, with its creator, Itziar Okariz, attempting to prove 'this is not just a man's world' by standing up for a slash in the north of Sweden. But her thunder was stolen by another artist, bearded Terry Waite clone Dorinel Marc, who placed a cup under her leaking body, before scooping it up and having a drink. If this was his vile stab at trying to re-establish men as the dominant race, then I'm all for parity with the fairer sex. This was madness. I needed the confined safety of the temperance hall.

30　Gothenburg Goodbye

Wheeling towards Gothenburg at full steam, Rhys uttered three words I had been dreading more than anything else. 'I'm going home.' Running low on funds, my cycling sidekick had made the difficult decision to bail out, with the Swedish port offering a ferry journey back to England. We had spent just over three weeks together and I couldn't imagine not having Rhys by my side now. He was my wing man, part of the baggage and had become key to the trip. My lonely solitary start to this marathon quest had been replaced by joking, moaning and leg busting comradeship. Every second of our two wheeled union, whether gut wrenching hard or fall off the saddle happy, had been memorable, eagerly embracing the thrill of steering twin handle bars towards strange destinations and quirky people come rain or shine. Together we had conquered countries undiscovered to us, and going on alone again, without my flesh and blood comfort zone, filled me with trepidation. But we agreed not to dwell on the negative. Bashing out the 60 kilometres to Gothenburg and getting settled in early for a farewell Saturday night drinkathon. It couldn't have worked out better.

Hills steeper than anything encountered so far rose up around the peculiar grave fields of Fjärås Bräcka. Huge jagged upright stones, oblong lumps of grey arrow pointed rock, patrolled the edge of the gradient, growing in even greater numbers down below in the retreating meadow. This was Halland's principal burial site, home to more than 100 death stones dating back to the Iron Age. The tallest of the collection was the road side slab, 'The Frode Stone' which was 4.7 metres high. Also nearby was *Limmahögarna*, a Bronze Age burial mound. The large raised grass bank demonstrated the importance of its unknown occupant, now preserved to keep treasure hunters at spade's length. Another morbid chapter could be read on the modest grave stones at *Kolera Kyrkogård*, belonging to 48 Fjärås residents who lost their lives in an 1834 cholera epidemic. At the long climb's summit, a spectacular view, added special credence to this beauty spot's continued popularity as a final resting place over the passing centuries. Catching your breath with a glimpse of the flawless shining blue waters of Lake Lygnern, running away forever along bristling banks of hairy pine, was a fine reward. The biggest lake in Halland, Lygnern was formed by a receding Ice Age glacier and provides drinking water for local communities.

Remaining disciplined to the task at hand, getting lost on a golf course and playing through the rough of Kungsbacka's bustling market town, we found ourselves taking on a series of back-breaking man-made inclines. The cycle path followed a busy dual carriageway, a feeder for the Gothenburg bound E06 motorway, defying geography with a lot more sinew straining ups than stamina regenerating downs. Some of the hills went up for more than a kilometre, with a significantly shorter descent from the top, rolling you towards the footing of another killer climb. The physical signals born out of such a heavy work load were disturbing. My arms trembled, legs quivered, and most concerning of all a violently pumping heart was throwing itself against my rib cage in a last ditch bid to escape and grasp oxygen. God knows what this meant about my general standard of health, but shouldn't I have been coping a bit better after cycling across four countries? I didn't spontaneously combust in a convulsing mess however, which I regarded as a positive sign. Must kick those social cigs into touch.

The concrete peaks mercifully levelled off into a maze of residential alleys and shared cycle/pedestrian paths where a heavily padded dad was pushing two sleeping toddlers along in a buggy on his rollerblades. Solving this puzzle with minimum fuss we exited into a large cluster of sea lagoons, weighted down by enormous weather dimpled islands of rock, on the fringes of Billdal. Red and white bathing huts offering private access to the mirror clear water took a leisurely pew at the end of stone groyne piers. Nautical themed houses with round port hole windows and anchors presided over a marina full of paint splattered men, gently brushing the bellies of small boats suspended on wooden legs.

Spiralling off into suburban verdant passages, the mechanical clunks of changing gear sticks and loudly ticking engines reverberated from the Gothenburg approach path. Claustrophobia reigned supreme as the two-way cycle track, hedge segregated from the frantic main road into the city, was attacked on all side by bikes, mopeds, skaters and people just using their legs for a stroll. Sometimes you feel as if you are the only cyclist in the world, spending long hours on a lonely furrow of dead country roads and muted forest paths. This was a suffocating shock to the system. And we weren't the only ones having trouble readjusting. Right out of nowhere, the furry behind of an adult deer burst past our front wheels, ploughing across the cycle lane and hopping head first into the thicket. Completely stunned I made an emergency stop. Wincing through gritted teeth I awaited the painful bellow of a mortally injured animal, way out of its natural element, battered by passing cars. But it never came. The wily old bugger obviously knew his Green Cross Code, patiently taking his time to look up and down the road for a gap in the traffic, before making a lightning break to the field on the other side. I couldn't believe this had happened less than a kilometre away from heavily populated streets, on a cycle path sandwiched between a housing estate and the screeching tyres of a city highway. Who needed Sir David Attenborough when you had 'The Life of Bikes'?

Gothenburg was a sprawl of a city, stacked high above the main artery of its historical lifeblood, the cargo pumping sea trading vein of the Göta Älv River. Blue and white trams criss-crossed wide avenues hemmed in by a mixed timeline of seven-storey buildings, 19th-century structures with grand entrances, and trendy glass and stainless steel bars. Sloping San Francisco style streets hurdled through the middle of tables and chairs, intimately entwined in the city's café culture. Imposing statues waded cold green feet through huge decorative shower bowls, gazing out across duck filled canals and the untainted lungs of tree heavy parks. In short this cosmopolitan hub had something for everyone, whether you craved fine art, meals cooked by some of the best chefs in the world, banging techno disco or just a little peace and quiet.

Gothenburg is Sweden's second city, behind the capital Stockholm, and is home to half a million people. Utilising the direct Kattegat feed into the Göta Älv River, Gothenburg has flourished, with its expanding crane covered harbour growing into the largest Scandinavian port. An important logistics centre for trains and lorries throughout Sweden and neighbouring Norway, the port has an annual 37 million tonne turnover of ship cargo. But progressive Gothenburg has made great strides away from the shipping industry too. Multinational businesses SKF, Volvo and Ericsson have think-tanks here, developing their reputations as field leaders in the lucrative hi-tech manufacture of motor vehicles and electronics. Who knows what future technological advances the collective brains of Gothenburg will deliver, with a 50,000 strong student population forming the biggest university in Sweden.

Sun drenched *Slottsskogen Park* was swarming with a multicolour of shirt numbered athletes and ice cream licking spectators. It was half marathon day in Gothenburg, an annual event contested by 40,000 runners, but I couldn't work out if the race had started, finished, or was still to begin. One set of smiling competitors were sharing an athletics track with a group of inflatable waffles, chips and bananas. Others limbered up outside the enormous park, jogging down the street for a few hundred yards, before sharply turning back on themselves as if they had bashed into an invisible force field. A vibrant crowd revelling in the carnival atmosphere cheered on road runners behind a taped off kerb, with the tempo set by a jazz quartet and Roy Orbison covers band playing their instruments outside closed shop windows.

Taking a few pointers from the road wise deer, we made a 360 degree sweep of the non-racing traffic cluttered streets, crossing part of Gothenburg's 80 kilometre double tram track, while keeping our eyes peeled for cars, buses and other bikes. It wasn't easy. The Slottsskogen hostel was conveniently placed for all the city's amenities and rightly advertised its immaculate lodgings as: 'Just like staying in a hotel, but a lot less expensive.'

You could get a dormitory bed, sharing a room with 14 over sweaty travellers, for less than a tenner, but we opted for a double bunk room, which was only a couple of quid more and had a TV set. Yipee!

After launching a frenzied man hunt for a cobweb covered cycle shed key, we settled into our quarters. The other two beds were already taken, booked out in advance by a pair of Swedish runners who return to the city every year to compete in the half marathon. They were both in their seventies. As we unpacked our bags, one of the ageing athletes sat in the corner. He looked, and probably ran, like a tortoise and I could picture him slowly chewing a lettuce leaf. But he was terribly thin. I'd seen more meat on a chicken nugget. He didn't speak a word of English, but was eager to show off his chunky gold sprayed medal attached to a blue ribbon. His mate was nowhere to be seen. Maybe he'd keeled over and died stretching a withered hand towards a hydration drink. Silly old fool.

It seemed everyone was a winner in this race. Legions of athletes dressed up for a night on the town limped down the street, all swinging huge *Jim'll Fix It* medallions around their necks. Sitting at a tarpaulin covered decked restaurant court, we tucked into a fish and pasta dish, plus a few drinks, again dispelling whispered horror stories of inflated Scandinavian bar bills. If you shopped around in Gothenburg it wasn't difficult to pay just over £2 for a bottle of lager. But eateries were an even better option, offering special meal package deals of two beers, a pint and a bottle almost able to fill your glass again, for £3.50. Most importantly, it tasted nice and wasn't cheap shit specially reserved for clueless tourists.

But even this couldn't cheer Rhys up. He wasn't looking forward to dissolving our partnership. And he must have been the only bloke in history to visit Gothenburg and not be able to get on a boat. Despite being clearly marked on the giant fold-out North Sea Cycle Route overview map, the DFDS Seaways sailing to Newcastle had been permanently cancelled in October, blaming budget air fares for its demise. Rhys didn't mind flying, it was just the hassle. He had to cycle to the airport, which was a 40 minute bus ride out of town, and ahead of that mission locate a sheet of bubble wrap big enough to cover his dismantled bike and meet strict air transit safety guidelines.

We walked deeper into town, past basement Goth rock stores, tattoo parlours and skateboard shops, even popping in to Gothenburg's porn megastore. But a selection of luminous pink dildos, butt plugs shaped like dummies, nurse uniforms, black whips and the curiously named DVD 'Weird Gay Cocks', failed to put a smile back on his face. Edging closer to the trendy, *Kungsportsavenyen,* a clustered strip of bright lights, pubs and clubs, known among the city's night crawlers as 'The Avenue', we tried to drown Rhys' sorrows. Drawn into a darkened bar by the excited screams of young blonde fillies and tanned well chiselled guys watching a giant TV screen, we wondered what was causing all the commotion. Never in my wildest nightmares could I have guessed the Eurovision Song Contest, but the packed drink clutching congregation were loving every minute of it.

Back at home, nobody would be watching this in a pub. It was a competition we didn't take seriously. Partly because we were hated by the rest of Europe and the other nations relished the annual opportunity to gang together and spank our latest entry from a musical factory conveyor belt of mediocre cringeworthy losers. I think it used to be called Stock, Aitken and Waterman. Anyone who watches the Eurovision Song Contest in England does so behind locked doors and for two reasons only; to hear Terry Wogan take the piss out of the countries who hate us and witness which stone deaf realm gives us more than Nil Pwa on the final leader board. There was fervent solidarity from the drinking Swedes, as neighbouring Finland were the hosts, following the terrifying victory of their head banging heavy metal trolls in the previous competition. This contest offered the usual selection of Ricky Martin wannabes, Goths dressed like undertakers, pink wearing Frenchmen, Romanian gypsies and a blue-eyed German Frank Sinatra. And let's not forget the hysterical interludes giving an insight into the host nation, which this time peaked with a load of muddy old men playing football in a bog and having their nude behinds whacked by a thorny branch, before diving through an ice hole.

A huge shout and raised glasses greeted Sweden's entry, a poor Marc Bolan rip-off, including the panda eye make-up. After watching our lukewarm welcomed flag bearers, Scooch, a rabble of cheesy orange-faced dance retards dressed up as air cabin crew struggling to reach half mast, we retreated to the toilets in embarrassment. Serbia's female Joe Pasquale look-a-like Marija Serifovic took first place, narrowly edging past a Ukrainian transvestite wearing an umbrella on his head. We came second from bottom, thanks to a vote of full marks from Malta, where Scooch can now be found on tour.

Eurovision had done little to lift Rhys' sullen, drunken mood, and he sloped back off to the hostel, leaving me to investigate 'The Avenue' on my own. I had to get used to it I suppose. Loud music pumped out of bars and queues of short skirted sexy young things, covered in war paint, queued for numerous clubs. A girl I chatted to in the Eurovision bar (who went to great pains to make me aware Gothenburgers couldn't stand the snobs of Stockholm) had vouched for *The Lounge*. The bouncer didn't want to let me in at first, telling me my trainers, light weight trousers and fleece weren't casual enough to gain entry. After threatening to return in pants, socks and a vest he changed his mind.

The Lounge was nothing like a traditional English disco, full of drunken idiots jumping up and down to 'Baggy Trousers' by Madness and couples necking over their glasses. It was all far more civilised. Soft trance music floated through the dimly lit air, allowing Swedish clubbers to squat on black square poofs around low tables chatting away over drinks. A giant plasma screen filled one white wall, projecting close-ups of beautiful women mouthing muted words. A steep staircase climbed up to a brightly lit smokers' penthouse, with wall grills filtering the cigarette fumes outside, beating the ban on lighting up in public places across Sweden. The heavens had broken with a vengeance outside, transforming the streets of Gothenburg into a running river, drench fed by gutters filled to bursting point and overflowing drains. I staggered into bed quietly at 1.30am, trying not to disturb Rhys or the geriatric road champs, soaked to the skin by rain and beer.

Bang… Thud… Clump! Oh my poor head. Who the fuck's making that racket? Clump… Thud… Bang! For fuck's sake, what is going on? Thud… Bang… Clump! It was 6-fucking-30am! Pulling the bed covers off my thumping head, I drearily found a fuzzy focus. It was the missing running pensioner with a medal around his neck. Had he only just finished the race? Still wearing his shorts and vest, a brown head band was slapped back over a few remaining grey hairs. The tortoise was nowhere to be seen, leaving his colleague behind to stamp around the room, making more noise than a pair of hobnailed boots.

The hammering was complimented by the tossing of coins on the table, turning the wall sink taps on and off, rustling food wrappers and the zipping of bags. Every irritating action was punctuated by the inconsiderate old wanker mumbling under his breath. This went on for two hours, broken up by short intervals of shuffling across the floor, leaving the room and slamming the door shut, before returning 10 minutes later. Really wishing I knew basic Swedish words, I wanted to threaten to show the rude arsehole the finishing line by chucking him out the window. Next time I make a late night return to a room full of grumpy old runners, I'm going to smash pots and pans above their resting heads. Knowing my luck, they'll be tone deaf and sleep straight through it.

Katie was already in the air. She would be touching down in under an hour and I felt like an excited child, not a travel hardened adventurer. My immediate attention returned to Rhys, whose timely arrival in Germany had pulled me away from the teetering brink of quitting prematurely and returning home. He had lifted my spirits when they were drowning, giving me the renewed desire to keep biking on. How was I going to cope without him? As we stood hugging each other goodbye outside the hostel doorway like a couple of big girls' blouses, all the things I was going to miss most about Rhys flashed through my mind. The early morning moans, spitting in the road and an uncanny ability to bang his head on random lamps, bunk beds and branches. There was the frenzied teeth brushing, admirable attempts to communicate with wildlife and the creepy hmmmm sounds he made after spotting a beautiful woman or enjoying a nice meal. He made the same noise in his sleep too, but I didn't want to know about that. I was going to badly miss the other person who had shared in most of the magic and mediocrity of the trip so far. An easy going fella and a first rate companion who had played a key role in the conquering of my travelling fears. Pedalling towards my romantic rendezvous, abandoning Rhys to a lonely bubble wrap hunt, it felt like I was losing a brother.

31   Love will tear us Apart

First date butterflies fluttered uncontrollably around my stomach. Leaning against Erika, outside the 18th-century covered platforms of Gothenburg's central station, I nervously awaited Katie's grand entrance. She had called from the airport in a right old flap, making sure I would be at the bus stop when she arrived blind in a strange country. And it just felt weird. This was the human being who shared my most intimate secrets, a soul sister and the love of my life, so why was a deep insecurity washing over me? We were inseparable at home and never spent a night apart. But here I was, 34 days down the line from abandoning her in England to pursue my personal quest, and I wondered if everything would be the same. We hadn't been separated completely, like the classic pioneering adventurers of the developing world, relying on the occasional letter to give them comfort every few months or years. Modern day mobile phones had kept the sound of our voices alive to each other every day. It also made things extremely difficult, especially during lonely spells and at night time, wishing you were curling up next to the warm body on the other end of the receiver. I was starting to get paranoid. Having been away for what seemed an eternity, would Katie feel different about us? Would the girl still fancy me? Would she still love me?

Bags tossed to one side after running off the bus, a leaping, kung-fu style flying cuddle and kiss instantly allayed my worst fears. It was incredible to smell her hair again, grip that body tightly and swap smiles set to full heart longing beam. Releasing herself from another crushing bear hug, Katie took two steps back and laughed: 'You look really different.'

'So do you. Talk about freaky,' I chuckled, before moving in for another compassionate round of smoochy hugs.

The missus had pulled off a blinder. Using her travel booking secretarial contacts to steal two discounted nights at the plush five star Radisson SAS Hotel opposite the station. The smartly turned out receptionists had never watched a guest try to wrestle an overloaded bike through their revolving glass doors before. Even more shocked were the cluster of suitcase pulling aeroplane captains in well starched uniforms, momentarily distracted from booking a pretty stewardess in for a spot of overnight hanky-panky behind the wife's back. But the polite staff couldn't have been more helpful (opening a side door for starters), ticketing my bags for storage and allowing Erika to be stabled in a back room, tied to a radiator. After more than a month on the road the Radisson was a welcome taste of luxury. A spotlessly dusted brown wooden lobby viewed a spacious open plan ground floor collection of bars, dining areas and a piano treading water in the middle of a sunken white pool and fountains. Fast glass elevators raced up to a catacomb of 349 rooms, climbing onwards and upwards towards a ceiling with a steady head for heights.

The sleeping quarters were a psychedelic acid trip from the 60s. A tiger striped headboard growled above the bed, big swirling circles rolled across the carpet, draped by rainbow coloured curtains facing cylindrical lamps, red sloping chairs and a huge plastic chilli pepper stapled to the wall. Visually intoxicated by such vivid decoration and furniture, I could have sworn I chucked out George Best and two giggling blondes drinking champagne under our bed sheets. Quickly returned to reality by another vision, Katie's naked body, it was time to play catch-up.

The Radisson conjured up the other two things I had nearly missed as much as Katie since leaving home. The room had a bath. A long, relaxing soak in a tub full of bubbles, sipping a cup of coffee, beat a shower any day of the week. The other stolen joy was a fried breakfast. It wasn't quite a full English, with small frankfurters substituting bangers, but there were fried eggs, tomatoes, mushrooms, bacon and beans, which was good enough for me.

Not all of our two and a bit days together were spent storing up the love bank behind closed doors. Gothenburg was the biggest port of call so far and a hypnotic setting for romantic liaisons, boasting attractive architecture, lively entertainment and a mouth-watering variety of restaurant menus. I tried to impress Katie with the knowledge gleaned prior to her arrival, showing her around the sights of this wonderful city. But, being a woman, she was only interested in the hive of clothing and footwear shops, joining the throng of other girls buzzing in and out of doorways. Dragging Katie kicking and screaming away from the fashion houses for a stroll to the other end of town we passed the curving buckled wheel shaped roof of the *Ullevi* Stadium. A European football temple,

Ullevi was built for the 1958 World Cup finals in Sweden and is still the highest capacity ground in Scandinavia. Able to seat 43,000 spectators, *Ullevi* is the sometimes home of top Swedish football club IFK Gothenburg, depending on the importance of the match dictating crowd demands, whisking me back to my childhood. I can still remember IFK beating Dundee United on TV in the UEFA Cup final in 1987. Two years later I was awe struck when the Swedish footballing Gods visited Roots Hall to play Southend United in a friendly fixture. I managed to bunk over fences, hurdling three sides of the ground, to reach the IFK bench and plead for one of their shirts as a reward. 'Sorry, English boy. We are not allowed,' I was told by an eloquent blond giant. *Ullevi* has hosted UEFA Cup finals, World Athletics Championships, ice skating and speedway races. It was also the venue for the first NFL match on European soil in 1988 when the Minnesota Vikings took on the Chicago Bears in a pre-season game. The attendance record was set in 1985, but not by a sporting event. It was a Bruce Springsteen concert played to 64,312 rowdy rockers, strumming their air guitars in tune with The Boss. A walk of stars rings the pavement around the ground, paying homage to members of football's most successful elite, Brazil, who won their first World Cup in 1958, beating Sweden 5-2 in the final, inspired by a 17-year-old Pele. I wonder how arguably the greatest player ever would feel about the build-up of bird shit taking the shine off his star. Next door to the stadium is *Liseberg*, the biggest amusement park in Scandinavia, but sadly for Katie it was closed. I was pleased. I didn't do fairground rides either.

Walking hand-in-hand along the city centre's street splitting canal, we gave two roaring teethy lion busts a wide berth, before saluting a fading green statue of Gothenburg's bearded founder, King Gustaf II Adolf, who, dressed up like one of the Three Musketeers, posed in front of the city hall and stock exchange. Gothenburg was a jumble of different architecture. The sophisticated tall glass panelled panes of the slanting boat shaped opera house docked next to the Göta Älv River demonstrates the best in ultra modern design. As does the skyline dominating *Götheborgsutkiken*, known as the lipstick (but actually looking more like a building in disguise Transformer), an 86 metre high structure with a restaurant crow's nest offering a panoramic view of the city.

There are very few structures remaining from when the city was founded in 1621 because all but the military and royal houses were made from wood. But a layer cake of the old can be viewed at *Masthugget Hill*. Houses from the 19th century sit at the bottom, with the repetitive concrete piles of Brutalistic modernist design from the 1950s in the middle and older *Landshövdingehus* buildings the icing on the top. These houses are unique to Gothenburg. Bylaws at the end of the 1800s prohibited homes made of wood being higher than two storeys. Crafty builders got around this problem by throwing the wooden floors on top of a brick ground storey, giving birth to the *Landshövdingehus*.

One of the most striking edifices stands shoulder to shoulder with other imposing walls of solid stone lining the canal. The chiselled features of crabs, fish and mermaids still occupy a lofty perch on the façade of the former Swedish East India Company headquarters. The shipping venture was formed in 1731, operating lucrative long haul voyages to the Far East and establishing Gothenburg as Scandinavia's trade gateway to the West, until its demise in 1813. The building has been the home of Gothenburg's City Museum for 150 years, modelled on the British Victoria and Albert. The prize exhibit is the *Äskekärr*, the only Viking era ship on display anywhere in Sweden.

An excited run up marble stairs to a gloomy chamber ended in disappointment. I was expecting something slightly intact, along the lines of the *Mary Rose*. What I got amounted to a scattering of broken, rotting fence posts, laid out across an alarmed red sheet. I suppose it kept firewood poachers at bay. The cargo vessel's skeleton dated back to the year 900 and was recovered from a clay river bed 30 kilometres from Gothenburg in the 1930s. *Äskekärr* would have been 16 metres in length and able to carry 16 tonnes of goods under the strength of a single sail, with small oars only used for landing. It is the only Viking ship in the world to hold runic inscription markings, believed to brand it as a livestock carrier. This area was the border between the three strongest Viking colonies of west Sweden, Denmark and Norway, known then as Tanmaurk, Nuruiak and Gautland. Plenty of scabby double-edged Viking swords and jewellery filled other glass cases, found in abundance here because of Gothenburg's past geographical status.

Hungry after our final day sightseeing we hunted out some evening grub. Gothenburg serves up all sorts of food, ranging from traditional fish dishes, to Thai and Italian cuisine. You really can find anything you want to suit your stomach. Close to the Radisson, on the other side of a covered shopping arcade, the *Sense* bar in *Östra Larmgatan* had become our favourite haunt. Lip shaped velvet red chairs, wooden chests and candlelight beckoned you towards the beer pumps inside. A quirky pink side room restaurant of old pictures hanging in fat golden frames was an added sideshow and the food was not only delicious, but amazing value for money.

Sense must have the most generously competent sushi chef in town, with eight huge chunks of tiger prawn, avocado, tuna and crab costing less than £10. In the day time it was even better. A pick-it-yourself buffet of creamy hot soups, a fresh salad bar, pasta, noodles, meat, cheese and crusty bread, all swimming in long ship wooden bowls, plus a beer, for only a few quid more. After stuffing all those combinations down our faces, it was time for a calorie burning last night hotel workout.

It was the early evening Tuesday bus queue at Gothenburg's central station. Hold on a minute! This couldn't be right! It only seemed a few hours ago that Katie had arrived on a Sunday morning over the other side of the concourse. Katie couldn't be jetting out again already. Despite being apart for so long, everything had slipped effortlessly back into gear, with both of us scared to admit the hours of our short reunion were flying past far too quickly. If we didn't mention it, then maybe time would freeze still and we wouldn't be separated again. I really didn't want her to go. But she had to.

Spending the last few days together had been incredible. But at what cost? It had reminded me of all the things I was sacrificing for my big adventure. Having someone to cuddle up to at night, randomly geeking off together and even being pulled protesting around girly clothes shops, had all sowed a seed yearning for home. If I'm honest, Katie coming to Gothenburg did me absolutely no favours at all. And her imminent departure, on top of losing Rhys, was seriously questioning my desire to continue.

Old women cast us sympathetic glances as we welled up, holding each other closely, the minutes ticking away like seconds. It could have been an emotionally charged scene from a tear jerking Hollywood love story. It certainly bettered my favourite spot of big screen romance when Princess Leia shouts 'I love you' to space pirate Han Solo before he is carbon freezed on Cloud City and gift wrapped by the evil Empire as a wall decoration for Jabba the Hutt's palace. When the film rights are sold to this book, Julia Roberts will play Katie and Mel Gibson will fill my shoes. Green Greedo will make a cameo appearance as Rhys.

The screech of a breaking airport bus signalled the moment we had been dreading, huddled there, firing off endless goodbye kisses, as the skin around Katie's eyes turned pink under a torrent of tears. This was so cruel. I didn't know when I was going to see her again, it could be weeks or even months. At that moment I could have buried my flying fears and boarded the plane with her. And then, with a last disappearing wave from the bus steps, she was gone. I'd never felt so alone in the world.

A miserable climb over the long Göta Älv River bridge headed towards mountainous tree dotted rock cakes. A depressing backdrop of shabby edge of the city apartment blocks, water towers and industrial units did little to lift the mood. And Erika's tyres were wining too. She was pining for Rhys' bike Globe, who I presumed was a man, following the severing of their own two wheeled bond, spending romantic nights together under the stars and intimately chained together in cycle sheds.

245

We were a right sorry pair. Following a path next to the E06 motorway, which stretches all the way from Malmö in the Swedish south up to the Norwegian capital of Oslo, I was following the provincial cycle route of Bohuslän.

A morbid 20 kilometre shunt led to Kungälv, an attractive riverside town dominated by the intimidating figure of the *Bohus Fortress,* one of history's great survivors. Casting a powerful figure on a raised grass embankment, the sturdy rounded stone tower and thick defensive walls were painted blood red by the setting sun. The building of *Bohus* got underway in 1308 when this area was the most southern part of Norway. The Norwegian monarch, King Hakon V Magnusson, had the original construction made out of wood after a bust-up with the Swedish dukes. The outer walls were later reinforced and surrounded by ramparts of earth and stone mounds. In the middle of the 14th century the wooden buildings were replaced by stone. The defence works outside the circular walls, with its casemates, embankments and barracks were erected towards the end of the 16th century.

Bohus revelled in its fearsome reputation as the largest and strongest fortress in Scandinavia. In some places the impenetrable walls are nine metres thick. In 1389, the Swedish king, Albrekt of Mecklenburg and his son, Erik, were imprisoned at *Bohus* for insulting Queen Margareta, the figurehead of a unified Sweden and Norway, accusing her of being 'trouserless'. In the words of an English queen, Victoria, she definitely wasn't amused. And they had little chance of escape. *Bohus* has been put under siege 14 times, but never conquered. The Swedes even tried to burn it down unsuccessfully in the 16th century. Sweden finally got its hands on the stronghold after making peace with their neighbouring enemies in 1645. But the scheming Norwegians and Danes teamed up together, launching a devilishly fiendish plot of stealing the new owners' socks, mittens and blankets ahead of winter. Now that really showed the shivering Swedes who was boss!

Bohus was taken out of active service and used as a prison for 130 inmates in the 18th century, after being stripped of its canons by King Christian XII, eager to renew old hostilities with Norway. Nowadays, the fortress is of scientific botanical interest, with the old cement wall joints providing nourishment to lime demanding plants. Rare lichens and moss thrive on the shadow covered side of the battlements, but it is forbidden to pick plants around the walls. *Bohus* is open to visitors, who are guided around damp dungeons and across the walls and, if they're really lucky, treated to a good old-fashioned medieval sing-song.

Home for the night was an old 18th-century school house, complete with a bell on its roof, opposite the fortress. The hostel interior was a reconstructed medieval museum piece of candle chandeliers, wall tapestries of old crowned kings served cups of mead, coats of arms and there was even a dark wooden banqueting hall. The sort of place the Sheriff of Nottingham would take his mistress for a dirty weekend. It was a shame my room never had the same charm. I'd been placed in solitary confinement, sat in my pants staring at two empty bunk beds, a small table and four blank white walls. It really wasn't going well being back on the road alone. I was desperate for a bed time conversation, even a winge and a moan. But there was nobody else here and it was soul destroying. It was only a few hours since I'd left Katie, who had touched safely back down in England now, but I didn't know how much more of this I could take.

32   Bridge over card shark infested Waters

The crown forest of *Svartedalen* lifted up from the quiet riverbanks of Kungälv along an incline of solid rock teaming with pine. The gentle trickle of knoll hidden brooks followed a worn out road littered with fallen fragments of stone, twisting and turning past crystal clear lakes. No other signs of human activity crossed my path all morning, but a patchy pointed gravestone from 1843, resting under the branches, proved somebody else had trod, or maybe even cycled, here before me.

Back on the road towards civilisation a new vision of dazzling beauty took top spot on the leader board. The *Hakefjord* was the single most stunning piece of eye candy I had seen since Freddy Eastwood's rocket of a free-kick dumped Manchester United out of the Carling Cup at Roots Hall. A seemingly limitless pool of clean blue water, matched only by the wide open roof of sky above, full of tree condensed islands and tiny red houses. Spongy brown moss and petite purple headed flowers sprouted out of a rock strewn shore of sleeping hippo's hides, with a tiling of mussel shells coughed up on the beach. The approaching petrochemical town of Stenungsund did its best to tarnish the view, with four dirty great power plant chimneys craning unwelcome necks on to the horizon. But that was the least of my worries. Had I mentioned I hated heights?

The gigantic orange cable supported *Tjörn* bridge raised its capital H shaped shoulders above the fjord. A transport cradling colossus, it lifted vehicles over to a large island of the same name, the gateway to a complicated archipelago of sea bordered settlements of all shapes and sizes.

More than 650 metres in length, the bridge pylons are 114 metres above the sea below. The bridge was opened in 1981, the year after its predecessor was knocked down in a collision with a ship, claiming the lives of eight people whose cars fell over the edge. Gulp!

I used to have a real problem driving over high bridges, particularly the QE2 crossing between Essex and Kent. Steering wheel gripped with fear on the initial ascent, I worried that my crazy brain would take control, forcing sharp turning arms to crash the motor through the barrier, nosediving into the Thames below. Funnily enough, I never mentioned this to any of my passengers, keeping the car in the middle twos lane, with a defensive escort of traffic either side blocking any attempts to fly. Practice makes perfect and I eventually got over it. But this was very different, riding the humped back of a gleaming steel giant in the open air, without the security of a locked door to prevent me tipping over the edge and plummeting to my doom. My padded shorts had taken on some extra padding.

This trip was supposed to be about defeating all anxieties and I just had to go for it. Facing straight ahead, no looking left or right, and definitely not down, I pedalled frenetically as fast as my legs could manage, breathing as heavily as an overweight rhinoceros with sweat dripping down my front horn. Cars and lorries flew past my right shoulder, I could hear them, but couldn't see them, and it was all over in a matter of minutes. Shattered and arms shaking I looked back triumphantly at the conquered car hungry metal monster. Noticing the low metal rail between the edge of the cycle track and oblivion for the first time my heart skipped a beat. Now that really could have been far too tempting an invite to refuse hurdling.

Tjörn was the number two island of superiority on an archipelago necklaced by an abundance of tiny islets. The daddy of land masses in this part of Sweden was Orust, accessed by the much shorter, smaller and less nerve wracking *Skåpesund* bridge. Down below the water course overpass chalets balanced on rocky shelves and boats were tied up next to jetties waiting for some exercise. Fertile dried mud infested farm roads led to the reedy lakes and wet dripping tunnel walls of the Boxvik promontory and into the wilderness of Stocken. A countryside lawn covered in grassy marbles of rock reclaimed by nature after falling loose from the split bag of a giant on his way to an important game against Scandinavian trolls many centuries ago.

Right in the middle of this lush nowhere land was another example of unique youth hostelling. A sentry of thin trees marched past a red barn and up to the front door of a matching coloured two-storey wooden farmhouse dating back to 1774. The islands were historically a poor area of Sweden and the fishermen would supplement their meagre incomes by working extra hours on the farm. Nowadays, *Tofta* is a picturesque summer wedding venue with couples whose family roots are buried in this forlorn outback, committing to each other under the barn roof, out on the curving gardens or down by the cliffs at the sea. As I lugged my gear across a living room and kitchen into a second floor bedroom, numerous thank you cards and wedding pictures adorned the walls. I wondered how many happy pairings had sealed the deal in my bed!

There was a big bridge game in town. It was Wednesday night and ruthless card sharks were swimming to this remote corner of Sweden from all over the country, crack teams of mixed doubles partners hell bent on getting their teeth into a 4,000 krona cash-pot. Just over £300 to you and me. *Tofta* would be bursting to the rafters with a loaded weekend deck, but the hustlers were arriving early, desperate to get in some last minute practice. And absolutely blind drunk of course.

Six noisy laughing and joking players, three men, three women, had laid a banquet out on the kitchen table. The sextet were munching away on meatballs, giant prawns, cocktail sausages, cheese, salad and bread sticks, all washed down with copious amounts of red plonk. I was sitting alone, through the doorway, curled up in an armchair, trying to plan the next stage of tomorrow's journey, when the high spirited diners issued a hollered invitation to break bread with them. Peter was in his late thirties, shaven headed with glasses, and more than happy to satisfy my lust for conversation. He could talk for Sweden. His girlfriend, Inga-Lis, was from the dark frozen wastelands of the far north and struggling to keep up with the other drinkers, punctuating her stammering English with bizarre bird tweeting sounds. The other two couples were in the senior bracket, Jan-Olov and Elisabeth, plus Roger and Joyce, all equally courteous hosts.

Roger had a well lived cheeky face and more than a slight touch of the Sean Connery's about him. He was in his sixties and had a hearing aid, but was a loveable rogue and a definite ladies' man. A former hand tool technician, Roger said he had lived in 78 different countries, including stints in Argentina, Belarus, Ukraine and glamorous Rotherham. Maybe it was all porky pies, rounded off by the claim he married the glamorous Joyce, who had a Michael Parkinson obsession, on the runway at Stockholm airport in 2000. But his table stories were all very entertaining.

In the meantime, Inga-Lis was getting more fascinated with me, poking and prodding at my chest, as she slipped further into touchy-feely intoxication. 'Why are you wasting time here? You should come to the north of Sweden. Cheep-Cheep. The land of the Midnight Sun. Tweet-Tweet. You can stay with my family if you like.' It was a kind offer, but it would all be forgotten in the morning. But Inga-Lis was just getting warmed up for a verbal offensive. 'What is it with you English and your upper class? It's all a load of southern European macho bullshit. Cuckoo-

Cuckoo. And the Chelsea Flower Show. Towitta-woo. I would love to go there, but it is wrong. Cock-a-doodle-do. Too artificial. Not real.'

Peter interjected, quickly changing the subject by explaining Scandinavians all spoke English so fluently because their TV schedules were dominated by it. Inga-Lis spent a lot of time glued to Terry Nutkins and Johnny Morris. 'I love English shows,' explained Peter. 'We have them on all the time. Inspector Morse, Frost, and Helen Mirren in *Prime Suspect*. I love them all.' However, Peter was concerned his English was not varied enough and asked if he had a decent grasp of its vocabulary. 'If I said to you, Peter, that your bird has had one too many, would you know what I mean?' I asked.

'Yes. She is getting too pissed,' he smiled. 'It is a shame you are not here tomorrow. Then you will really see the Swedes partying. We are a controlled people, but sometimes we have to lose control and we will.' I couldn't have summed the Swedes up better myself, just as friendly as the Danes, but more reserved initially, before letting their hair down wildly.

Suddenly the conversation turned serious and the cards came out. It was training time. The entire party held up cards in front of stony poker faces, not giving any hint of advantage to their rivals. It was quite scary. If this was how they practised they must have looked terrifying when the action got underway for real. 'Bridge is a very serious game,' Peter explained with a furrowed brow. 'The more experienced the opponent, the more serious you must take them. You cannot take chances and must have a system. This is a big competition, with the best players from west and south Sweden coming here. It will be tough, but we will do our best.'

To be honest, I think Peter was more interesting in speaking to me than playing cards. He was out of more than the bridge game anyway. Squinty eyed behind steel rims, he was staggering around the room chuckling and demonstrating his growing affection by massaging my shoulders. Waiting for a chance to escape, Peter wobbled off to the toilet, and I bolted for bed. Knock-Knock! Surprise, surprise, it was swaying Peter at the door. 'I am not sure if this is appropriate to be here, but we must get serious now and practise some more,' he slurred.

I was starting to get a little bit concerned about my heterosexuality remaining intact at this point. 'No problem, Peter. I was going to turn in anyway. Goodnight.'

But my new best friend was persistent. 'No! You must join us and drink lots more of our wine. Please come and join us.'

Sitting back at the table with a full glass in hand, the card school tried to get me involved. I declined by informing them I was still having trouble mastering snap. Peter had clunked down the outside stairs, hot on the trail of Inga-Lis, who had been missing for 30 minutes without anybody even noticing. Probably crashed out in a bush somewhere, he was homing in on her drunken mating calls and didn't come back. It was getting on for midnight and I needed to get my head down, thanking the remaining four players for their wonderful hospitality and wishing them the best of luck in the competition. 'You do not need to thank us,' said Jan-Olov. 'Thank you for joining us.'

Light rain patted away at my water-proof jacket, waiting in front of a car ramp for a small cable pulled yellow ferry to put me down on Malö. A slow jerky shunt released a motor vehicle cargo up the opposite bank, gifting me a traffic free start to hopping over a group of smaller islands, stepping stones cut off from each other by a complicated fjord flow system. Narrow roads, not much wider than a car, bored their way through weaving roofless tunnels of wrinkled rock, opening up occasionally for a sea pool parking bay for yachts. A miserable morning had failed to completely shift the dark blanket of the sleeping hours, leaving a dull grey haze hanging over this lamp free zone. The fine drizzle tagged along for another push-and-pull boat ride from the stony outcrop of Flatö to another island connection Dragsmark, past the foundations of a grass covered 13th-century monastery, buckling under the weight of gravestones stacked against its ruins.

Another mind manageable bridge, the *Skaftöbron*, stretched its finger over the bordering waters to the old shipping community of Fiskebäckskil. Red fishing huts clung tightly together around a wind blasted cauldron of a harbour. Dark blue waves were kicking up a head of steam, forcing half drowned orange plastic buoys to struggle treading water. Above the blustery quayside, thin cobbled streets bent around the sheltering stack of ornate seagull white wooden houses, fighting for every inch of space the town could spare. A choppy 20-minute ferry ride, the third of the day, carried me to Lysekil. Talk about beauty and the beast. Lysekil lacked all of Fiskebäckskil's appeal as a rundown seafront of tacky kiosks and grotty fat loaded take-aways greeted a disappointed dismount.

Disappointment soon turned to despair and then major doubts about what I was still doing here. Forced on to the hectic 162 main road, I was now expected to continue north towards Norway, keeping within the perimeters of a 20 centimetre wide dotted line, immediately broken by my bulging pannier bags without trying. The difficulty levels of a finely executed balancing act were handicapped by the battering wind rush of passing juggernauts and car driving jokers coming within a whisker of brushing my packs. The gravel and bottles filling a stinky brown stream in the verge between Erika and a painfully sturdy train track didn't offer an appealing landing pad. The rocky peaks continued to reach upwards, now taking on a reddish tint, as I escaped the chicken run highway intact and pedalled on past the sunken hill dwarfed village of Hamburgsund.

A freshly laid section of black tarmac rolled down to Fjällbacka, taking over from the red carpet its most famous visitor was used to treading on a regular basis. Another quaint seaside town, with the flower shaped stained glass windows of a church tower straining to achieve parity with the rocky shelving, it provided the doorway to another west coast cluster of sea islands. A bust of Sweden's Hollywood leading lady Ingrid Bergman sits in a small square by the harbour. A favourite holiday destination of the three time Academy Award winning actress, who brought a mixture of innocence and beauty to the big screen, she could switch off from the stresses of movie glitz and glamour in perfect isolation here. Bergman, whose most famous role was alongside Humphrey Bogart in the 1942 classic *Casablanca*, would spend her summers in a cottage on the nearby island of Danholmen. Ranked the fourth greatest female star of all time by the American Film Institute, following a career spanning more than 50 movies, Bergman died in London in 1982, aged 67, after a long battle with breast cancer. Her ashes were scattered in the waters of her beloved ridged sanctuary around the Fjällbacka archipelago.

A boat taxi will whisk you off to the most well known of these sea outcrops, the Väderöarnas. Also known as the 'Weather Islands', they attract the windiest and warmest climates in Sweden and even have a unique type of tropical vegetation. But be warned, the weather can change very quickly, with naughty clouds breaking open without a second's warning, ready to drench the unprepared traveller to the skin.

I was planning to stay on one of the islands, Valö, but a phone call ahead declared no room in the hostel inn. Early evening was falling fast, but luckily I had a back-up plan, a promise of a bed for the night at the next town Tanumshede, home to a UNESCO World Heritage Site of Bronze Age rock carvings. Unfortunately, I couldn't get through to Katrin, who worked for the local tourist board and had offered to put me up. A Swedish answerphone message wasn't really helping me, but I left a reply, hoping she would get back to me at the end of a 100 kilometre total for the day. She didn't!

There was a campsite next to the carving centre, which was at a place called Vitlycke, two kilometres outside of Tanumshede. It was getting on for 9pm and I needed to get set up for the night. I could catch up with Katrin in the morning. The campsite was dead. Not one paying guest. Red wooden cabins passed out with boredom, a closed reception and an empty field crying out for some canvas company. There was a house at the end of the ground so I went and knocked. And knocked. And knocked a bit more. Eventually, an irritated brown-bearded head popped through a skylight in the roof. 'Sorry. We are closed. Two more weeks we will be open,' the head said, struggling to pull together a most unconvincing smile.

This head was going to be trouble. 'I see,' I replied. 'I'm supposed to be staying with a lady from the carving centre, but I can't get through to her until the morning. It's getting late and I'm running out of options. Could I just put my tent up here? It is very small.'

'That is very sad,' said the head. 'But I can't help I'm afraid. I am closed.'

'Come on, mate. You've got this massive empty field here and I'll be gone early in the morning. I'm happy to pay.'

'No. That would be bad. People would see you and then think I am open. Very bad for me.' Vitlycke was in the middle of a forest and there was nobody around for miles. It wasn't as if there were 10 caravans and a scout troop hiding in the bushes, waiting to pounce at the first sign of tent pegging encouragement.

Tired with pleading, I called up to the roof top: 'Thanks a lot, you toss pot!'

The head, which had now sprouted a waving hand, thought I was paying him a compliment. 'That's OK. Good luck.'

Salvation was delivered by a till attendant at Tanumshede's *Bilisten 6* petrol station. After listening to Katrin's phone message, which was a tourist board information recording, he tapped away at a computer keyboard, tracking down her home number on an internet directory. It was gone 10pm now and I was scanning outside for a road side grass verge big enough to put my tent on. As long as it was 50 metres away from a house it would be OK. A startled Katrin picked up the phone, took my number, rang back 10 minutes later and saved my bacon, giving directions to a friend's house. 'You can't miss it. It is the only yellow house in town.'

33 Messages from the Past

'I have just been awoken by the sound of your voice and the smell of my urine,' read the text on my mobile. An early breakfast show call from *BBC Essex* had prompted the message beamed over from a Southend bathroom. Two radio presenters, keen to get the inside studio track on my trip, had fired off questions into a half-asleep fuddled brain. Ten minutes after the interview, I was still lying under the duvet, reading the bleeped alert on my phone. The yellow house had turned into a musty yellow cabin at the bottom of a garden opposite a redundant petrol station, obviously put out of business by the overly efficient *Bilisten 6* franchise. A woman in a black pin-striped suit, covered in muddy paw prints, had turned up with her husband in a Land Rover to give me shelter. I had to share the single bed and an old TV set with a family of fat hairy spiders, who discussed my arrival around the plug hole of a shower floor conference. It was warm and I was shattered. My arms were still stuck in the handlebar gripping position when I got into bed. It looked like I had a shopping trolley under the covers. Watching spiders sprinting over the end of the bed sheet buffed up my wailing technique, which, combined with my new outstretched posture, would help me get work as an extra in zombie movies.

Sunlight poured in through yellow and white squared curtains, urging me to haul my lazy backside out of bed. The door lock was jammed. The key wouldn't turn. I'd have to climb out the window, taking care not to trip over a TV aerial lead going the same way and breaking a flimsy cracking ledge under my feet. Just as I squeezed half my body out the gap, balancing on my knees and wondering what to do next, I was rumbled. 'Do you not usually use the door?' asked my puzzled host.

'Yes. Of course. Sorry. It is jammed.' I felt so embarrassed.

'Come inside the house and have some breakfast,' said the wrinkly faced woman, who was wearing a fleece covered in dog hairs.

Stone steps led up to the kitchen of a rundown yellow house in desperate need of a facelift. Hundreds of porcelain dogs were kennelled on wall shelves and the real thing was sitting in a carry cage, a skinny sad looking black mutt with big bulging eyes. It reminded me of Rhys, but was in fact an expensive prize Italian pooch. The whole place stunk of dog shit and hygiene concerns were surpassed by hunger as I scoffed down a slice of ham and cheese topped bread handed over by Zelda. Mrs Dog's Muck lived on a farm outside Tanumshede, renting out the ramshackle Terrahawks Towers and yellow cabin to tourists. She bred pedigree dogs for shows all around Europe and was a regular visitor to Crufts. The St Bernard was her speciality, but new plans were afoot to start mating British Bull Terriers. 'They are lovely dogs, but I am worried they will chew the house to pieces,' she told me. I think that is what's know in the trade as finishing off the job.

An effortless downhill freewheel through the woods of Vitlycke led back to the rock carving centre. A merchandise packed museum sits by the road, attached to an impressive outside facsimile Bronze Age farmstead. Bone-like wooden supports criss-cross a cluster of thatched roofs, while Gotland sheep native to the period and crop studies from the same age give this living and breathing project authenticity. It certainly did the trick for a couple of middle-aged Yanks holding Premier membership cards with DENSA. 'Do you think this is real mi-de-evil fur, Hank?' asked the woman as she stroked gold ring encrusted fingers through a replica fur coat.

'I don't know. Maybe, dear. Now come and finish your cappuccino.'

The remarkable carvings date back a lot later, some 3,000 years ago, with the last engraving believed to have been chipped away just before the birth of Jesus Christ. Opposite the museum, lying in the high grassy banks of Vitlycke is the real crowd puller, annually attracting hundreds of thousands of visitors from all over the world. A flat slab of smooth granite, 20 metres long and seven metres high, containing 400 petroglyphs, a World Heritage classification gives this site the same historical importance as the pyramids of Egypt or India's Taj Mahal. Offering a fascinating insight into the social, working and religious lives of these ancient people, the most famous carving is of an embracing bridal couple in the upper part of the rock face. A stick woman with a dog-shaped head and a man, who appears to have an erect penis coming out of his backside, depict a holy wedding or a sexual intercourse ritual. This ceremony would be used to safeguard the fertility of men and animals, probably carried out on May 1 each year, with cult priests taking on the mantle of Gods.

This spot rested next to a coastline of fjord during the Bronze Age, allowing sailing chieftains to trade for copper with Italy and tin with Britain. It is no surprise then that many of the carvings are related to the sea, with boats and whales predominant features. Another shows a man lying down attached to a boat by his legs and a woman kneeling by his head. This is believed to symbolise the journey to the kingdom of death. Another set of pencil-thin worshipping figures are holding lollipop suns on sticks, praying for healthy crops. Nature plays its part, with birds and huge curly snakes, chasing terrified men, knocked into the stone. But the strangest of all is a horned devil-like creature with a tail and spear towering over a much smaller man (with an erection) fighting back with a wooden staff.

All the carvings have been painted red to make them more visible, an action frowned upon by many archaeologists, and need to be constantly cleaned to combat erosion pollution. As I walked around these strange symbols, wondering what made the Bronze Age people carve out so much of their primitive graffiti in this one place, I collared a member of the rock spraying sterilisation team for an opinion. 'I think there are lots of messages here,' said the pony-tailed Andreas. 'Maybe they are signs of past things or offerings to Gods. The rock is in an accessible place and was meant to be seen by lots of people, otherwise it would have been hidden away somewhere else. These carvings were made to stand the test of time and there could be a message here specifically made for us.' What a chilling thought. Could these Bronze Age symbols be a special code, sent down the corridors of time and still uncracked, trying to warn us about future threats and dangers? Did these prophetic stone scribes know something about global warming and other natural disasters? Or were they just a load of primitive old superstitious scrawlings? I doubt we will ever know for sure.

Ouch! Fuck it! Something had managed to crawl into the inside of my knuckle covered cycling gloves and leave behind a nasty sting. It really hurt, making my blood boil, before a manic grin broke out. Yeah, it was painful, but I wasn't getting paranoid about it. I wasn't feverishly gabbling down the phone to Katie, pleading with her to carry out an internet diagnosis of any fatal allergic reactions caused by the stings of all rare breeds of northern European bee, wasp and hornet. I wasn't worried that the lethal poisons of nature could be pumping quicker into my veins, aided by a heightened cycling pulse rate. I was OK. There was no panic.

I just got on with it, pedalling past pine forests and rolling green meadows where playful foxes skipped about in broad daylight around the dandelions. Farming shacks set their creaking doors at the foot of the ever climbing rock, turning whiter now and partially hidden by a balaclava of dark moss poking out of its nose and ears. The familiar sight and shape of wooden houses sat quietly in a selection of picture postcard poses. The Swedes really were a nation of shed dwellers with almost click-on model kit garages, conservatories and wood lockers, all cloned to the same triangular design. Variety accessories included clamp on porches, shutters and decking. It was like playing dolls houses for adults. But Crystal Ken and Barbie were nowhere to be seen.

Taking my life into my own hands, sorry, trusting the speeding bodies of cars, trucks and motorbikes not to kill me, I had to cross and pedal along an active stretch of the E06 Oslo highway for 15 minutes. This wasn't a short-cut, it was part of the official route unbelievably. A rural plod led to a circling of the *Kosterfjorden*, another refuge of island sheltering open water, revealing a train line carved around a curving rocky hump of wall into Strömstad. Sweden's most westerly town was an upward shift of bistros, kiosks, shops and sailing stores, window displaying a selection of chunky ropes, golden lanterns, life jackets and rubber dinghies. Everything you could need for a life at sea, most important to this town. A small harbour was cloaked by red fishing shed restaurants (didn't they have any other paint in Sweden?) and packed with white yachts, mostly displaying the flag of Norway, which was only 13 kilometres across the border. Bargain hunting Norwegian skippers wheeled trolleys full of beer crates and spirit bottles around the dock's wooden decking, beating the vertical inflation rate at home by tipping booze run bounty into empty cabin stores.

Strömstad was an island hopper's paradise, sea surrounded sanctuaries of seclusion begging to be explored. The most popular of these are the Koster islands, home to Sweden's most westerly population. Beaches, brushwood, heather clad moors, cobblestone fields and antique lighthouses welcome travellers curious enough to catch a boat out to their shores. But the most interesting outpost award goes to *Alaska Lodge* on Nord-Långö. The grand design of former gold digger Hilma Svedal, who inherited a tenth of the island, everything is made from rocks and shells; terraces, flower pots, tall arches, benches and even temples. Aged 26, Hilma sailed to America to seek out her fortune in 1896, spending 12 tough years sifting through the Alaskan wilderness to find it. In 1928 she returned to Nord-Långö and got to work on transforming the island into her own private piece of Alaska with a sunny Californian style, piecing her creation together with glue bought in Strömstad. Hilma died in 1965, but her floral surrounded dream lives on as a bizarre summer tourist attraction.

Strömstad had been reared on the financial income generated by its alliance with the Skaggerak, growing from a population of a mere 300 inhabitants in the 18th century to just over 6,000 today. Governed by Norwegian rule until 1658, the town was handed back to the Swedes by a battered and bruised King of Denmark/Norway as part of the *Treaty of Roskilde*. Up until this point the harbour had been used for the transport of lumber, but things picked up after the handover with Stockholm's hierarchy keen to establish the town as a west coast shipping trade centre. Strömstad flourished under its new directive, particularly during the great herring fishing period in the second half of the 1700s. It was also at this time foundations were laid for alternative revenues, key to this fishing settlement's transformation into a thriving spa town. Mineral rich springs were first visited in 1782, with pilgrims believing the magical water could cure illnesses such as epilepsy, paralysis and rheumatism. Outdoor and indoor baths were built with relaxation seeking Swedes flocking to the town for mud, seaweed and shower therapies. Still as popular today, a new open air bath opened in 2005.

An air of healing floated around the flawless walls and staircases of the *Crusellska Hemmet* hostel, a timber dwelling presiding at the top of Strömstad's steep lanes. A black iron rail and stone steps lead to the front door of this 17th-century guest house, which has a long history of finding peace for its occupants. Slowly burning candles decorate the sterile white reception counter and gold leaf swirls of wallpaper border beige polished floorboards and calming blue room doors name-tagged after past residents. *Crusellska* cashed in on the alternative therapy boom by starting life as a health centre, before turning its attention to conventional medicine as a hospice for the terminally ill in the 1930s. It has now returned to its original roots, combining hostel accommodation with stress relieving services such as massages and seaweed treatments in a pure white bath with curving lips, designed to apply tender kisses to the back and shoulders of aching bodies.

The soft skinned receptionist was the picture of health, a woman in her fifties, who looked a good 10 years younger, surely a stunner in her heyday. 'Are you going to Norway?' asked the attractive Gilf (excuse me for borrowing and revamping Rhys' crude Milf terminology, but there was a good chance she was a granny).

'Yes. I'm going to catch the ferry to Sandefjord first thing in the morning,' I replied. 'I hear it is very expensive over there.'

'Oh yes! At least double the prices of everything here. I hope you have lots of money.'

'But why is it so expensive?'

'I don't know. The Norwegians have plenty of money. Their oil makes them one of the richest nations in the world. But we like them making everything expensive at home, it means they come and spend their money here. A lot of Norwegians come here to buy houses and they will pay more than double its market value, which is crazy, but very good for us Swedes.'

'So you like the Norwegians then as a people, not just their cash?' I enquired.

'Yes. We are very close as we are so near the border. There are as many Swedish flags in Strömstad as Norwegian ones.'

'And would you say you are similar people?'

'I suppose so. We share a similar language, but they have always been like our little brother. Simpler people.'

'What? Stupid?'

'No. Easier to please. Swedes expect everything to be just right and we will grumble if it is not. Norwegians will just get on with things. Such perfection doesn't bother them. They are more laid-back than us.' It sounded to me like big brother was taking advantage of little stupid brother.

A fine spray of rain accelerated into a full-scale downpour. Wet drips fell down from the pond overflow of my water-proof hood, breaking out into dribbling ice cold nose rivers. Desperate for company and mingling with the empty stool legs of a partially open roofed boat bar, I stared into the gloom with a beer in my hand. It was Friday night and everything was far from alright. Feeling like a social outcast, I listened grumpily to the sickening sound of happy families down below, huddled together under lantern lit cabin coverings singing songs together. Two soaked satchel carrying teenagers were dicing with death, skidding over the bodies of drenched boats to collect parking permit fees, only a slide footing away from plunging into the freezing dark waters around them. Across the harbour, tongues of mist devoured the remains of a skeletal head and body sign advertising the Cod Bar. That's where I would have been heading tonight if Rhys was still by my side, another drunken swing of the pants at a Shakin' Stevens revival night. But I wasn't in the mood for partying on my own.

Descending twisting stairs below deck to a swanky restaurant, I invested in my own Strömstad therapy, three courses of expensively priced sea cuisine comfort eating, tailored for the bulging wallet of Norwegian night-trippers. As I dined alone, starting with the smallest bowl of soup in northern Europe, accompanied by two French bread crumbs, a feeling of sea green nausea drilled into the pit of my stomach. The floating restaurant was moving, only slightly at first, but building up into a forceful enough tilt to enter my fork and knife into the cutlery leapfrogging championships. A sprayed-on muscle top wearing barman was relaxed about the whole thing, continuing to laugh and joke with a couple of waitresses spellbound by his bulging tanned biceps. The unconcerned air of cool evaporated a few minutes later. The chinking of wine glasses above Muscle Man's head signalled the dining room's intention to set sail, persuading the big poser to scramble outside in a panic to check the rope lashings cradling this baby to the dock.

Managing to keep down all three courses, I walked off the food with a despondent trudge to the other side of town as amplified winds whistled around the streets and squares. Buying cigarettes and chocolate I sparked up in a shelter, watching leaping waves slapping against the fences of restaurants and bars on the other side of the bay. Merry groups of people sat behind windows in bars, sipping glasses of beer and hot cups of coffee, but I couldn't be bothered to join them. Capitulating into a wallow of self-indulgent misery, my thoughts increasingly turned to home, being back in my flat, clasping hold of Katie and returning to normal life. It all seemed such a long way from here. And who wanted to speak to a shower coated black cloud of walking depression anyway? Leaving the rosy faces to remain cheery behind a protective glass shield, I headed back to HQ to pull off my soaking clothes before a stinking cold set in. Climbing the *Crusellska* stairs, the basket chairs and couches of the living room were all taken by a silent diving team, relaxing ahead of tomorrow's plunge into Strömstad's rocky pools by crowding around a laptop computer to watch a movie in the dark. I prayed it was *Jaws* so they all went to bed and had nightmares.

Throwing a downcast frame on the bottom bunk of my room, I got stuck into the first of three bars of rapidly demolished chocolate. Alone, tired and cold, I was reaching the end of the road. The buzz of adventure was more of a whispery blown raspberry and I really needed something special to happen and keep me on track with the North Sea Cycle Route. Norway was under pressure already.

34   Whale of a Time

Fierce waves lashed windswept stony feet outside the rain splattered window of the Color Line ferry as it lurched through the rocky sea canyon towards Norway. Utilising body origami, I was folded into a compact seat melting stress ball, specially designed to cope with two hours of rough and tumble to Sandefjord. Insane screaming gales banged on the side of the boat, preventing me from sleeping this one off as I did between Grenå and Varberg. The boat carried on rocking and even a trip to the toilet for a time wasting number two failed to help matters. The washroom was moving about more than the lounge on the other side of the boat, the jerking conjuring a sinking drunken sensation inside your head. Some poor sod in the cubicle next door was obviously feeling it too, throwing his guts up loudly in perfect harmony with the rolling ship.

Returning to my seat, I tried to phone Katie, my brother, anybody to take my mind off things, but there was no signal. Bollocks! I really hated Scandinavian ferry travel. Spending a Saturday morning towards the end of May being tossed around an angry sea like a plastic toy boat in a bath tub hit by a torrent of running tap water. Spring was meant to be handing the baton over to summer for God's sake, so where was the fucking sunshine? But it didn't seem to bother my fellow passengers, cross-legged Swedes and Norwegians reading their newspapers and magazines in dignified fashion, completely untroubled by the rocking and rolling outside.

Then the banging stopped, the jolts subsided and the rain smears on the window ran for the increasing number of hills, scared off by the intense glare of a brilliant sun. Huge brown cliffs rose out of the water, lying on their sides like sleeping giants, with trees and houses taking root in rapid numbers as the ferry advanced on Sandefjord. The dock wasn't what I expected at all, the usual glum mixture of car parks, storage containers, cranes and warehouses, sulking miles away from anything else. The boat stopped slap bang in the middle of a vibrant town square, pretty much shunting its nose across the traffic, allowing passengers to run down straight into the shops.

Following a motorcade of lowered Volvos pumping out techno music, temporarily halted by one conked out old wreck needing a push start down the ramp, I took my first pedals on Norwegian soil. Instantly different to Sweden, everything was peaking on a much grander scale, with Sandefjord enclosed by a crown of mountainous guardians drinking along the troughs of huge fjords. The town square had been commandeered by resting Saturday shoppers and a dog clutching crowd lining up for a best pooch competition, compéred by a wireless microphone salesman buttering up the owners to shift some of the big bags of food behind him. A pin-striped, paw covered, Zelda was nowhere to be seen.

The town's most eye-catching feature was a dramatic sculpture of desperate men in a capsizing boat attempting to plunge harpoons into the monstrous tail of a whale, all brought to life by the spray of fountains. The monument could have been a scene cut straight out of Moby Dick, paying homage to Sandefjord's past life as an important commercial whaling town. Ships began embarking on lucrative expeditions to the Arctic in 1850, with voyages to the Antarctic following in 1905. Towards the end of the 1920s, Sandefjord had a fleet of 15 factory ships and nearly 100 whaling boats. Twenty-five years later, 2,800 men from the town were hired as crew for these bloody journeys. But this was down scaled from the mid 1950s, before grinding to a complete halt in 1968 following international conservation outcries over drastically dropping whale numbers.

Unsurprisingly then, Sandefjord is home to Europe's only whaling museum, *Hvalfangstmuseet*, a gruesome, but thought provoking gallery of horrors, charting the growth of whaling throughout the world, from primitive beginnings in the Stone Age to Norway's rise to the top of the industry ladder. Rooms full of models, pictures, props and destructive weapons illustrated the tragic plight of these beautiful creatures. The curse of the whale was possessing a giant multi-purpose carcass able to reap man huge profits at the world market place. And nothing was wasted. Most important was the blubber, which was cooked and boiled into whale oil, used for lighting and lubricant, as well as margarines, soap and paint production. Other commodities were the meat, utilised for human consumption, animal fodder and fertilisers, plus the bone, used in the production of everything from brushes to umbrella ribs.

Reading the history text next to a glass case holding grenade harpoon made you realise these poor bastards never stood a sporting chance. The inhumane invention of Svend Foyn, christened the founder of modern whaling after valuing the blue whale equal to 400 seals, the weapon didn't explode until it was inside its target's body. But it didn't always kill straight away, especially if fired by an inexperienced gun man, leaving the whale to die in extreme pain. Another ugly display of clamps, spikes and chains showed the devices of torture used to hold the wounded whales in tow, caught on film by a monitor screen zooming in on one distressed captive fighting for life in a rough sea bleeding red. A macabre fishermen's family album captured old black and white photos of whaling stations in the Antarctic outpost of South Georgia. Slaughtered corpses with their guts exposed were laid out on frozen beaches surrounded by their proud bearded conquerors and the oil drums they were fated to fill. Even more gory were the pictures of massive bodies slung on a factory ship, a 24-hour operation, allowing whales to be caught, carried and boiled on the move day and night, their lifeless mouths wide open in surrender.

The back room of the museum was a taxidermist's heaven, a parade of stuffed Arctic animals, polar bears, seals, walruses and penguins, bringing the curtain down on this grisly show. Above my head was a replica model of a Blue Whale, at 33 metres long, weighing 181 metric tonnes, the biggest mammal on the planet (or, according to the gift mugs on sale, the equal weight of 25 elephants and 150 bulls). Before ceasing commercial activities in the late 1960s, Norway played a key role in driving this wondrous beast close to extinction, with population numbers falling from 200,000 to just a scattered 1,000 specimens. It is believed the Blue Whale has recovered over the last four decades, but only to a maximum of 12,000 heads. And Norway is still dabbling in its heritage, turning a blind eye to the International Whaling Commission's prohibition of commercial whaling. In 1993, Norway resumed catching whales for profit, hounding Northeast Atlantic Minke whales, with a limited export to Iceland and the Faroes Islands. Norwegian catches have expanded to 546 victims in 2006, which has angered whaling protesters, but is still no way near the genocide threatening totals of the past.

It was FA Cup Final day, Chelsea against Manchester United, at the new Wembley Stadium. Trouble was, 25 kilometres separated me from the next town, Larvik, cornered in by the huge bows of trees and struggling to make the almost vertical climbs in front of my handlebars. Norway was more up and down than a pair of knickers in a Jackie Collins novel. It was really hard work, a tougher grind than the previous four countries put together, and threatening to finish me off. The Norwegians were another nation of shed shelterers, but some residents had broken the mould, bashing a High Chaparral series of Wild West style brown shuttered ranches into the hills. The forests were beautiful, tall, thick, dark and endless, but sadly littered with old TV sets, pots and smashed plates in some places. Great chunks had been bitten out of the surrounding cliffs by diggers and drills, with huge slabs of granite stocked up for delivery to the local stonemason.

The village of Tjølling presented me with a Rimi store, Norway's answer to Aldi. Shame the prices weren't the same. As I mused around the refrigerator section, trying to suss out which pack of salami was going to cost me less than my shirt, women opened up hatches and started shovelling frozen pink shrimps into carrier bags. I didn't want to hazard a guess at how much they cost. Grabbing a banana and a small loaf of bread to accompany the salami, tilling in at an extortionate £5, it was time for a quick bite (the other half would be rationed for tonight at those prices) ahead of resuming the search for a TV screen and a heated bar.

Dead as a factory ship whale, cold, grey and wind bruised, Larvik didn't seem an accommodating venue for English football's end of season showpiece. Half demolished buildings towered over their rocky strewn innards, next to a shabby ferry terminal and train station, while all the pubs and shops looked shut. There wasn't a soul to be seen anywhere on this side of the railway bridge. But I was saved by a bastion of light across the tracks, a square of modern high rise blocks fighting a bricks and mortar crusade for hospitality, harbouring a hotel, health centre and the swish *Becks* brassiere and bar. The man in charge was a suave, tanned chap (and weren't they all!) in a smart dark suit, who obviously had his pick of the Larvik ladies, unless he was gay, and pillared me with free coffees. Maybe he was. He explained Larvik was in a state of transformation, following a history of relying on the timber trade, boosted by the abundance of beach woodland in this area. Proud of his roots, he unsuccessfully tried to convince me major investors were tripping over themselves to reach Larvik and said the town was preparing to build one of the biggest music schools in northern Europe. Play the other one!

Sitting on a comfy leather armchair among a gang of *snus* suckers, I settled down to watch the game in the warmth, while an aggressive sea threw splashing arms on to the pavement outside. *Becks* had adopted the timber theme, with the TV at the centre of a wall of shaven rounded stumps, which were also glued to the ceiling. The game itself was boring, settled by a late Didier Drogba goal in Chelsea's favour, heralding a surprising cheer from the Norwegians. I took it for granted they would all be supporting Manchester United, as one of their favourite footballing sons, Ole Gunnar Solskjaer, was playing for the Red Devils. Watching the match sent thoughts spiralling back towards home again. I'd be sitting in a pub having a few beers with the boys right now, not worrying about where I was going to sleep or if I could stretch my meagre budget to Rimi's counter prices for the next few weeks, living on a diet of unbuttered bread and salami. Adding cheese was far too expensive. I wasn't a millionaire. Returning an empty coffee cup to the bar, I saddled up to Erika and pushed back into the howling wind, but my sense of adventure was draining away fast.

Helgeroa was a handsome village, resting at the bottom of a forest shielded slope, staring out across a horizon filling bowl of clear blue fjords and isolated island peaks. Little boats were moored in front of a gathering of red huts, one of which I hoped contained the skipper of a vessel ready to navigate these expansive fjords to Langesund, somewhere unseen on the other side. One of the shed traders was busy scraping away at a hot hamburger grill, threatening to melt the chocolate in the middle of his confectionery store. Even before the words had left my mouth, I already knew the predictable answer: 'Is the boat running to Langesund?

'No. It is not summer yet. It will be leaving in…'

'Two weeks?' I butted in.

'Yes. But how do you know this?'

'The experience gained from a lot of cycling, my friend,' I replied.

I'd have to bike it round the long way now. An energy conserving boat ride replaced by a 55 kilometre slog around the hilly banks of the fjords. Dejected and starting to crumble under the physical and mental exhaustion of a futile solitary campaign, I approached a lad in the outside cabin bar of an empty seated restaurant courtyard, asking if he could replenish my parched water bottle. Handing the cold plastic back into my hand, he asked: 'Are you OK? You don't look very happy?'

'I'm not,' I agreed. 'I've been on this great adventure for the last 40 days, but now my thoughts are full of home and I'm not sure if I want to be here anymore.'

'Then why do you not go home?'

'Because I will feel like I have let myself down. That I have returned too soon.'

'Surely, that cannot be right. It can only be an adventure when you are truly still embracing the spirit of it, looking forward to the new choices each day will bring with passion. If that feeling has died then the adventure is finished. Remember, life is full of adventures and they all have an ending, but there will always be another just around the corner.'

Blimey, I felt like I had just been treated to a rare spiritual audience with a mystical holy man, not some young dude pulling pints in an open faced wooden shack. Waving farewell, I pushed back on, past the droopy nose and antlers of the moose warning signs and deep into the heart of real mountains. Skirting around sneaked peeks of the fjord shrinking to a puddle below, the rocky frontier road climbed higher and higher through thick vegetation and mighty trees.

It was getting on for 8pm and there was a chill in the air, intensified by the eerie silence of this old mountain road, with its small waterfalls dripping sad tears down rough cliff faces. The upward grafting was agonising, remaining on a long, steep course for leg destroying periods. The trail wound on and on, as if it was never going to relent, growing wilder and darker under a blanket of quiet intermittently pierced by the call of an invisible bird hiding anywhere among thousands of branches. This was both tougher and more awesome than anything I had come across so far, a real slice of raw nature testing my endurance, which I was failing physically, but still straining to enjoy visually. Dropping down into the lowest possible gears, I circled around a corkscrew of hill, pulling itself upwards beside the colossal arms of a viaduct bridging a shortcut between the powerful peaks for cars. I could barely move as the ligaments clicked painfully in my left knee-cap, struggling to pull body, bike and luggage forwards. But carrying on pedalling slowly, barely turning the pedals, I made it to the top of the climb, soaked in a deeply personal shower of sweat.

Gratefully turning downhill, desperate gasping mouthfuls of cold night air sent icicles arrowing into my oxygen hungry lungs as a shivering freeze shot through a perspiration drenched body. I rolled limply towards a petrol station outside of Nystrand. My first sign of human life for two hours was the Saturday night attendant taking a five minute break to stage a spitting contest on the forecourt with his friend. A nice chap, he interrupted another noisy throat and nostril generation of ghastly sticky green ammunition, to point me in the direction of Langesund. Moving along the shores of a dark fjord, painted in orange stripes of street light, towards the Brevik bridge, the black banks of hill dwelling houses shone like candles below the white metal frame. Everywhere I turned, bright window twinkles of fairy lights illuminated tree covered lumps of broccoli, rooted to the mainland or consumed by the fjord far away in the distance.

I needed to stop. It was getting late and I was achieving absolutely nothing, resisting the aching nagging of my legs to turn it in, for the sake of storing away a few extra kilometres. I'd covered 90 kilometres of Norway on my first day, usually nothing out of the ordinary on this trip, but the under pedal terrain had been the most difficult to impress. Not far short of midnight and without a camp site anywhere to be found, I broke off the main road cycle path and set up in a field opposite well lit buildings hemmed in by pitch black forest. Clutching the torch between my legs, I polished off the remainder of my bread and meat, before sliding into unconsciousness smelling like a skunk. My first day in Norway was over. It would also be my last.

I was going home. Woken by a bunch of nursery rhyme singing kids on a set of swings, I packed up my stuff under their curious gaze. The journey was over, it was time to return to the bosom of my loved ones. Being back on my own was no fun at all and I'd fallen out of love with the journey just outside Langesund, as good a place as any to call it a day as it was almost half way around the 6,000 kilometre North Sea Cycle Route circuit. Initial feelings of disappointment turned to pride after breaking the news to an excited screaming Katie on the phone. I hadn't let anybody down and most importantly I had proved myself, showing that I could hack being away on my own, or in the company of friends, without disintegrating into a wobbly mess of hyperventilating skin and bone rolling about on the floor. I had made life changing progress, pushing myself to achieve something I had previously convinced myself was impossible, by dragging a knackered carcass over the mental finishing line. I had finally managed a proper adventure, emulating the achievements of Jesus Christ himself by fasting in the wilderness for 40 days and 40 nights. And if that was long enough for the Son of God, then it would do me fine.

Sunday morning service church bells rang around the rooftops as I pedalled through nearby Porsgrunn, ready to jump on the next available train. One house in particular caught my eye. White painted wooden letters were arranged above the door to spell out 'Odd Fellow', like some sort of final farewell tribute. I smiled at those two words, which probably summed me up perfectly, basking in the personal glory of knowing the job was done. Here I was hundreds of miles from Leigh-on-Sea, gliding along alien streets without a care in the world, ready to return home triumphantly. I'd achieved so much, but was still allowed to have a few qualms. I was disappointed not to be seeing more of country number five unfold, as Norway's untamed landscape had promised so much in just 24 hours and would undoubtedly deliver more. I was gutted about missing out on the remoteness of the Shetland and Orkney islands, before seeing more of my own native Scotland and England on the way home. But there was no need to harbour regrets, remembering the words of the holy barman of Helgeroa: 'As one adventure draws to a close, another will soon begin.' I'd had my fill of adventure this time round, I was contented, and there was no need to continue just for the sake of it. But this wasn't game over, just unfinished business. Stealing the catchphrase of another great wordsmith, Arnold Schwarzenegger in Terminator mode: 'I'll be back!'

Epilogue

There had been no rush to get back to Katie before the wedding. We'd already tied the knot the previous summer. The cruellest twist had entwined the fate of Katie's mother, Marion, with the premature suffering and death of my own dear mum. Marion, only 52, was diagnosed with a brain tumour just a few weeks after my mother slipped away, triggering a groundhog calendar of trips to the same cancer ward, doctors and nurses. The final verdict for Marion was only slightly better, a lower grade secondary tumour which killed slower, but allowed her to hang on for the wedding. And what a perfect summer's day it was, beautiful sunshine, a packed church and a wonderful evening which could live on in Marion's soul forever.

I took the new mother-in-law for a spin around the dance floor minus the wig, affectionately labelling Marion a chinchilla because of the short grey fur growing on her head, the result of chemotherapy. The future was grim and I was taking part in a final dance with a woman on death row, but I was so pleased to be holding her there, overjoyed she was getting the opportunity to witness the happy union stolen away from my own mother and father on this mortal earth. Marion was an intelligent woman who I'd struck gold with straight away, right from the first dinner table introduction. She wasn't anything like the scary tyrant Katie built her up to be. Marion knew her time was running out, but she put on such a brave face, laughing and joking throughout the wedding day, alongside her husband Tom, who must have been going through pain and anguish I couldn't even start to try and comprehend. On those sort of magical occasions, it's hard to believe something so dark and final is lurking around the corner. But it was. Six months later Marion was gone, swiftly following a second difficult Christmas in a row, climbing upstairs to join the party with both of our families.

When people hear this story they can't believe it's true. How unlucky can you be to lose two mothers, in the prime of their lives, within 12 months of each other to the same terrible disease? The bookies wouldn't take a bet on it. But that's the question I often ask myself. Would this have happened if Katie and I hadn't got together? We'd known each other for years without any attraction at all, ahead of eventually starting dating. Did God bring us together for this very reason, knowing terrible things were going to happen and our bond of love would get us through it all?

I don't know if any of these things are true, but watching two special women die in such a tragic way really does make you realise we must make the most of cherishing our precious lives. There's no room to take anything for granted. I've witnessed first hand how suddenly it all changes for the worst, previously active healthy people pulled towards death's door at the bat of an eyelid. The balance of life can change for good or bad in a split second, you have no prior warning and there is nothing you can do about it. So get out into the world now and do all those special things you want to do while you can. You might live to 123, but you might not make 23, and the last thing anybody wants is regrets on their death bed.

That's why I got on my bike and had this adventure and I hope there's going to be plenty more ahead. I proved to myself I could set aside any previous anxieties to go it alone across foreign fields, but I also learned a valuable lesson. An adventure shared is twice as rewarding, solving problems on the road in combo and taking on the highs and lows with a smile on your faces at the end of most days. Being alone is boring, comradeship and watching the positive effect of a journey help and enlighten another person is an amazing thing to see. Rhys, God bless him, 9 out of 10 North Sea cyclists who have read this book will never leave home without someone like him.

The physical demands were a big challenge, but again a remarkable achievement. When you are on the road it doesn't seem that big a deal, you are just sweating through each day, trying to hit a distance target and reach your bed for the night. But on returning home and letting everything gradually sink in to place, the penny drops on how awesome it was to use nothing but your body (boat rides not included, all you clever clogs out there) to cross five countries and thousands of kilometres with a raw fusion of pumping muscle and pedal power alone. People I met on the road would say to me: 'You must be a serious cyclist at home to have come all the way to my country.' They would nearly fall off their chairs in shock when I told them I never used a bike at home, demonstrating that this is an eventful journey anyone, young or old, can take at their own pace.

And what about God? Had this experience brought me any closer to answering questions about life after death? Had I 'found' myself climbing up northern Europe? The honest answer is a big fat juicy no! I'm always going to be scared stiff about whatever happens next, but taking this trip made me realise that time is too short to wallow in the unknown. There is a beautiful random world out there and you don't have to fly to Australia, Canada or the Far East to see it. There are hundreds of astounding places stacked full of stunning scenery right on our own European doorstep. Curious misty islands, quirky villages, tree heavy mountains, moving sand dunes and most importantly hospitable strangers, who will let you sleep in their back garden overnight and give you a free bowl of hot grub. Life is an adventure, just get out there and taste it for yourself. The North Sea Cycle Route is a great place to find your feet. It certainly did the trick for me.

North Sea Cycle Route Kit Check

Kit:
Trek 7.3FX bicycle with Schwalbe Marathon Plus tyres.
2 x 28 litre Altura back panniers, Altura clip-on front box and map carrier.
Cat Eye rear and front lights, tyre pump, 1 litre water bottle.
Vango Banshee 200 tent (one man), sleeping bag.
Altura water proof trousers, 2 x gloves fingerless and full finger, Regatta hooded water-proof jacket, Diadora Chili water-proof cycling boots.
Altura padded shorts, 3 x Altura padded cycling shorts. Bell cycling helmet and Abus lock.

Spares and tools:
Chain and cable lubricant, two spare 28 inch inner tubes, tyre lever set, self-adhesive puncture patches, Topeak multi-purpose bike tool, V-brake shoe set.

Medical supplies:
Vaseline, Deep Heat, Savlon and Sudo creams, Anadin, Nurofen and Rennie tablets, Ibuleve gel, Lemsip sachets and plasters. Swiss Army knife.

Other clothes and extras:
2 x socks, 2 x football socks, 2 x boxer shorts, 2 x lightweight trousers, boardies, woolly hat, flip-flops, trainers, vest, fleece, 3 x T-shirts, 2 x long-sleeve shirts, electric shaver, shower gel, toothpaste and brush, towel, deodorant can, toilet roll, batteries, CD walkman and CD case, digital camera, mobile phone and charger, European plug adaptor, three notebooks, four pens, 18 maps, reading glasses, sun glasses, passport and wallet.

North Sea Cycle Route Itinerary

COUNTRY ONE: NETHERLANDS: (Total distance – 410 kilometres)

1	Harwich (England) – Zandvoort	*www.campingdebranding.nl*
2	Den Helder	*b.barend38@quicknet.nl*
3	Texel	*texel@stayokay.com*
4	Harlingen	*www.zeehoeve.nl*
5	Holwerd	*www.holwerd.nl*
6	Roodeschool	ten Harkels' garden

COUNTRY TWO: GERMANY: (Total distance – 910 kilometres)

7	Weener	Camping Weener
8	Norddeich	*www.nordsee-camp.de*
9	Wilhelmshaven	House Radmer
10	Wilhelmshaven	House Radmer
11	Bremerhaven	*info@jgh-bremerhaven.de*
12	Kollmar	*www.kollmar-elbe.de*
13	Büsum	North Sea Wife
14	Husum	Ganter's nest
15	Dägebüll	Camp Moin-Moin
16	Sylt	*www.campingplatz-westerland.de*

COUNTRY THREE: DENMARK: (Total distance – 810 kilometres)

17	Ribe	*www.danhostel-ribe.dk*
18	Ribe	*www.danhostel-ribe.dk*
19	Henne Strand	*www.hennestrandcamping.dk*
20	Søndervig	*www.sondervigcamping.dk*
21	Langerhuse	Vesterhavs Camping
22	Klitmøller	*www.nystrupcampingklitmoller.dk*
23	Klim Strand	*www.klimstrand.dk*
24	Løkken	*www.loekken-hytteby.dk*
25	Hirtshals	*www.hirtshals-camping.de*
26	Skagen	*www.pouleegcamping.dk*
27	Sæby	*www.hedebocamping.dk*
28	Hadsund	*www.hadsund-camping-og-vandrerhjem.dk*
29	Hadsund	Hadsund Camping
30	Grenå	*www.grenaastrandcamping.dk*

COUNTRY FOUR: SWEDEN: (Total distance – 400 kilometres)

31	Kärradal	Appointment with nature
32	Åsa	*www.kuggavik.se*
33	Gothenburg	*www.sov.nu*
34	Gothenburg	*www.Radissonsas.com*
35	Gothenburg	Radisson SAS Hotel
36	Kungälv	*info@kungalvsvandrarhem.se*
37	Stocken	*www.toftagard.se*
38	Tanumshede	Yellow cabin kennel
39	Strömstad	*crusellska.com*

COUNTRY FIVE: NORWAY: (Total – 1,130 kilometres…to be continued)

40	Langesund	Dark Norwegian woods

Other North Sea Cycle Route Links

The official website: www.northsea-cycle.com

Official Maps:
www.sustrans.co.uk (The Netherlands, England, Scotland, Shetland and Orkney)
www.esterbauer.com (The Netherlands, Germany and Denmark),
www.hallandsturist.se (Halland, Sweden)
www.vastsverige.com (Bohuslän, Sweden)
www.bike-norway.com (Norway).

Ferry operators:
www.stenaline.com (Harwich to Hoek van Holland, Grena to Varberg)
www.colorline.com (Stromstad to Sandefjord)
www.smyril-line.fo (Norway to Shetland, Scotland and Denmark)

Other useful links:

www.svenskaturistforeningen.se/sweden_youth_hostel.htm (Swedish Tourist Association/Youth Hostels) www.ctc.org.uk (UK National Cyclists' Organisation)

Tourism:
www.visitholland.com, www.germany-tourism.de,
www.visitdenmark.com, www.visitsweden.com, www.visitnorway.com,
www.shetland-tourism.co.uk. www.visitorkney.com,
www.visitscotland.com, www.visitbritain.com

Kit suppliers:
www.richardsonscycles.co.uk, www.skitopgear.com

Charity:
www.cancerresearchuk.org,
www.justgiving.com

Contact the author: berniebike@hotmail.co.uk

North Sea Cycle Route Soundtrack

The Specials – The Specials (Two Tone)

Badly Drawn Boy – The Hour of Bewilderbeast (XL Recordings)

Moby – Play (Mute)

The Killers – Sam's Town (Vertigo)

Chas 'N' Dave – Best of Chas 'N' Dave (Demon)

The Verve – Urban Hymns (Hut)

Happy Mondays – Pills, Thrills and Bellyaches (Factory)

Ian Brown – Golden Greats (Polydor)

Stone Roses – Stone Roses (Silvertone)

Johnny Cash – Wanted Man (Columbia)

Carter the Unstoppable Sex Machine – 30 Something (Rough Trade)

The Smiths – The Queen is Dead (Warner Music)

Queen – Sheer Heart Attack (EMI)

Billy Bragg – Must I Paint you a Picture? (Cooking Vinyl)

Gomez – Bring it On (Hut)

Beta Band – Zeroes to Heroes (Regal)

…and the pesky Ping-Pong Compilations (Keith Weller)